KÖNIGLICHE FAMILIE LEHRER

Higasa Akai

15

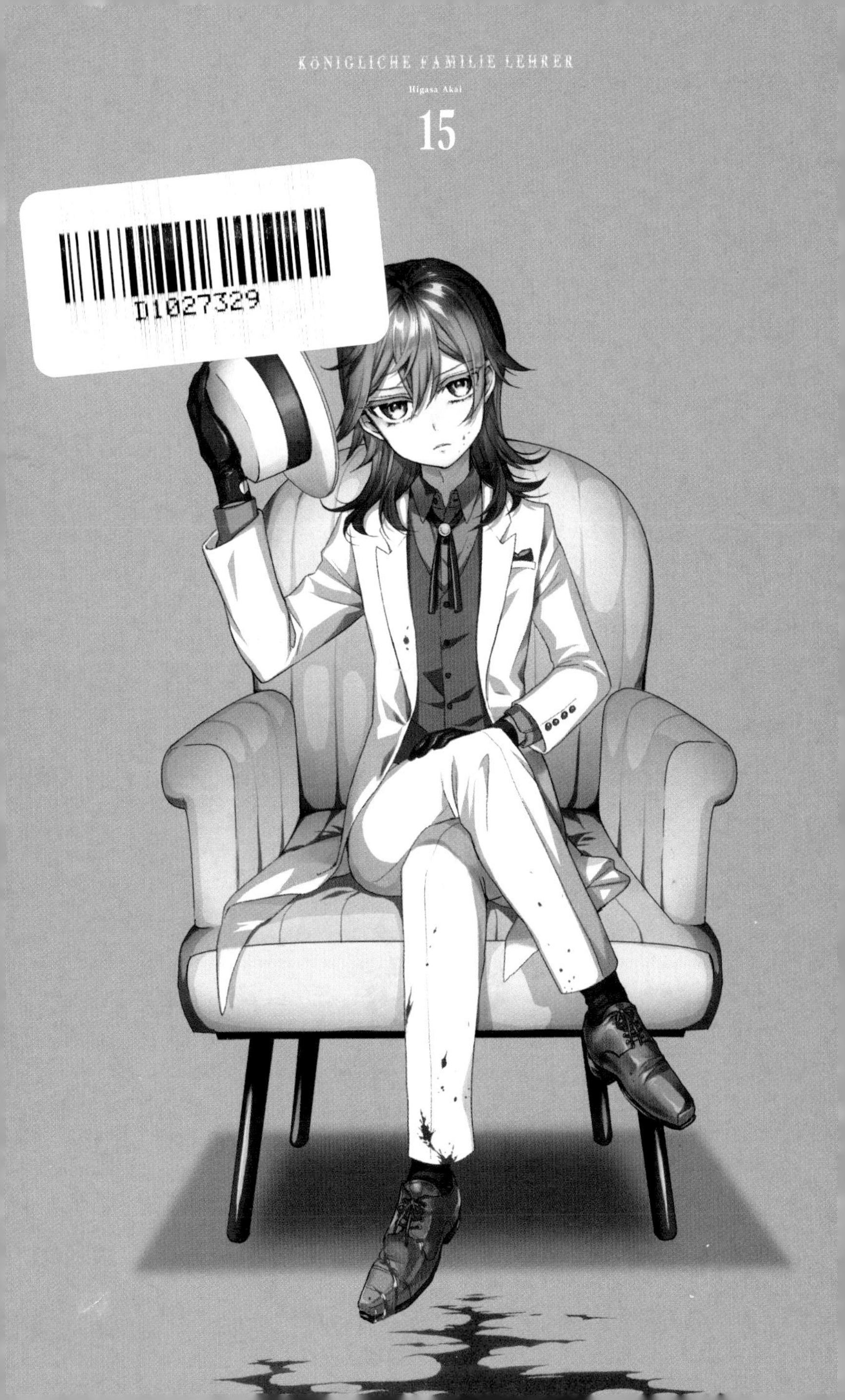

CONTENTS

KÖNIGLICHE FAMILIE LEHRER

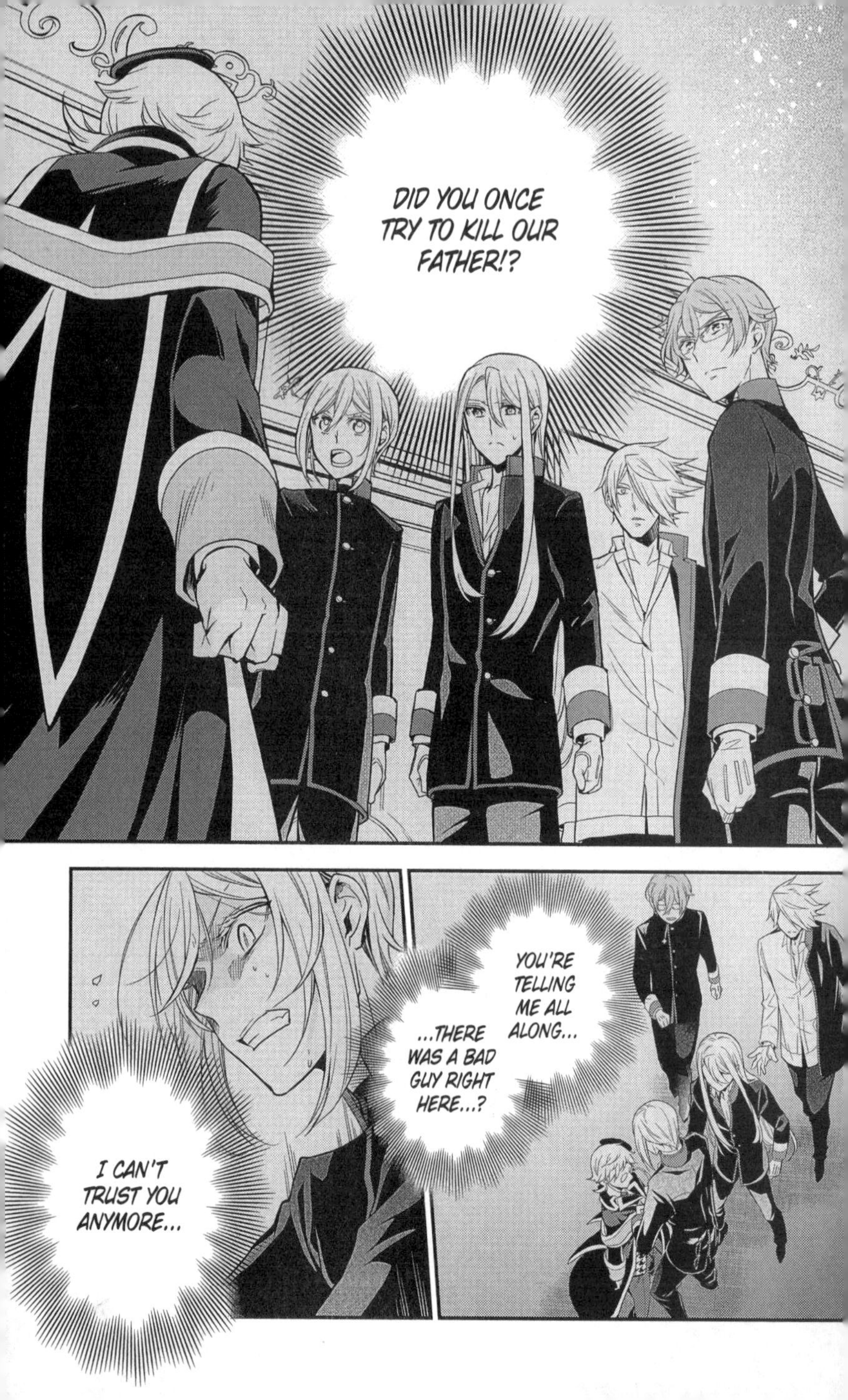
DID YOU ONCE TRY TO KILL OUR FATHER!?
YOU'RE TELLING ME ALL ALONG...
...THERE WAS A BAD GUY RIGHT HERE...?
I CAN'T TRUST YOU ANYMORE...

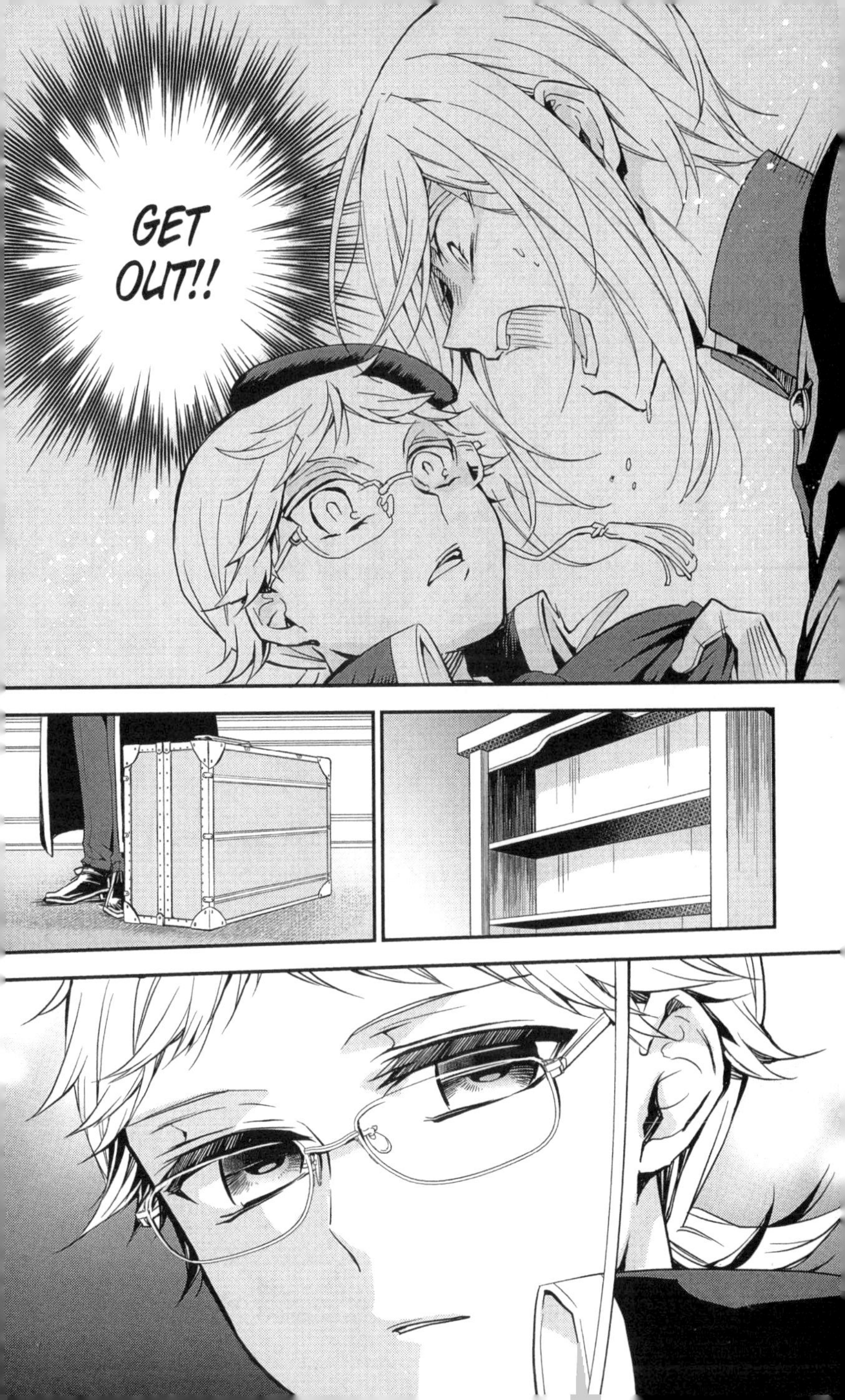
GET OUT!!

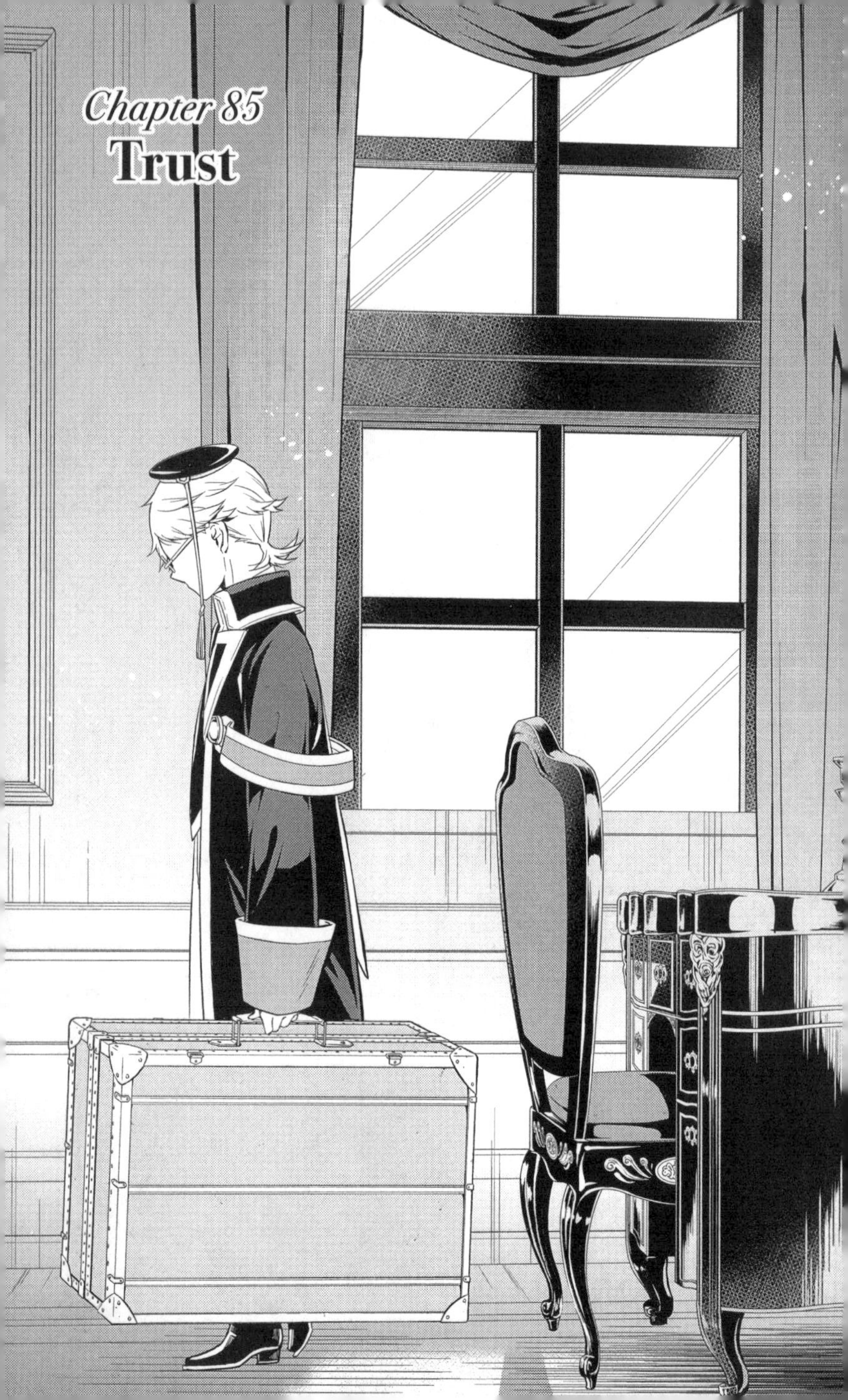
Chapter 85
Trust

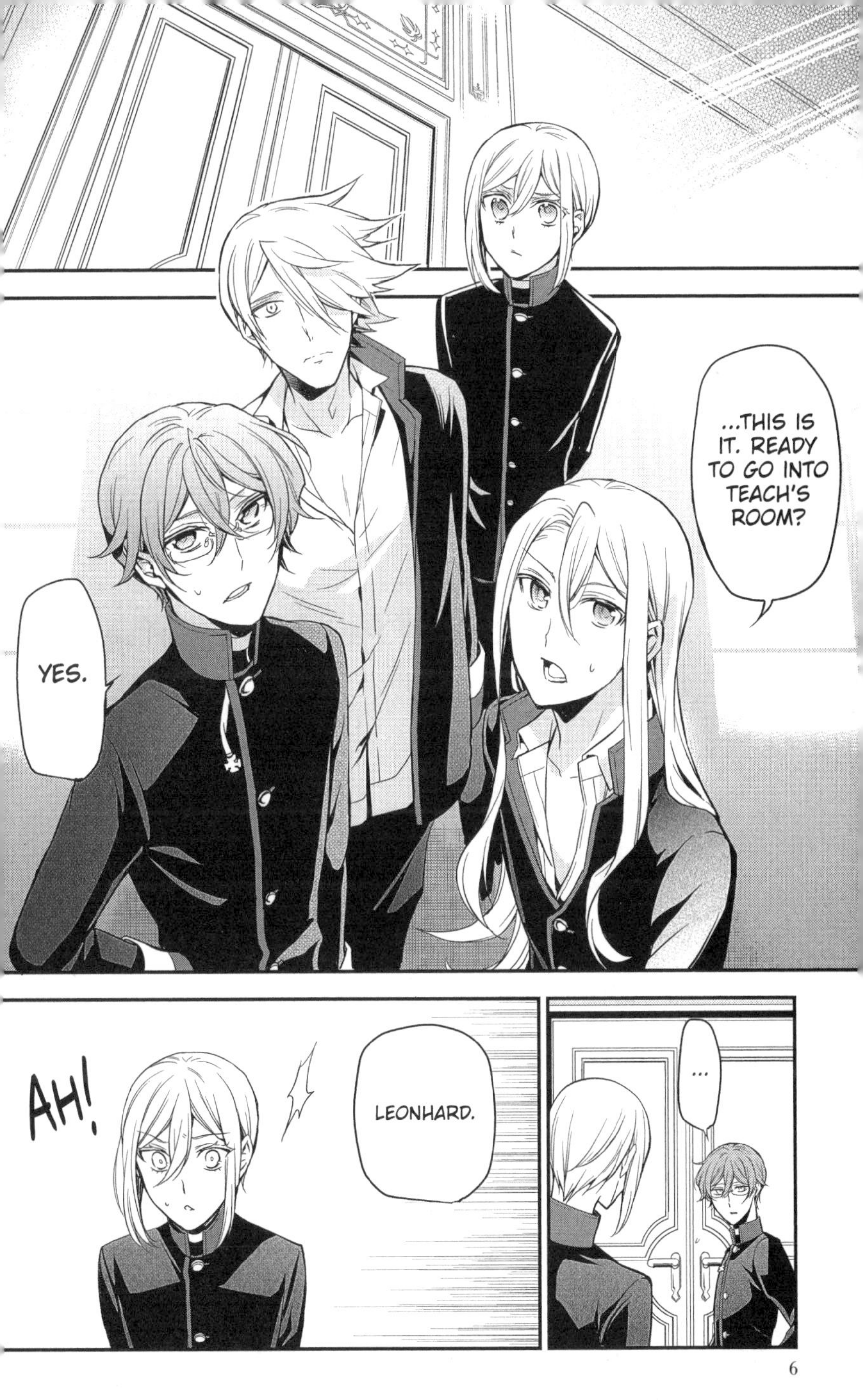
...THIS IS IT. READY TO GO INTO TEACH'S ROOM?
YES.
...
LEONHARD.
AH!

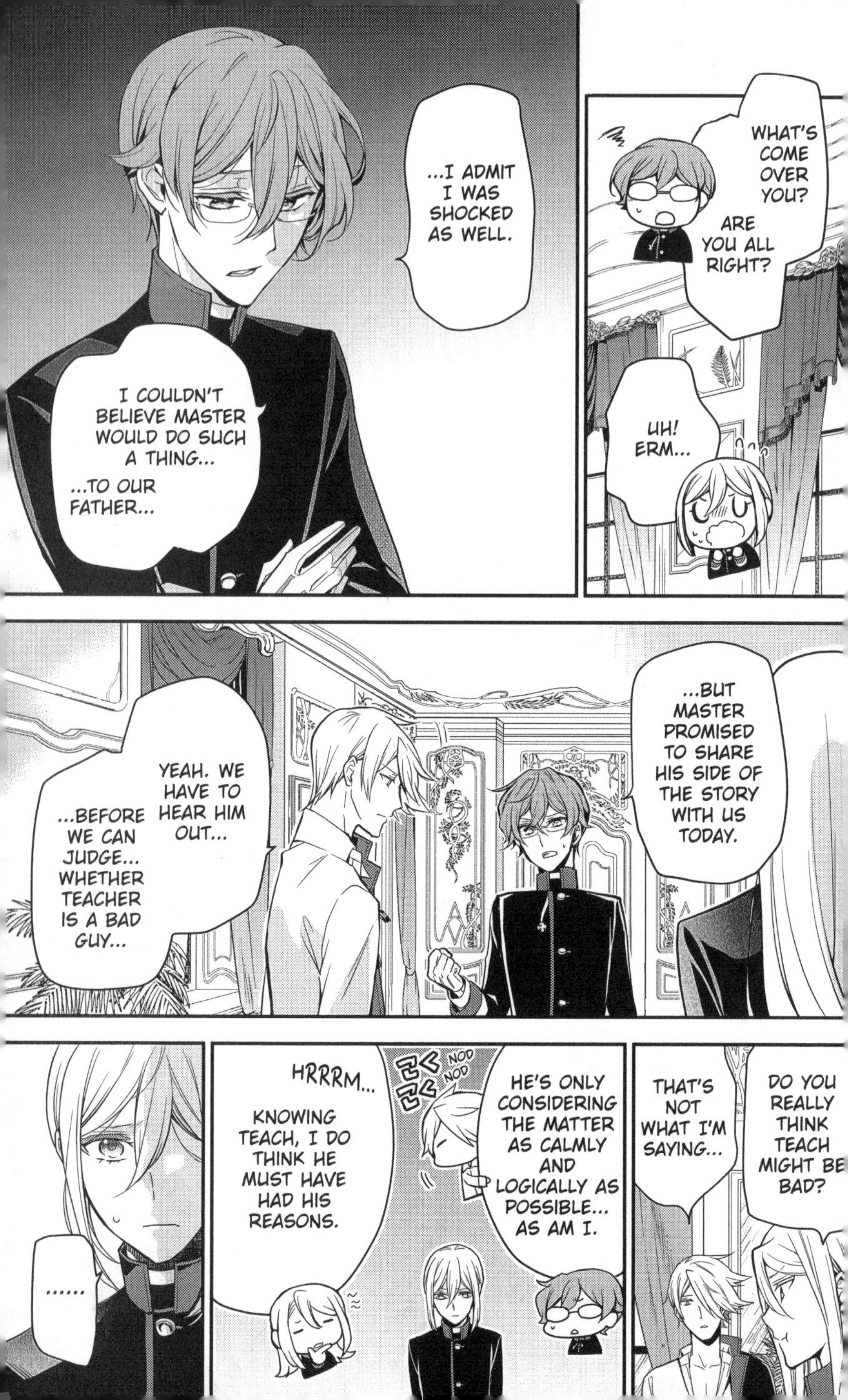

WHAT'S COME OVER YOU?
ARE YOU ALL RIGHT?
UH! ERM...
...I ADMIT I WAS SHOCKED AS WELL.
I COULDN'T BELIEVE MASTER WOULD DO SUCH A THING...
...TO OUR FATHER...
...BUT MASTER PROMISED TO SHARE HIS SIDE OF THE STORY WITH US TODAY.
YEAH. WE HAVE TO HEAR HIM OUT...
...BEFORE WE CAN JUDGE... WHETHER TEACHER IS A BAD GUY...
DO YOU REALLY THINK TEACH MIGHT BE BAD?
THAT'S NOT WHAT I'M SAYING...
HE'S ONLY CONSIDERING THE MATTER AS CALMLY AND LOGICALLY AS POSSIBLE... AS AM I.
NOD NOD
HRRRM...
KNOWING TEACH, I DO THINK HE MUST HAVE HAD HIS REASONS.
......

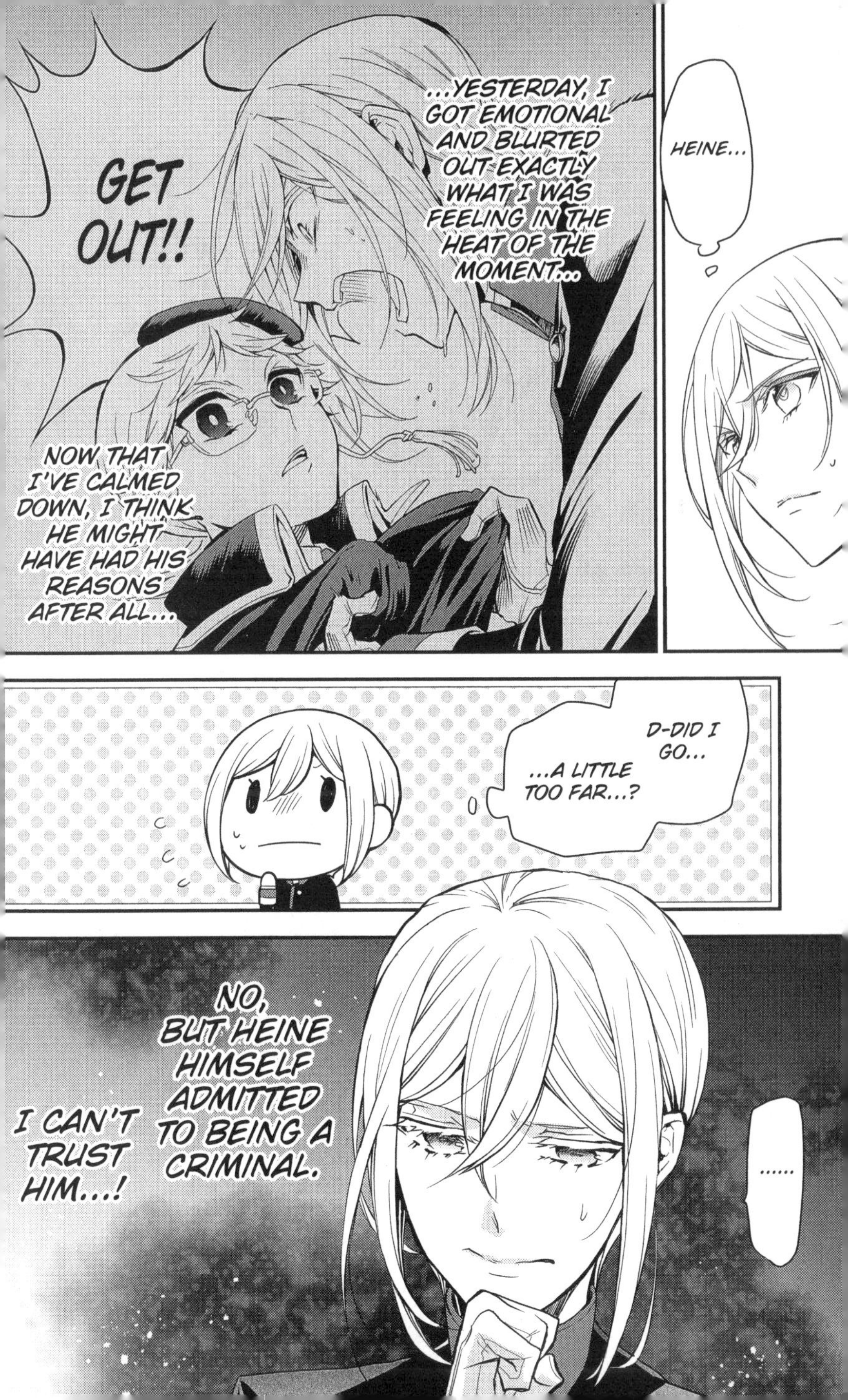
HEINE...
...YESTERDAY, I GOT EMOTIONAL AND BLURTED OUT EXACTLY WHAT I WAS FEELING IN THE HEAT OF THE MOMENT...
GET OUT!!
NOW THAT I'VE CALMED DOWN, I THINK HE MIGHT HAVE HAD HIS REASONS AFTER ALL...
D-DID I GO...
...A LITTLE TOO FAR...?
......
NO, BUT HEINE HIMSELF ADMITTED TO BEING A CRIMINAL.
I CAN'T TRUST HIM...!

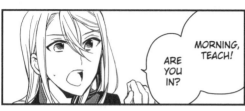

MORNING, TEACH!

ARE YOU IN?

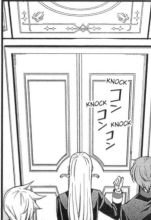

KNOCK コン

KNOCK コン

KNOCK

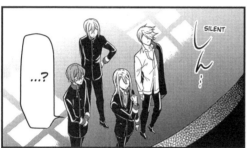

SILENT しん

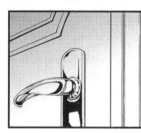

...?

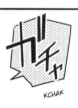

ガチャ

KCHAK

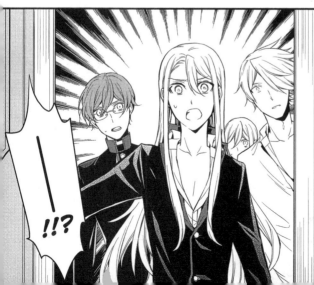

!!?

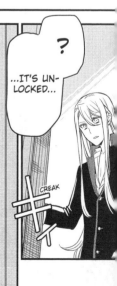

?

...IT'S UN-LOCKED...

CREAK

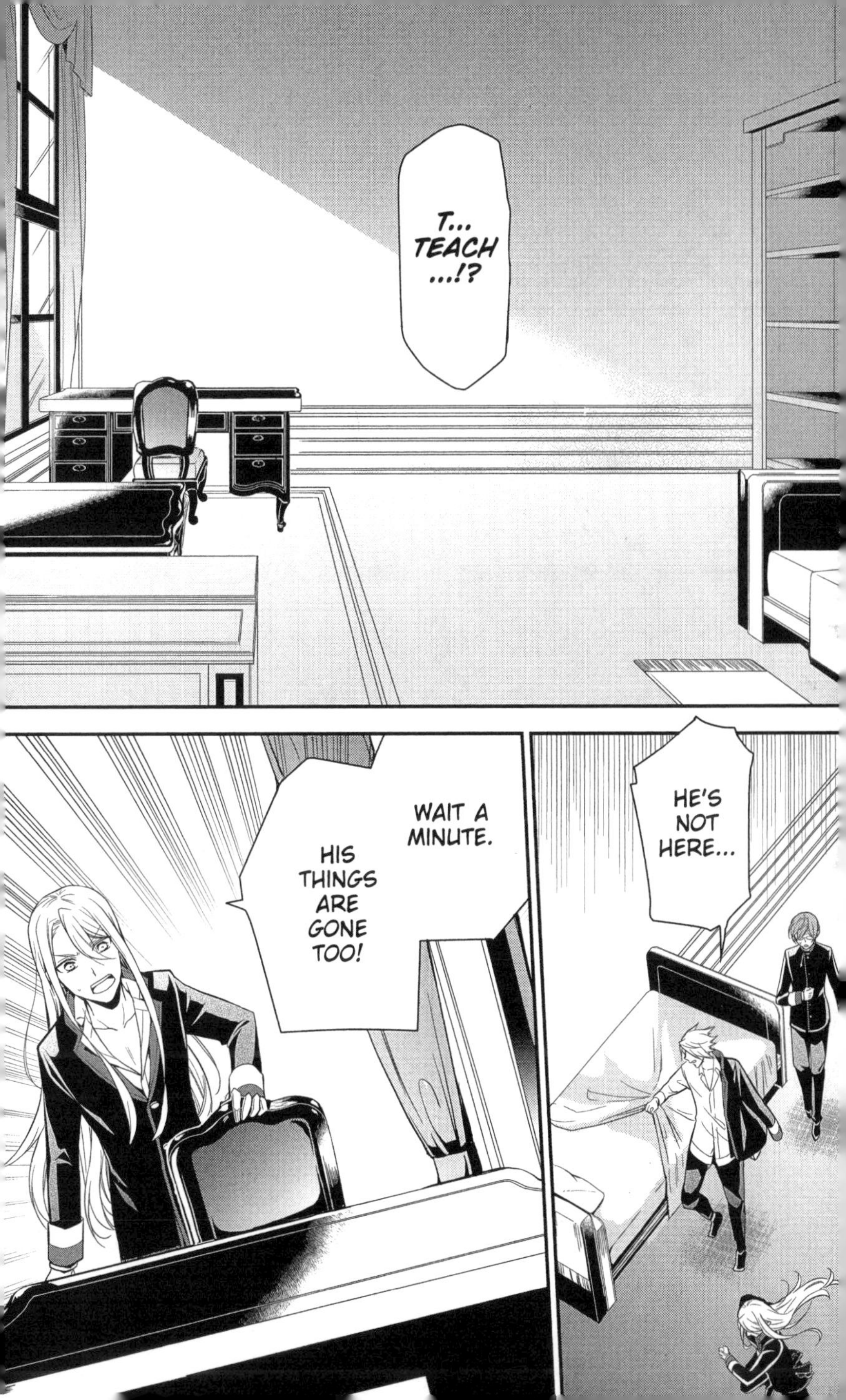
T... TEACH ...!?
HE'S NOT HERE...
WAIT A MINUTE.
HIS THINGS ARE GONE TOO!

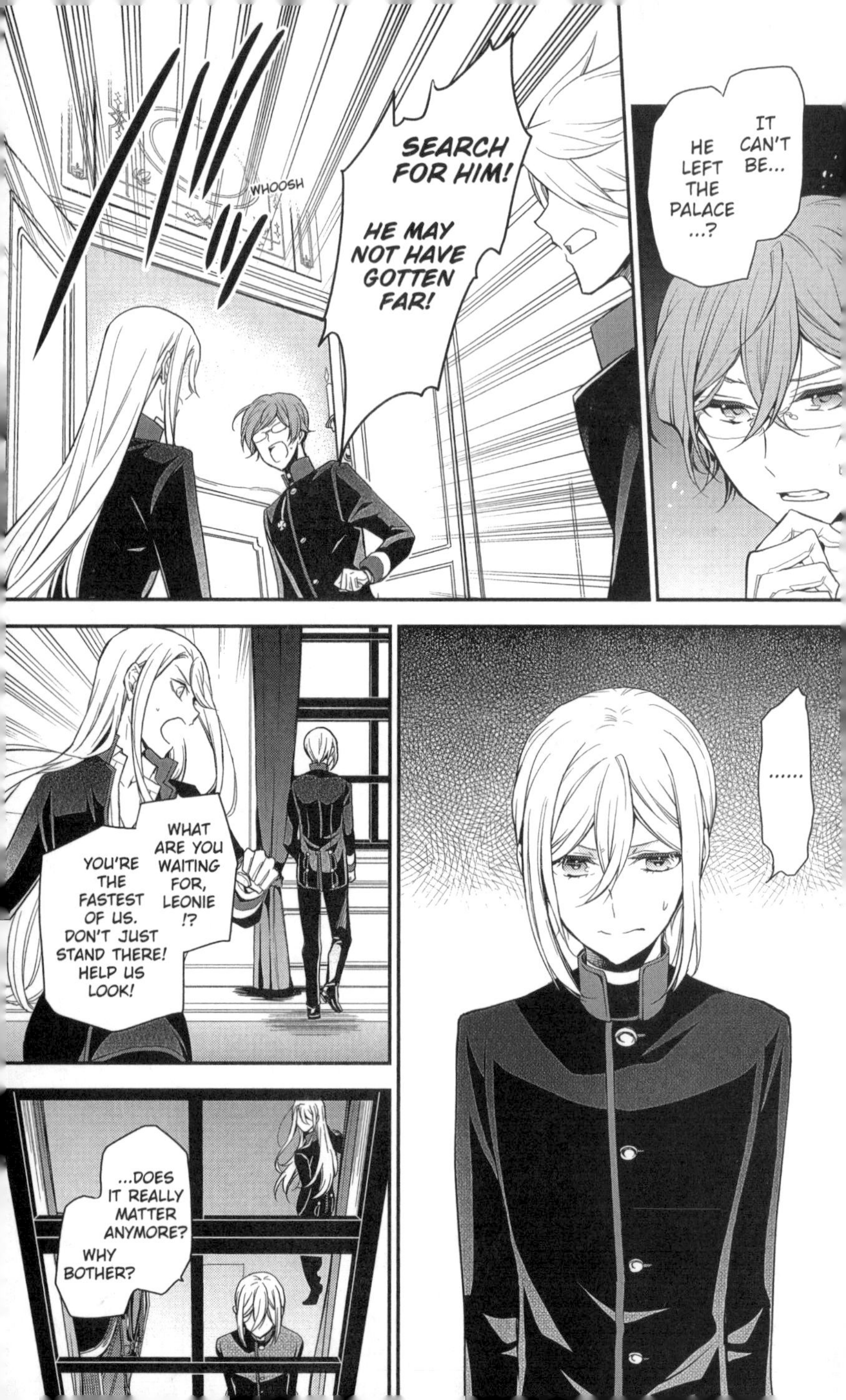
IT CAN'T BE... HE LEFT THE PALACE ...?
SEARCH FOR HIM!
HE MAY NOT HAVE GOTTEN FAR!
WHOOSH
......
WHAT ARE YOU WAITING FOR, LEONIE !?
YOU'RE THE FASTEST OF US. DON'T JUST STAND THERE! HELP US LOOK!
...DOES IT REALLY MATTER ANYMORE? WHY BOTHER?

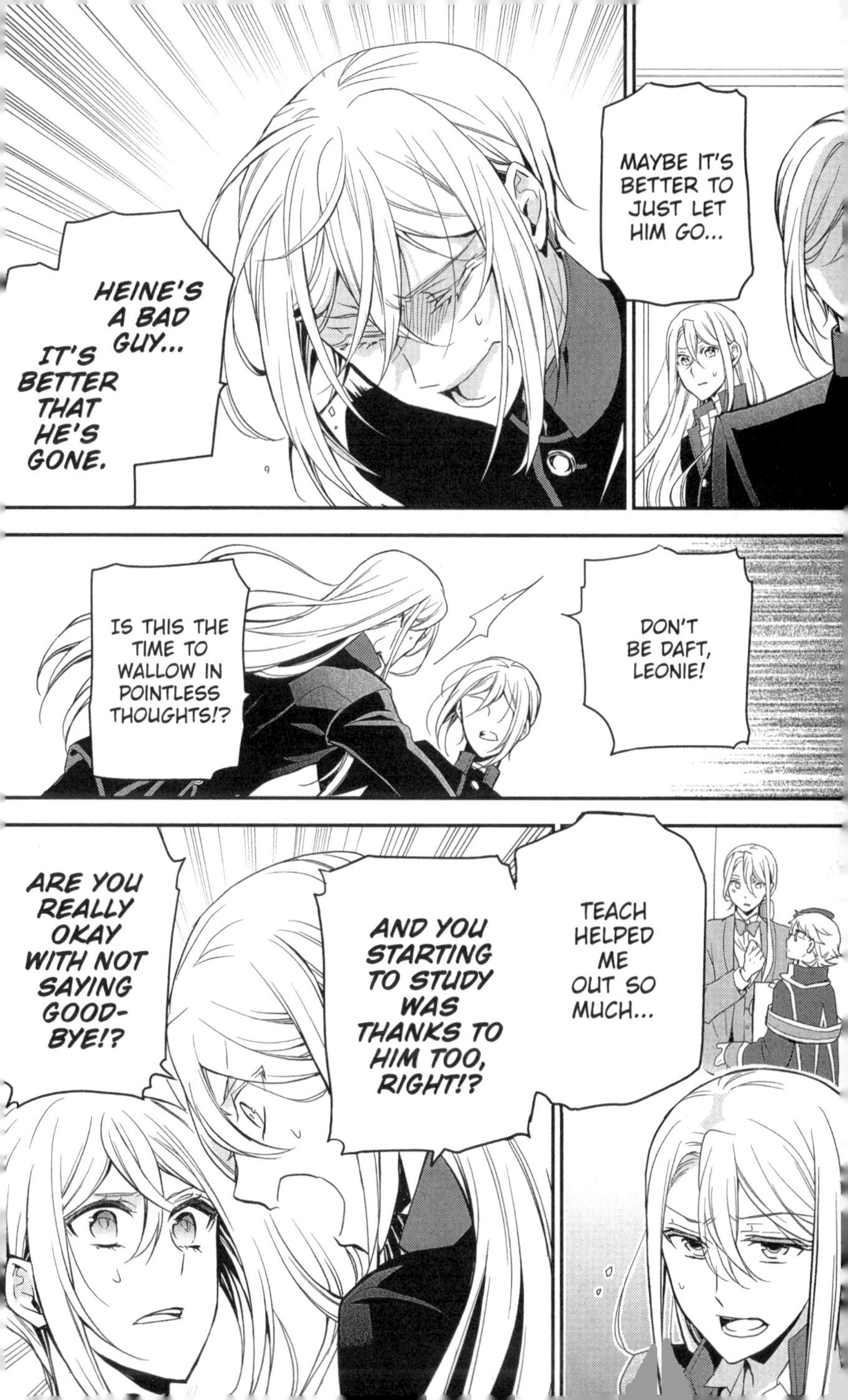
MAYBE IT'S BETTER TO JUST LET HIM GO...
HEINE'S A BAD GUY...
IT'S BETTER THAT HE'S GONE.
DON'T BE DAFT, LEONIE!
IS THIS THE TIME TO WALLOW IN POINTLESS THOUGHTS!?
TEACH HELPED ME OUT SO MUCH...
AND YOU STARTING TO STUDY WAS THANKS TO HIM TOO, RIGHT!?
ARE YOU REALLY OKAY WITH NOT SAYING GOOD-BYE!?

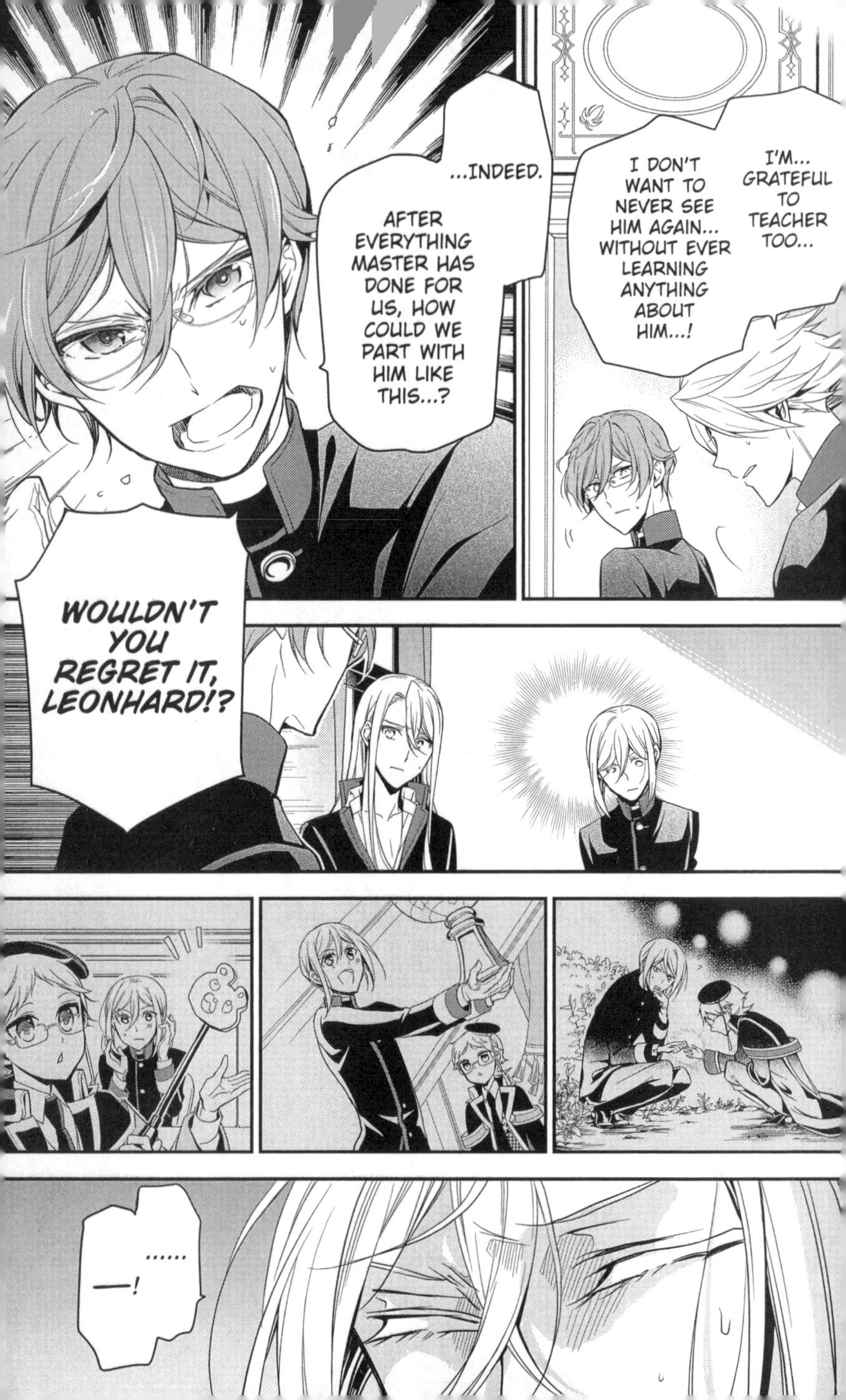
I'M... GRATEFUL TO TEACHER TOO...
I DON'T WANT TO NEVER SEE HIM AGAIN... WITHOUT EVER LEARNING ANYTHING ABOUT HIM...!
...INDEED.
AFTER EVERYTHING MASTER HAS DONE FOR US, HOW COULD WE PART WITH HIM LIKE THIS...?
WOULDN'T YOU REGRET IT, LEONHARD!?
......
—!

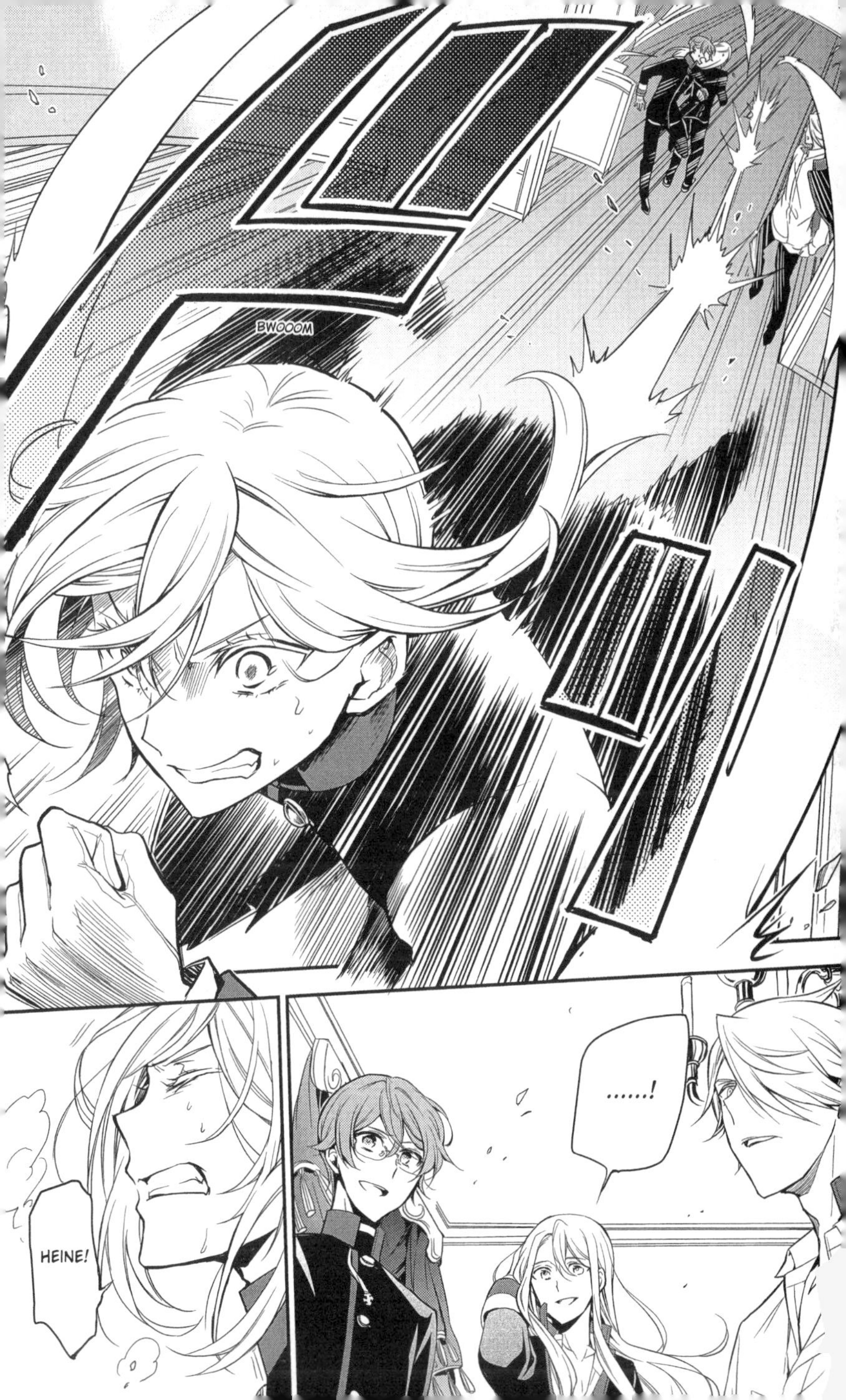
BWOOOM
......!
HEINE!

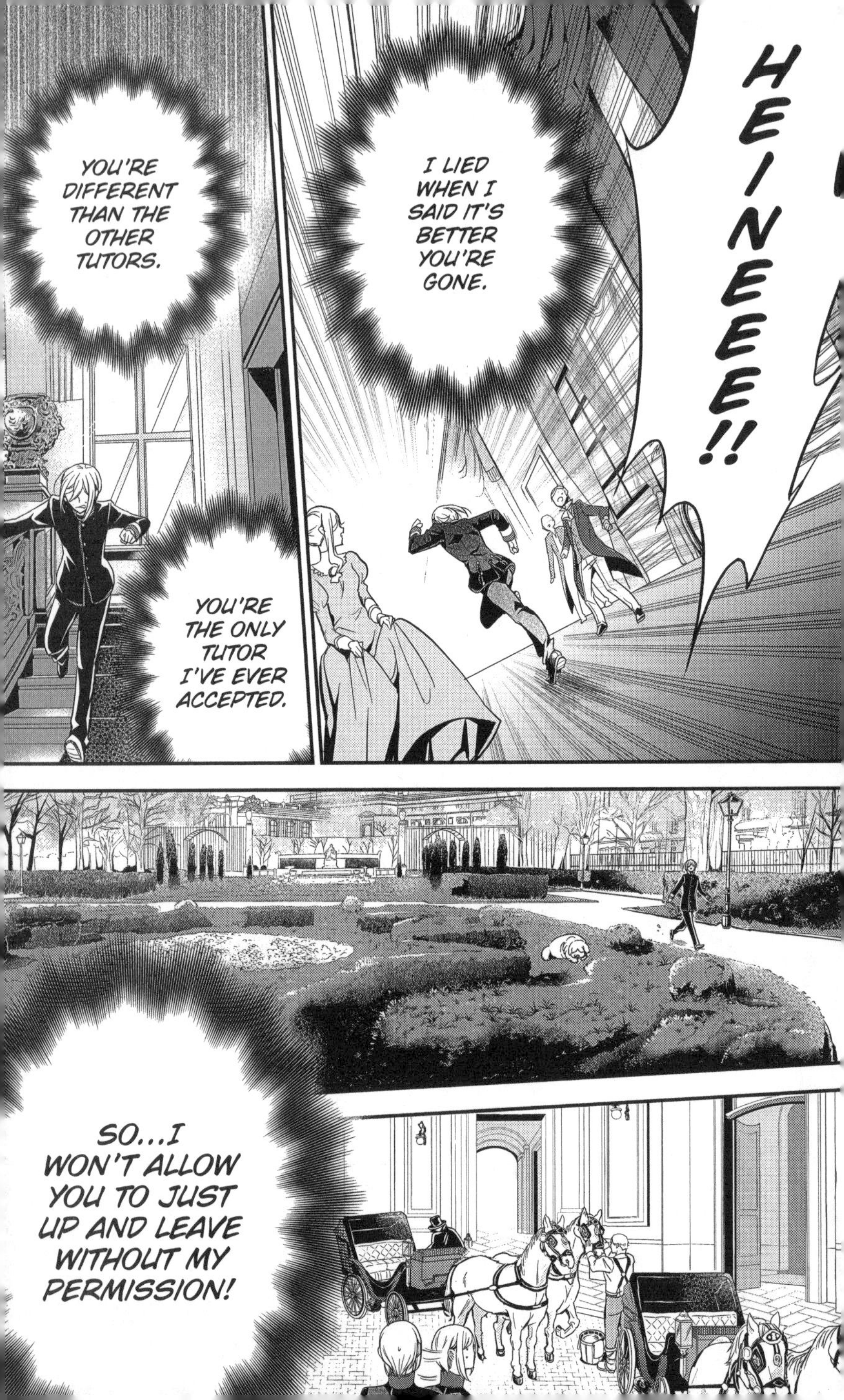
HEINEEE!!
I LIED WHEN I SAID IT'S BETTER YOU'RE GONE.
YOU'RE DIFFERENT THAN THE OTHER TUTORS.
YOU'RE THE ONLY TUTOR I'VE EVER ACCEPTED.
SO...I WON'T ALLOW YOU TO JUST UP AND LEAVE WITHOUT MY PERMISSION!

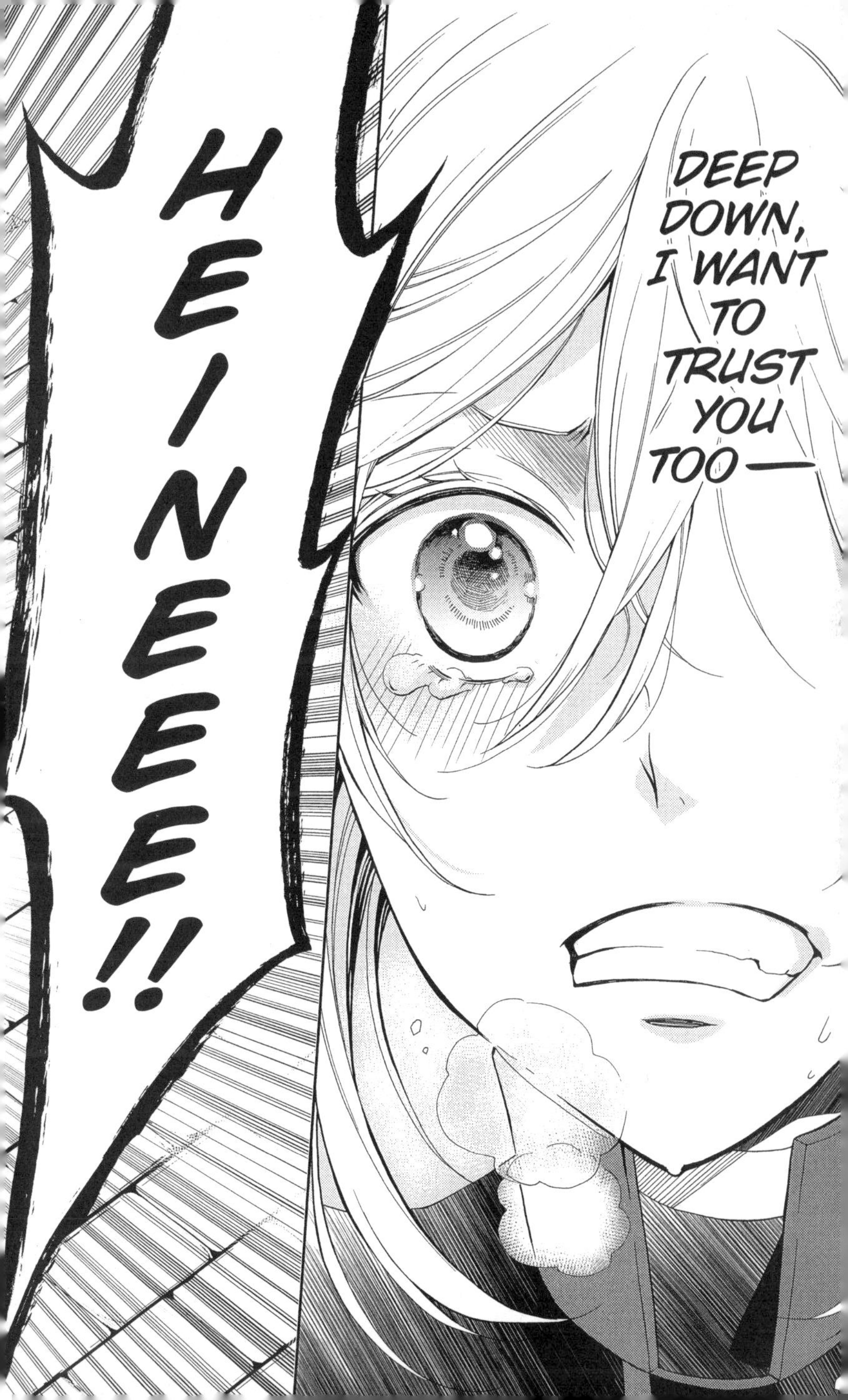
DEEP DOWN, I WANT TO TRUST YOU TOO—
HEINEEE!!

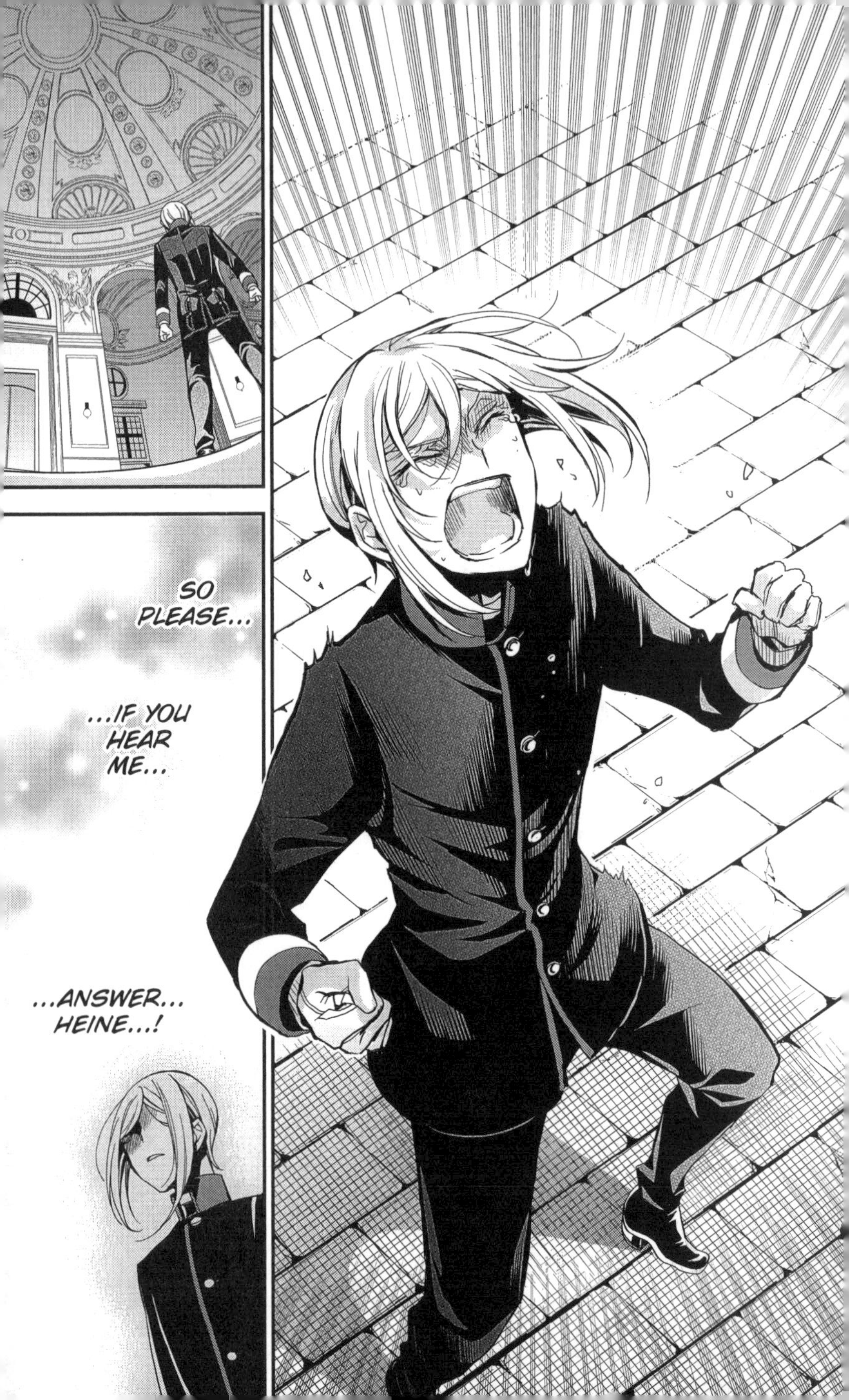
SO PLEASE...
...IF YOU HEAR ME...
...ANSWER... HEINE...!

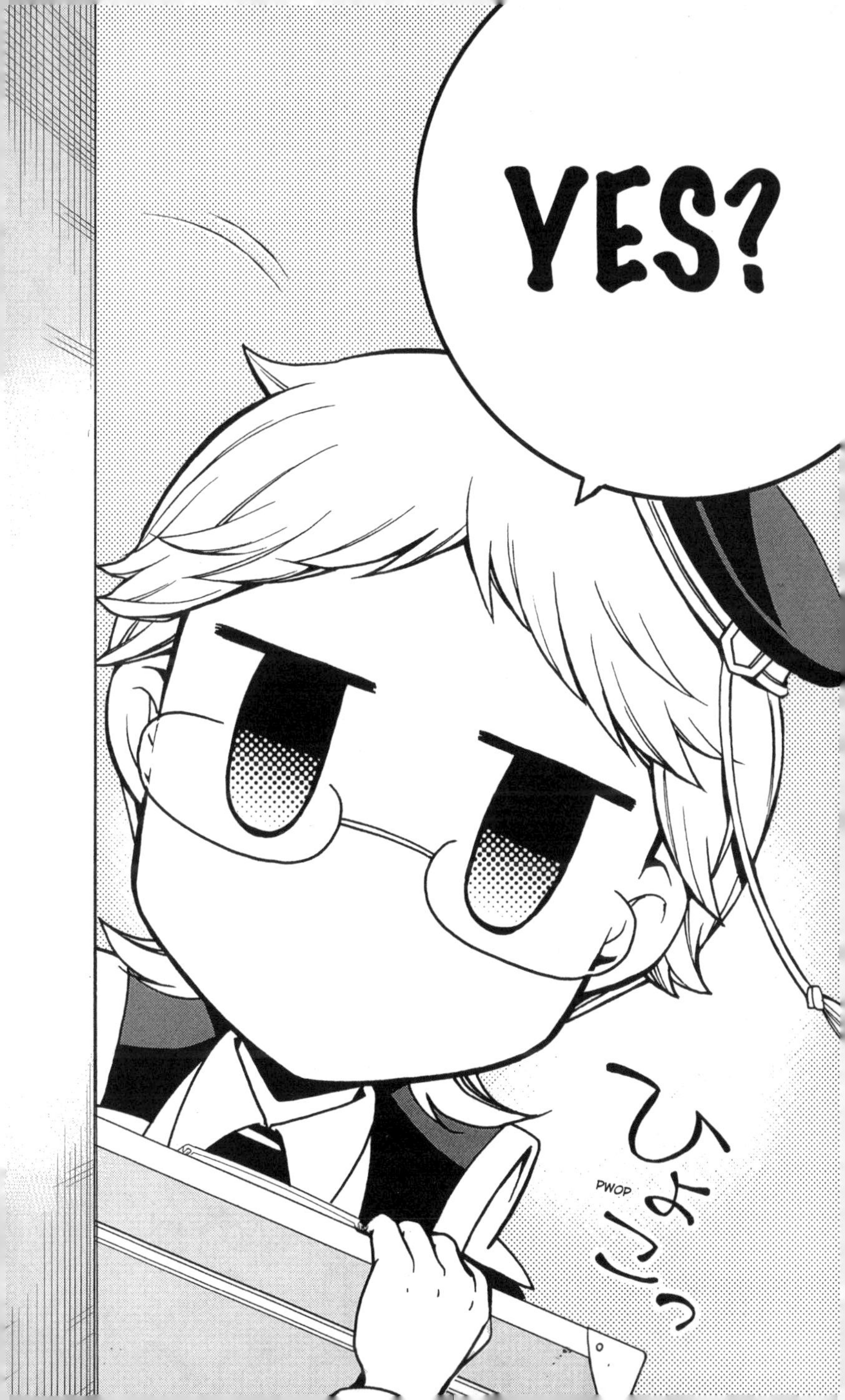
YES?
ひょこっ
PWOP

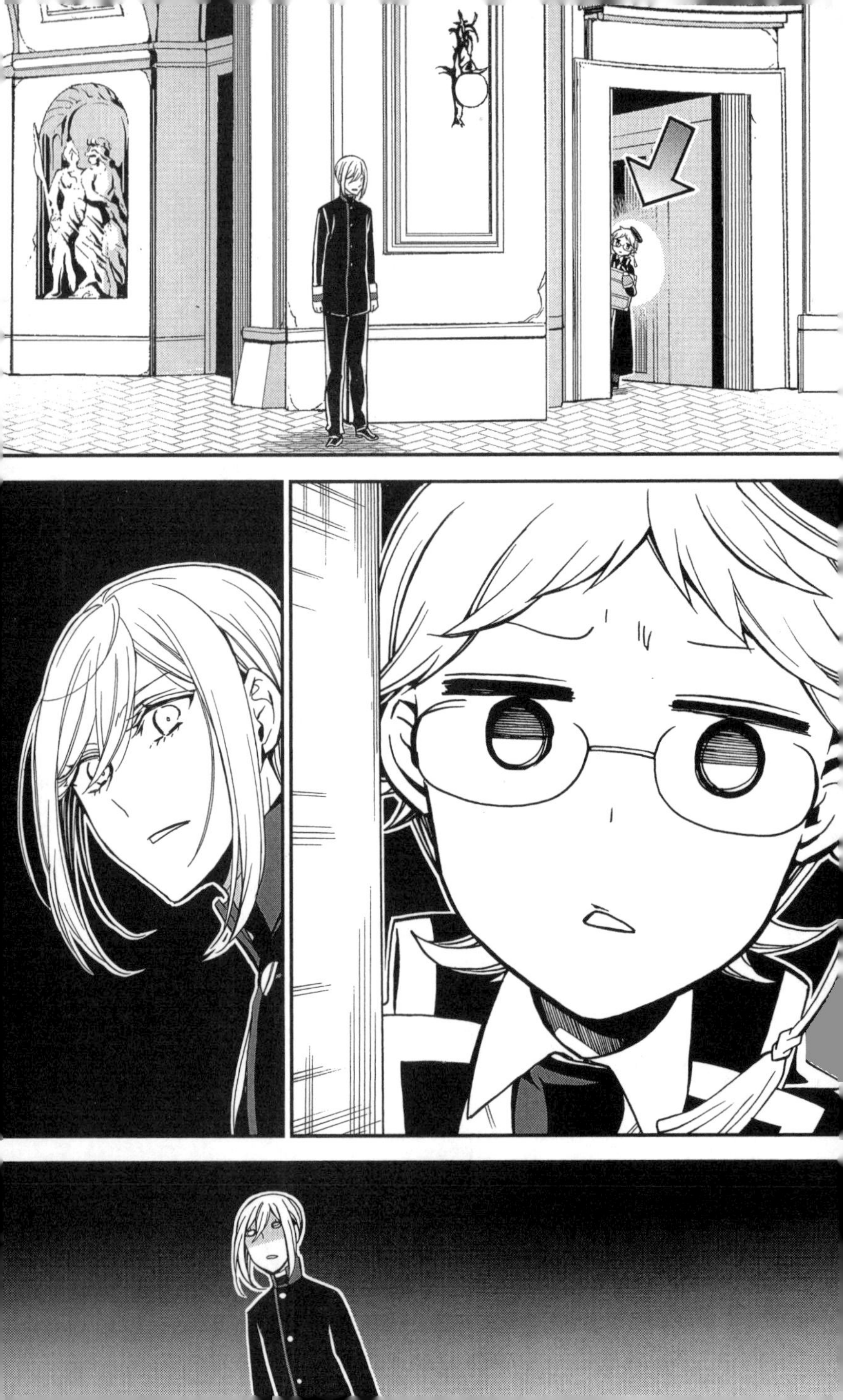

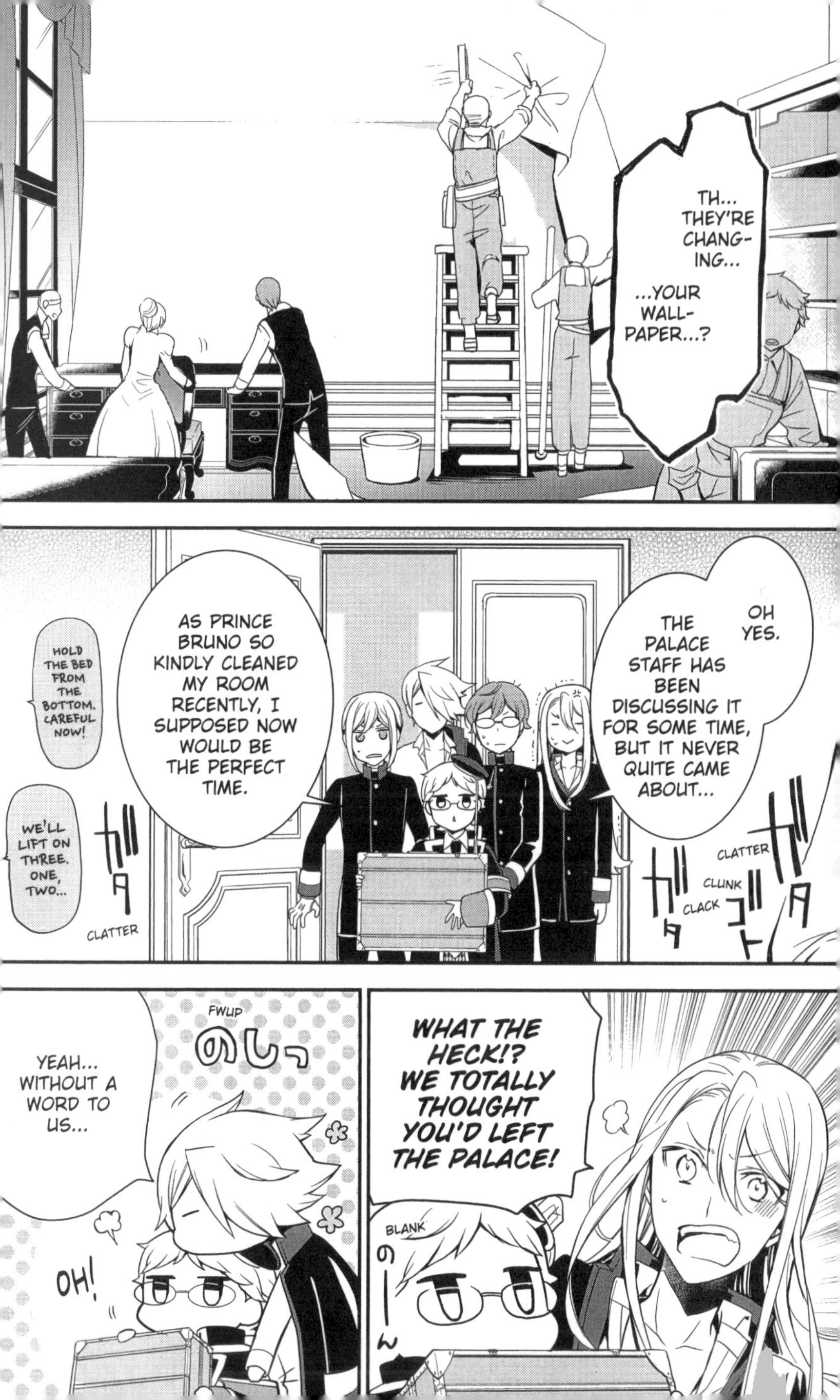
TH... THEY'RE CHANGING...
...YOUR WALLPAPER...?
OH YES.
THE PALACE STAFF HAS BEEN DISCUSSING IT FOR SOME TIME, BUT IT NEVER QUITE CAME ABOUT...
CLATTER
ガタ
CLUNK
ゴト
CLACK
ガタ
AS PRINCE BRUNO SO KINDLY CLEANED MY ROOM RECENTLY, I SUPPOSED NOW WOULD BE THE PERFECT TIME.
HOLD THE BED FROM THE BOTTOM. CAREFUL NOW!
WE'LL LIFT ON THREE. ONE, TWO...
ガタ
CLATTER
WHAT THE HECK!? WE TOTALLY THOUGHT YOU'D LEFT THE PALACE!
BLANK
の～ん
FWUP
のしっ
YEAH... WITHOUT A WORD TO US...
OH!

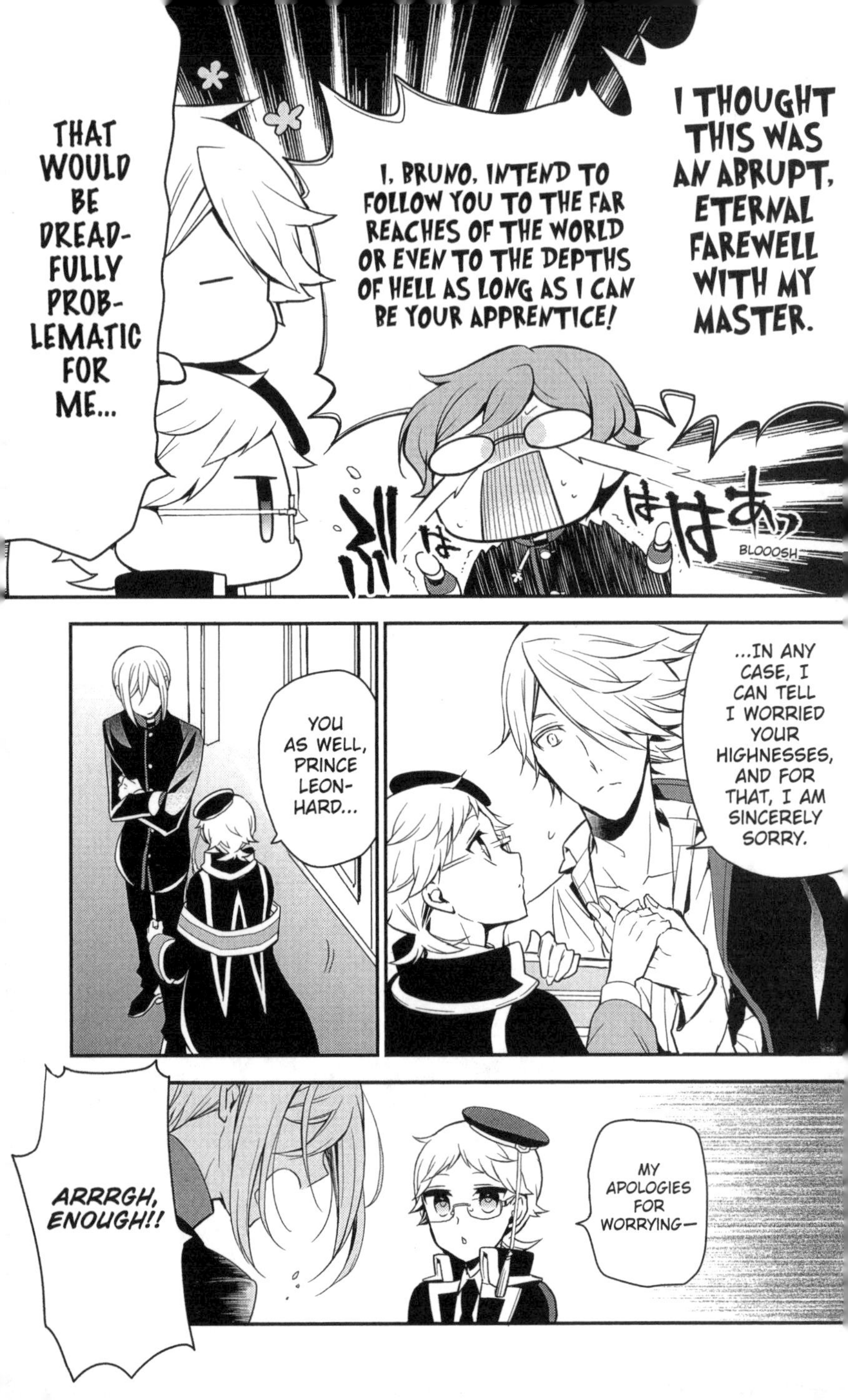
I THOUGHT THIS WAS AN ABRUPT, ETERNAL FAREWELL WITH MY MASTER.
I, BRUNO, INTEND TO FOLLOW YOU TO THE FAR REACHES OF THE WORLD OR EVEN TO THE DEPTHS OF HELL AS LONG AS I CAN BE YOUR APPRENTICE!
THAT WOULD BE DREAD-FULLY PROB-LEMATIC FOR ME...
BLOOOSH
...IN ANY CASE, I CAN TELL I WORRIED YOUR HIGHNESSES, AND FOR THAT, I AM SINCERELY SORRY.
YOU AS WELL, PRINCE LEON-HARD...
MY APOLOGIES FOR WORRYING—
ARRRGH, ENOUGH!!

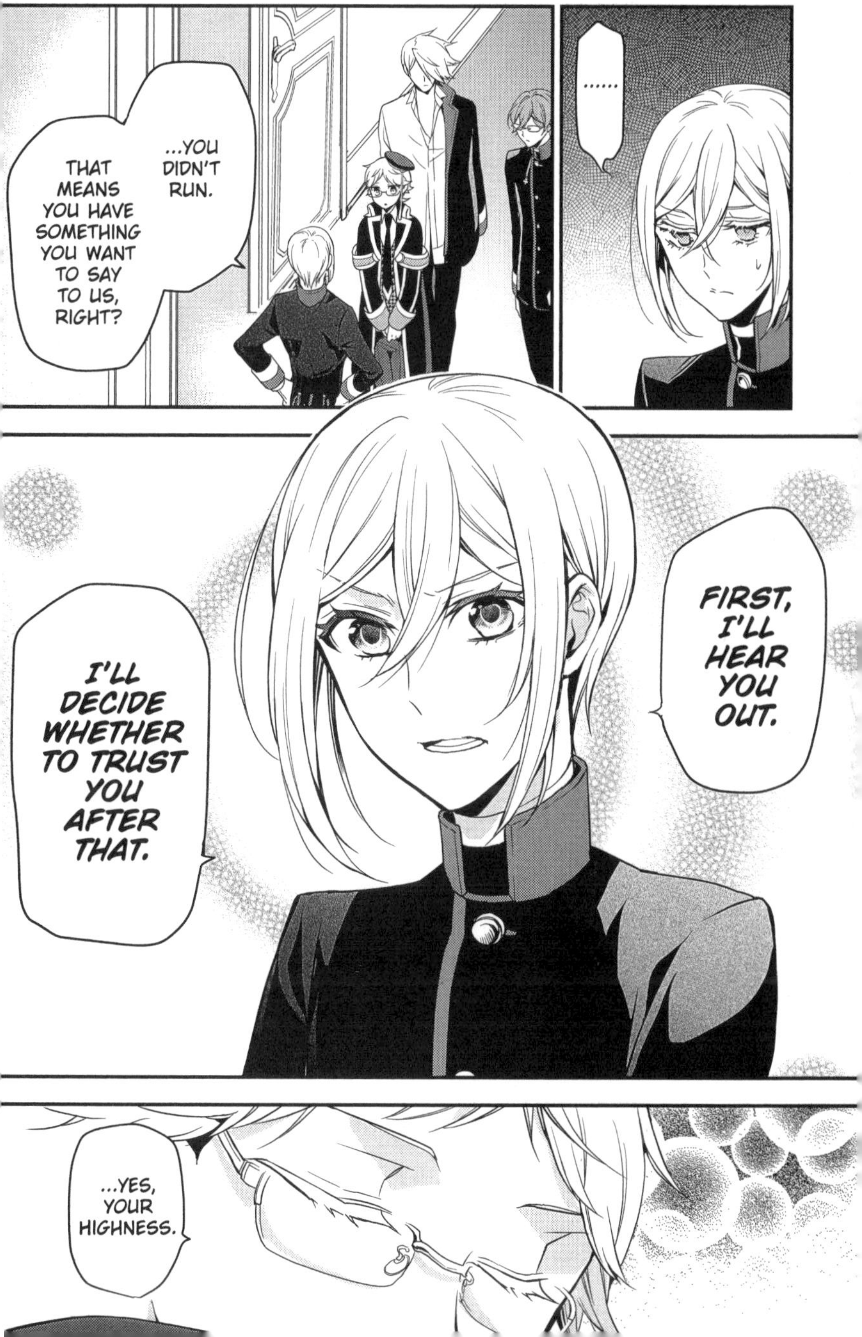
......
...YOU DIDN'T RUN.
THAT MEANS YOU HAVE SOMETHING YOU WANT TO SAY TO US, RIGHT?
FIRST, I'LL HEAR YOU OUT.
I'LL DECIDE WHETHER TO TRUST YOU AFTER THAT.
...YES, YOUR HIGHNESS.

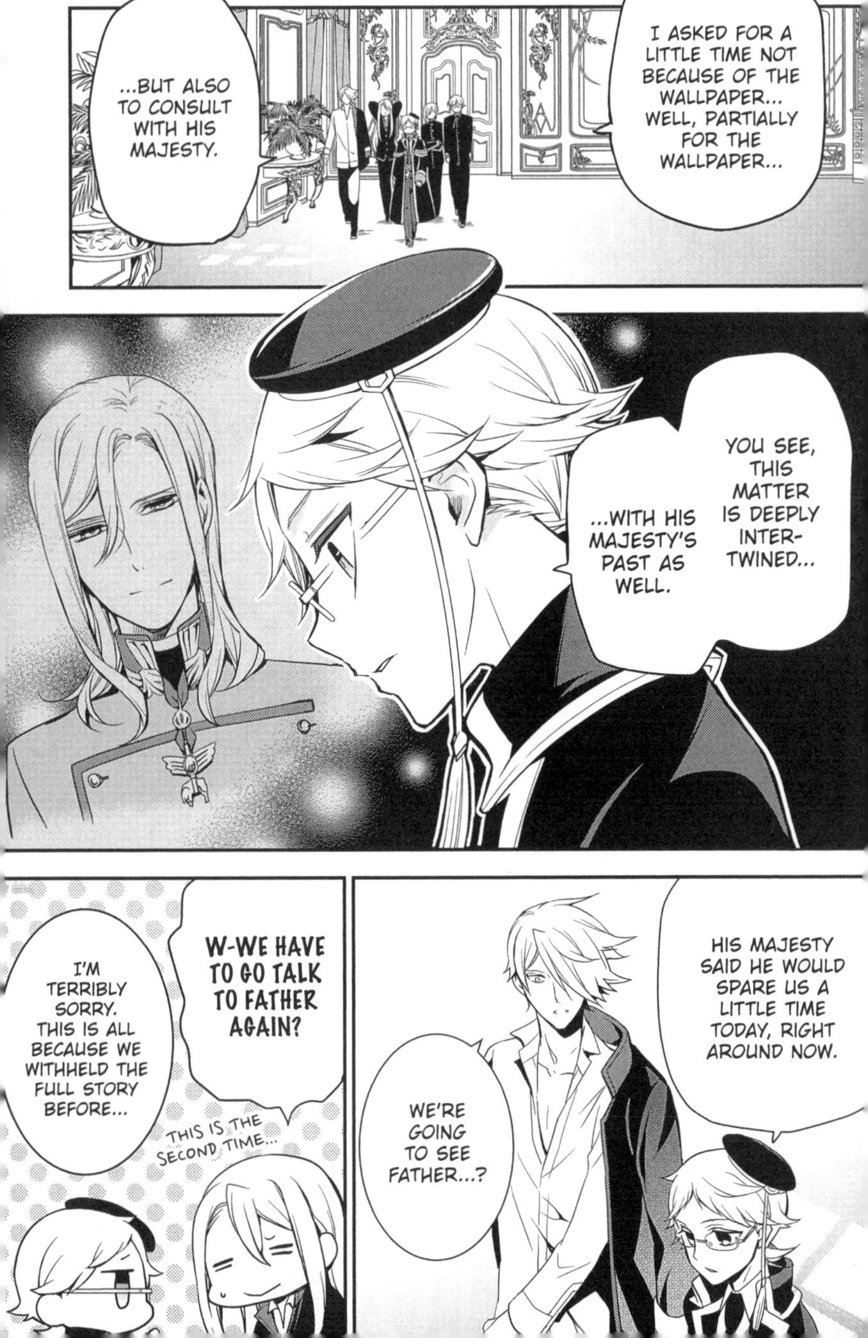
I ASKED FOR A LITTLE TIME NOT BECAUSE OF THE WALLPAPER... WELL, PARTIALLY FOR THE WALLPAPER...
...BUT ALSO TO CONSULT WITH HIS MAJESTY.
YOU SEE, THIS MATTER IS DEEPLY INTER-TWINED...
...WITH HIS MAJESTY'S PAST AS WELL.
HIS MAJESTY SAID HE WOULD SPARE US A LITTLE TIME TODAY, RIGHT AROUND NOW.
WE'RE GOING TO SEE FATHER...?
W-WE HAVE TO GO TALK TO FATHER AGAIN?
I'M TERRIBLY SORRY. THIS IS ALL BECAUSE WE WITHHELD THE FULL STORY BEFORE...
THIS IS THE SECOND TIME...

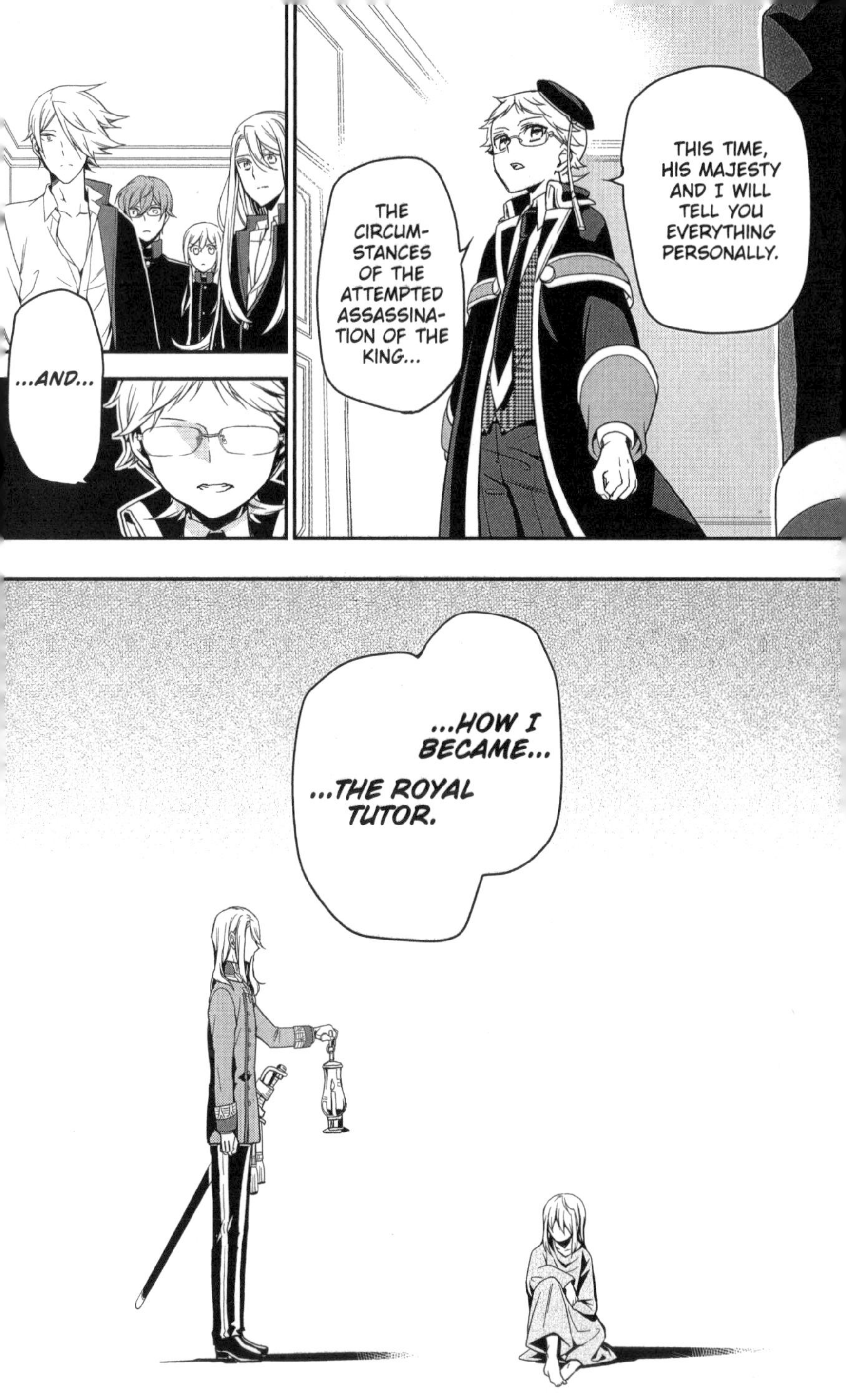
THIS TIME, HIS MAJESTY AND I WILL TELL YOU EVERYTHING PERSONALLY.
THE CIRCUM-STANCES OF THE ATTEMPTED ASSASSINA-TION OF THE KING...
...AND...
...HOW I BECAME...
...THE ROYAL TUTOR.

Chapter 86
A Fateful Encounter

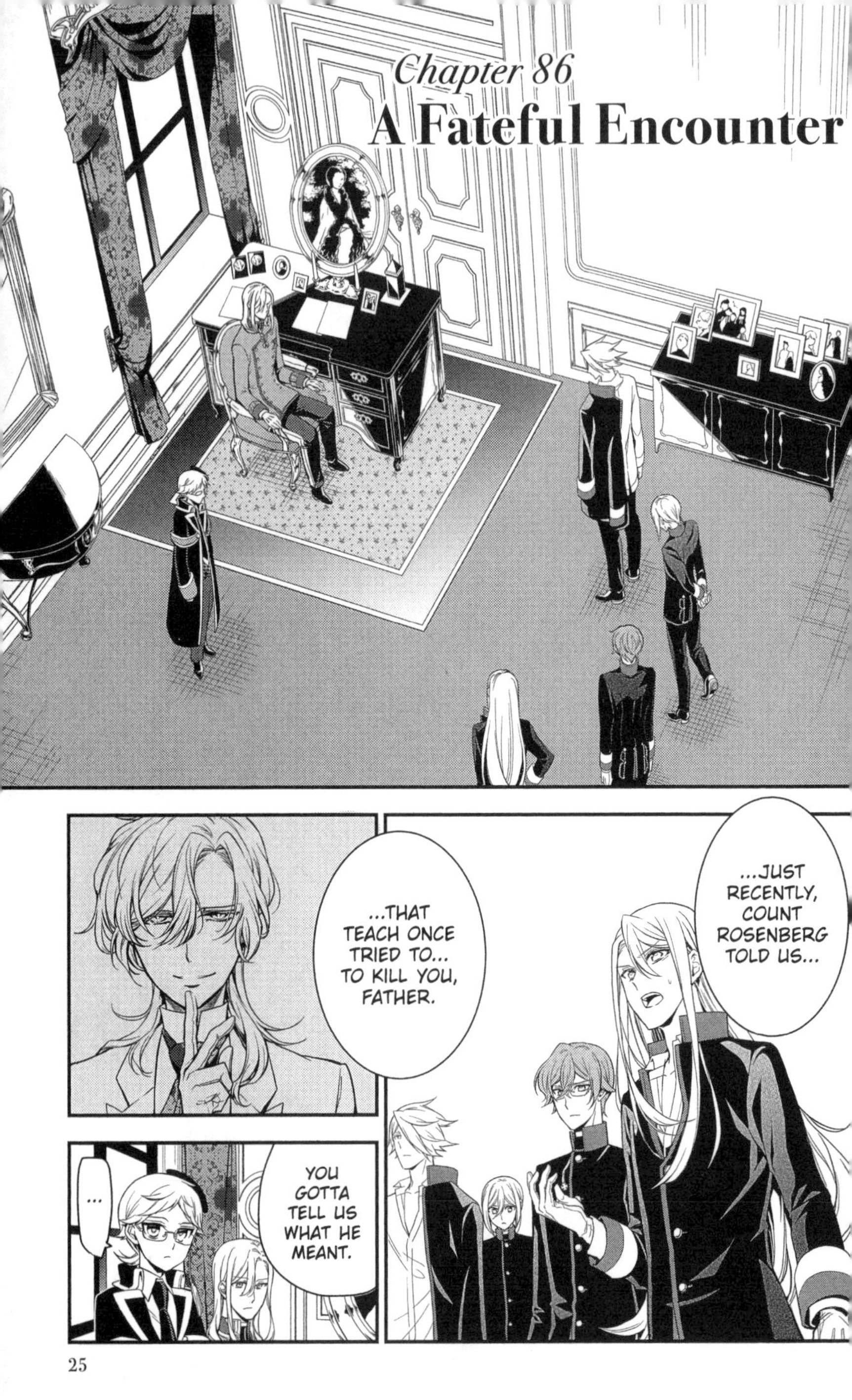
...JUST RECENTLY, COUNT ROSENBERG TOLD US...
...THAT TEACH ONCE TRIED TO... TO KILL YOU, FATHER.
YOU GOTTA TELL US WHAT HE MEANT.
...

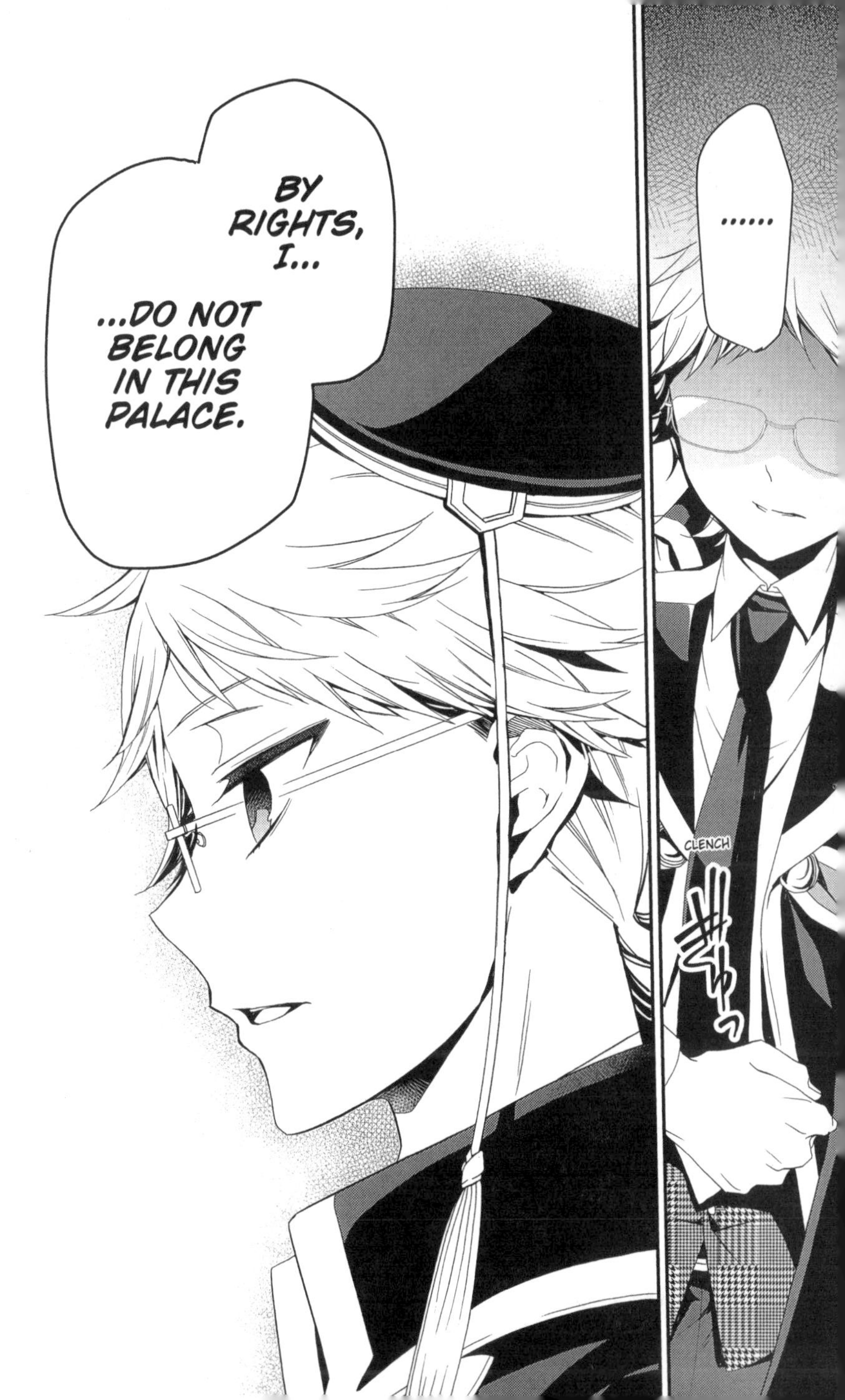
......
CLENCH
ぎゅっ
BY RIGHTS, I...
...DO NOT BELONG IN THIS PALACE.

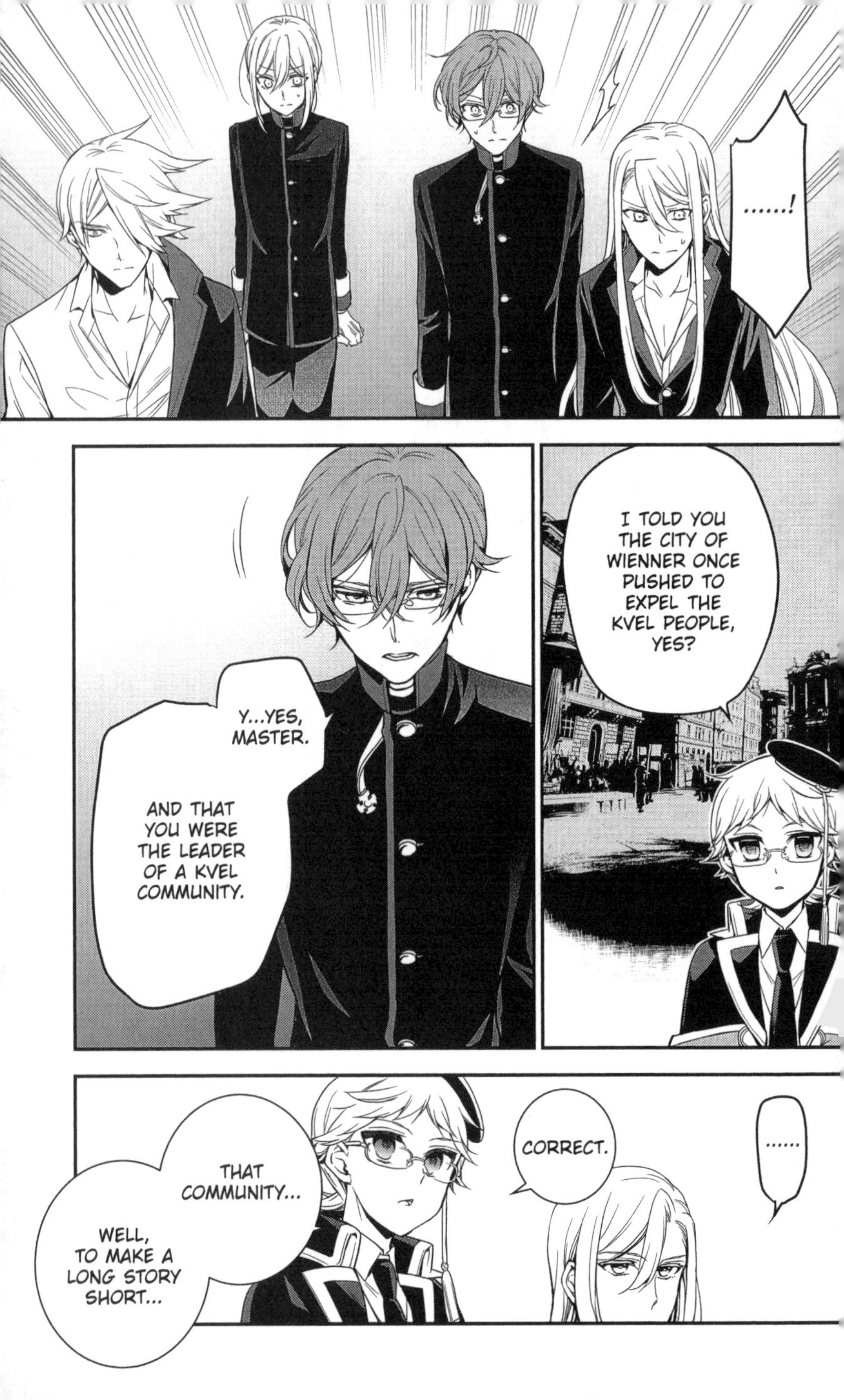
......!
I TOLD YOU THE CITY OF WIENNER ONCE PUSHED TO EXPEL THE KVEL PEOPLE, YES?
Y...YES, MASTER.
AND THAT YOU WERE THE LEADER OF A KVEL COMMUNITY.
......
CORRECT.
THAT COMMUNITY...
WELL, TO MAKE A LONG STORY SHORT...

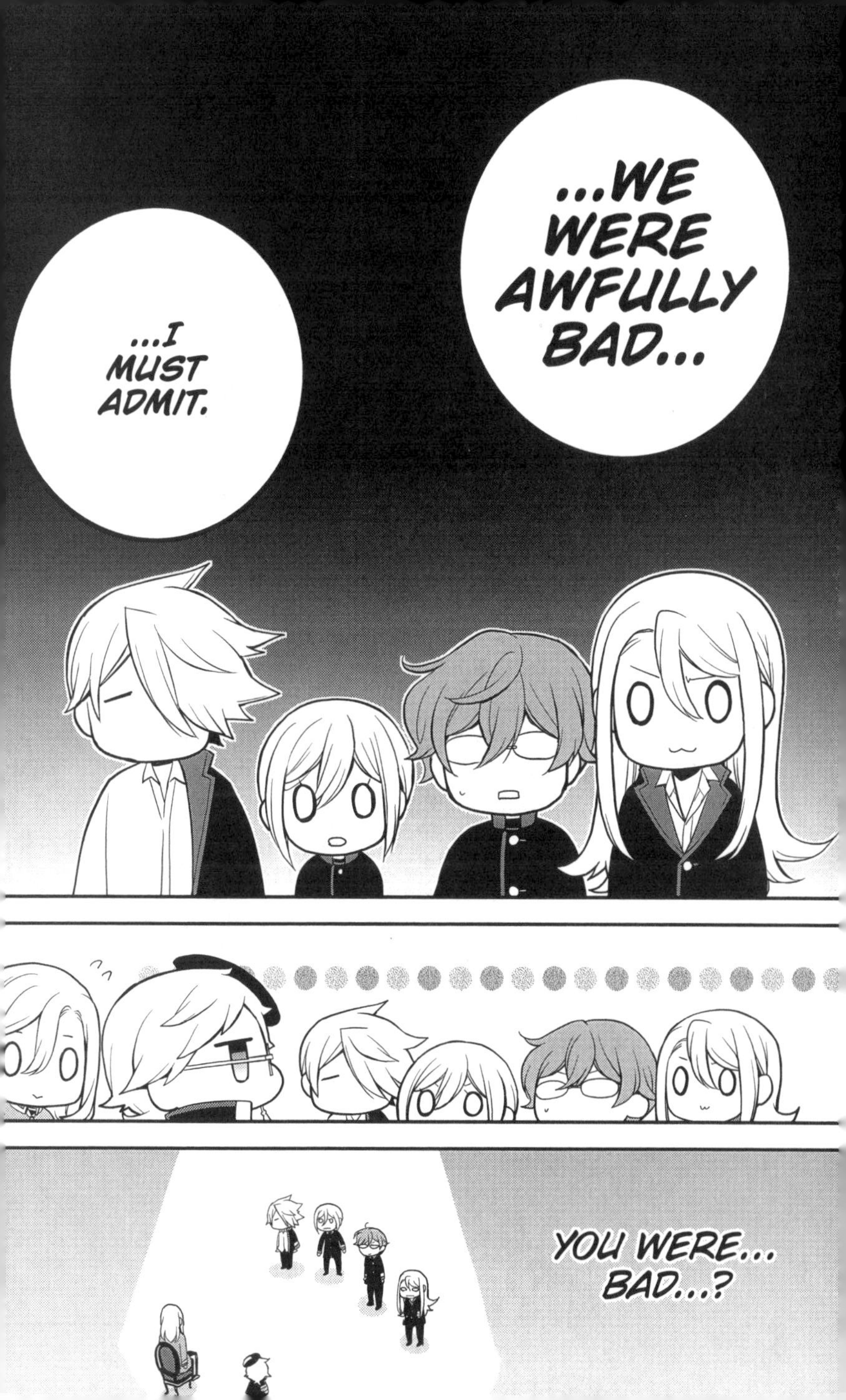
...WE WERE AWFULLY BAD...
...I MUST ADMIT.
YOU WERE... BAD...?

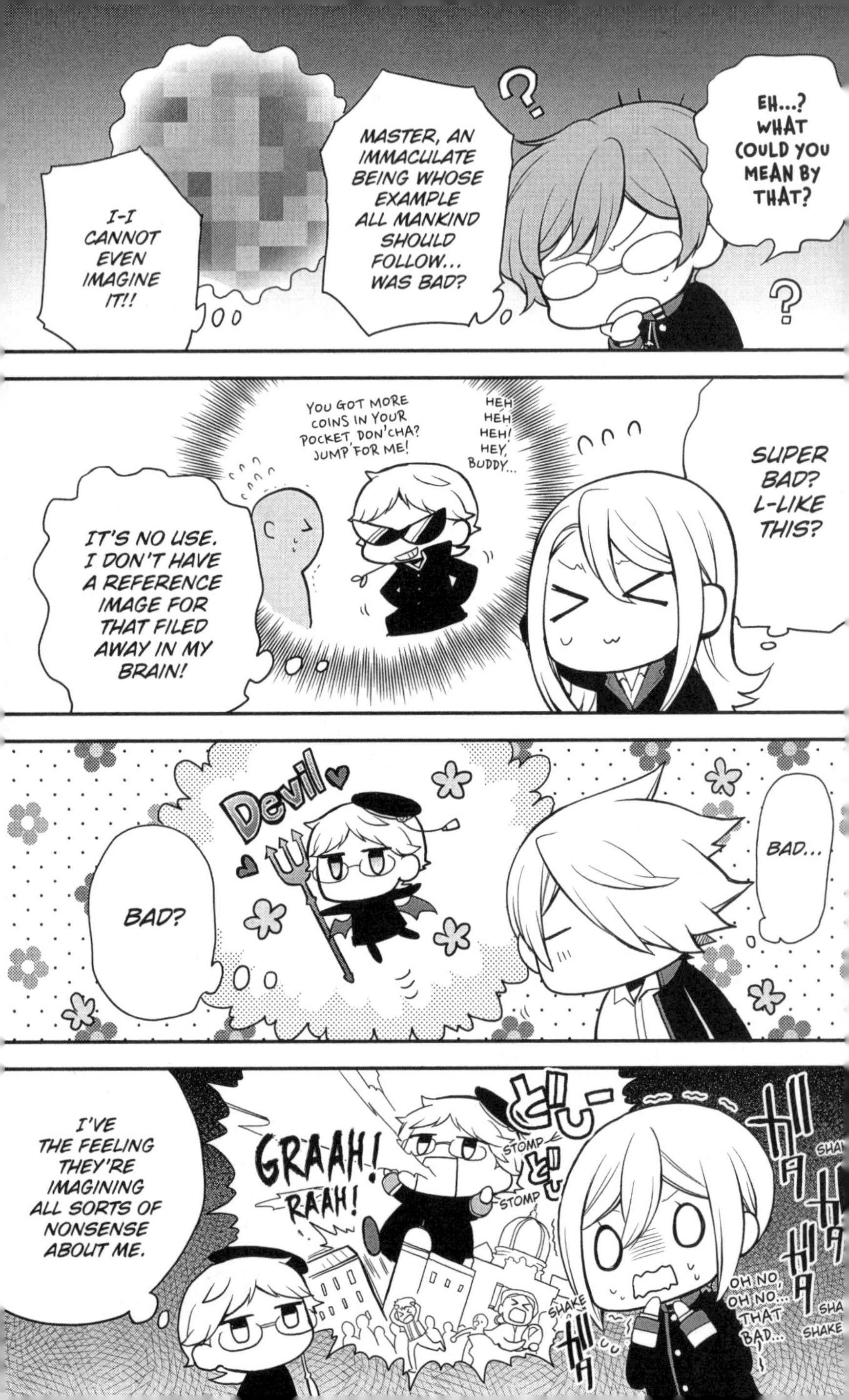
EH...? WHAT COULD YOU MEAN BY THAT?
MASTER, AN IMMACULATE BEING WHOSE EXAMPLE ALL MANKIND SHOULD FOLLOW... WAS BAD?
I-I CANNOT EVEN IMAGINE IT!!
SUPER BAD? L-LIKE THIS?
HEH HEH HEH! HEY, BUDDY...
YOU GOT MORE COINS IN YOUR POCKET, DON'CHA? JUMP FOR ME!
IT'S NO USE. I DON'T HAVE A REFERENCE IMAGE FOR THAT FILED AWAY IN MY BRAIN!
BAD...
Devil
BAD?
SHAKE
SHAKE
OH NO, OH NO... THAT BAD...
SHAKE
STOMP
STOMP
GRAAH!
RAAH!
I'VE THE FEELING THEY'RE IMAGINING ALL SORTS OF NONSENSE ABOUT ME.

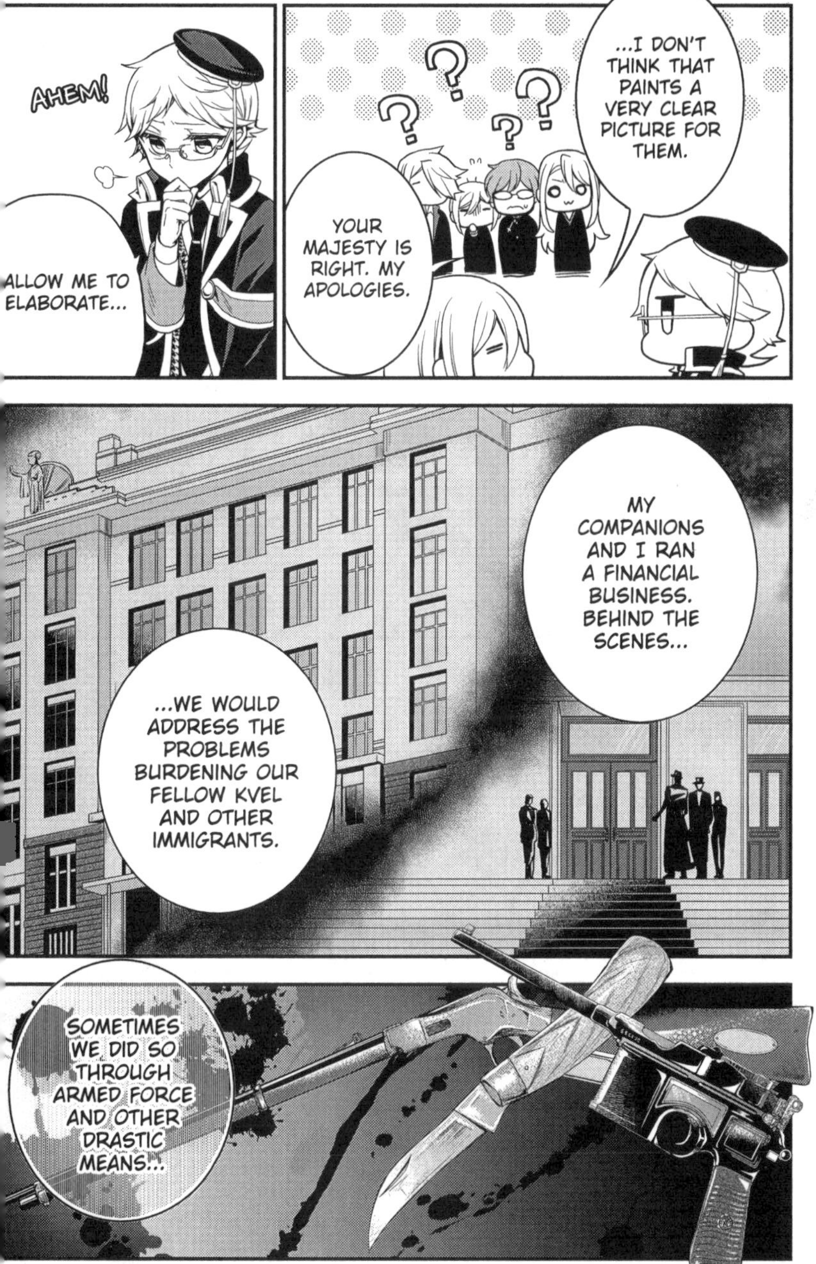
...I DON'T THINK THAT PAINTS A VERY CLEAR PICTURE FOR THEM.
YOUR MAJESTY IS RIGHT. MY APOLOGIES.
AHEM!
ALLOW ME TO ELABORATE...
MY COMPANIONS AND I RAN A FINANCIAL BUSINESS. BEHIND THE SCENES...
...WE WOULD ADDRESS THE PROBLEMS BURDENING OUR FELLOW KVEL AND OTHER IMMIGRANTS.
SOMETIMES WE DID SO THROUGH ARMED FORCE AND OTHER DRASTIC MEANS...

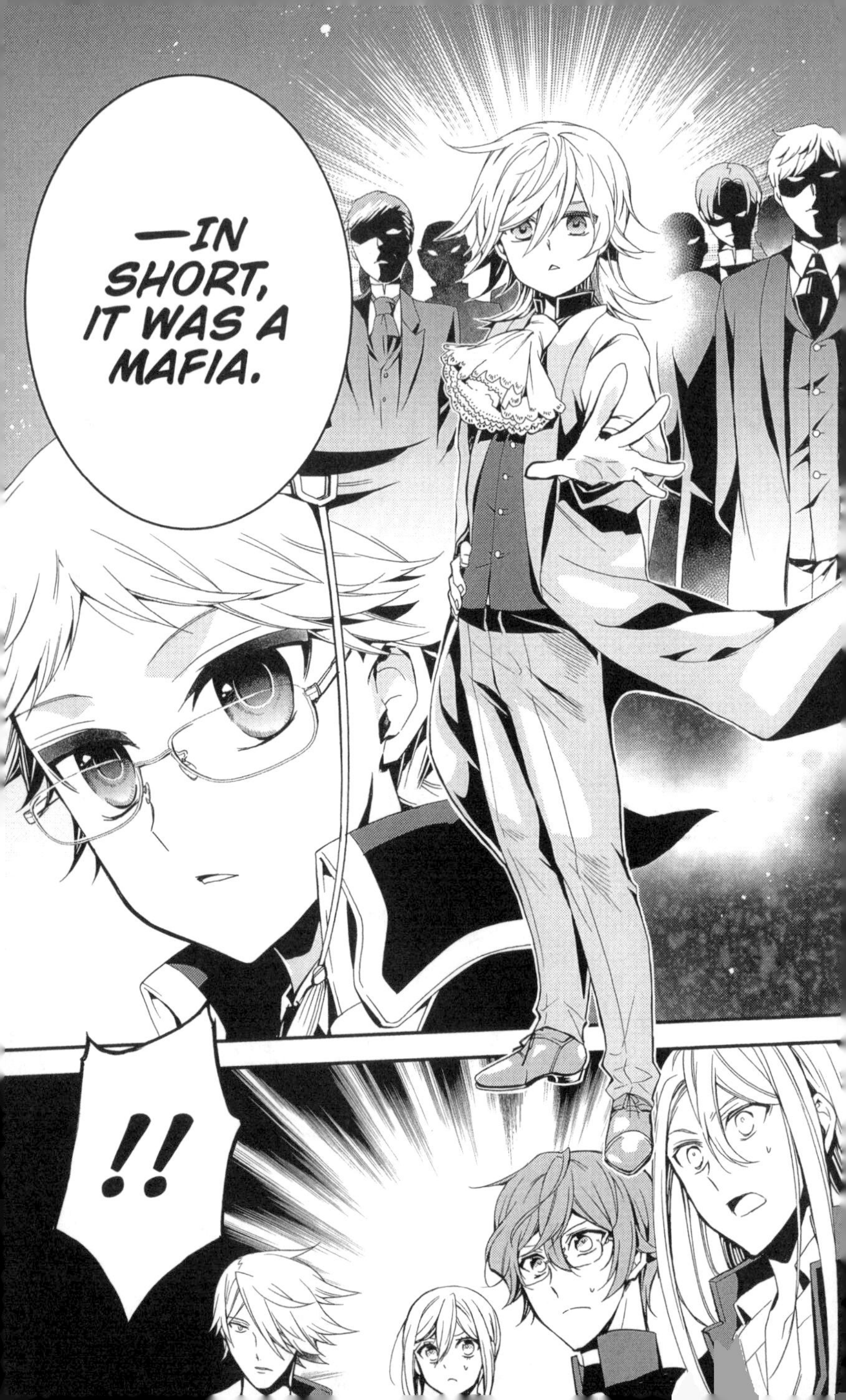
—IN SHORT, IT WAS A MAFIA.
!!

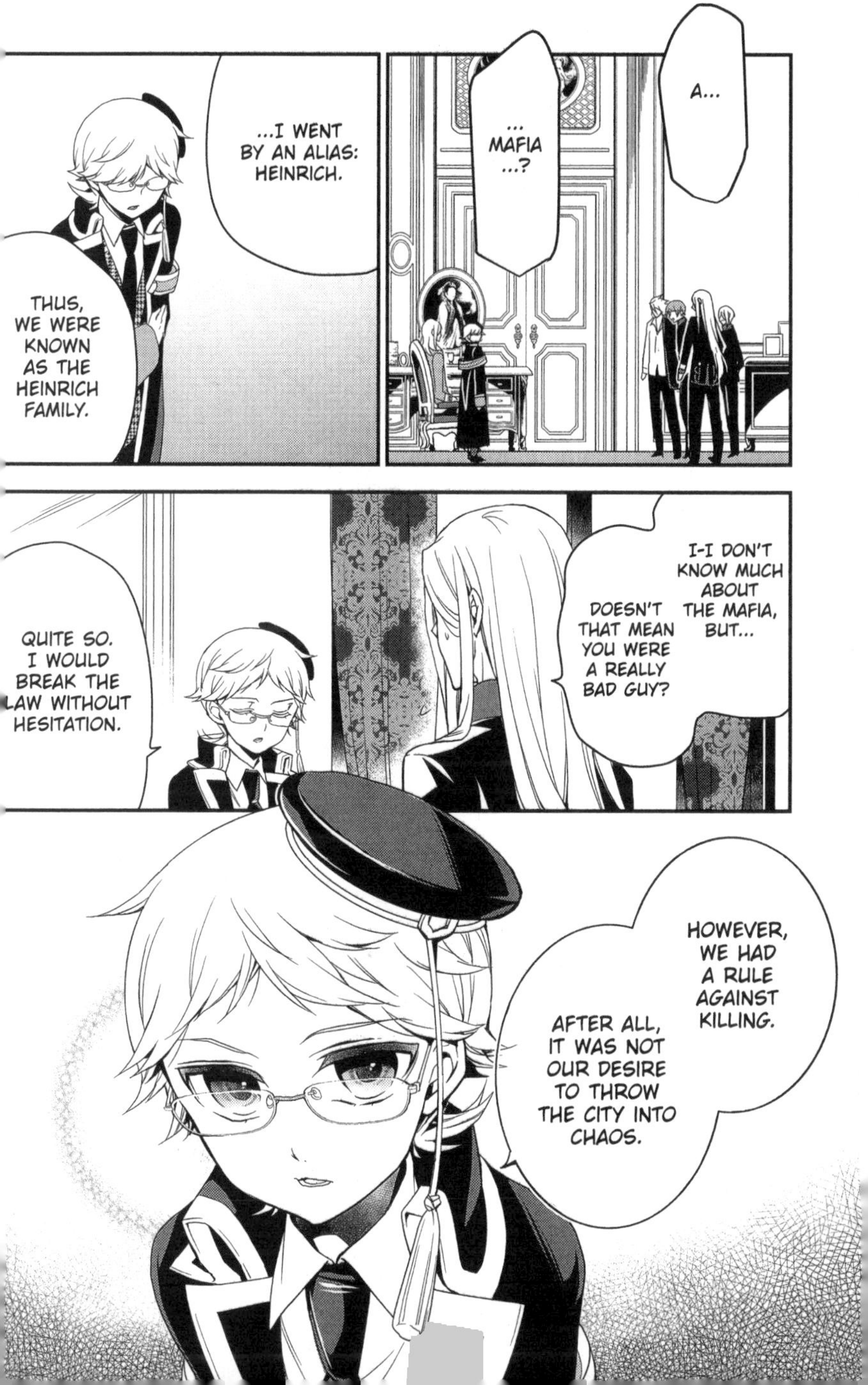
A...
...MAFIA...?
...I WENT BY AN ALIAS: HEINRICH.
THUS, WE WERE KNOWN AS THE HEINRICH FAMILY.
I-I DON'T KNOW MUCH ABOUT THE MAFIA, BUT...
DOESN'T THAT MEAN YOU WERE A REALLY BAD GUY?
QUITE SO. I WOULD BREAK THE LAW WITHOUT HESITATION.
HOWEVER, WE HAD A RULE AGAINST KILLING.
AFTER ALL, IT WAS NOT OUR DESIRE TO THROW THE CITY INTO CHAOS.

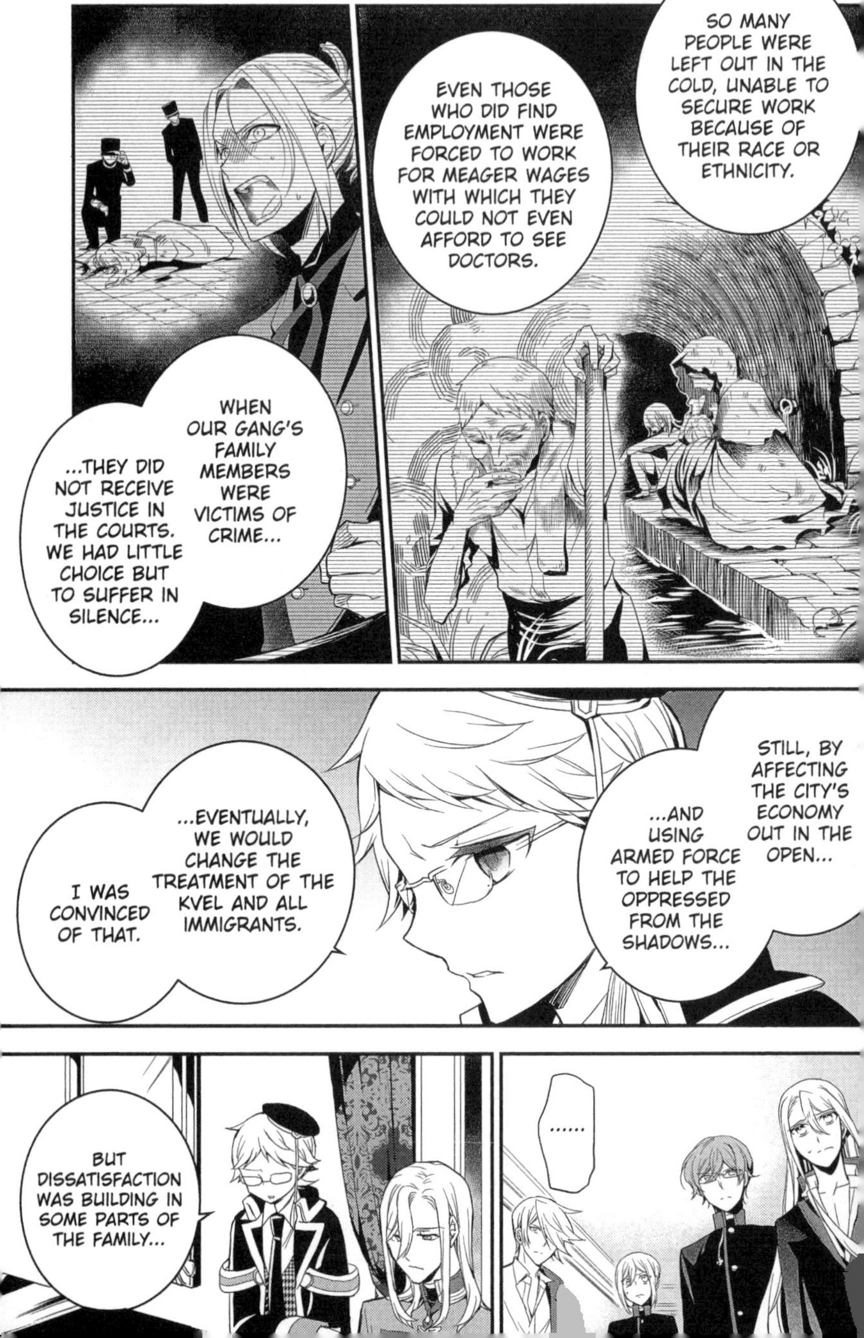
SO MANY PEOPLE WERE LEFT OUT IN THE COLD, UNABLE TO SECURE WORK BECAUSE OF THEIR RACE OR ETHNICITY.
EVEN THOSE WHO DID FIND EMPLOYMENT WERE FORCED TO WORK FOR MEAGER WAGES WITH WHICH THEY COULD NOT EVEN AFFORD TO SEE DOCTORS.
WHEN OUR GANG'S FAMILY MEMBERS WERE VICTIMS OF CRIME...
...THEY DID NOT RECEIVE JUSTICE IN THE COURTS. WE HAD LITTLE CHOICE BUT TO SUFFER IN SILENCE...
STILL, BY AFFECTING THE CITY'S ECONOMY OUT IN THE OPEN...
...AND USING ARMED FORCE TO HELP THE OPPRESSED FROM THE SHADOWS...
...EVENTUALLY, WE WOULD CHANGE THE TREATMENT OF THE KVEL AND ALL IMMIGRANTS.
I WAS CONVINCED OF THAT.
......
BUT DISSATISFACTION WAS BUILDING IN SOME PARTS OF THE FAMILY...

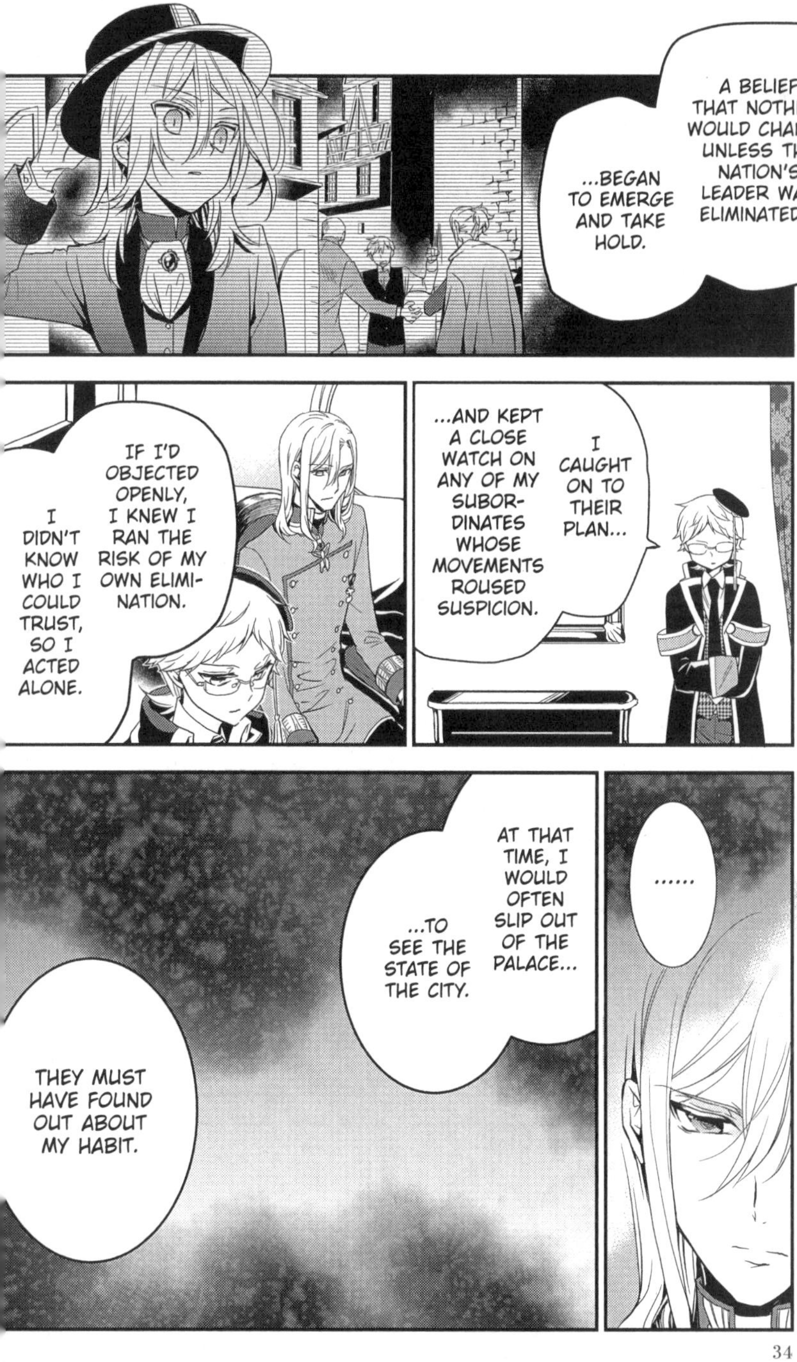
A BELIEF THAT NOTHING WOULD CHANGE UNLESS THE NATION'S LEADER WAS ELIMINATED...
...BEGAN TO EMERGE AND TAKE HOLD.
I CAUGHT ON TO THEIR PLAN...
...AND KEPT A CLOSE WATCH ON ANY OF MY SUBOR-DINATES WHOSE MOVEMENTS ROUSED SUSPICION.
IF I'D OBJECTED OPENLY, I KNEW I RAN THE RISK OF MY OWN ELIMI-NATION.
I DIDN'T KNOW WHO I COULD TRUST, SO I ACTED ALONE.
......
AT THAT TIME, I WOULD OFTEN SLIP OUT OF THE PALACE...
...TO SEE THE STATE OF THE CITY.
THEY MUST HAVE FOUND OUT ABOUT MY HABIT.

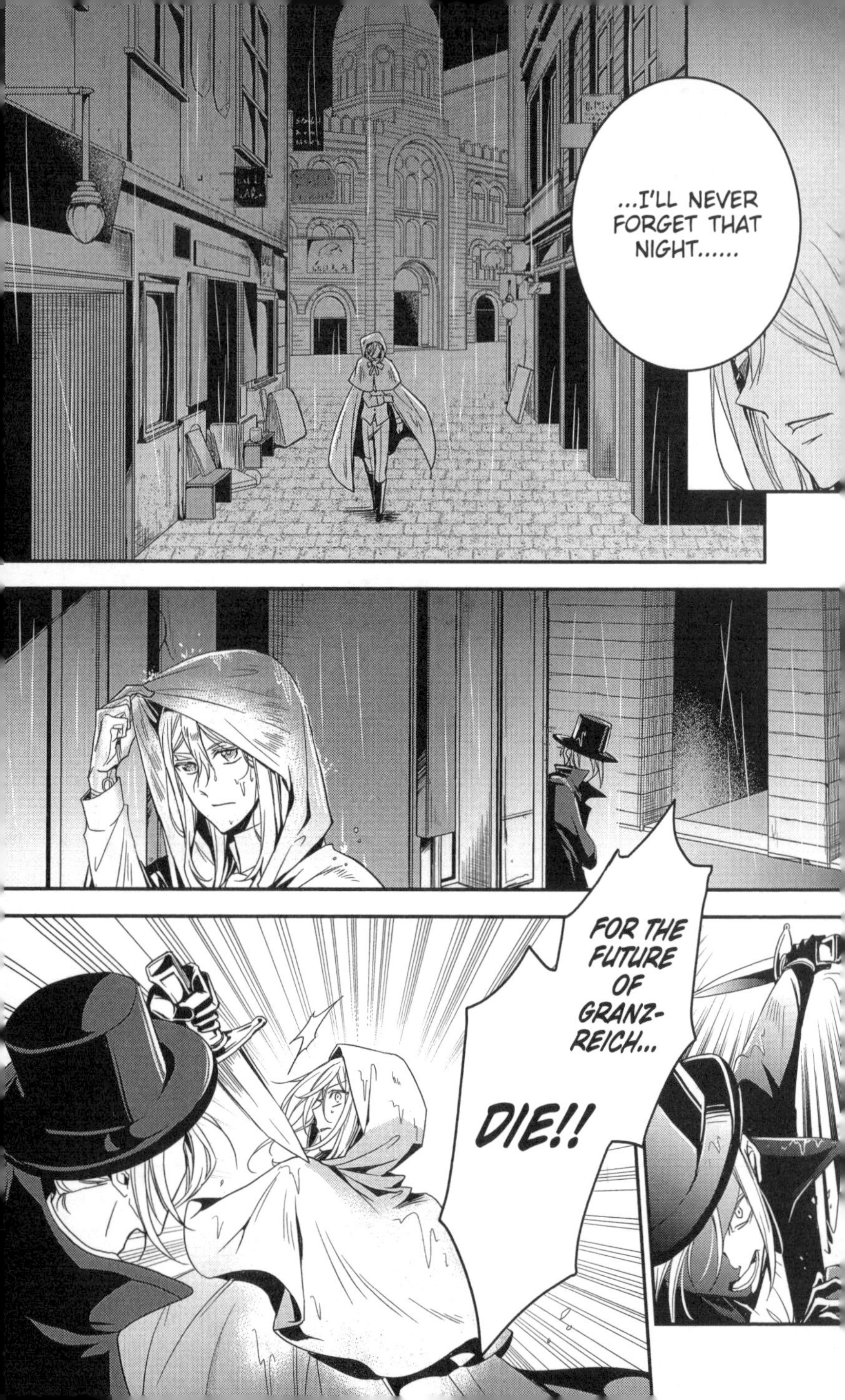
...I'LL NEVER FORGET THAT NIGHT......
FOR THE FUTURE OF GRANZ-REICH...
DIE!!

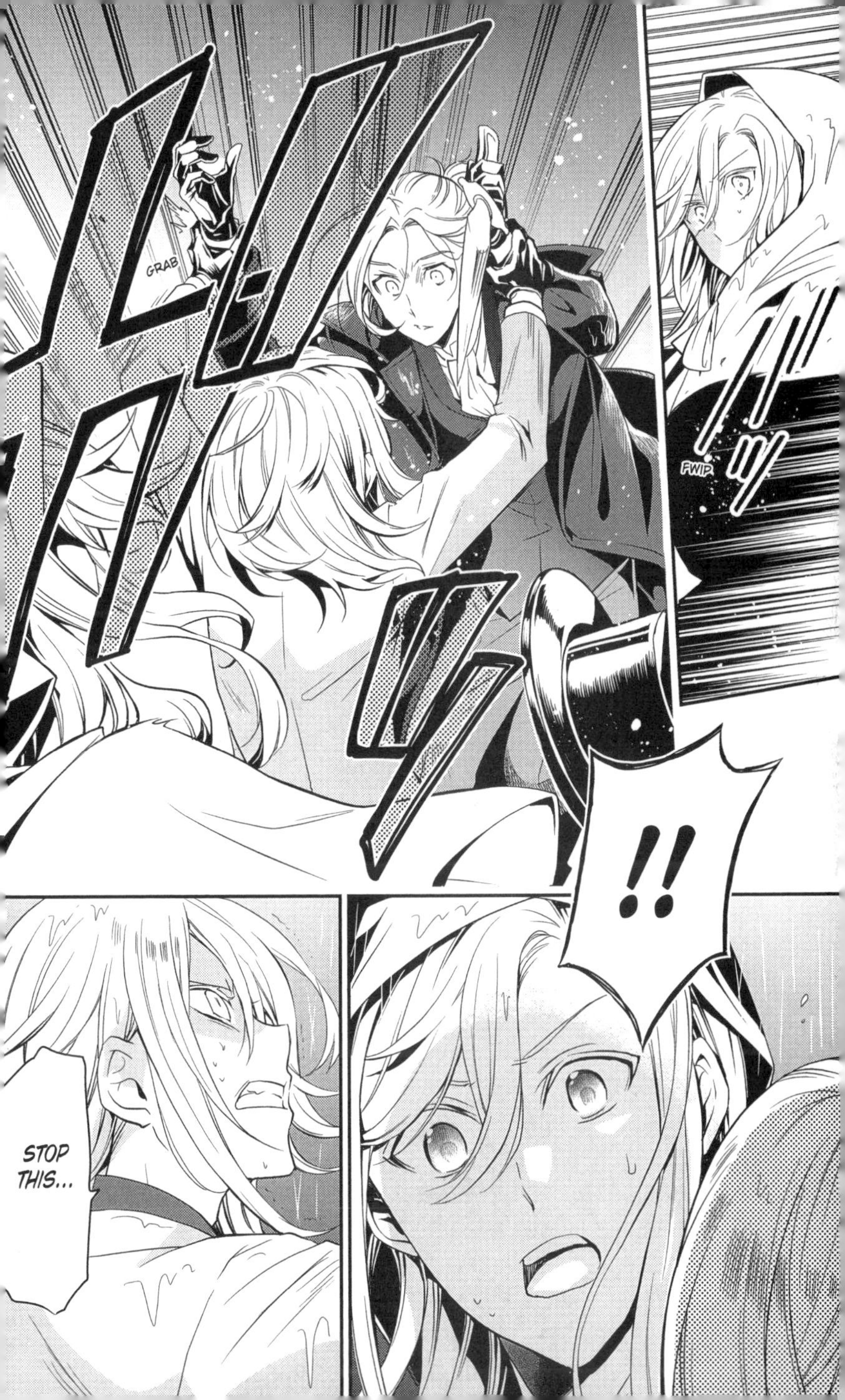
FWIP
GRAB
!!
STOP THIS...

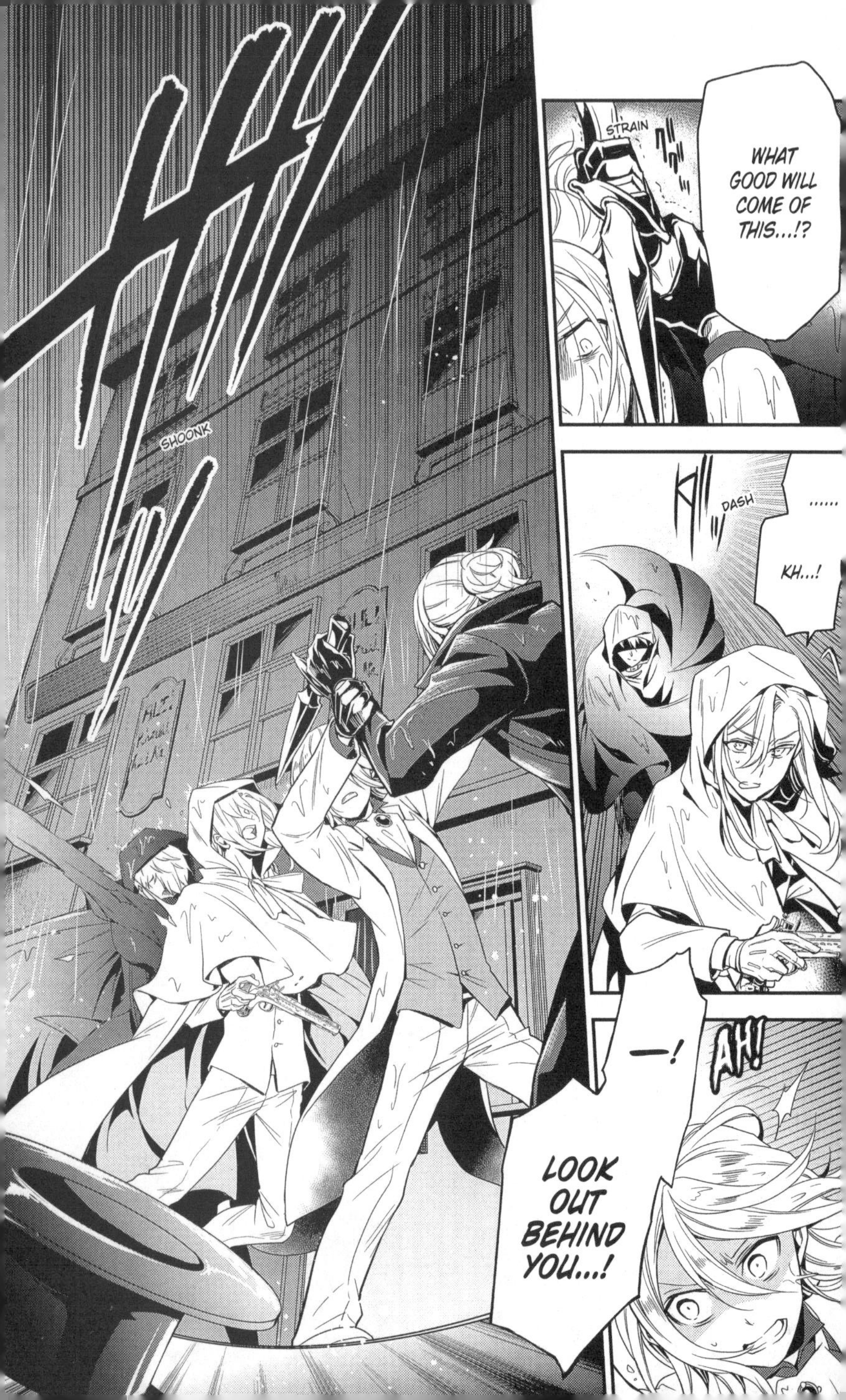

WHAT GOOD WILL COME OF THIS...!?
STRAIN
......
DASH
KH...!
AH!
—!
LOOK OUT BEHIND YOU...!
SHOONK

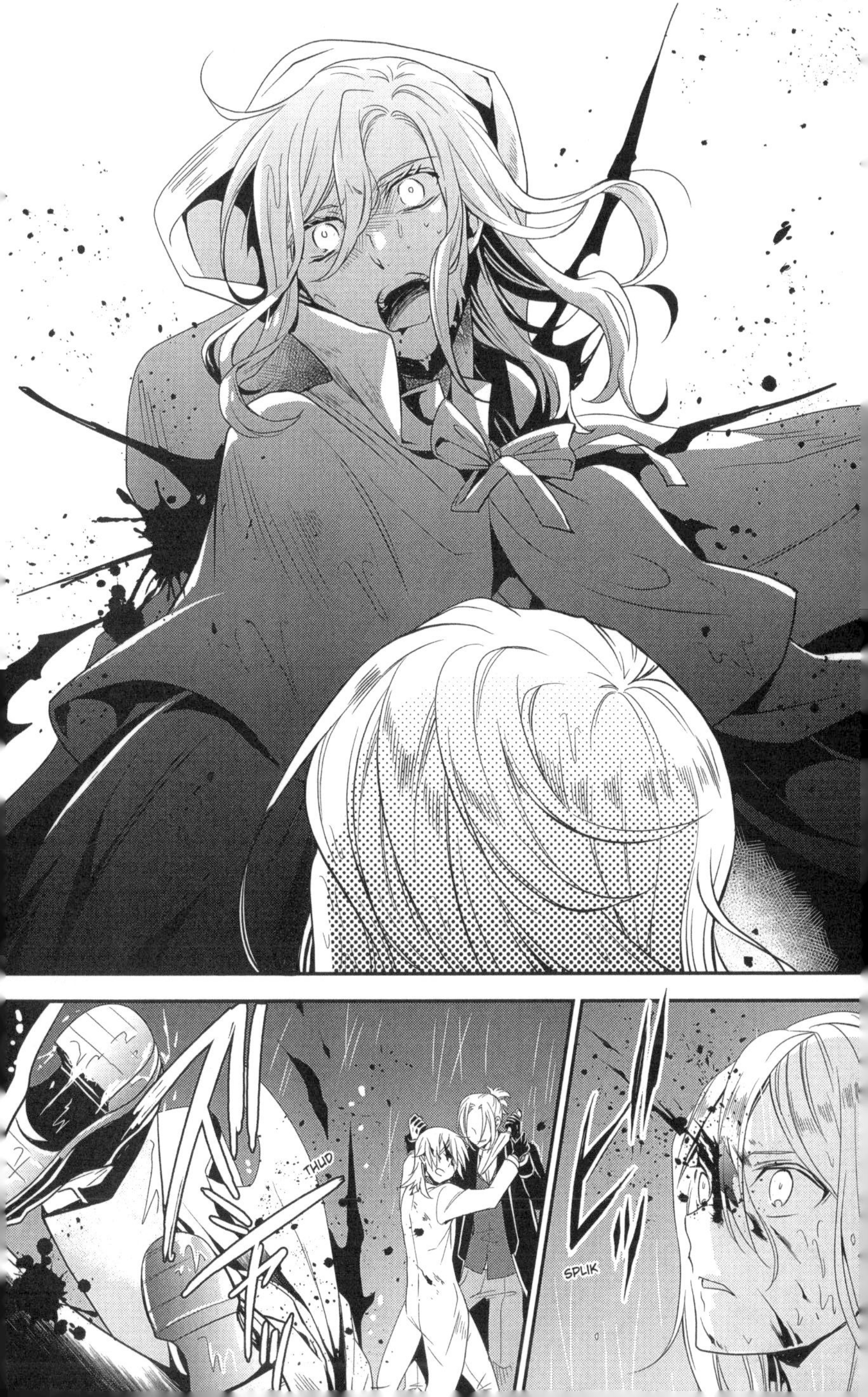
SPLIK
THUD

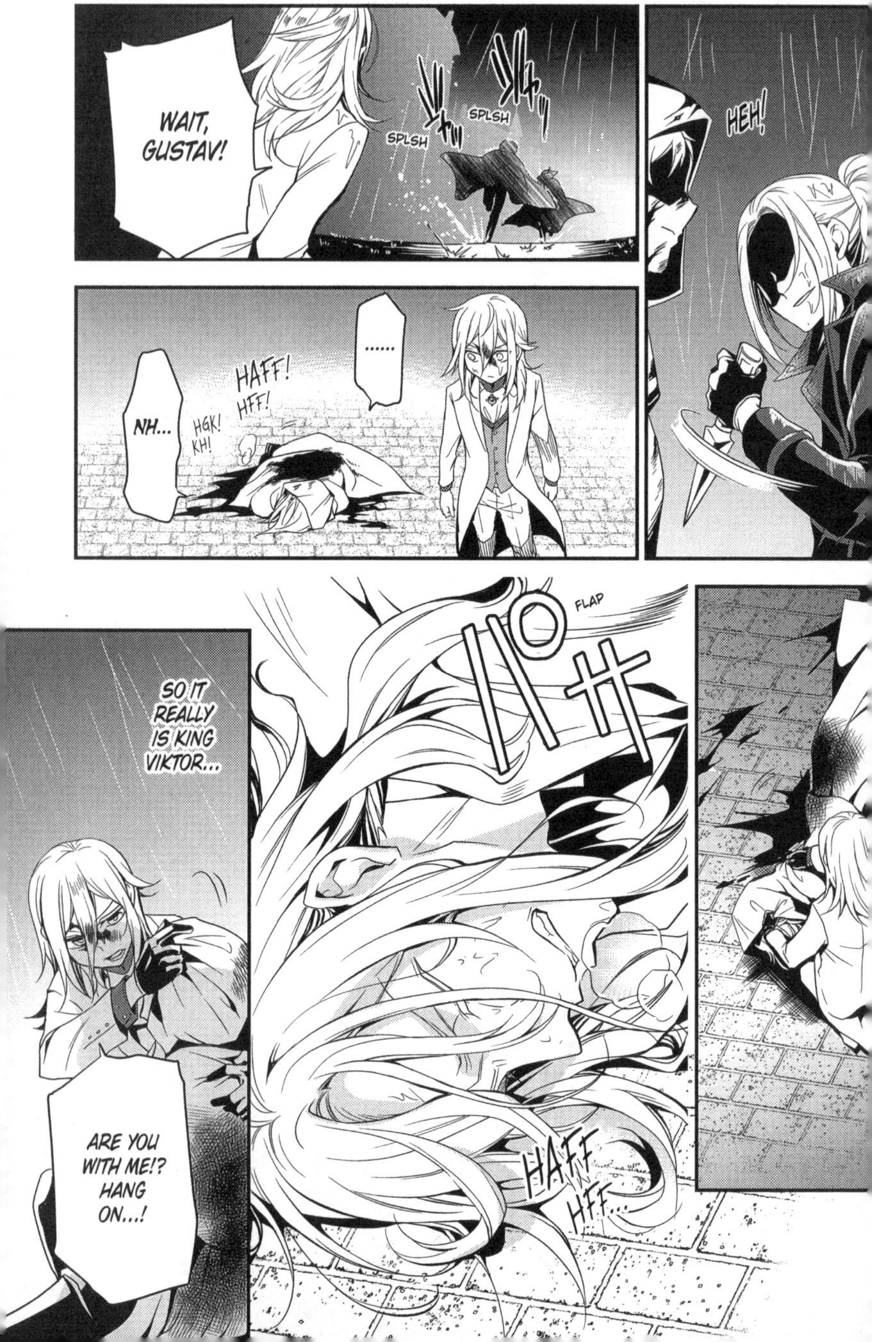
HEH!
SPLSH
SPLSH
WAIT, GUSTAV!
......
HAFF! HFF!
HGK! KH!
NH...
FLAP
HAFF HFF...
SO IT REALLY IS KING VIKTOR...
ARE YOU WITH ME!? HANG ON...!

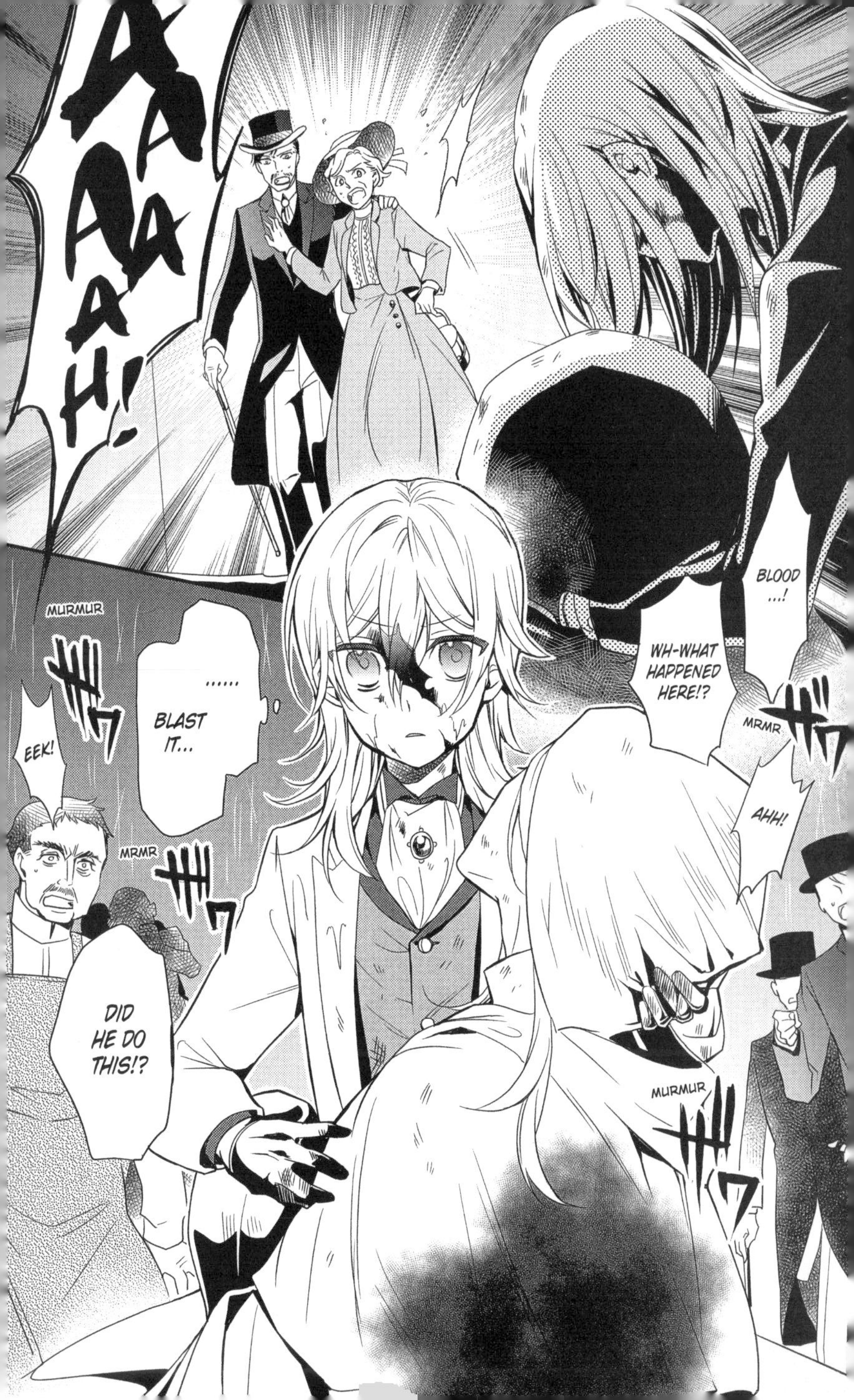
AAAAAAH!
BLOOD ...!
WH-WHAT HAPPENED HERE!?
MRMR
AHH!
MURMUR
......
BLAST IT...
MURMUR
EEK!
MRMR
DID HE DO THIS!?

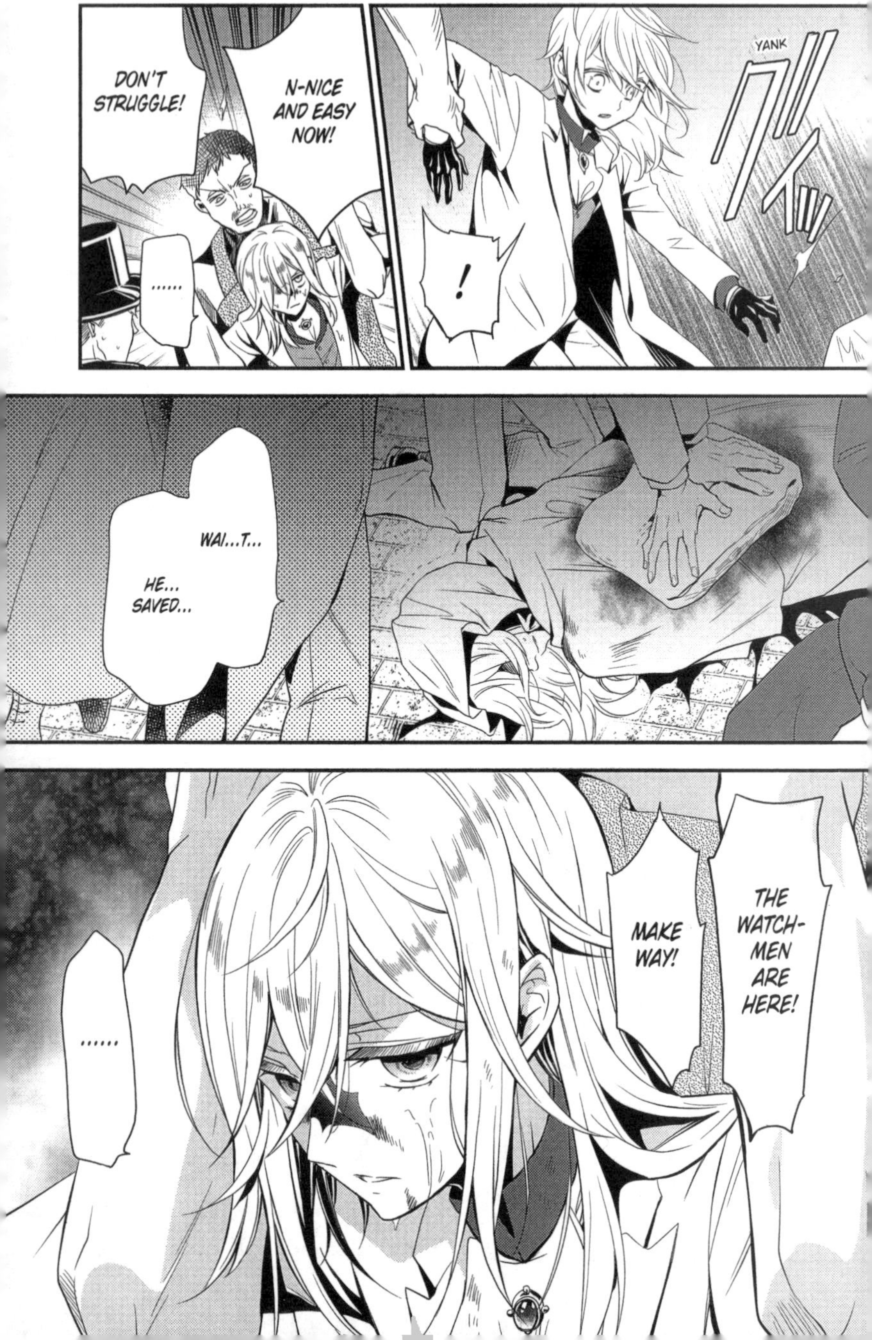
YANK
!
N-NICE AND EASY NOW!
DON'T STRUGGLE!
......
WAI...T...
HE... SAVED...
THE WATCH-MEN ARE HERE!
MAKE WAY!
......

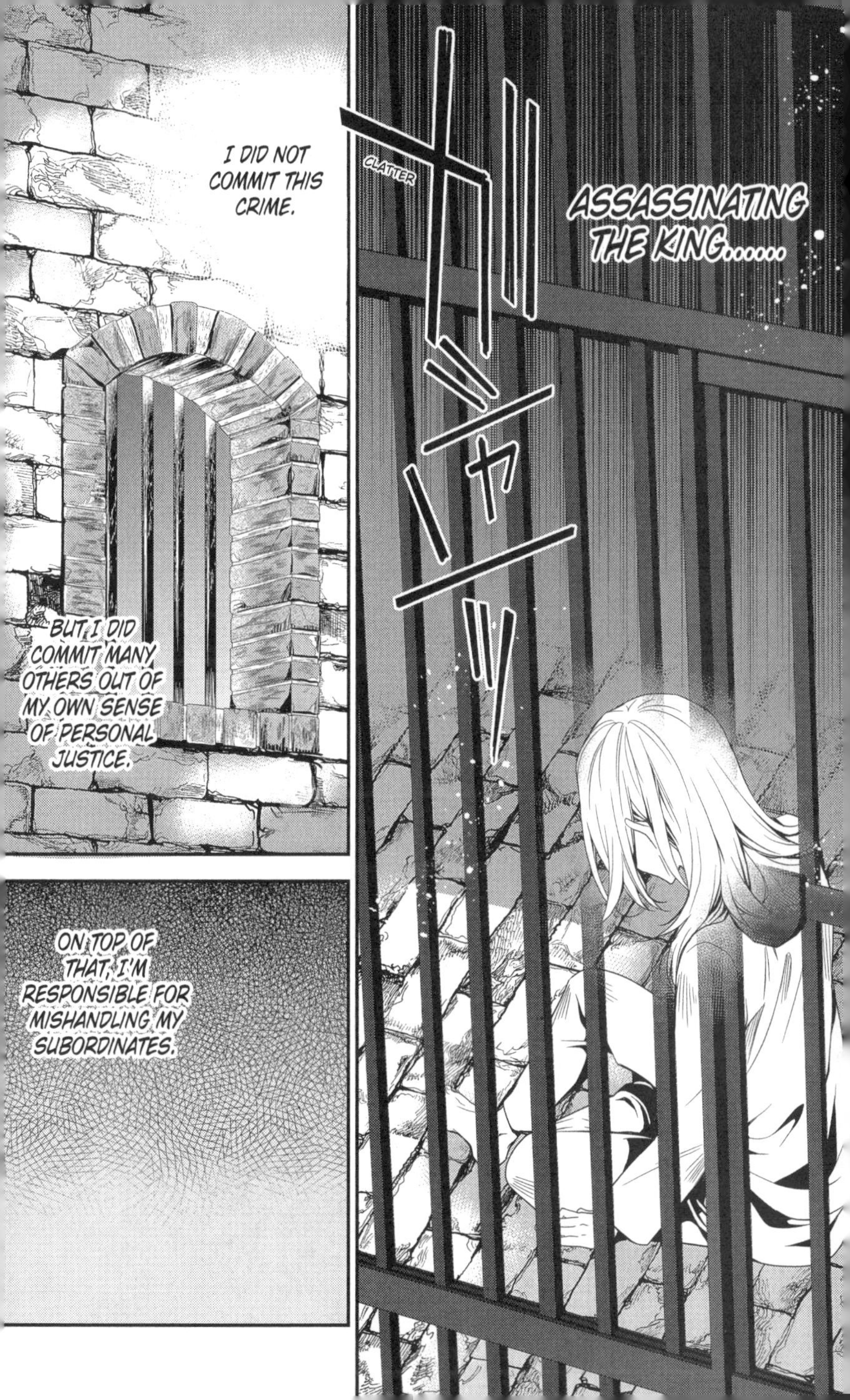
CLATTER
ASSASSINATING THE KING......
I DID NOT COMMIT THIS CRIME.
BUT I DID COMMIT MANY OTHERS OUT OF MY OWN SENSE OF PERSONAL JUSTICE.
ON TOP OF THAT, I'M RESPONSIBLE FOR MISHANDLING MY SUBORDINATES.

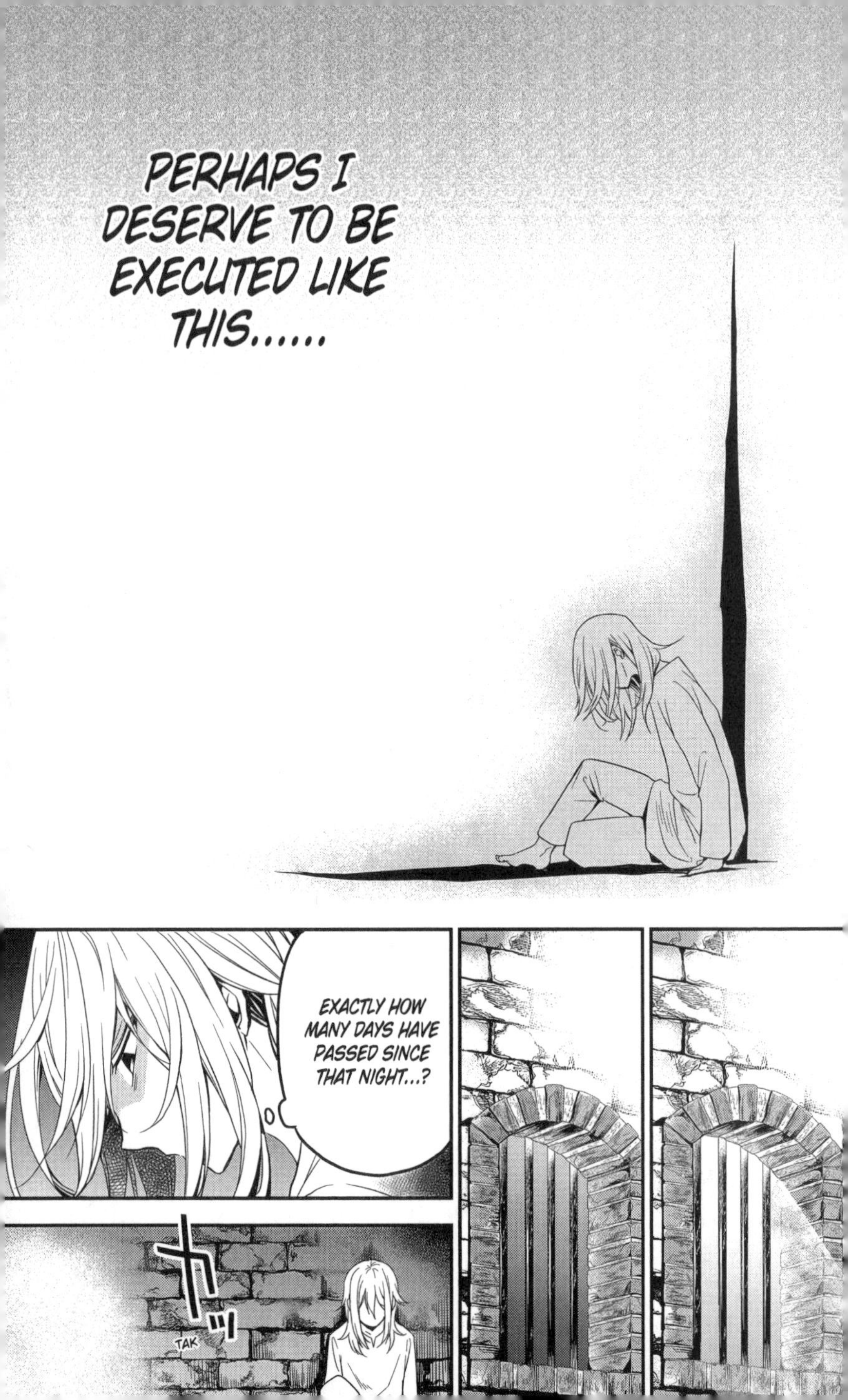

PERHAPS I DESERVE TO BE EXECUTED LIKE THIS......
EXACTLY HOW MANY DAYS HAVE PASSED SINCE THAT NIGHT...?
TAK

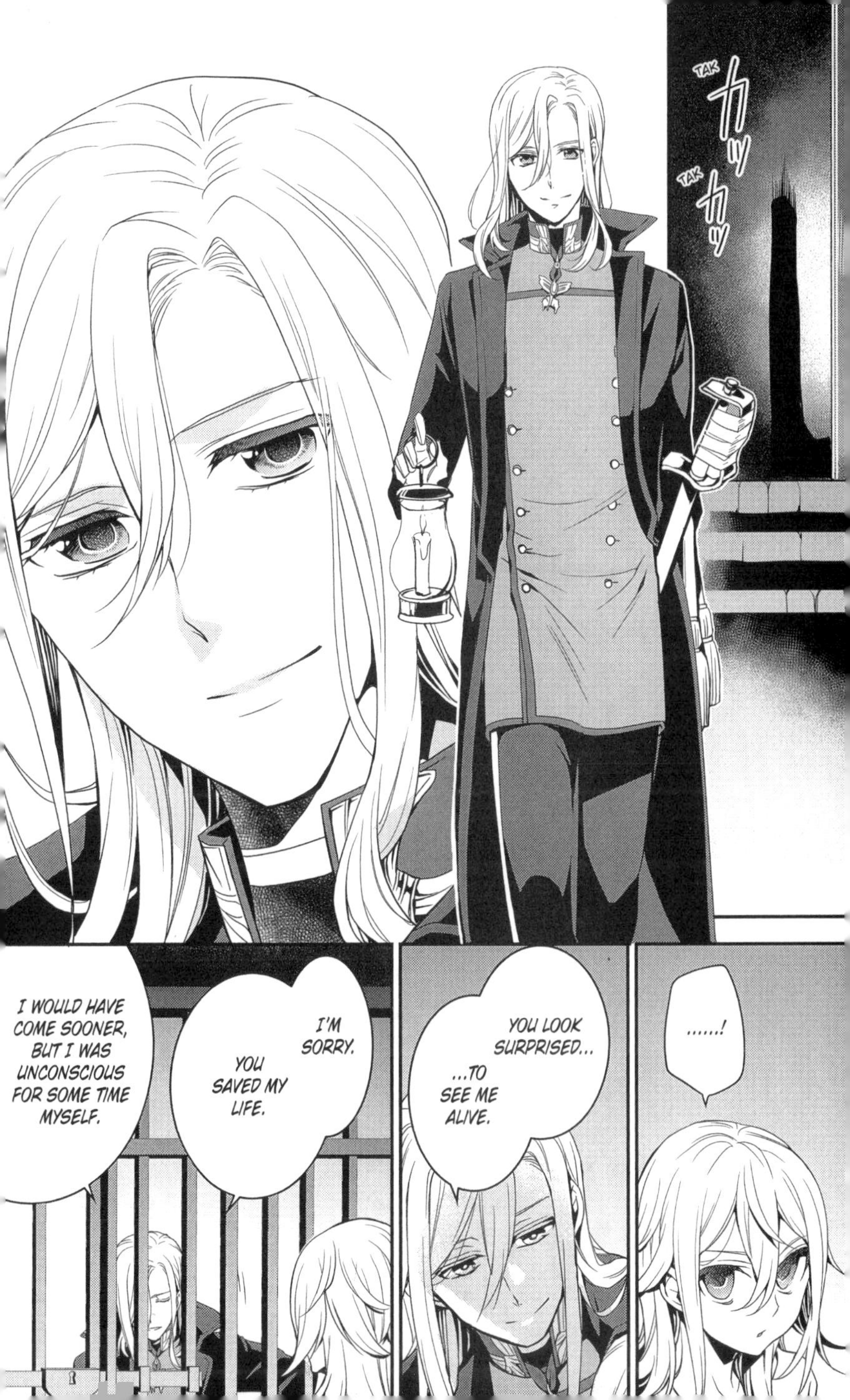
TAK
カッ
TAK
カッ
......!
YOU LOOK SURPRISED...
...TO SEE ME ALIVE.
I'M SORRY.
YOU SAVED MY LIFE.
I WOULD HAVE COME SOONER, BUT I WAS UNCONSCIOUS FOR SOME TIME MYSELF.

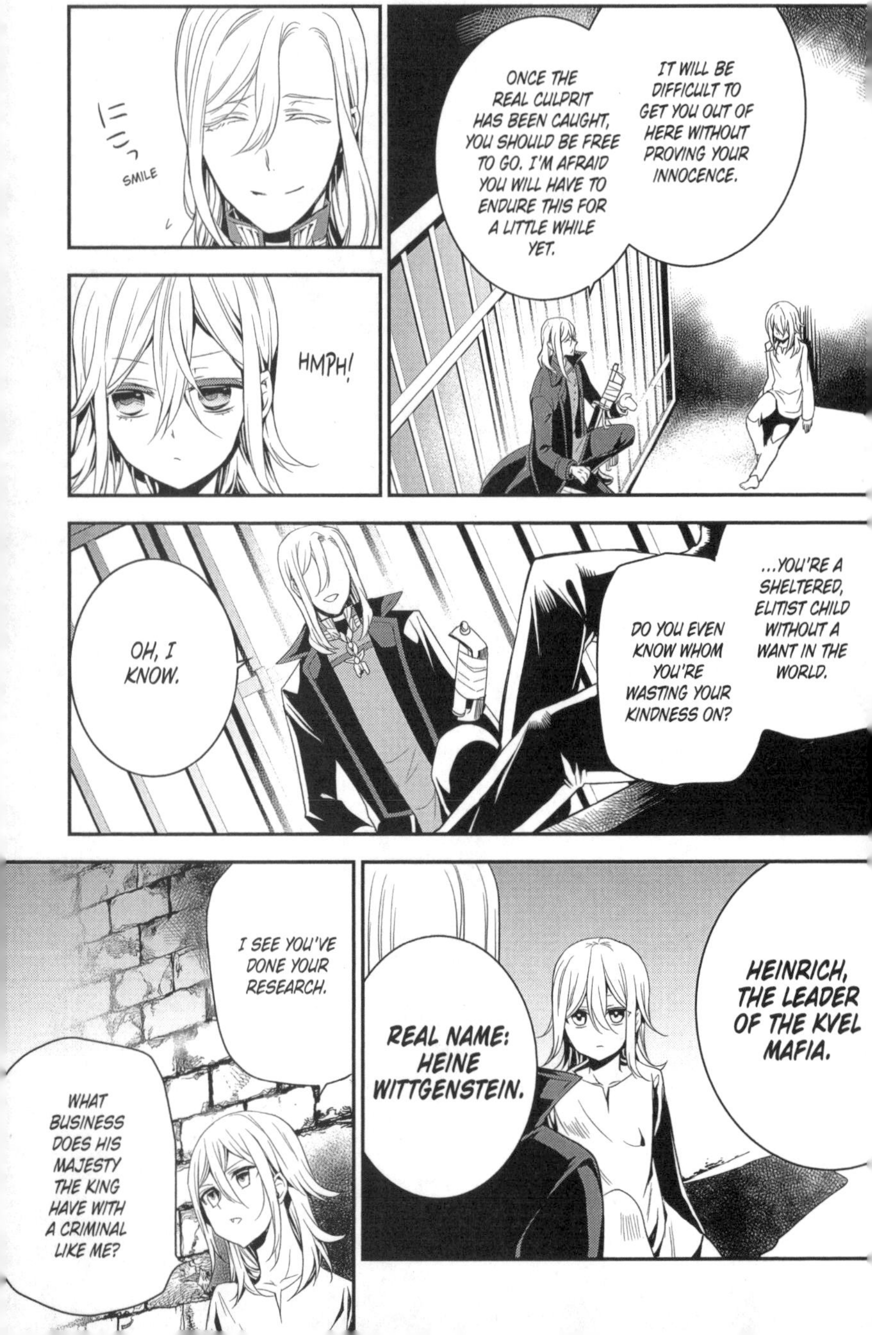
IT WILL BE DIFFICULT TO GET YOU OUT OF HERE WITHOUT PROVING YOUR INNOCENCE.
ONCE THE REAL CULPRIT HAS BEEN CAUGHT, YOU SHOULD BE FREE TO GO. I'M AFRAID YOU WILL HAVE TO ENDURE THIS FOR A LITTLE WHILE YET.
SMILE
HMPH!
...YOU'RE A SHELTERED, ELITIST CHILD WITHOUT A WANT IN THE WORLD.
DO YOU EVEN KNOW WHOM YOU'RE WASTING YOUR KINDNESS ON?
OH, I KNOW.
HEINRICH, THE LEADER OF THE KVEL MAFIA.
REAL NAME: HEINE WITTGENSTEIN.
I SEE YOU'VE DONE YOUR RESEARCH.
WHAT BUSINESS DOES HIS MAJESTY THE KING HAVE WITH A CRIMINAL LIKE ME?

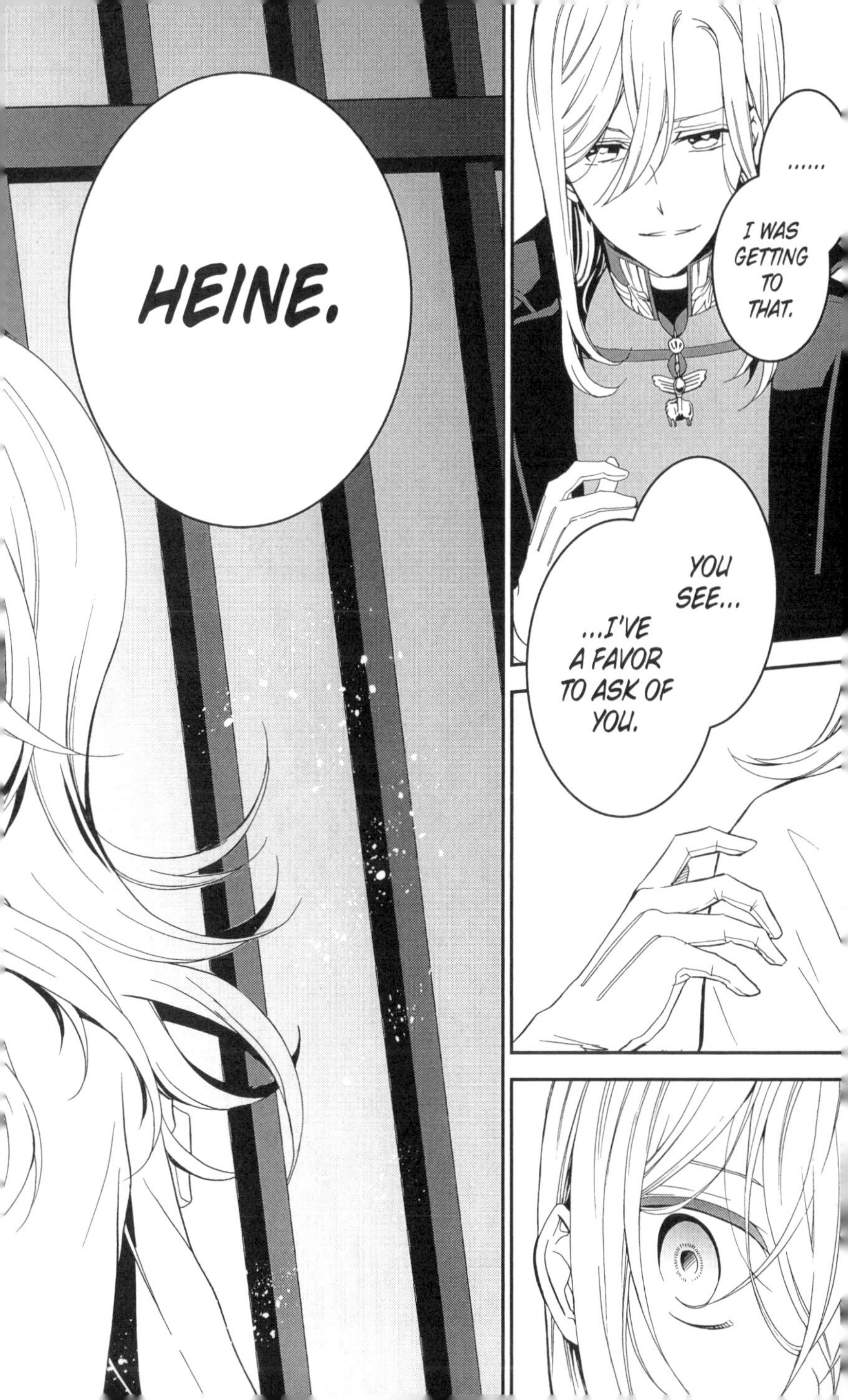
......
I WAS GETTING TO THAT.
YOU SEE...
...I'VE A FAVOR TO ASK OF YOU.
HEINE.

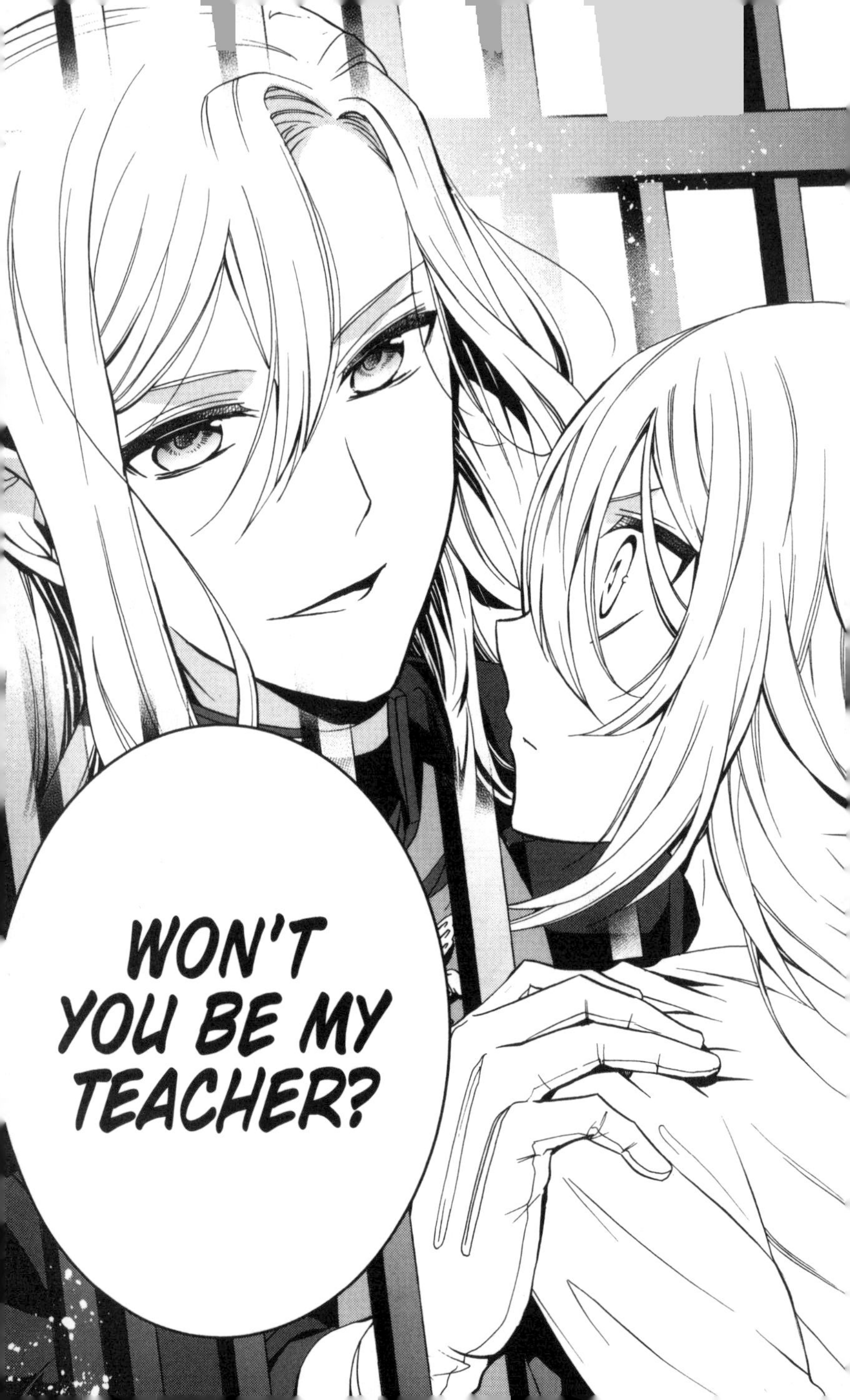
WON'T YOU BE MY TEACHER?

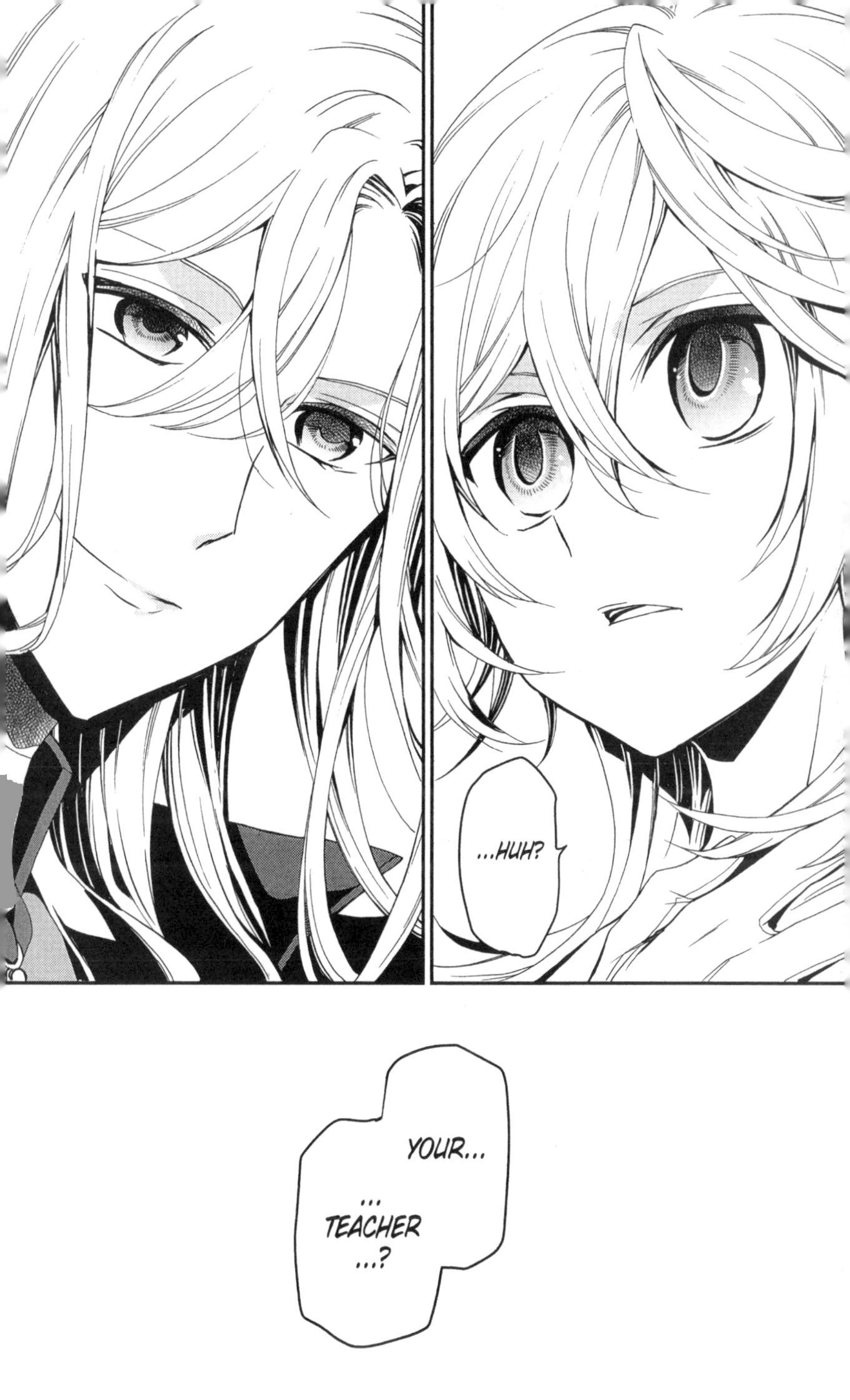
...HUH?
YOUR...
... TEACHER ...?

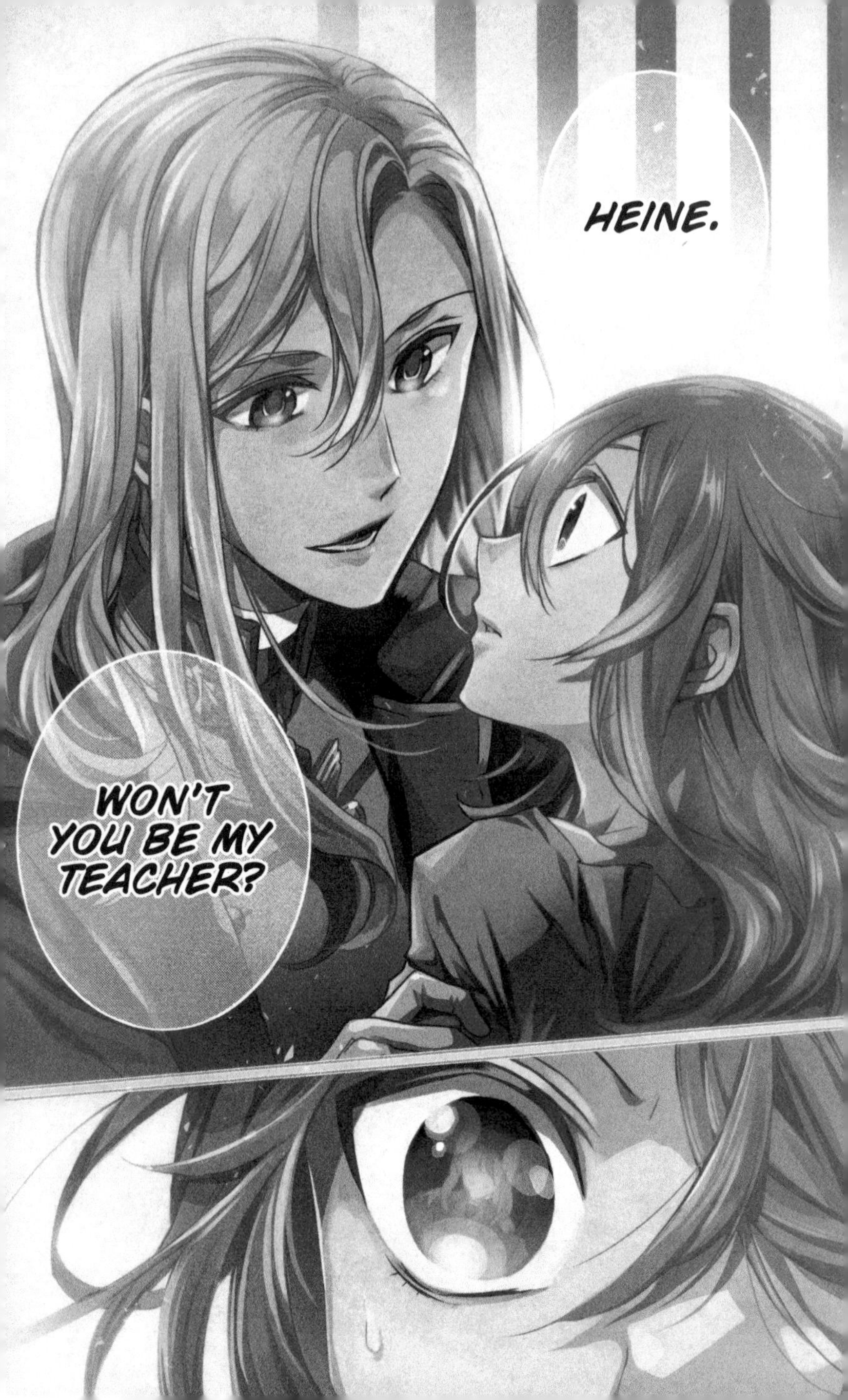
HEINE.
WON'T YOU BE MY TEACHER?

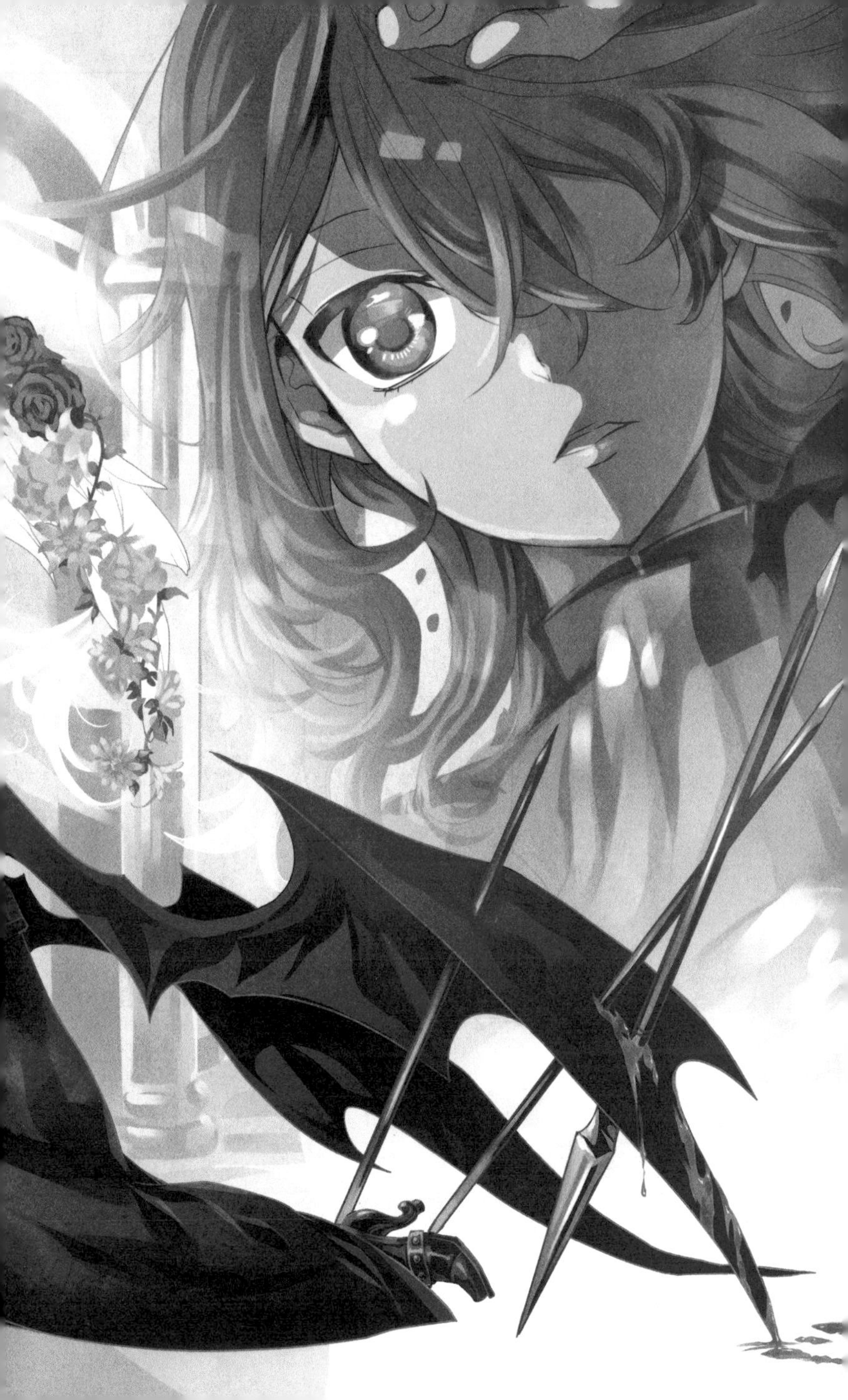

Chapter 87
I Want You Here

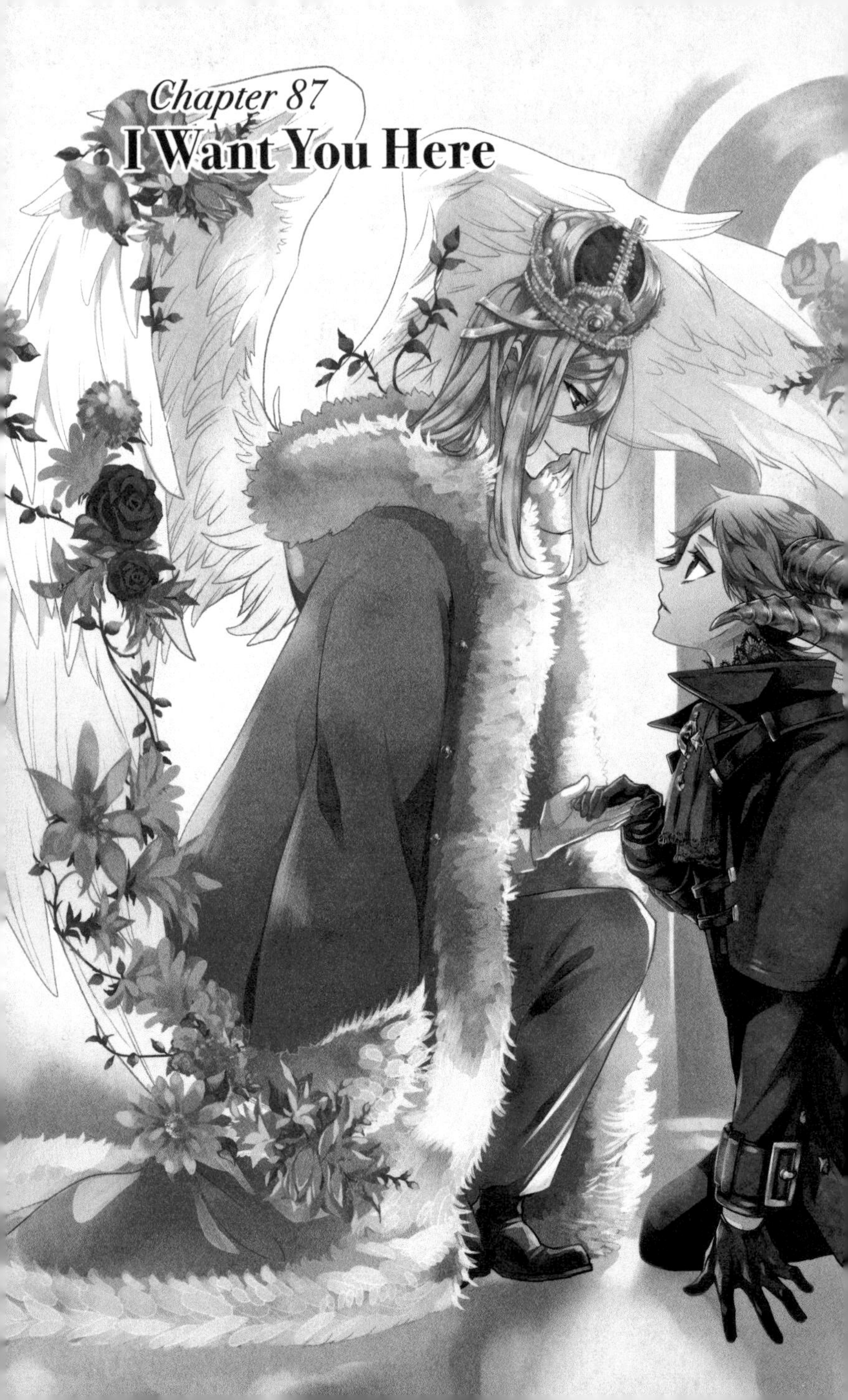

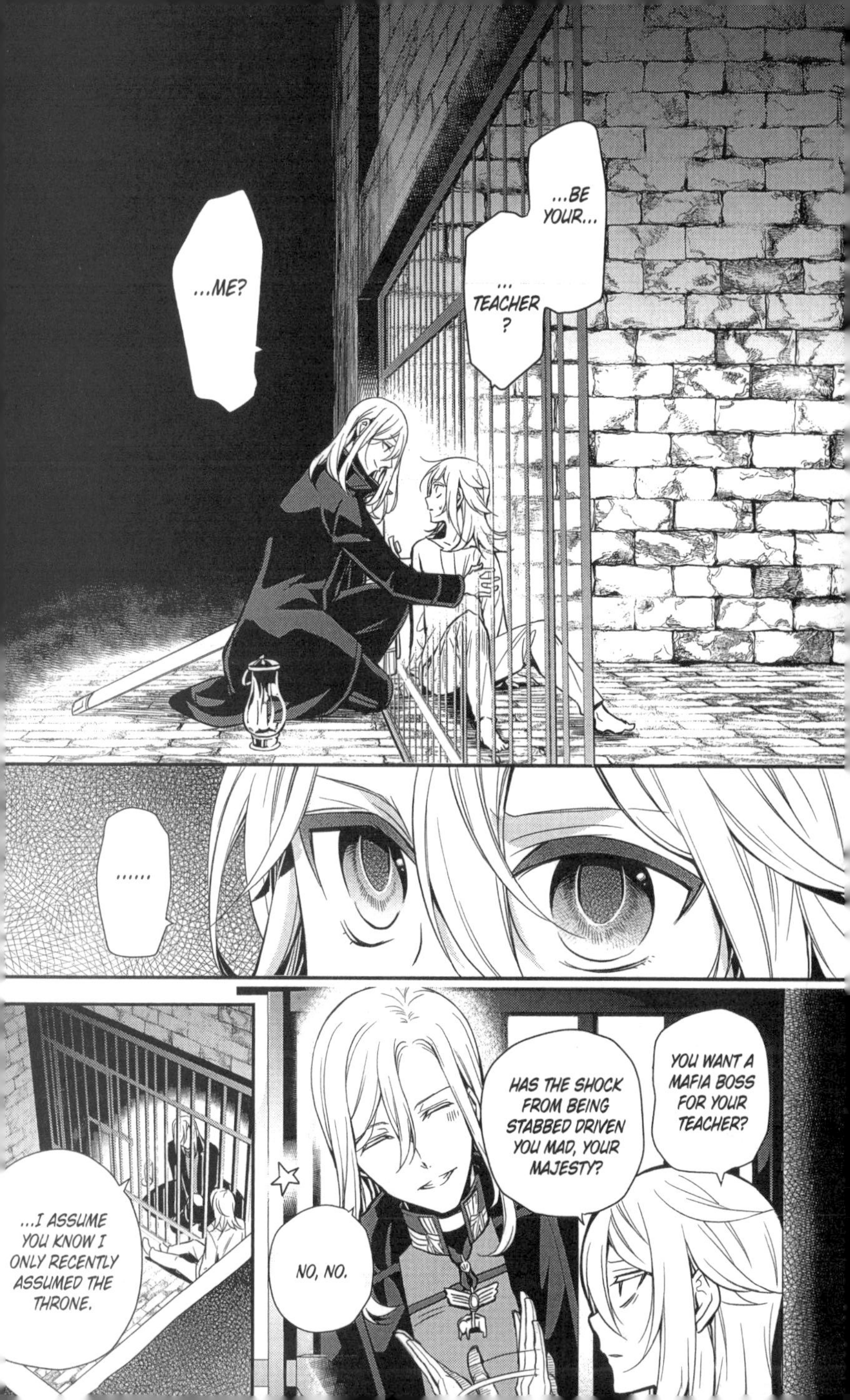
...BE YOUR...
...TEACHER?
...ME?
......
YOU WANT A MAFIA BOSS FOR YOUR TEACHER?
HAS THE SHOCK FROM BEING STABBED DRIVEN YOU MAD, YOUR MAJESTY?
NO, NO.
...I ASSUME YOU KNOW I ONLY RECENTLY ASSUMED THE THRONE.

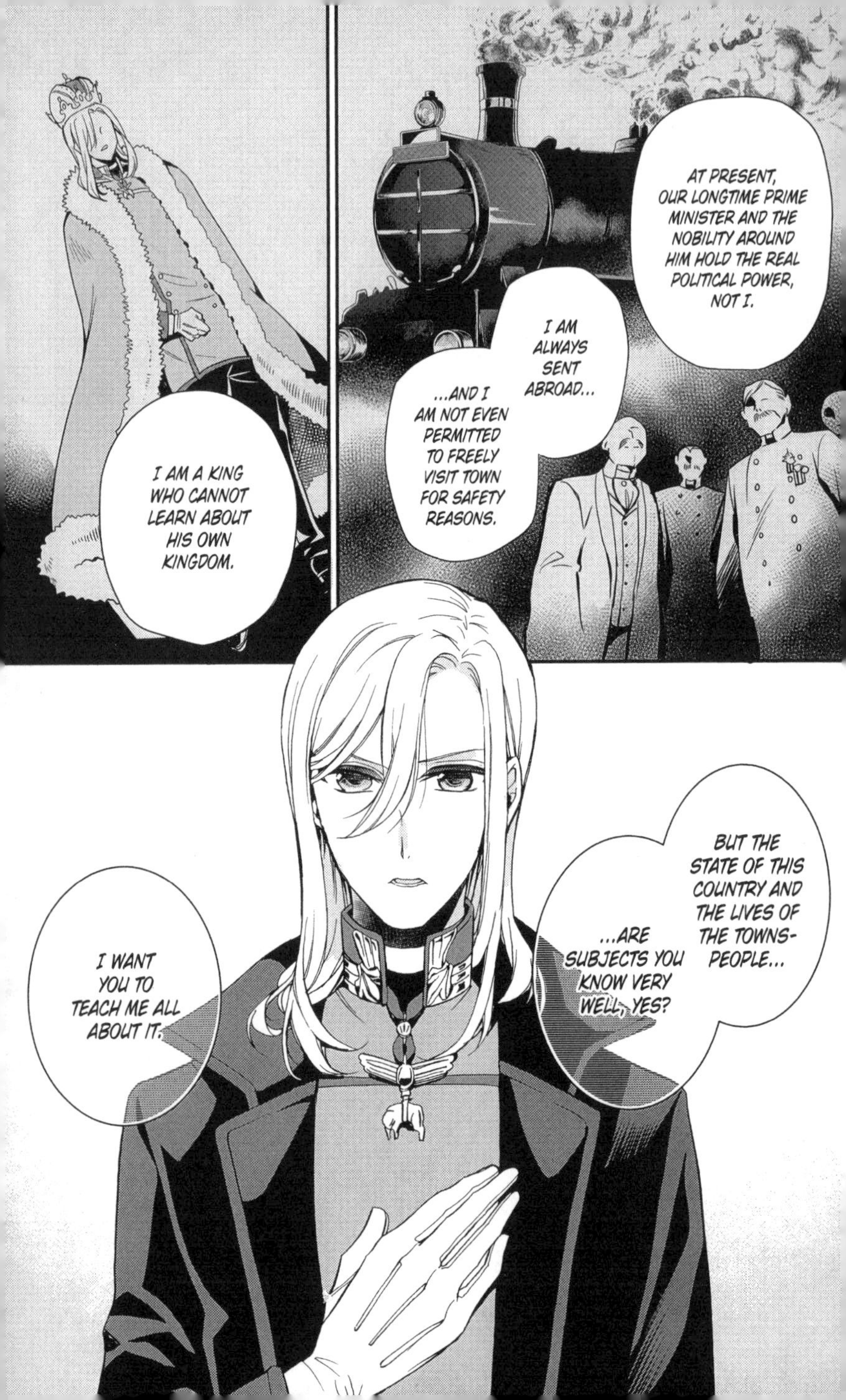
AT PRESENT, OUR LONGTIME PRIME MINISTER AND THE NOBILITY AROUND HIM HOLD THE REAL POLITICAL POWER, NOT I.
I AM ALWAYS SENT ABROAD...
...AND I AM NOT EVEN PERMITTED TO FREELY VISIT TOWN FOR SAFETY REASONS.
I AM A KING WHO CANNOT LEARN ABOUT HIS OWN KINGDOM.
BUT THE STATE OF THIS COUNTRY AND THE LIVES OF THE TOWNS-PEOPLE...
...ARE SUBJECTS YOU KNOW VERY WELL, YES?
I WANT YOU TO TEACH ME ALL ABOUT IT.

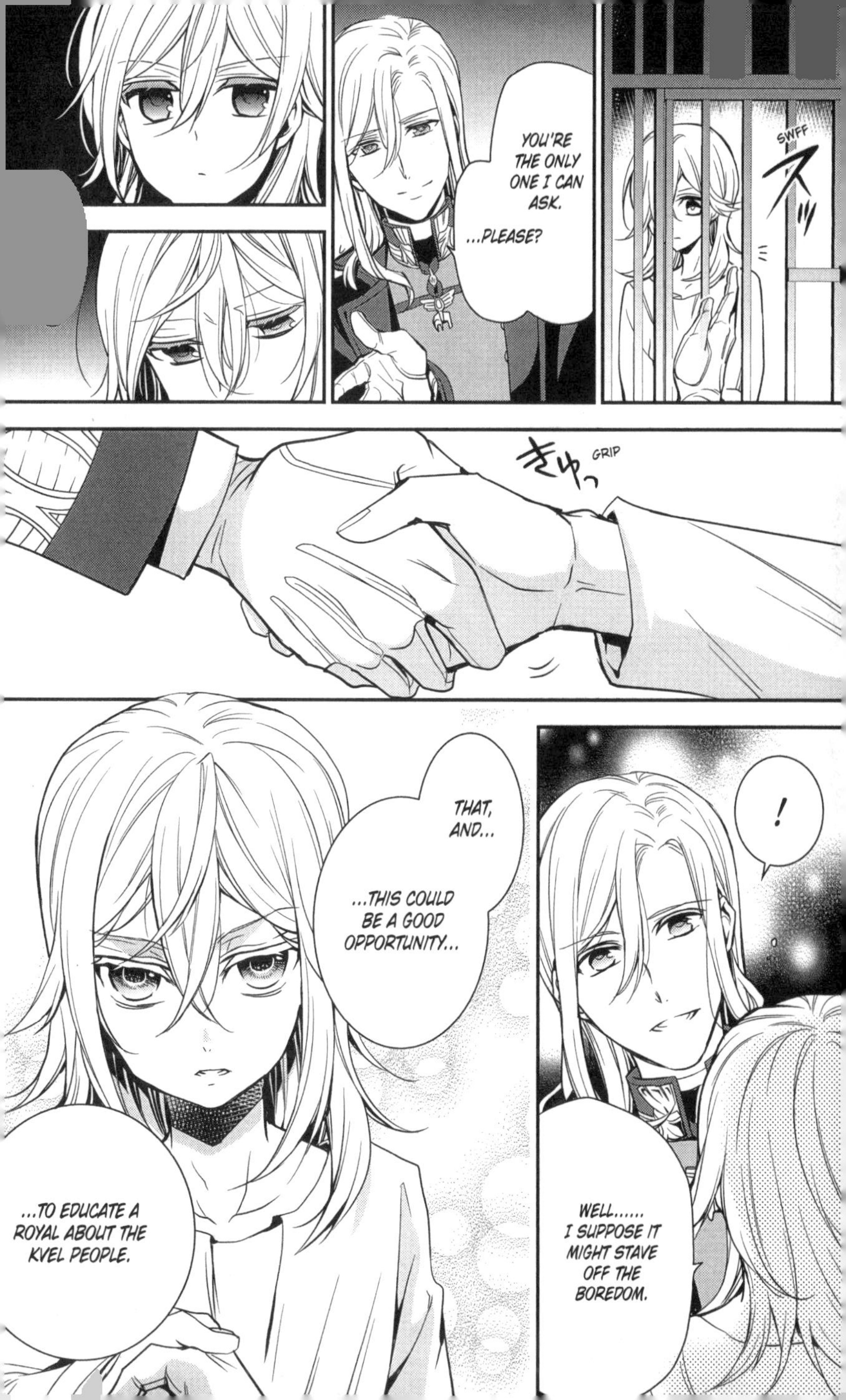
スッ
SWFF
YOU'RE THE ONLY ONE I CAN ASK.
...PLEASE?
きゅっ
GRIP
!
WELL...... I SUPPOSE IT MIGHT STAVE OFF THE BOREDOM.
THAT, AND...
...THIS COULD BE A GOOD OPPORTUNITY...
...TO EDUCATE A ROYAL ABOUT THE KVEL PEOPLE.

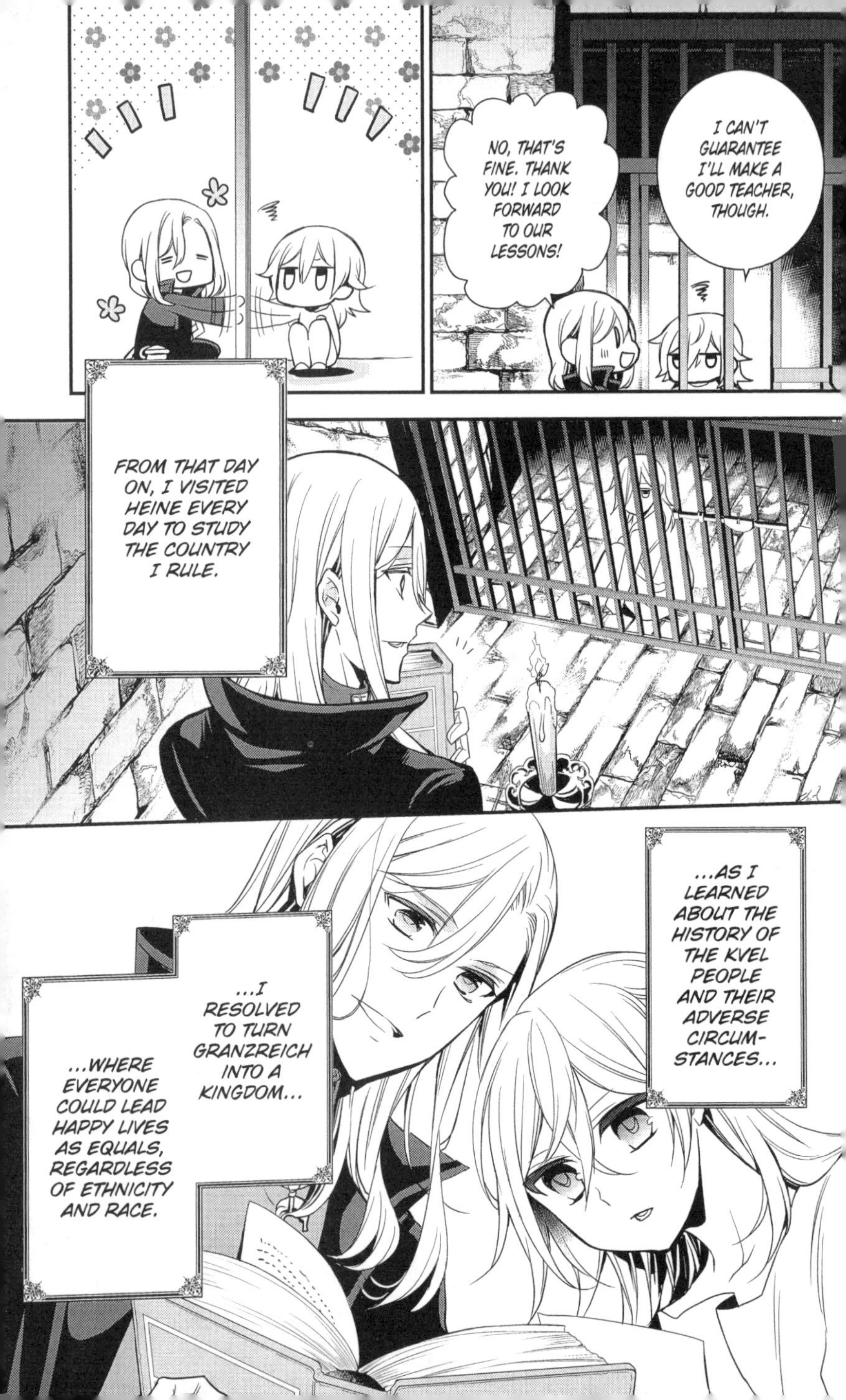
I CAN'T GUARANTEE I'LL MAKE A GOOD TEACHER, THOUGH.
NO, THAT'S FINE. THANK YOU! I LOOK FORWARD TO OUR LESSONS!
FROM THAT DAY ON, I VISITED HEINE EVERY DAY TO STUDY THE COUNTRY I RULE.
...AS I LEARNED ABOUT THE HISTORY OF THE KVEL PEOPLE AND THEIR ADVERSE CIRCUM-STANCES...
...I RESOLVED TO TURN GRANZREICH INTO A KINGDOM...
...WHERE EVERYONE COULD LEAD HAPPY LIVES AS EQUALS, REGARDLESS OF ETHNICITY AND RACE.

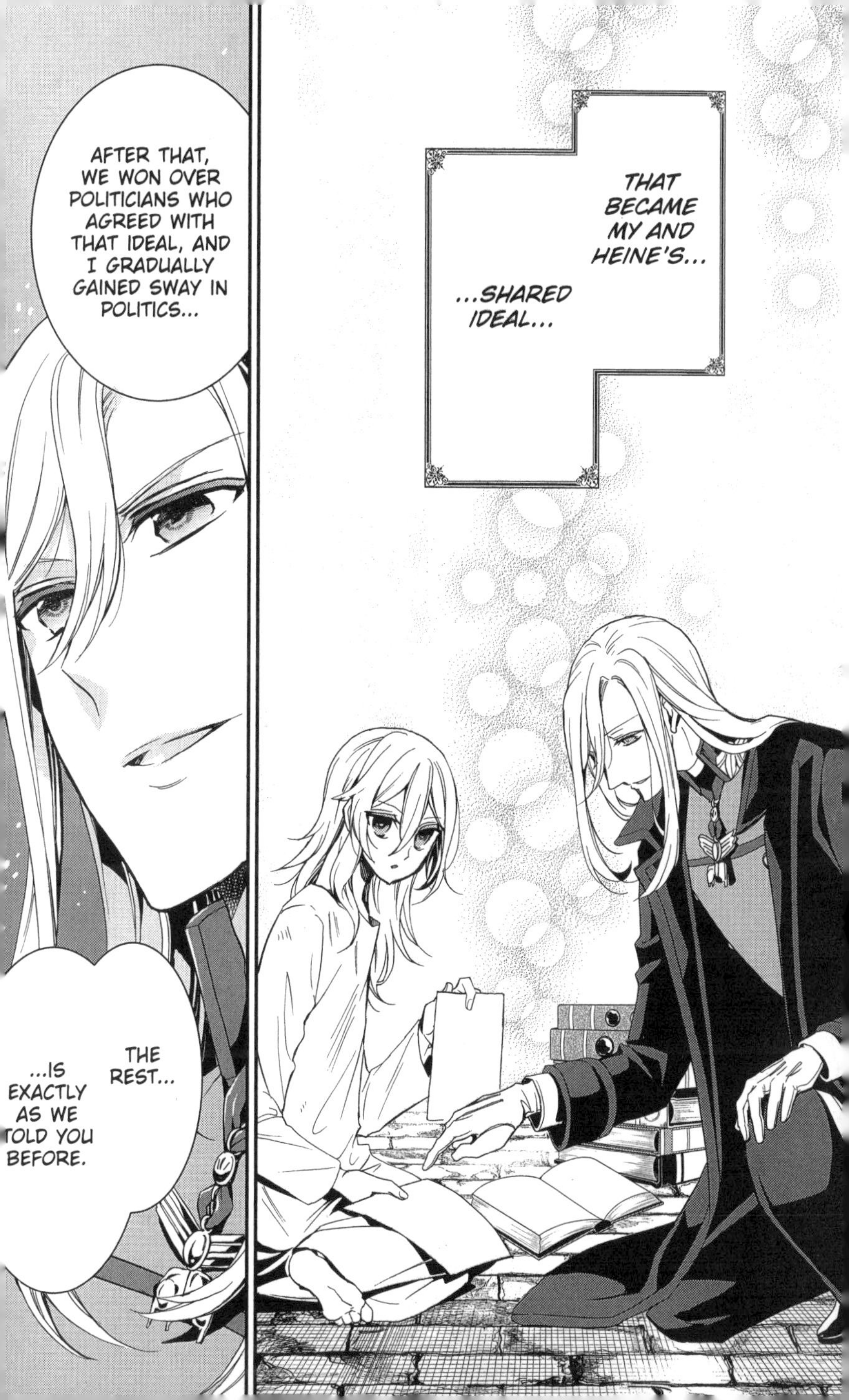
THAT BECAME MY AND HEINE'S...
...SHARED IDEAL...
AFTER THAT, WE WON OVER POLITICIANS WHO AGREED WITH THAT IDEAL, AND I GRADUALLY GAINED SWAY IN POLITICS...
THE REST...
...IS EXACTLY AS WE TOLD YOU BEFORE.

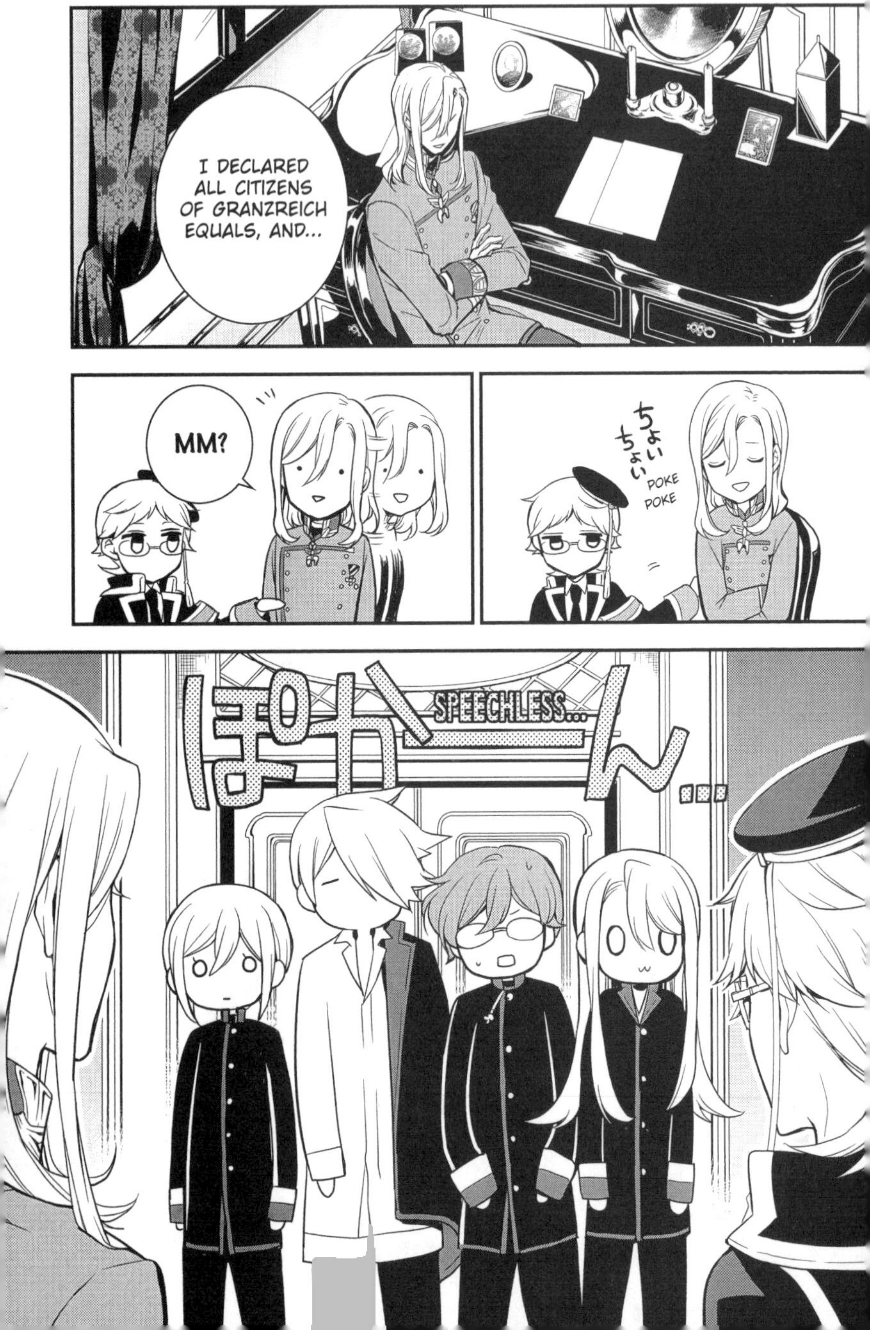
I DECLARED ALL CITIZENS OF GRANZREICH EQUALS, AND...
ちょいちょい
POKE POKE
MM?
ぽか～ん…
SPEECHLESS...

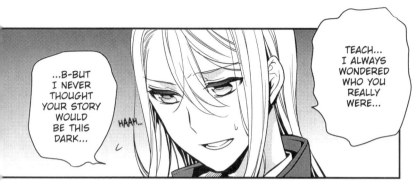

TEACH... I ALWAYS WONDERED WHO YOU REALLY WERE...
HAAAH...
...B-BUT I NEVER THOUGHT YOUR STORY WOULD BE THIS DARK...
どんより
GLOOM
I'D READ IN BOOKS... THAT EVEN GRANZREICH WAS ONCE EXCLUSIONARY AND UNSAFE.
BUT HEARING OF THAT TIME NOW IS...
FATHER... YOU WERE STABBED...?
ARE YOU OKAY...?
Y-YES, WHAT HE SAID!
WE HAD NO IDEA SOMETHING LIKE THAT HAD HAPPENED TO YOU!
HRRM...
ずーん...
GLOOM
わちゃ
FUSS
わちゃ
FUSS
あわ あわ
PANIC PANIC
......

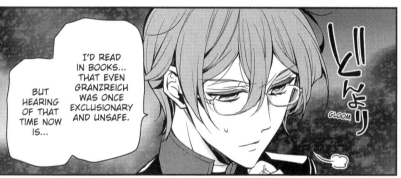

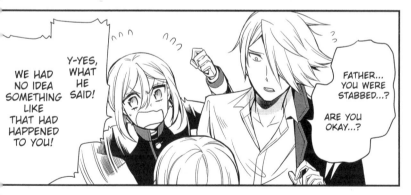

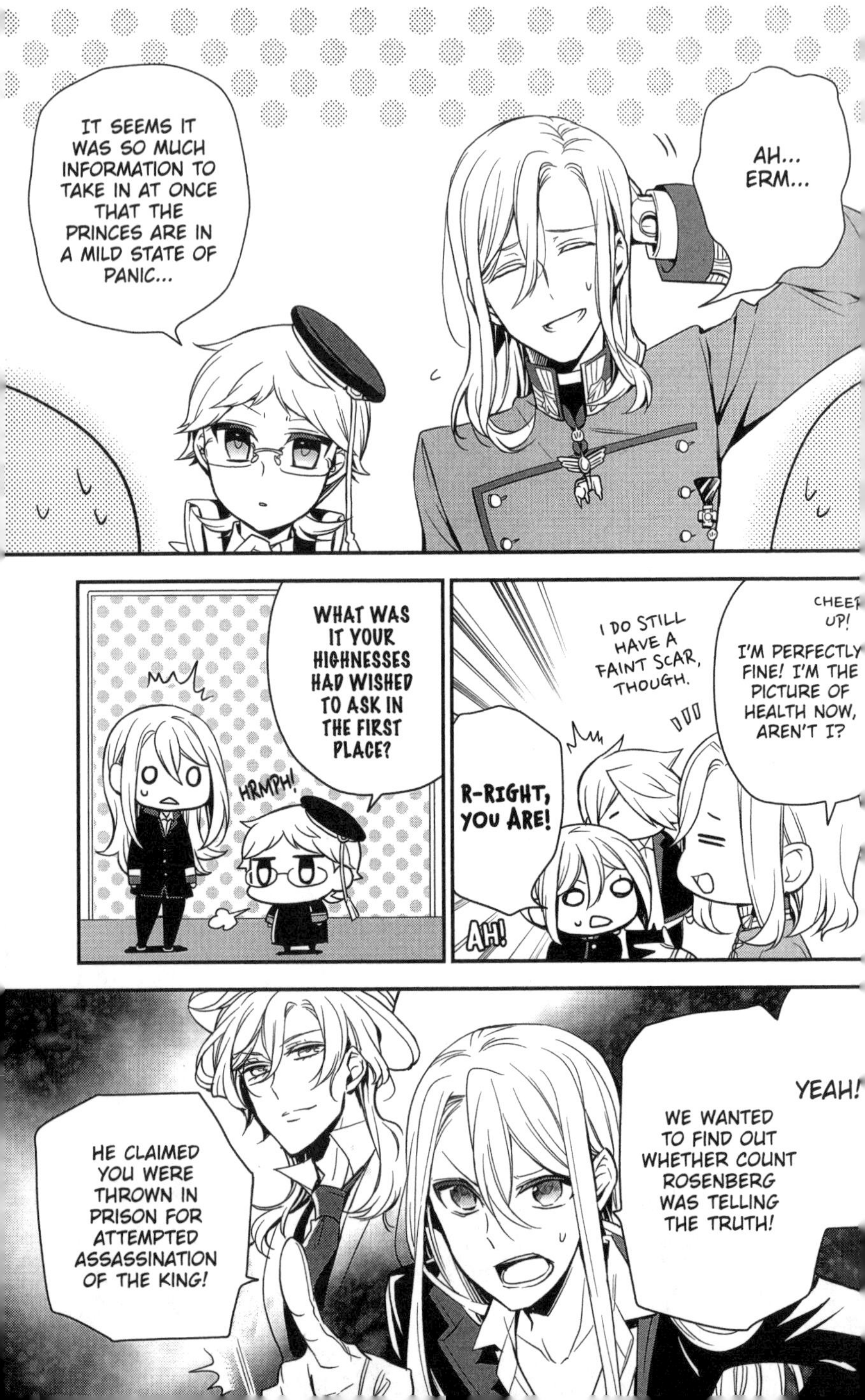
AH... ERM...
IT SEEMS IT WAS SO MUCH INFORMATION TO TAKE IN AT ONCE THAT THE PRINCES ARE IN A MILD STATE OF PANIC...
CHEER UP!
I'M PERFECTLY FINE! I'M THE PICTURE OF HEALTH NOW, AREN'T I?
I DO STILL HAVE A FAINT SCAR, THOUGH.
R-RIGHT, YOU ARE!
AH!
WHAT WAS IT YOUR HIGHNESSES HAD WISHED TO ASK IN THE FIRST PLACE?
HRMPH!
YEAH!
WE WANTED TO FIND OUT WHETHER COUNT ROSENBERG WAS TELLING THE TRUTH!
HE CLAIMED YOU WERE THROWN IN PRISON FOR ATTEMPTED ASSASSINATION OF THE KING!

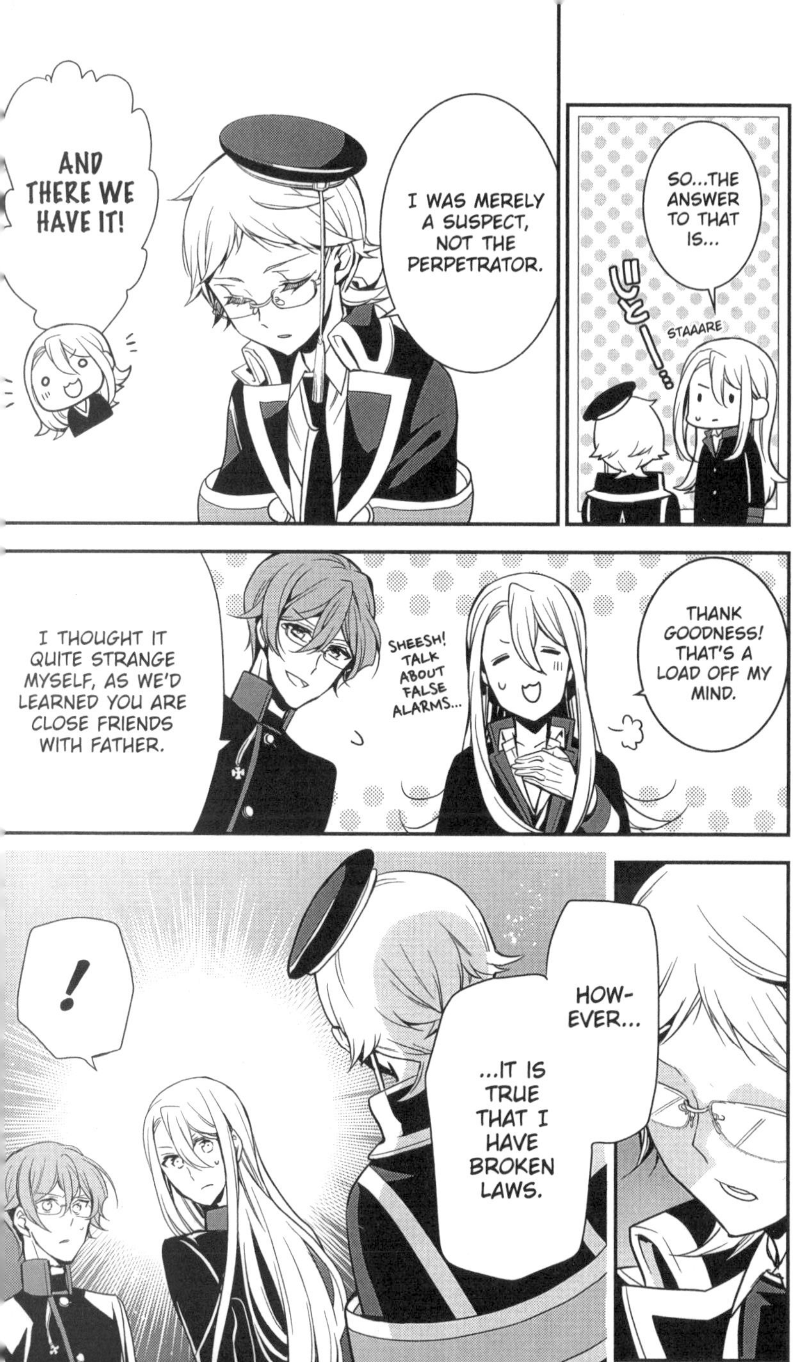
SO...THE ANSWER TO THAT IS...
STAAARE
I WAS MERELY A SUSPECT, NOT THE PERPETRATOR.
AND THERE WE HAVE IT!
THANK GOODNESS! THAT'S A LOAD OFF MY MIND.
SHEESH! TALK ABOUT FALSE ALARMS...
I THOUGHT IT QUITE STRANGE MYSELF, AS WE'D LEARNED YOU ARE CLOSE FRIENDS WITH FATHER.
HOW-EVER...
...IT IS TRUE THAT I HAVE BROKEN LAWS.
!

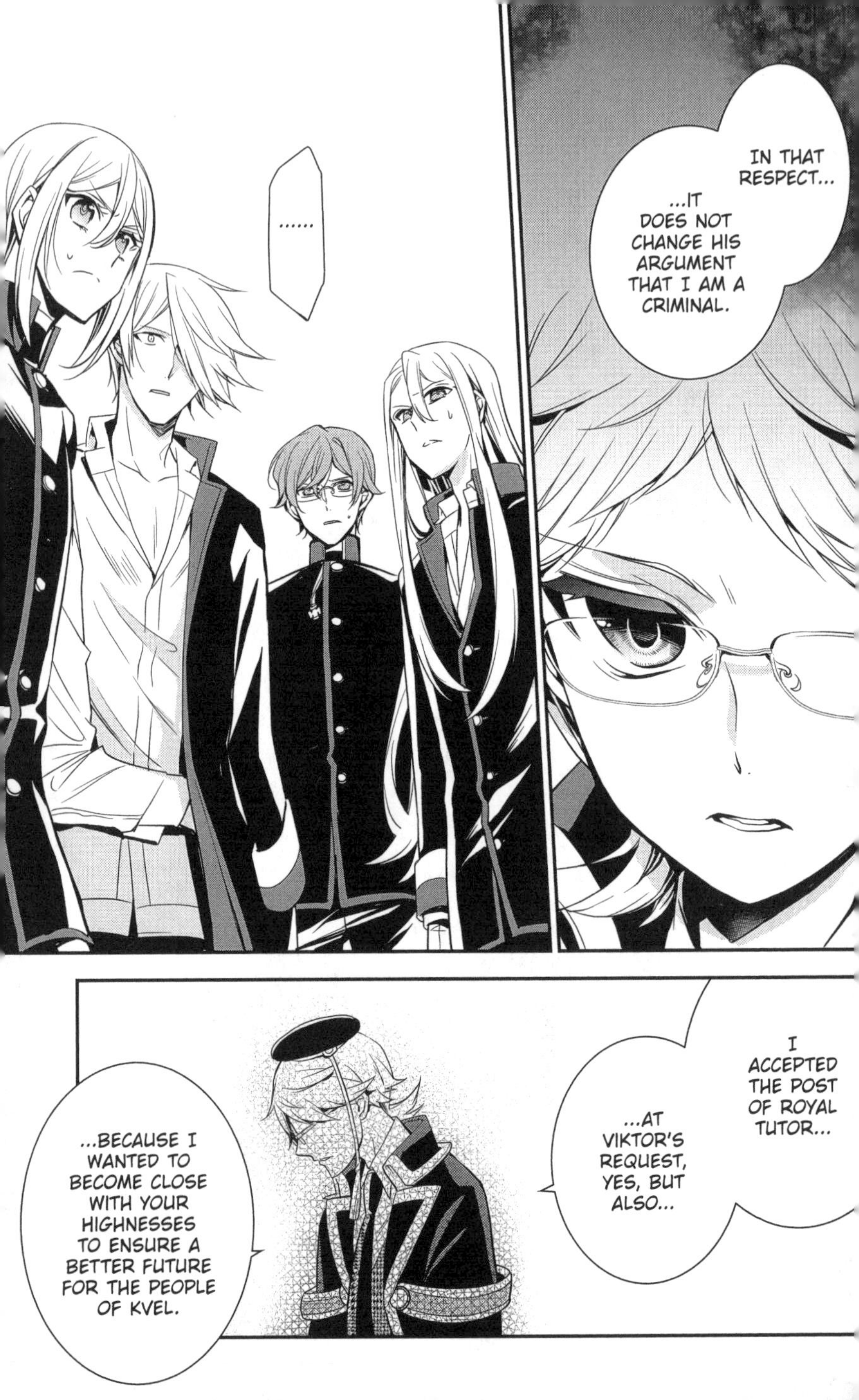
IN THAT RESPECT...
...IT DOES NOT CHANGE HIS ARGUMENT THAT I AM A CRIMINAL.
......
I ACCEPTED THE POST OF ROYAL TUTOR...
...AT VIKTOR'S REQUEST, YES, BUT ALSO...
...BECAUSE I WANTED TO BECOME CLOSE WITH YOUR HIGHNESSES TO ENSURE A BETTER FUTURE FOR THE PEOPLE OF KVEL.

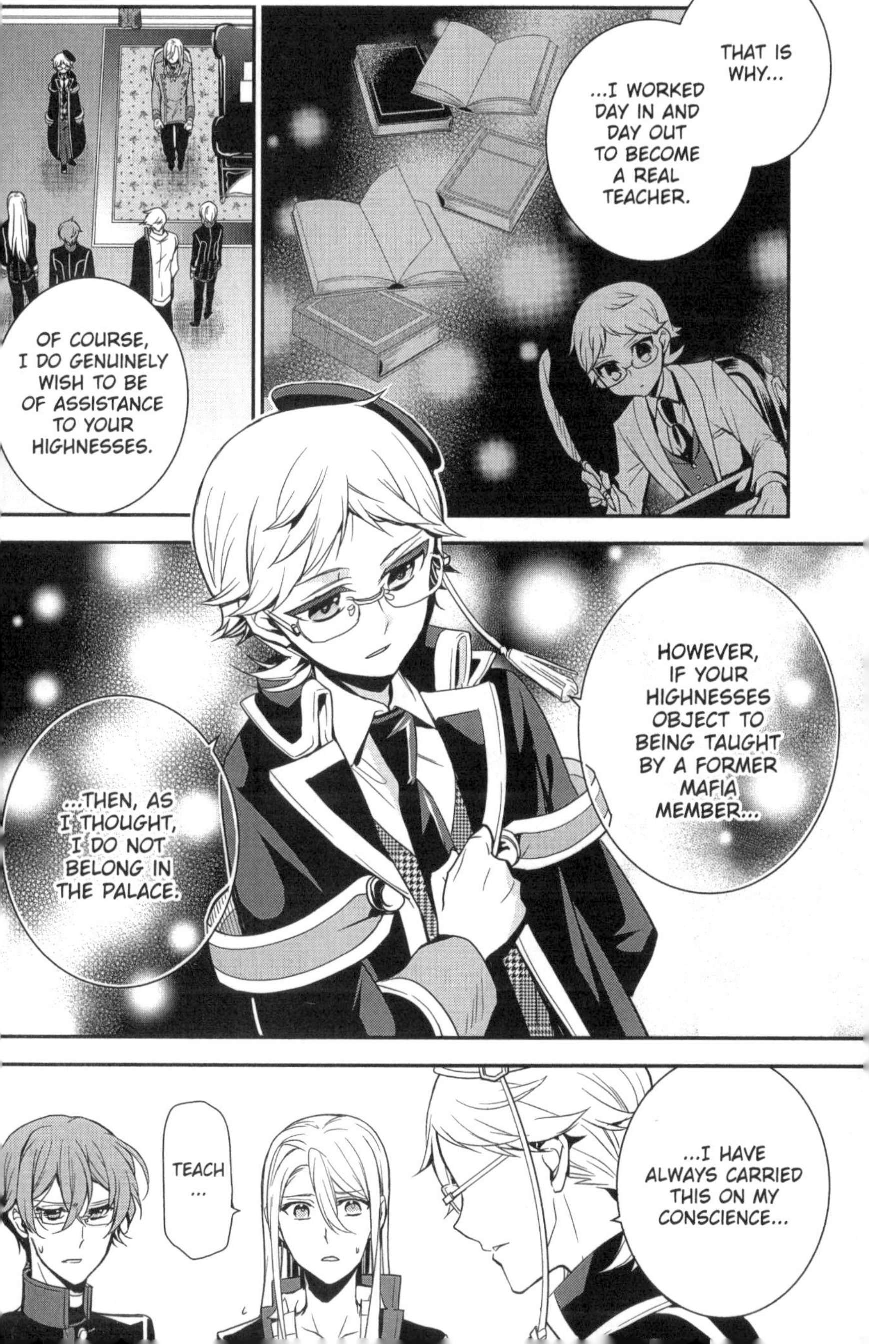
THAT IS WHY...
...I WORKED DAY IN AND DAY OUT TO BECOME A REAL TEACHER.
OF COURSE, I DO GENUINELY WISH TO BE OF ASSISTANCE TO YOUR HIGHNESSES.
HOWEVER, IF YOUR HIGHNESSES OBJECT TO BEING TAUGHT BY A FORMER MAFIA MEMBER...
...THEN, AS I THOUGHT, I DO NOT BELONG IN THE PALACE.
...I HAVE ALWAYS CARRIED THIS ON MY CONSCIENCE...
TEACH...

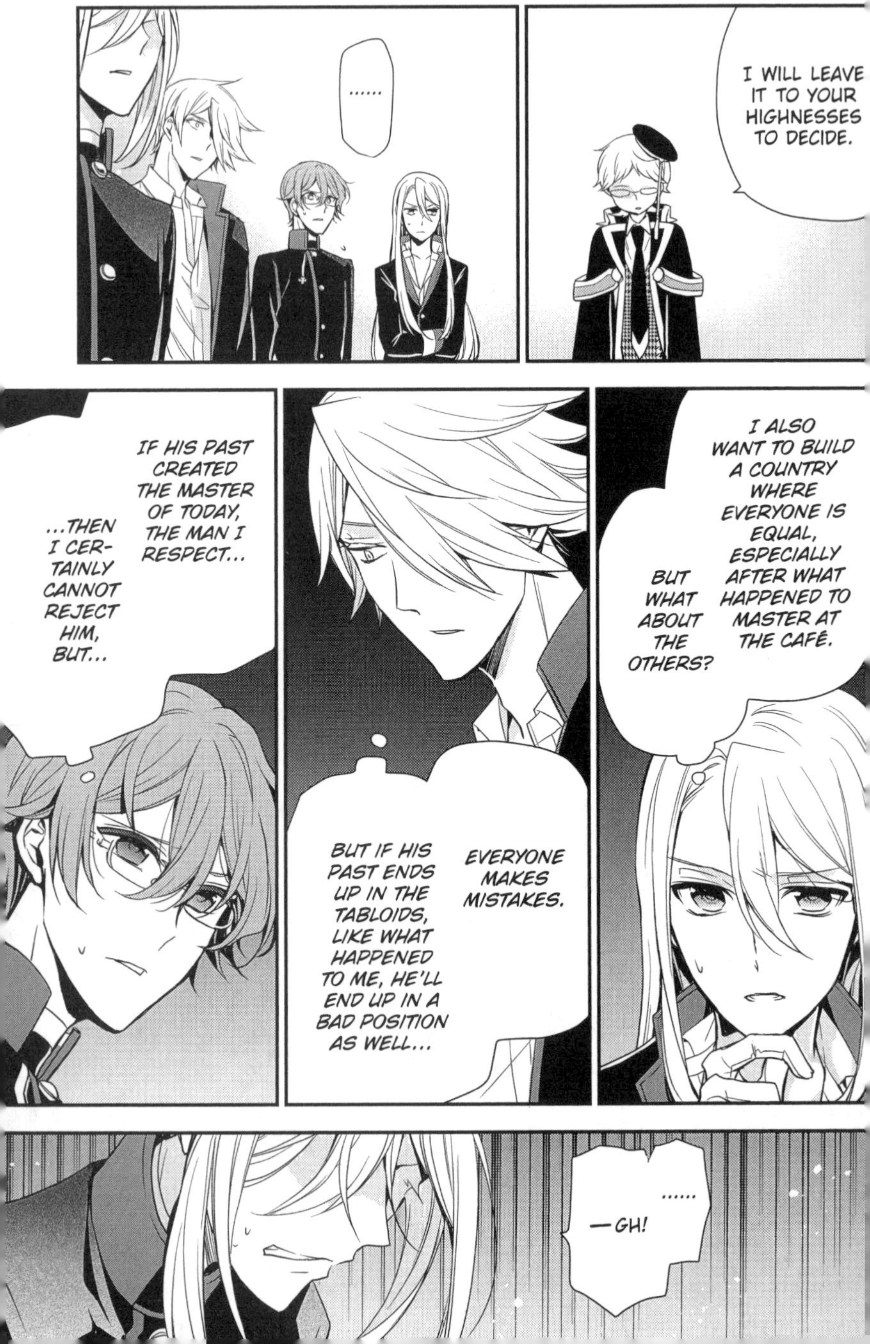
I WILL LEAVE IT TO YOUR HIGHNESSES TO DECIDE.
......
I ALSO WANT TO BUILD A COUNTRY WHERE EVERYONE IS EQUAL, ESPECIALLY AFTER WHAT HAPPENED TO MASTER AT THE CAFÉ.
BUT WHAT ABOUT THE OTHERS?
EVERYONE MAKES MISTAKES.
BUT IF HIS PAST ENDS UP IN THE TABLOIDS, LIKE WHAT HAPPENED TO ME, HE'LL END UP IN A BAD POSITION AS WELL...
IF HIS PAST CREATED THE MASTER OF TODAY, THE MAN I RESPECT...
...THEN I CERTAINLY CANNOT REJECT HIM, BUT...
......
—GH!

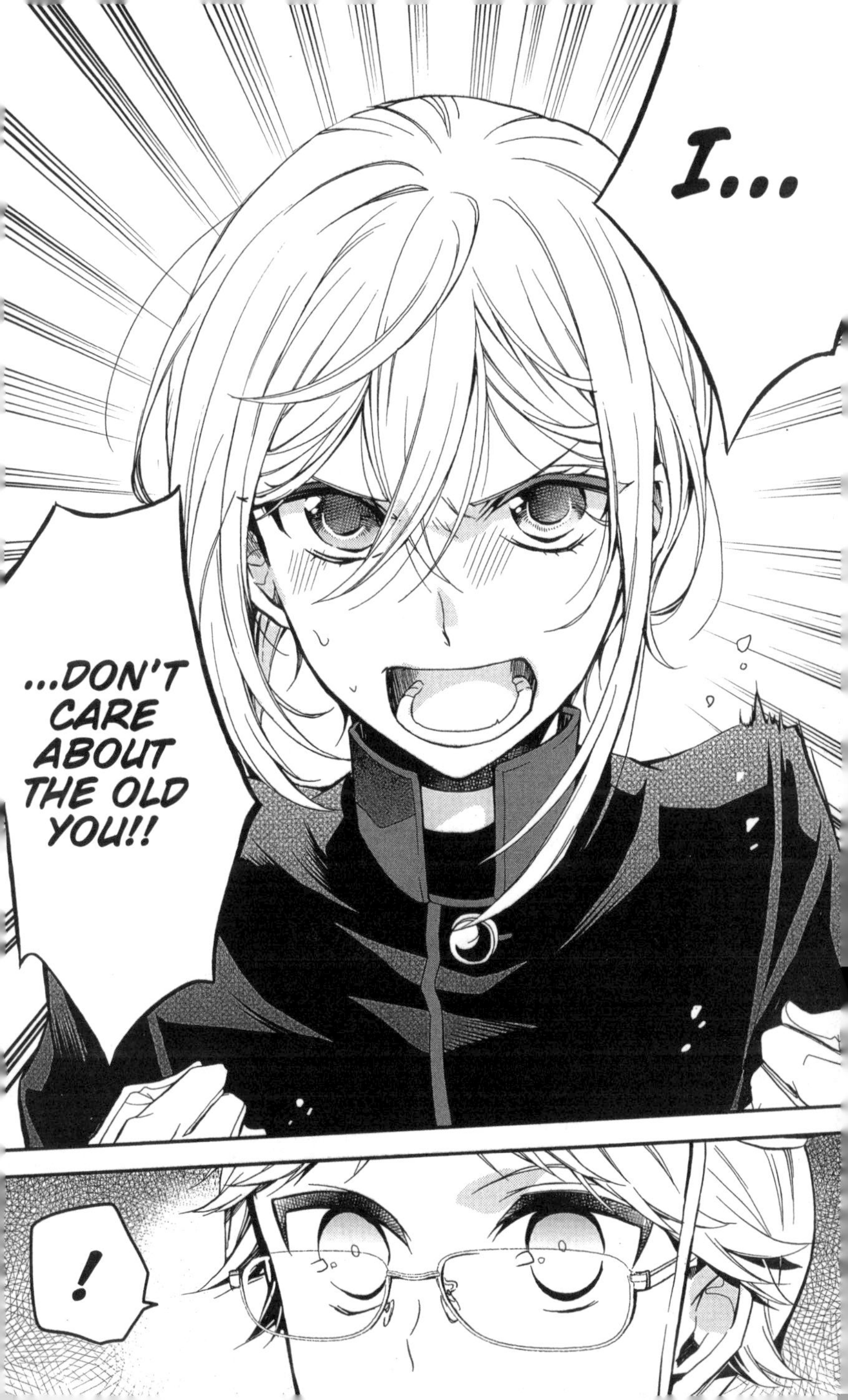
I...
...DON'T CARE ABOUT THE OLD YOU!!
!

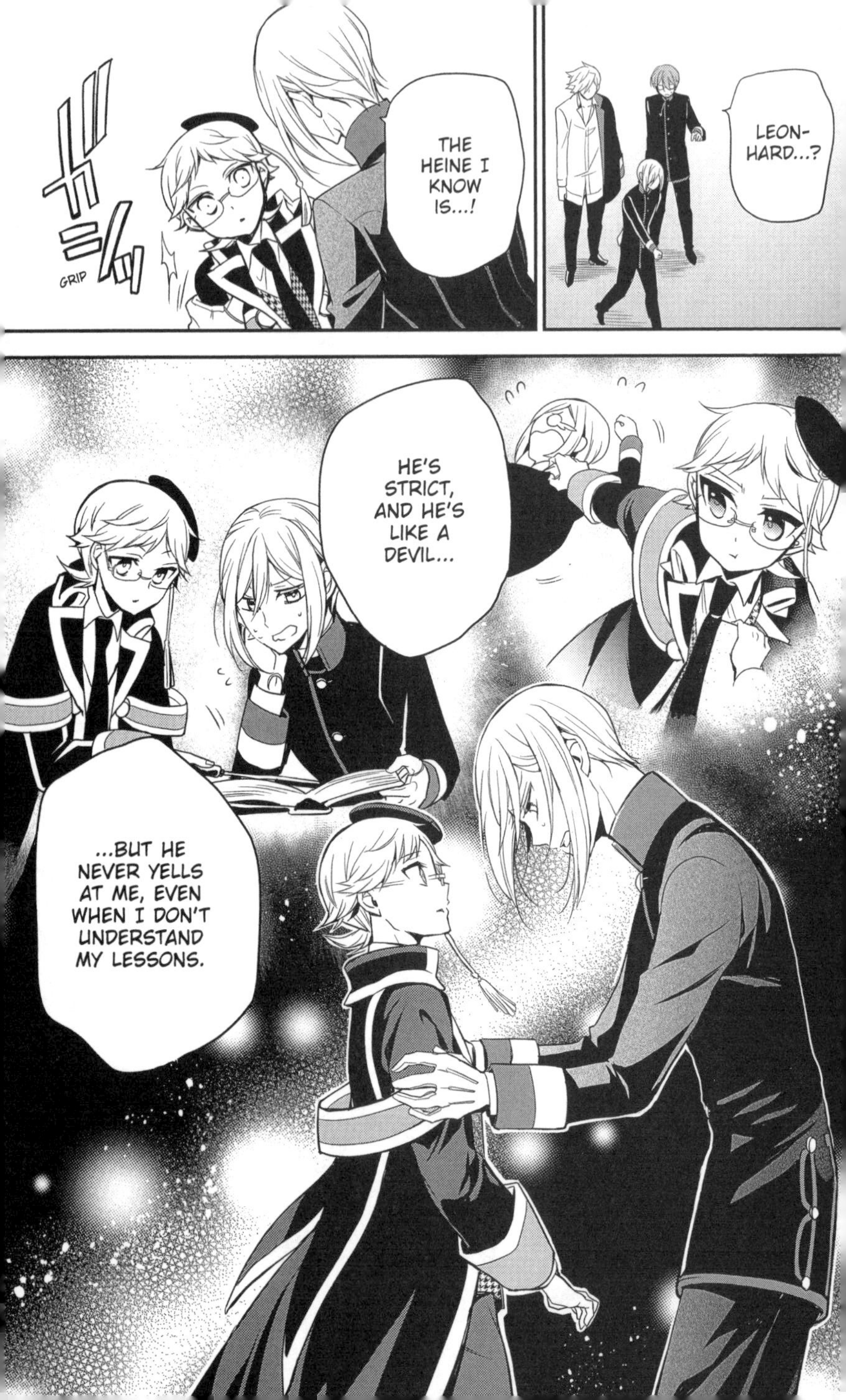
LEON-HARD...?
THE HEINE I KNOW IS...!
GRIP
HE'S STRICT, AND HE'S LIKE A DEVIL...
...BUT HE NEVER YELLS AT ME, EVEN WHEN I DON'T UNDERSTAND MY LESSONS.

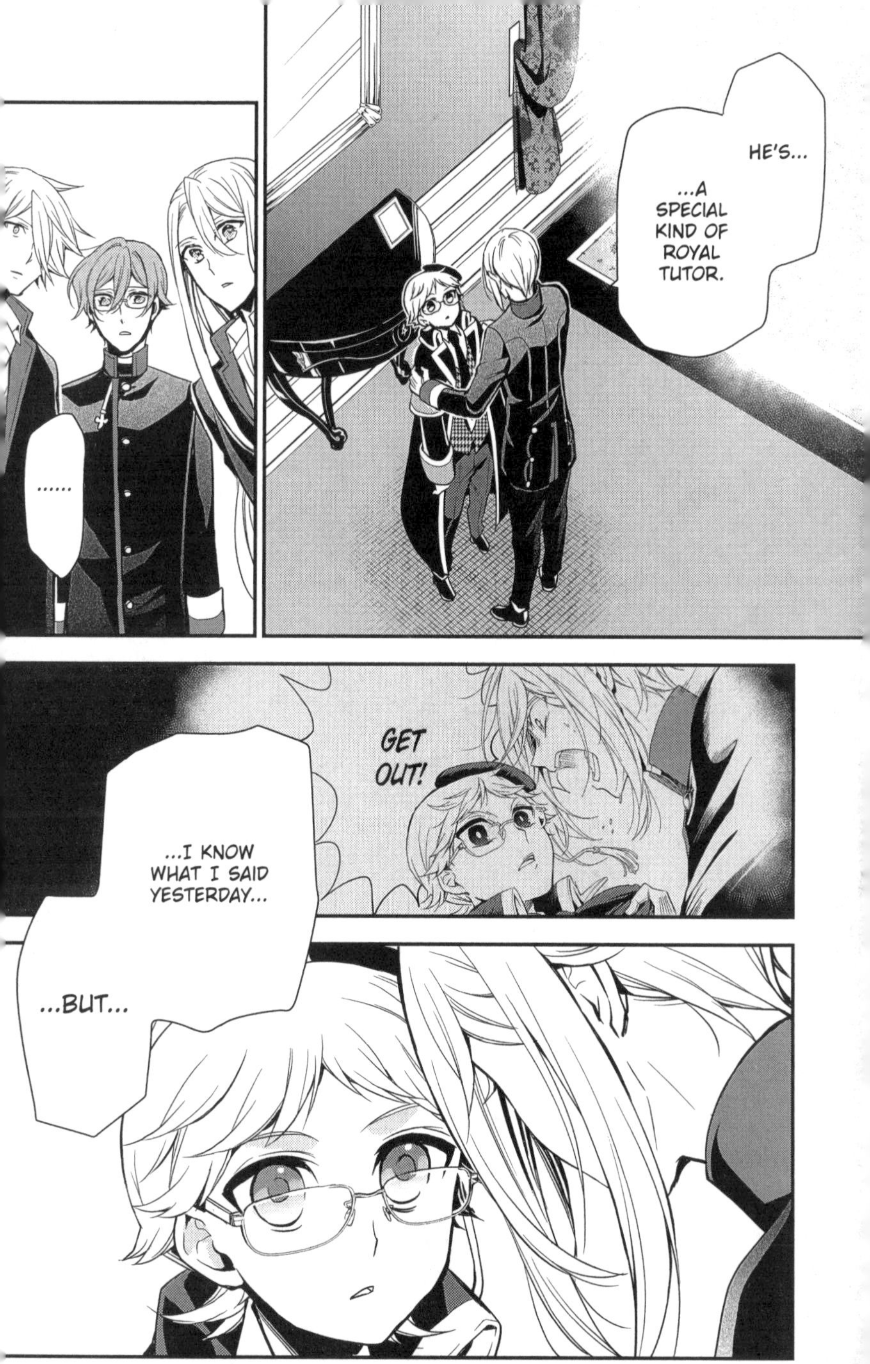
HE'S...
...A SPECIAL KIND OF ROYAL TUTOR.
......
GET OUT!
...I KNOW WHAT I SAID YESTERDAY...
...BUT...

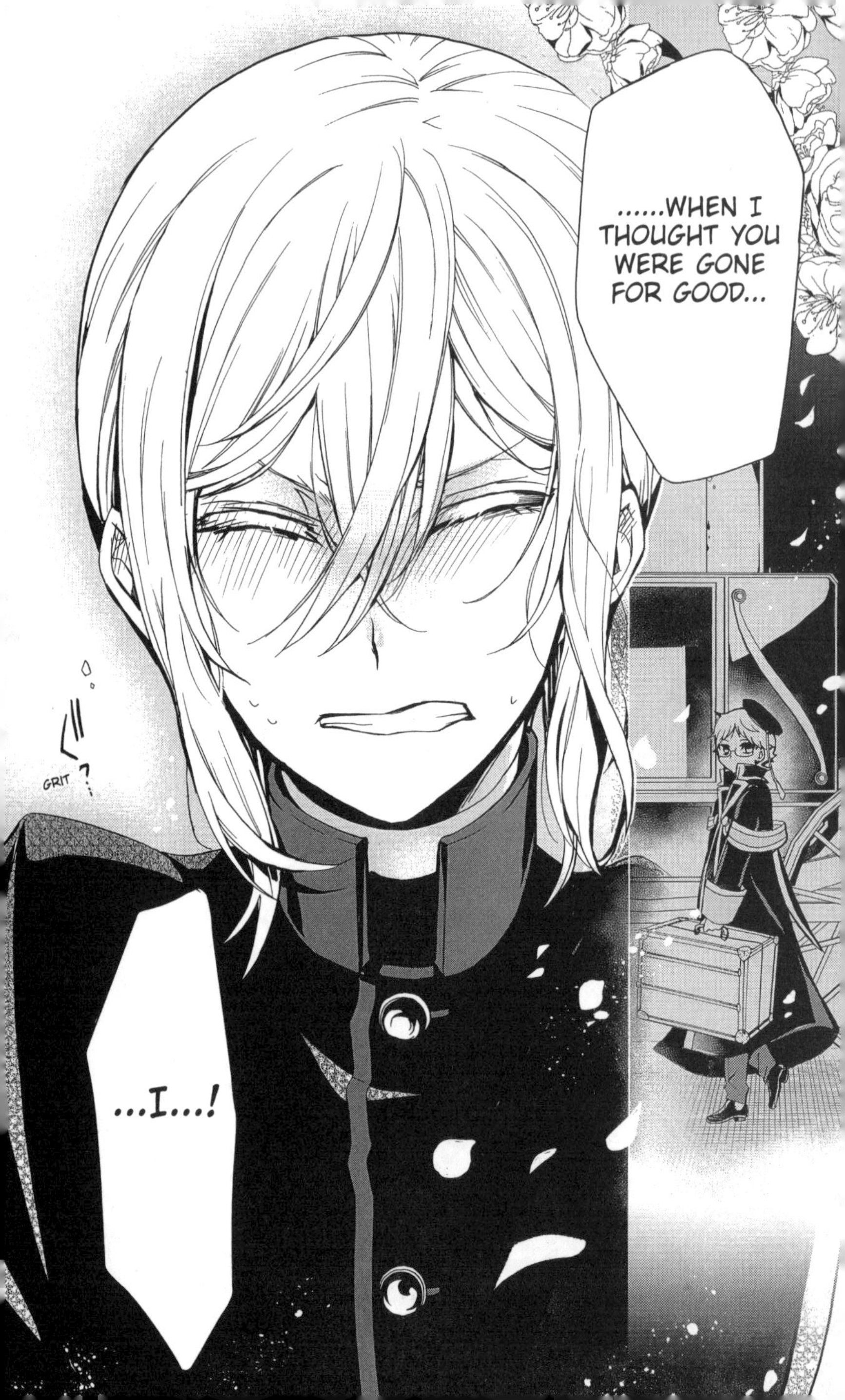
......WHEN I THOUGHT YOU WERE GONE FOR GOOD...
GRIT
...I...!

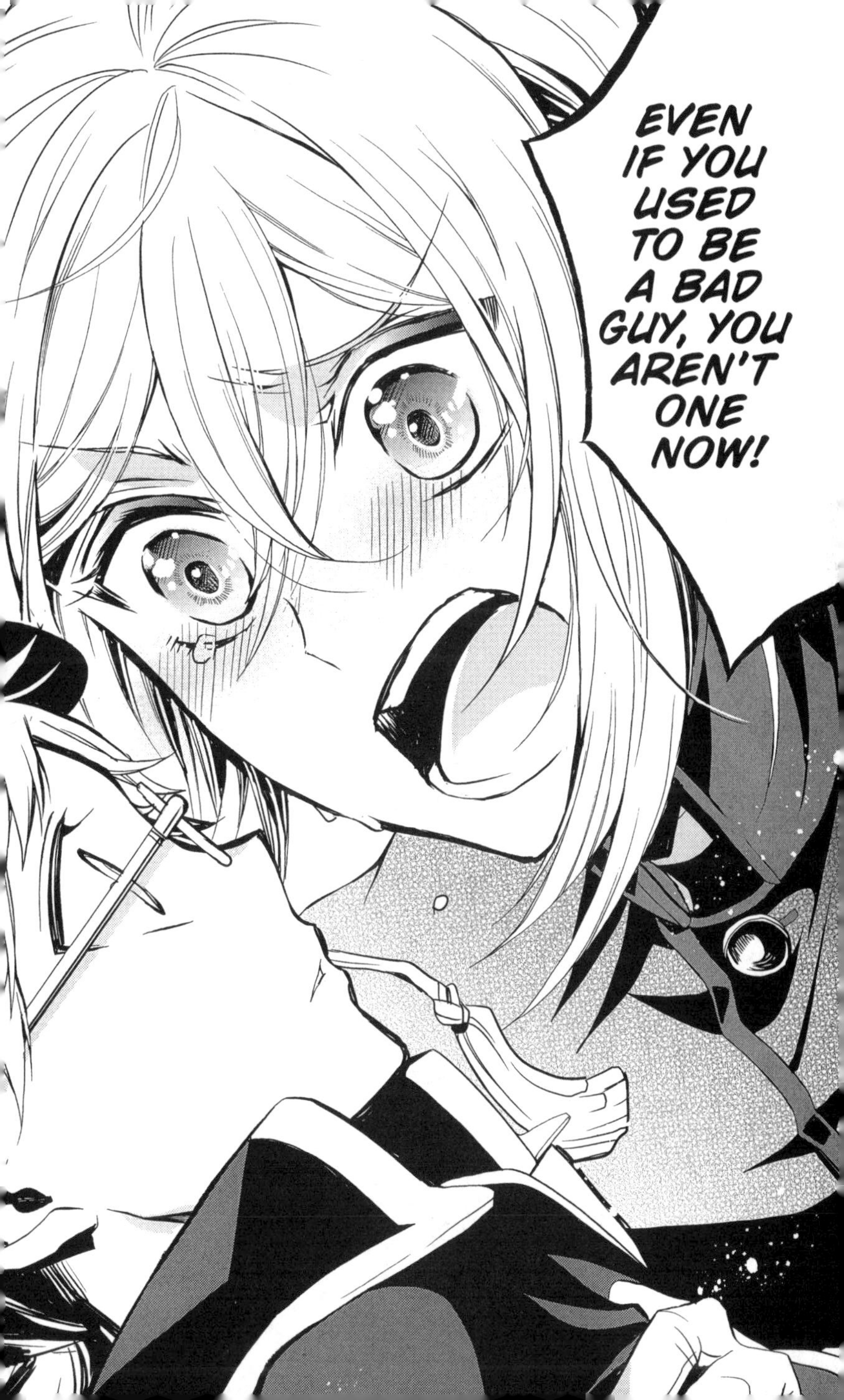
EVEN IF YOU USED TO BE A BAD GUY, YOU AREN'T ONE NOW!

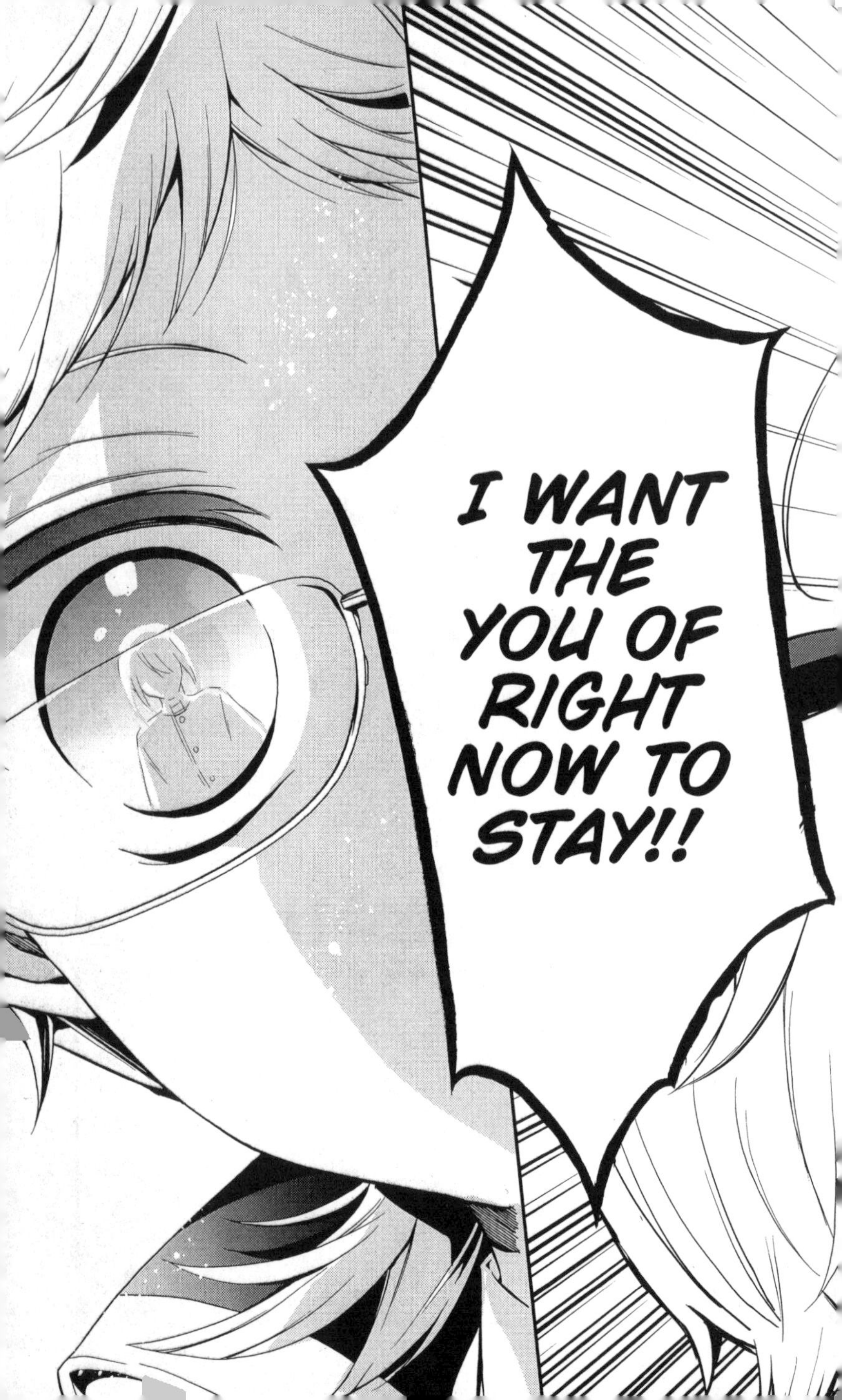
I WANT THE YOU OF RIGHT NOW TO STAY!!

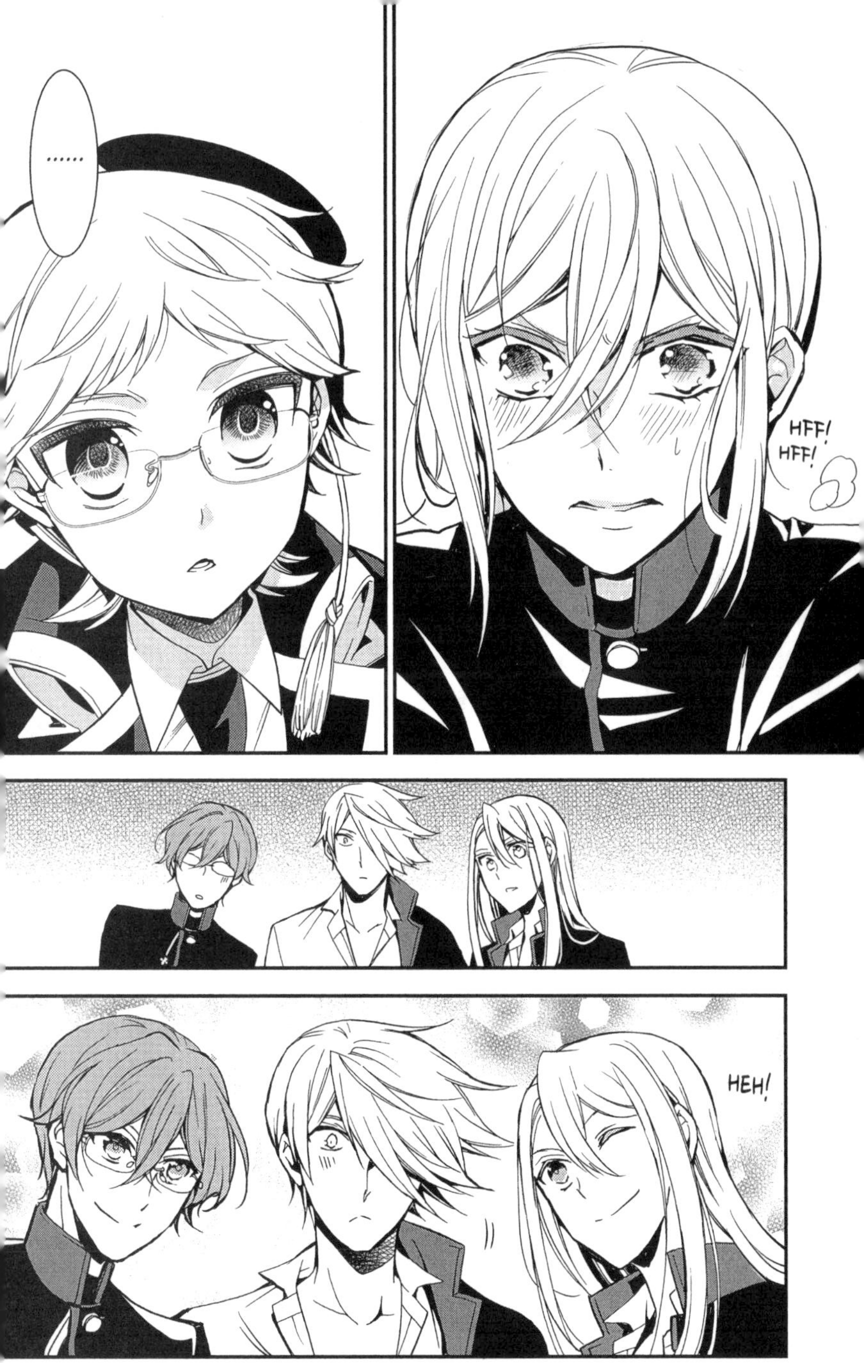
HFF!
HFF!
......
HEH!

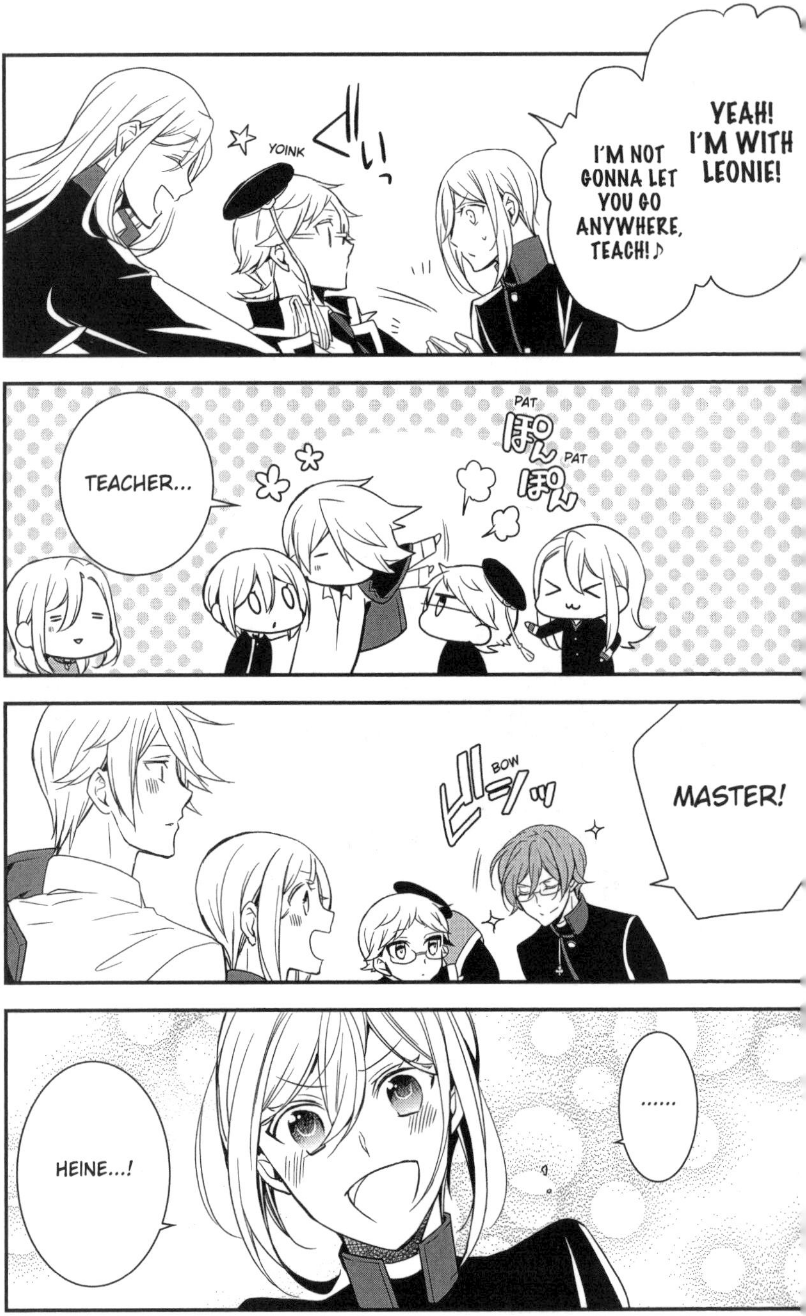
YEAH! I'M WITH LEONIE!
I'M NOT GONNA LET YOU GO ANYWHERE, TEACH!♪
YOINK
PAT
ぽん
PAT
ぽん
TEACHER...
MASTER!
BOW
......
HEINE...!

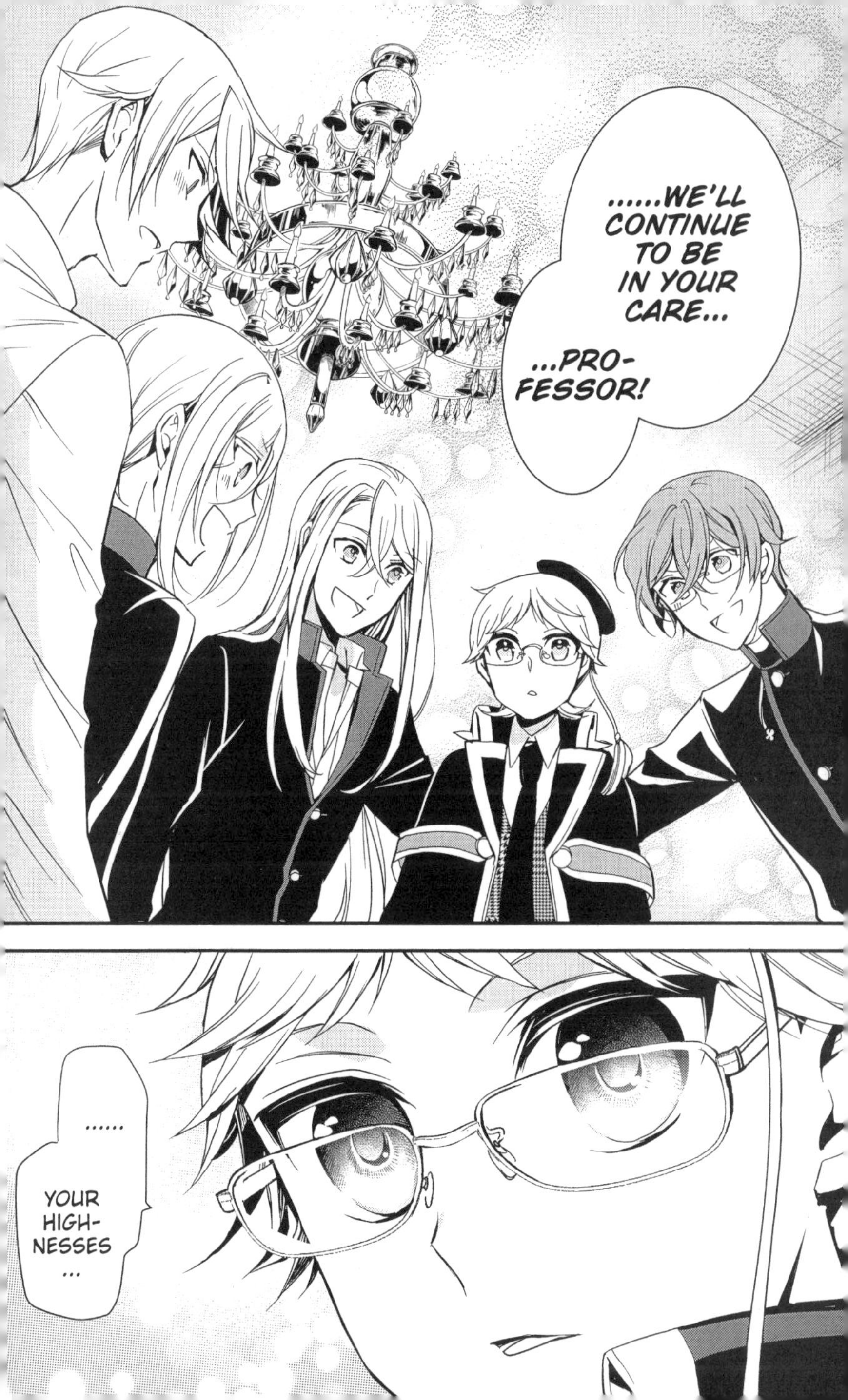
......WE'LL CONTINUE TO BE IN YOUR CARE...
...PRO-FESSOR!
......
YOUR HIGH-NESSES ...

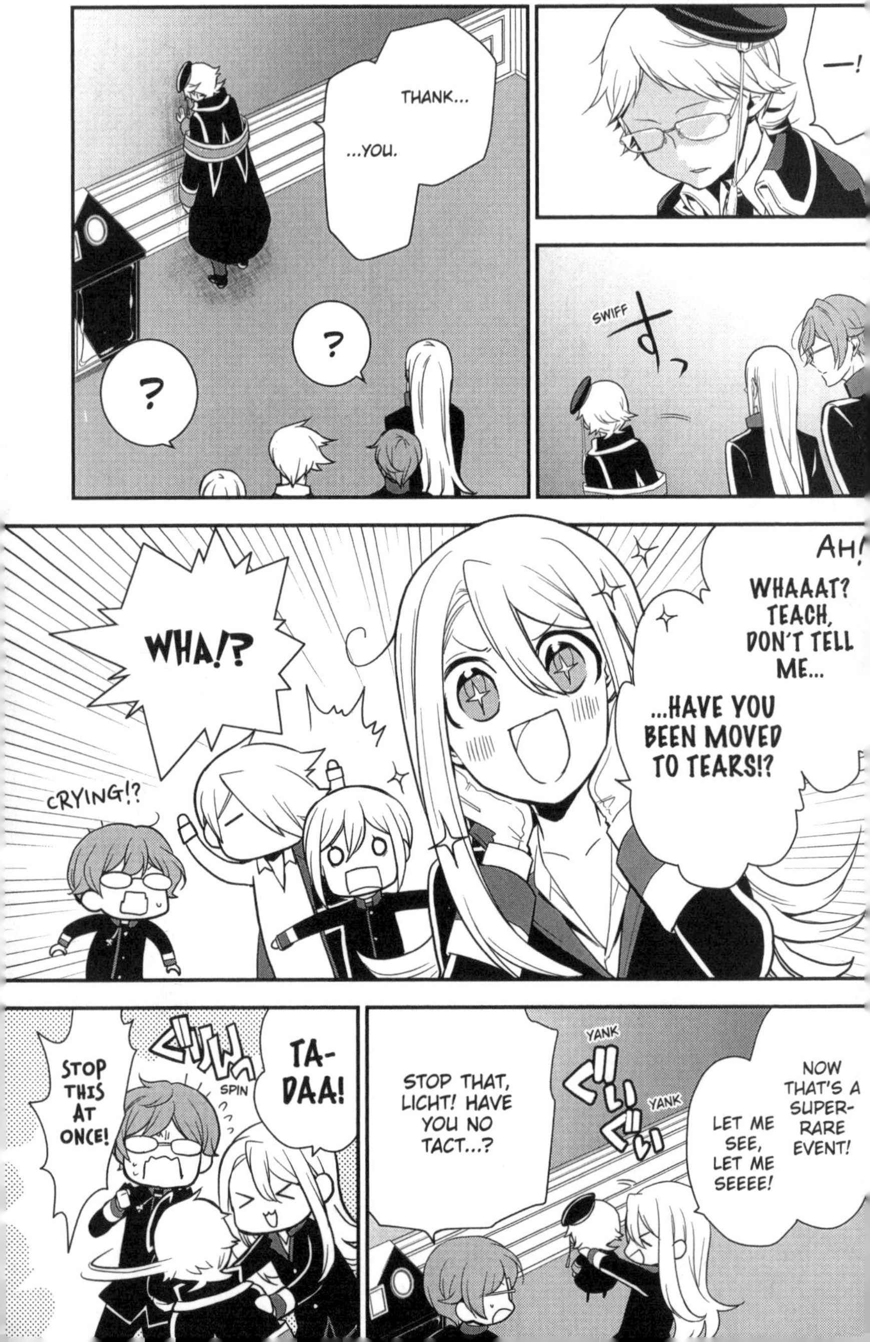
—!
SWIFF
THANK...
...YOU.
?
?
AH!
WHAAAT? TEACH, DON'T TELL ME...
...HAVE YOU BEEN MOVED TO TEARS!?
WHA!?
CRYING!?
NOW THAT'S A SUPER-RARE EVENT!
LET ME SEE, LET ME SEEEE!
YANK
YANK
STOP THAT, LICHT! HAVE YOU NO TACT...?
TA-DAA!
SPIN
STOP THIS AT ONCE!

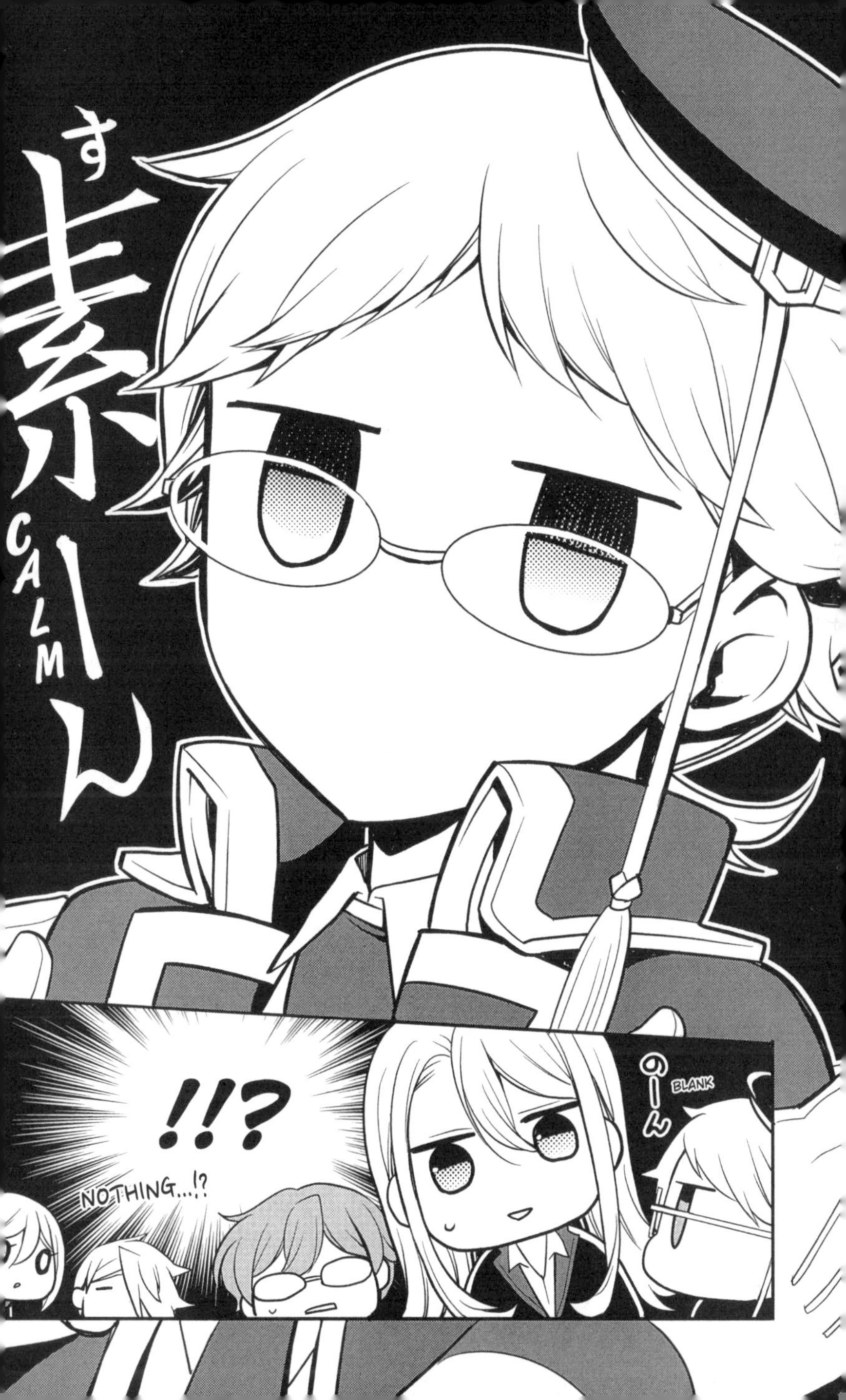
す
素ーん
CALM
のーん
BLANK
!!?
NOTHING...!?

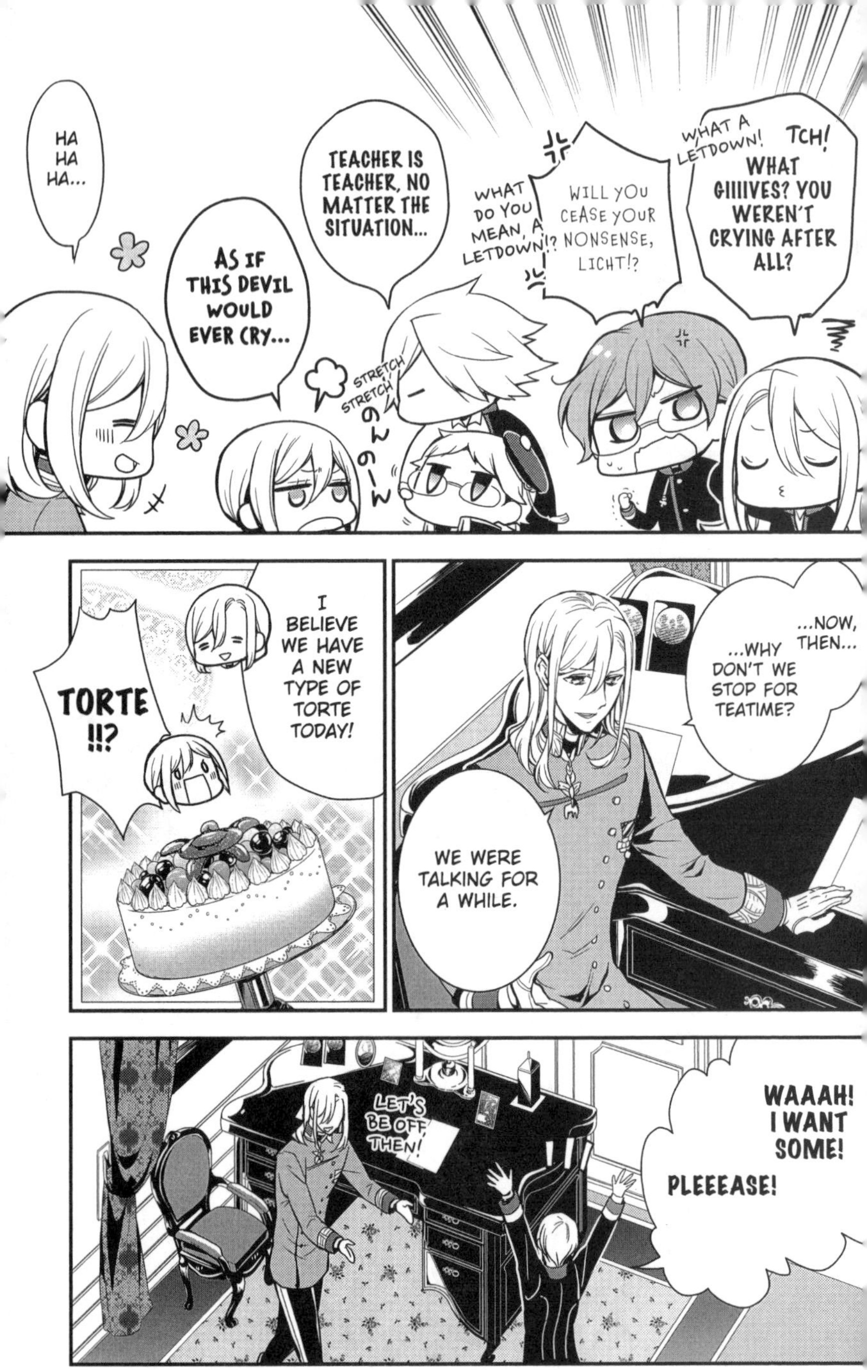
TCH! WHAT GIIIIVES? YOU WEREN'T CRYING AFTER ALL?
WHAT A LETDOWN!
WILL YOU CEASE YOUR NONSENSE, LICHT!?
WHAT DO YOU MEAN, A LETDOWN!?
TEACHER IS TEACHER, NO MATTER THE SITUATION...
STRETCH STRETCH
のんの～ん
AS IF THIS DEVIL WOULD EVER CRY...
HA HA HA...
...NOW, THEN...
...WHY DON'T WE STOP FOR TEATIME?
WE WERE TALKING FOR A WHILE.
I BELIEVE WE HAVE A NEW TYPE OF TORTE TODAY!
TORTE!!?
WAAAH! I WANT SOME!
PLEEEASE!
LET'S BE OFF THEN!

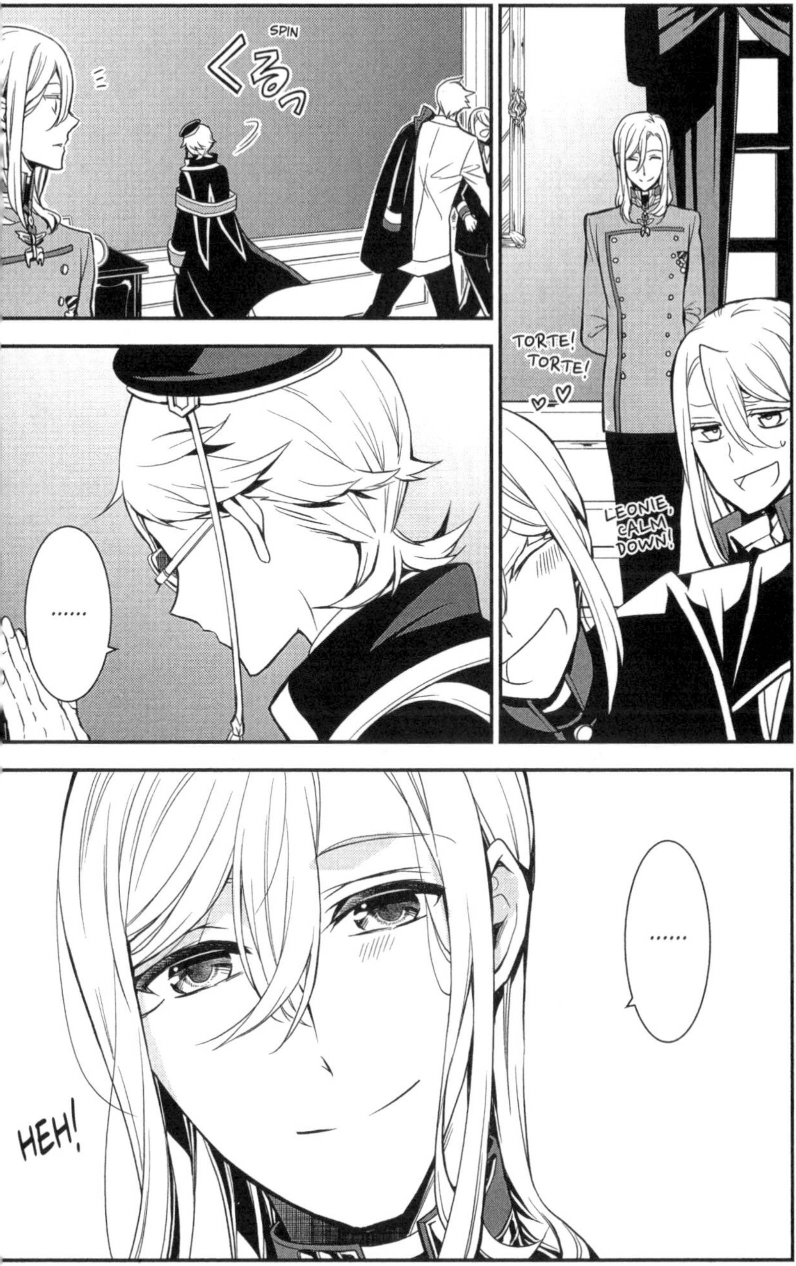
TORTE! TORTE!
LEONIE, CALM DOWN!
SPIN
くるっ
......
......
HEH!

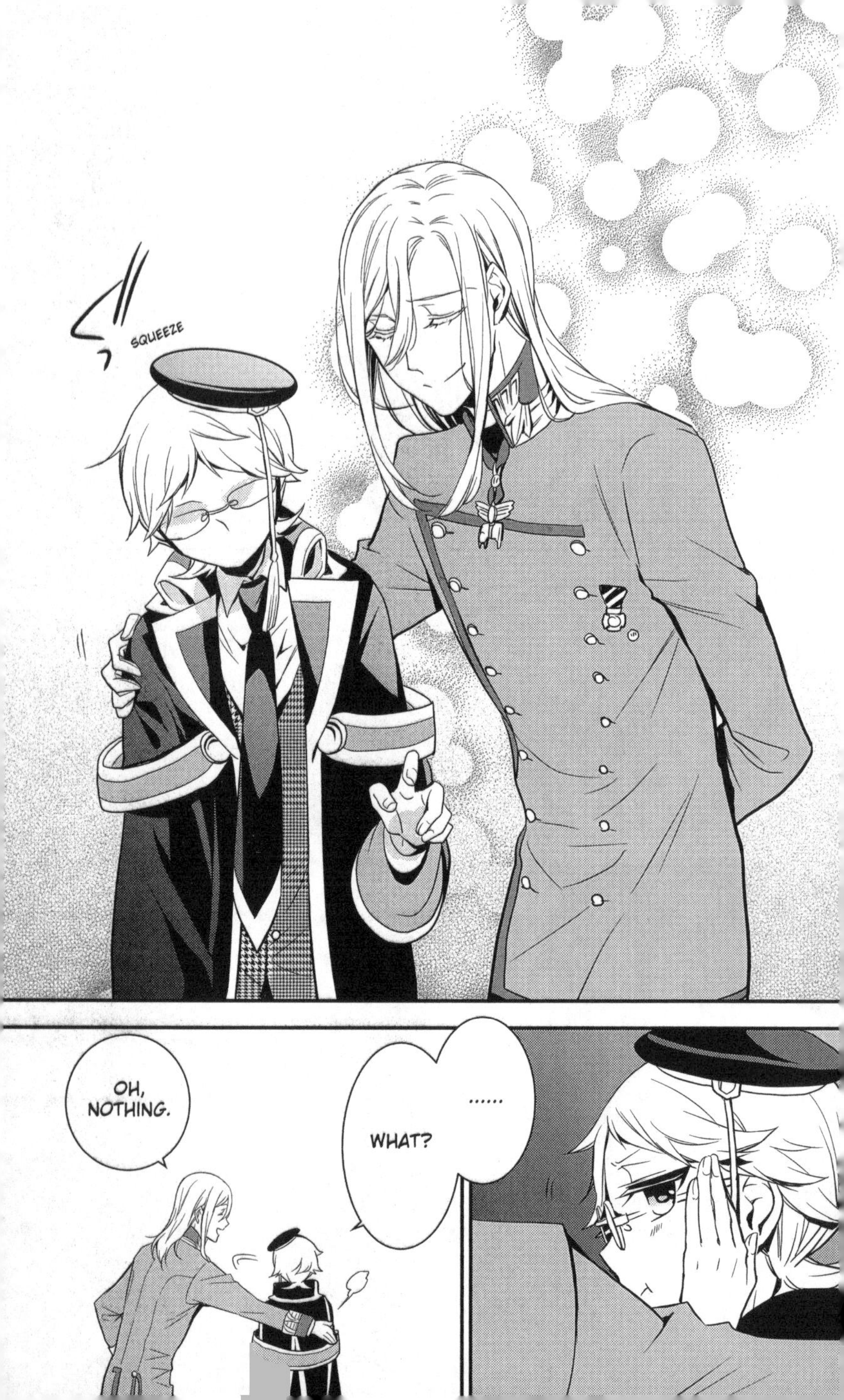
SQUEEZE
...... WHAT?
OH, NOTHING.

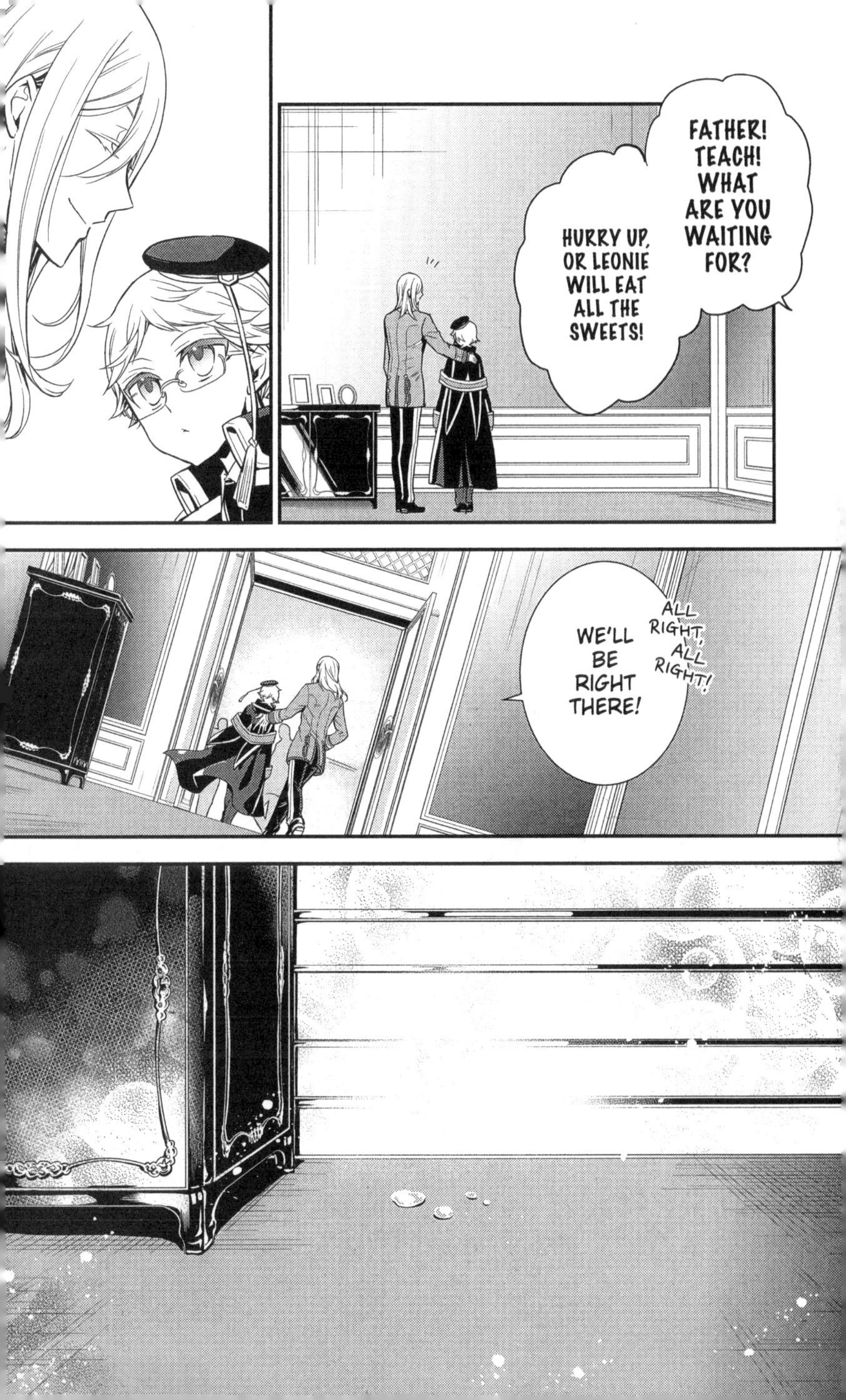
FATHER! TEACH! WHAT ARE YOU WAITING FOR?
HURRY UP, OR LEONIE WILL EAT ALL THE SWEETS!
ALL RIGHT, ALL RIGHT!
WE'LL BE RIGHT THERE!

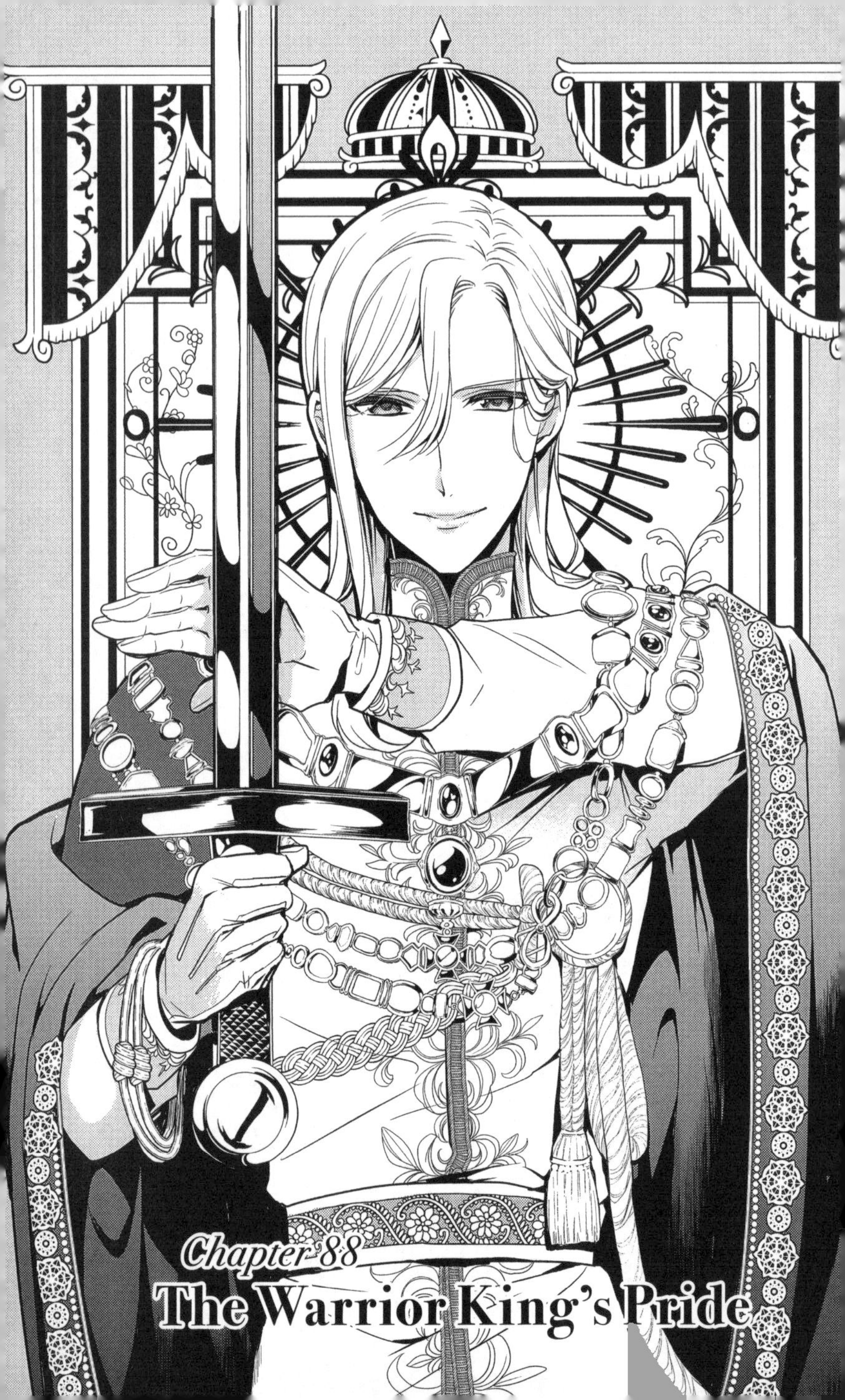
Chapter 88
The Warrior King's Pride

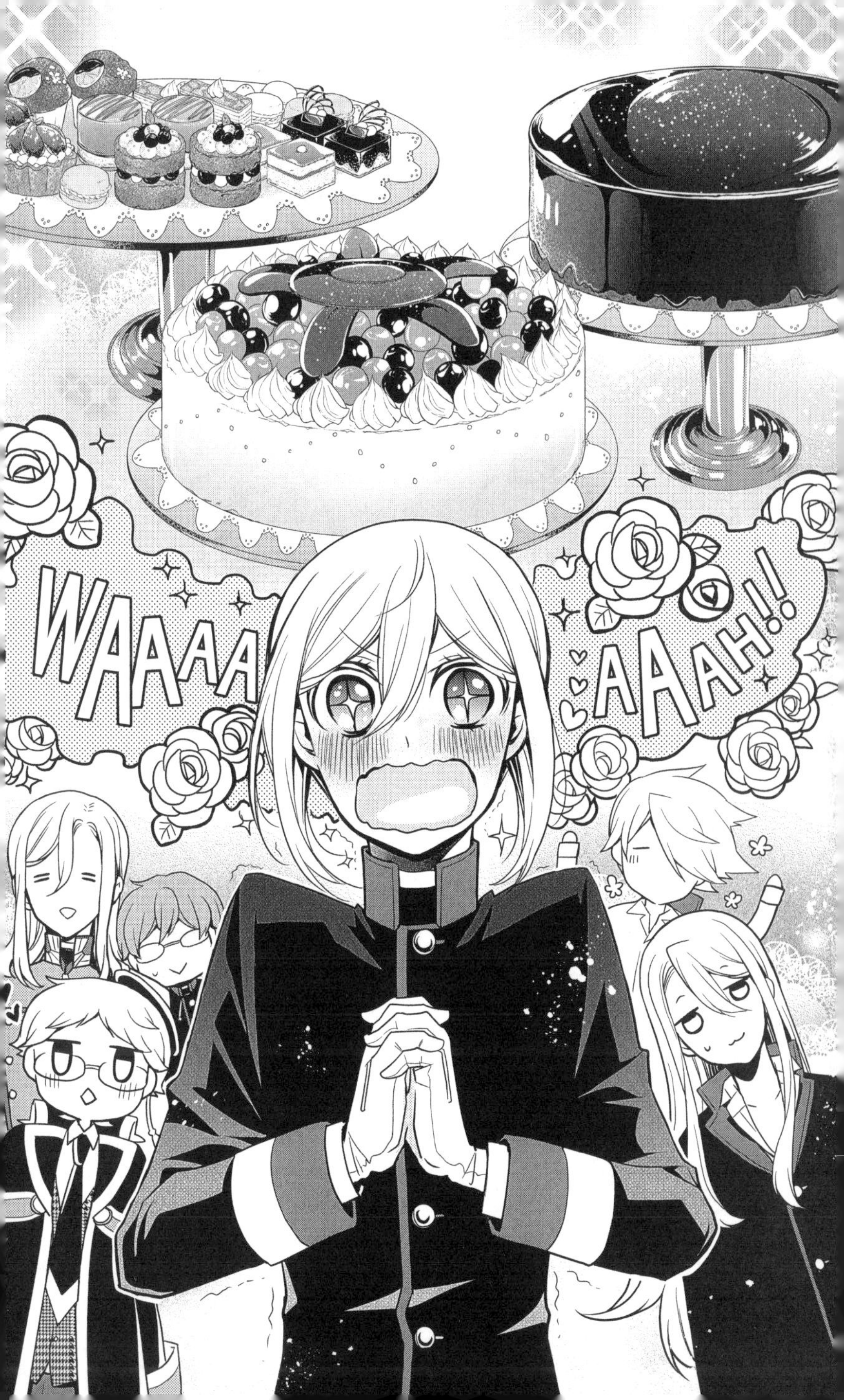
WAAAAAAAAH!!

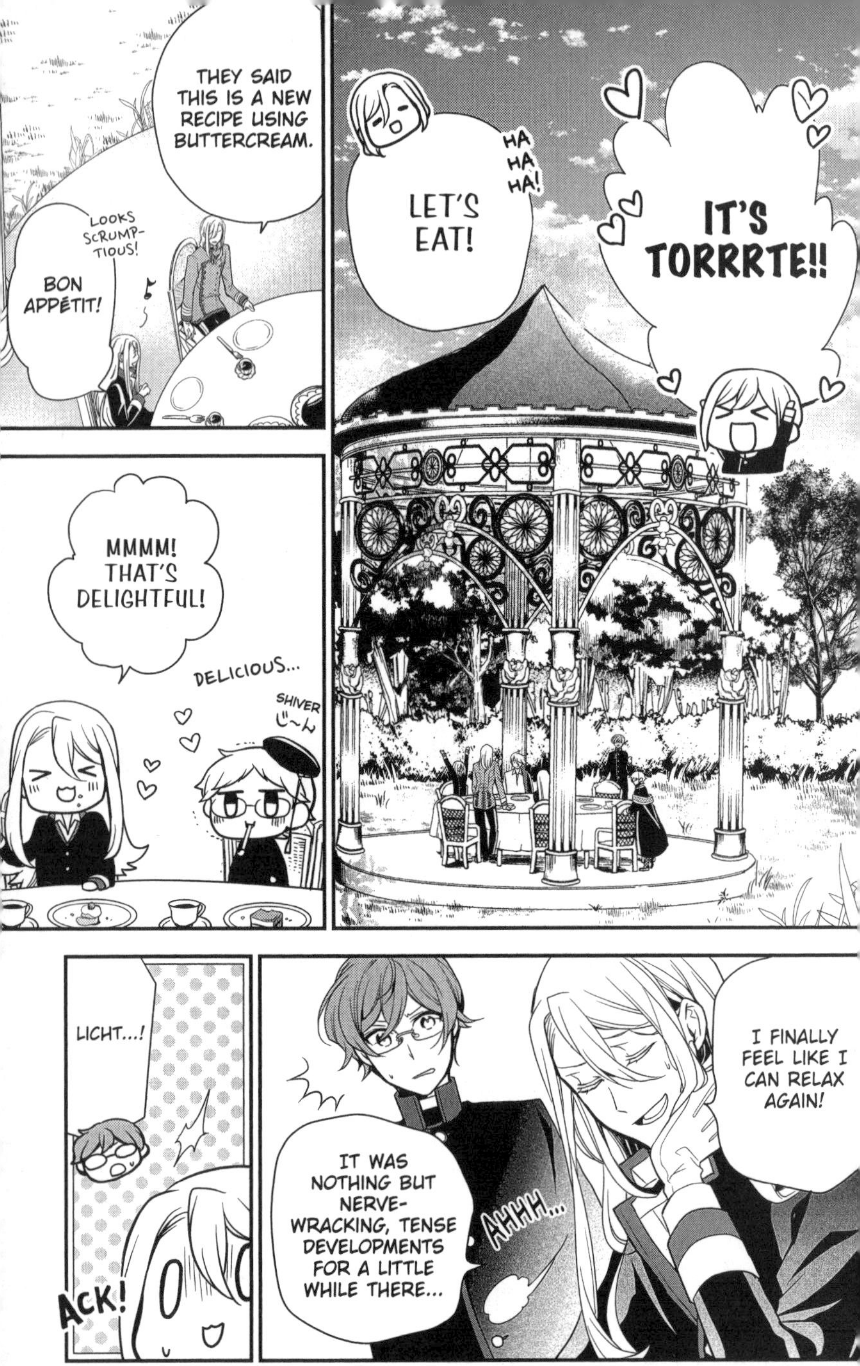
IT'S TORRRTE!!
LET'S EAT!
HA HA HA!
THEY SAID THIS IS A NEW RECIPE USING BUTTERCREAM.
LOOKS SCRUMPTIOUS!
BON APPÉTIT!
MMMM! THAT'S DELIGHTFUL!
DELICIOUS...
SHIVER
じ～ん
I FINALLY FEEL LIKE I CAN RELAX AGAIN!
AHHH...
IT WAS NOTHING BUT NERVE-WRACKING, TENSE DEVELOPMENTS FOR A LITTLE WHILE THERE...
LICHT...!
ACK!

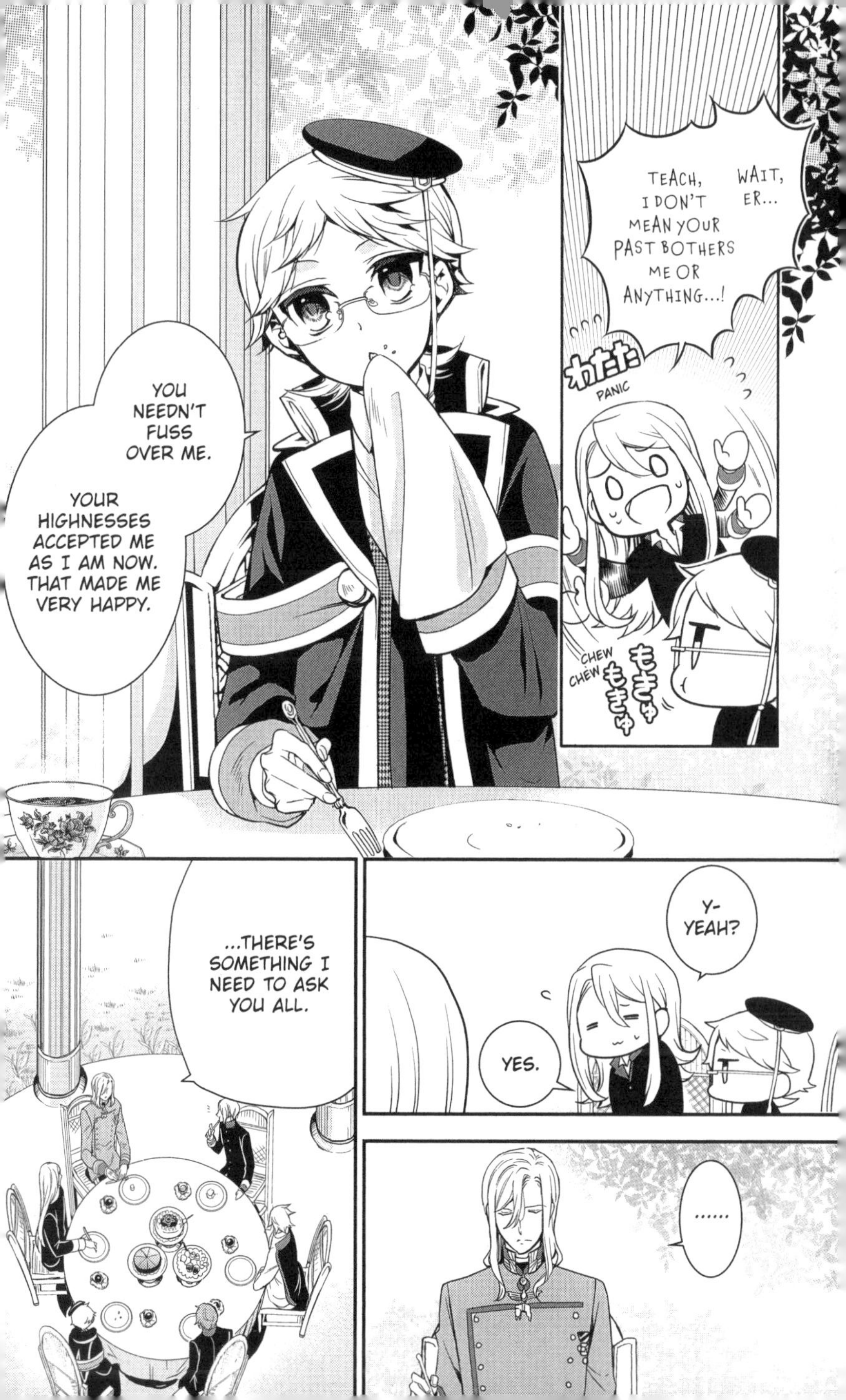
WAIT, ER... TEACH, I DON'T MEAN YOUR PAST BOTHERS ME OR ANYTHING...!
わたた
PANIC
もきゅもきゅ
CHEW CHEW
YOU NEEDN'T FUSS OVER ME.
YOUR HIGHNESSES ACCEPTED ME AS I AM NOW. THAT MADE ME VERY HAPPY.
Y-YEAH?
YES.
......
...THERE'S SOMETHING I NEED TO ASK YOU ALL.

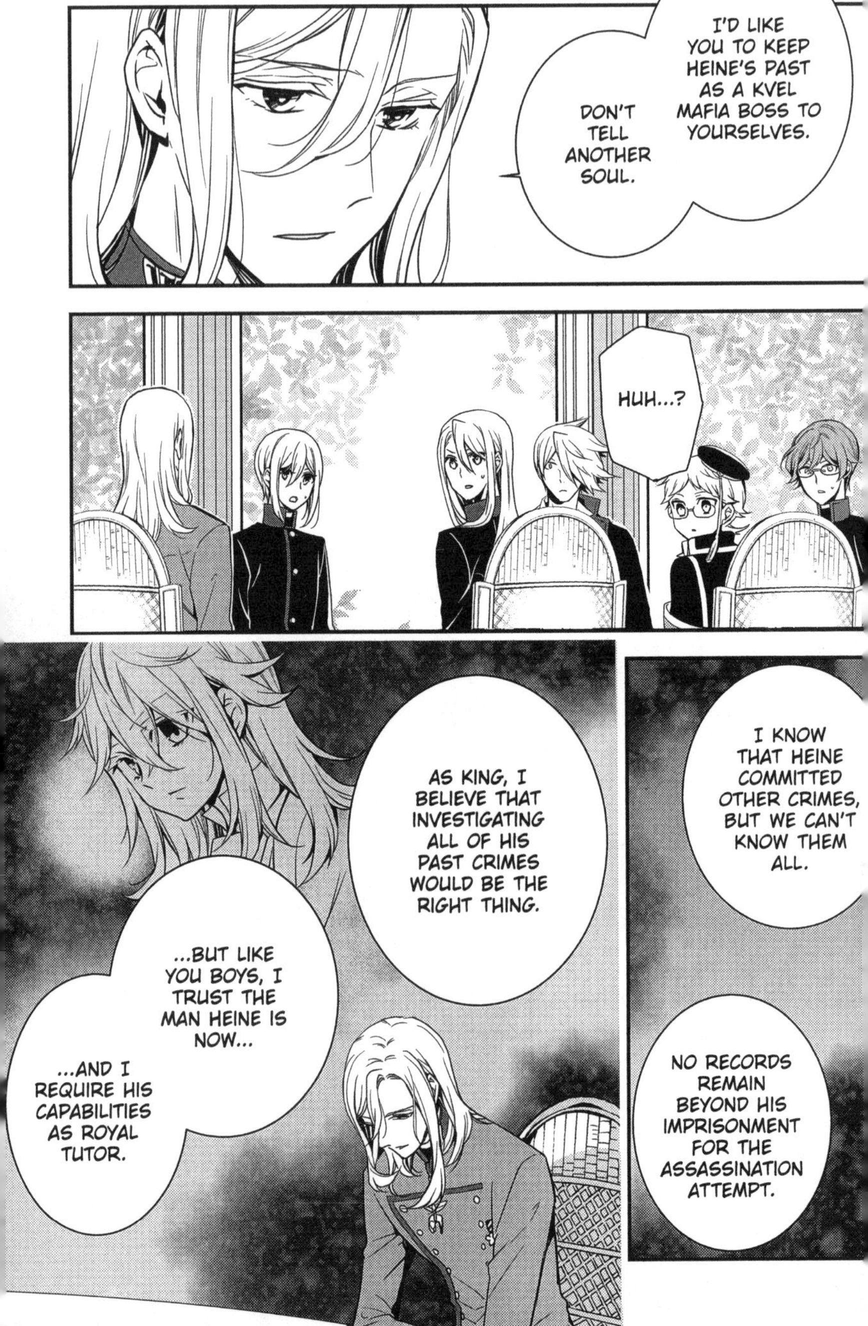
I'D LIKE YOU TO KEEP HEINE'S PAST AS A KVEL MAFIA BOSS TO YOURSELVES.
DON'T TELL ANOTHER SOUL.
HUH...?
I KNOW THAT HEINE COMMITTED OTHER CRIMES, BUT WE CAN'T KNOW THEM ALL.
NO RECORDS REMAIN BEYOND HIS IMPRISONMENT FOR THE ASSASSINATION ATTEMPT.
AS KING, I BELIEVE THAT INVESTIGATING ALL OF HIS PAST CRIMES WOULD BE THE RIGHT THING.
...BUT LIKE YOU BOYS, I TRUST THE MAN HEINE IS NOW...
...AND I REQUIRE HIS CAPABILITIES AS ROYAL TUTOR.

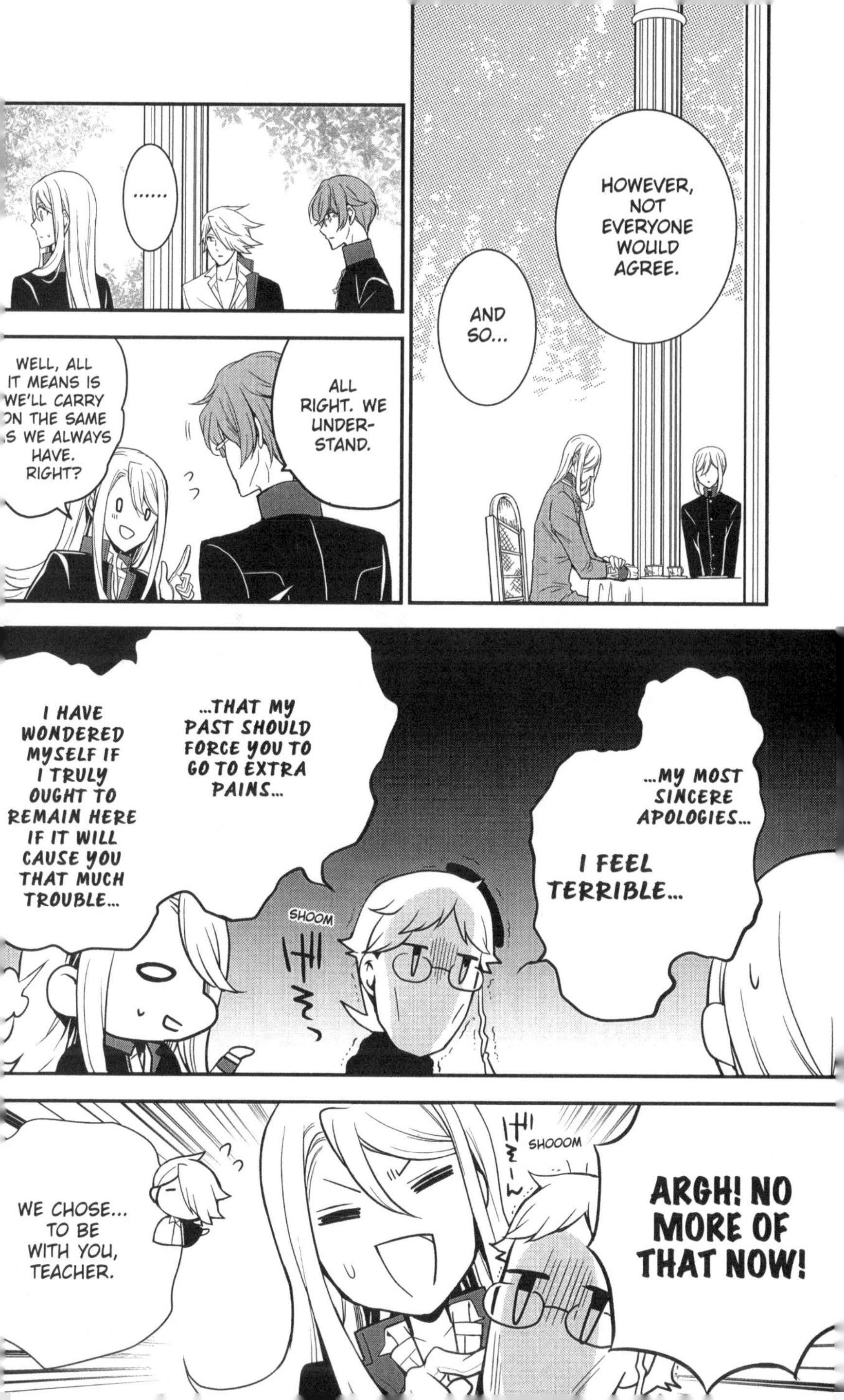
HOWEVER, NOT EVERYONE WOULD AGREE.
AND SO...
......
ALL RIGHT. WE UNDER-STAND.
WELL, ALL IT MEANS IS WE'LL CARRY ON THE SAME S WE ALWAYS HAVE. RIGHT?
...MY MOST SINCERE APOLOGIES...
I FEEL TERRIBLE...
...THAT MY PAST SHOULD FORCE YOU TO GO TO EXTRA PAINS...
I HAVE WONDERED MYSELF IF I TRULY OUGHT TO REMAIN HERE IF IT WILL CAUSE YOU THAT MUCH TROUBLE...
SHOOM
ARGH! NO MORE OF THAT NOW!
SHOOOM
WE CHOSE... TO BE WITH YOU, TEACHER.

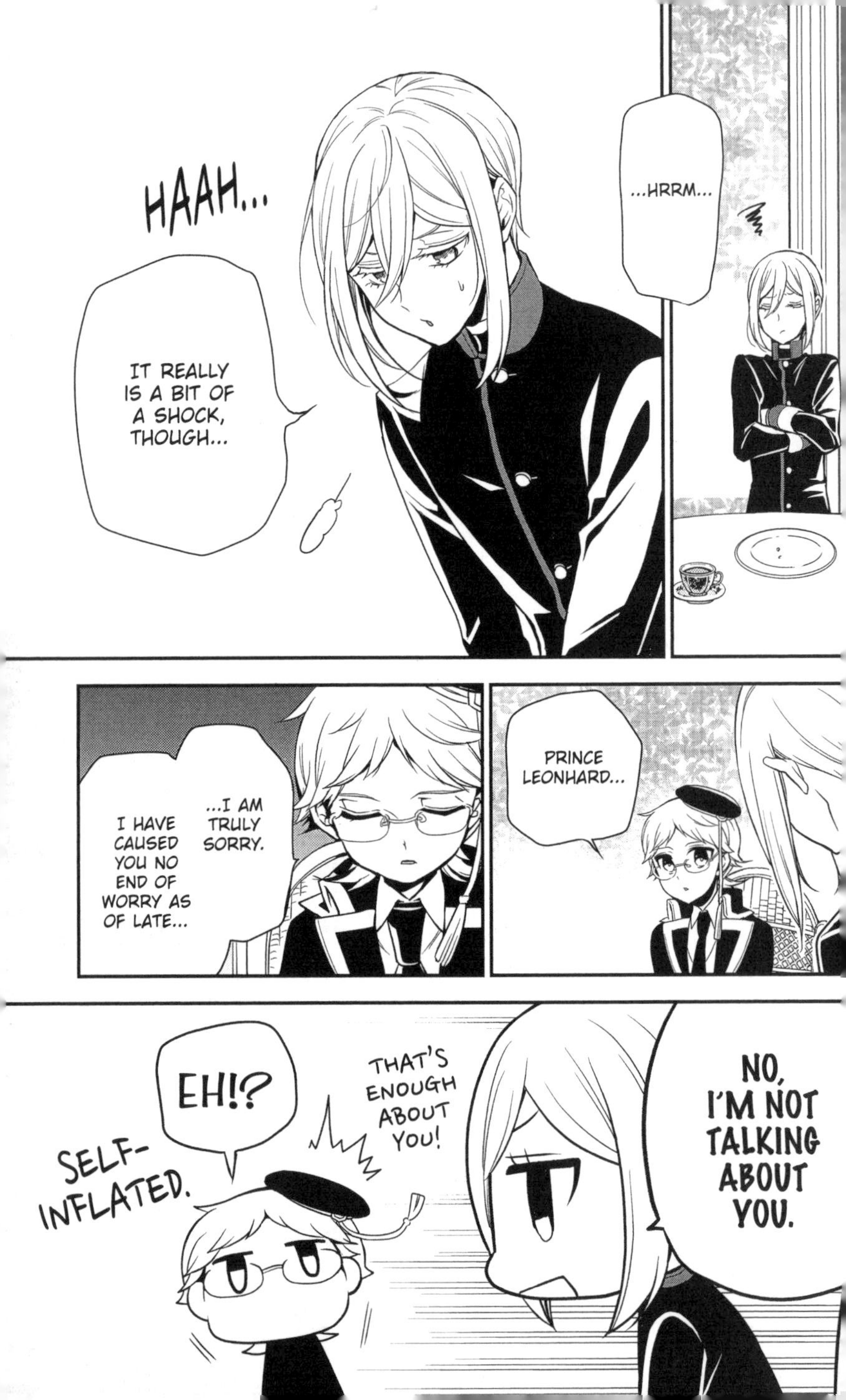
...HRRM...
HAAH...
IT REALLY IS A BIT OF A SHOCK, THOUGH...
PRINCE LEONHARD...
...I AM TRULY SORRY.
I HAVE CAUSED YOU NO END OF WORRY AS OF LATE...
NO, I'M NOT TALKING ABOUT YOU.
THAT'S ENOUGH ABOUT YOU!
EH!?
SELF-INFLATED.

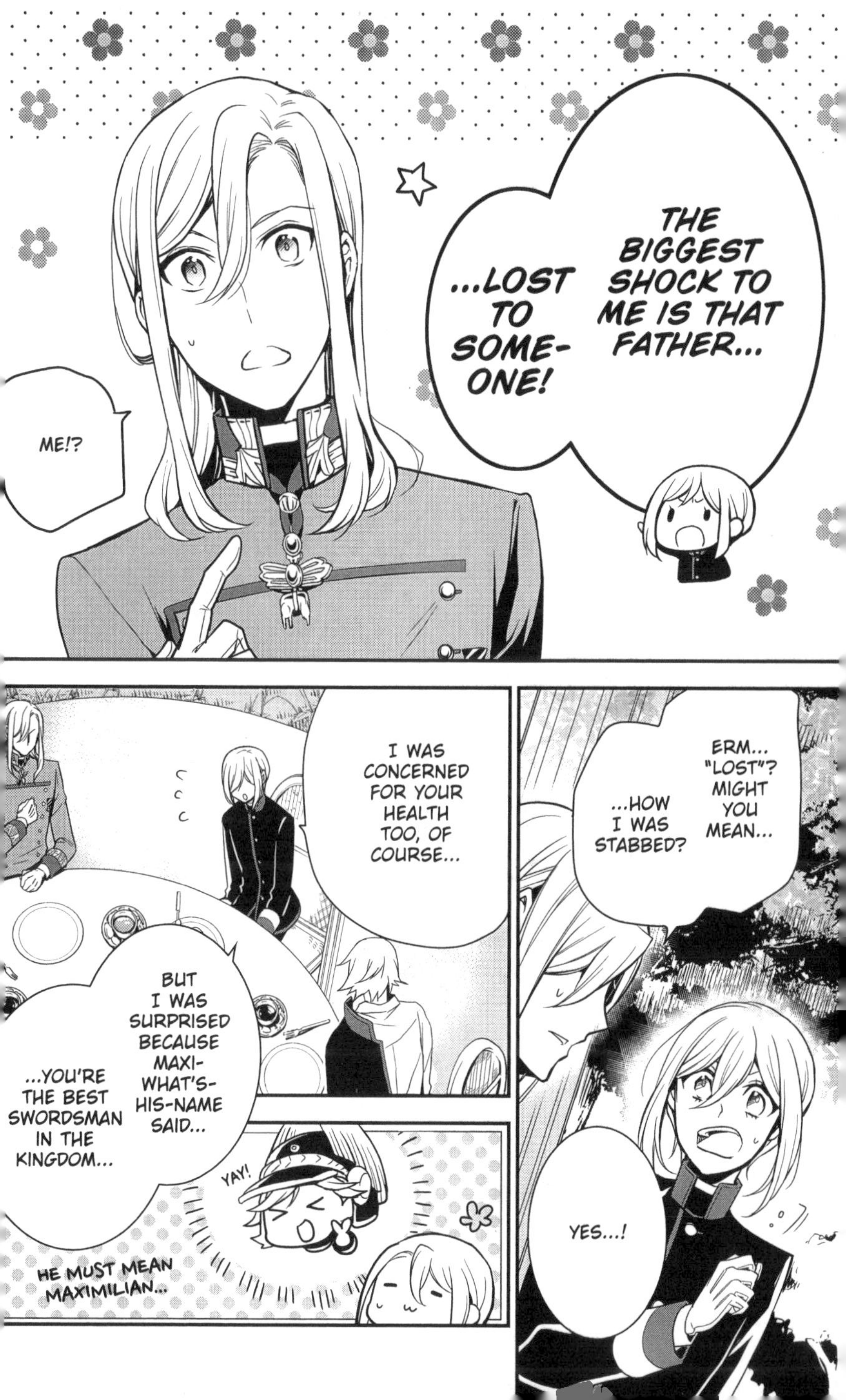
THE BIGGEST SHOCK TO ME IS THAT FATHER...
...LOST TO SOME-ONE!
ME!?
ERM... "LOST"? MIGHT YOU MEAN...
...HOW I WAS STABBED?
YES...!
I WAS CONCERNED FOR YOUR HEALTH TOO, OF COURSE...
BUT I WAS SURPRISED BECAUSE MAXI-WHAT'S-HIS-NAME SAID...
...YOU'RE THE BEST SWORDSMAN IN THE KINGDOM...
YAY!
HE MUST MEAN MAXIMILIAN...

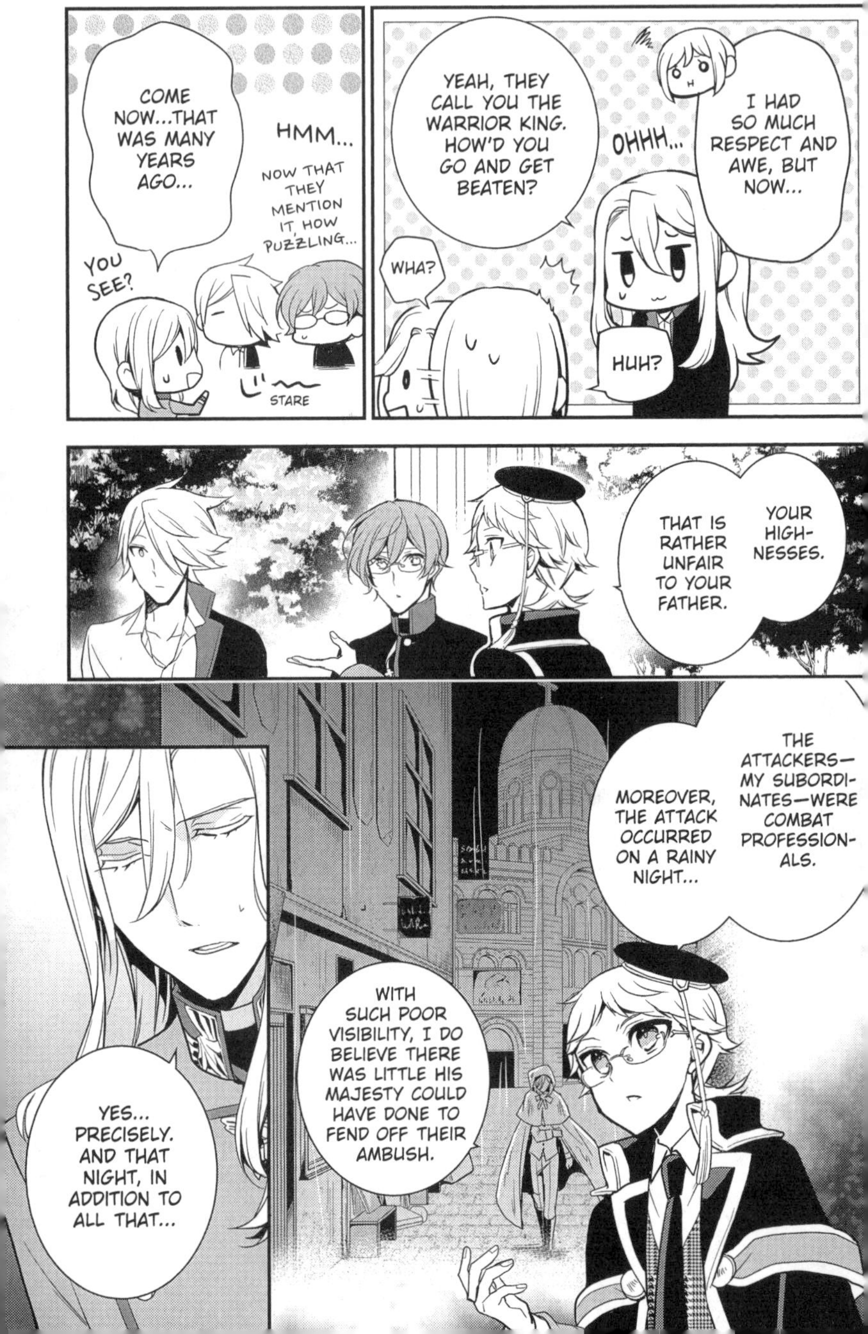
I HAD SO MUCH RESPECT AND AWE, BUT NOW...
OHHH...
YEAH, THEY CALL YOU THE WARRIOR KING. HOW'D YOU GO AND GET BEATEN?
HUH?
WHA?
HMM...
NOW THAT THEY MENTION IT, HOW PUZZLING...
COME NOW...THAT WAS MANY YEARS AGO...
YOU SEE?
STARE
YOUR HIGHNESSES.
THAT IS RATHER UNFAIR TO YOUR FATHER.
THE ATTACKERS—MY SUBORDINATES—WERE COMBAT PROFESSIONALS.
MOREOVER, THE ATTACK OCCURRED ON A RAINY NIGHT...
WITH SUCH POOR VISIBILITY, I DO BELIEVE THERE WAS LITTLE HIS MAJESTY COULD HAVE DONE TO FEND OFF THEIR AMBUSH.
YES... PRECISELY. AND THAT NIGHT, IN ADDITION TO ALL THAT...

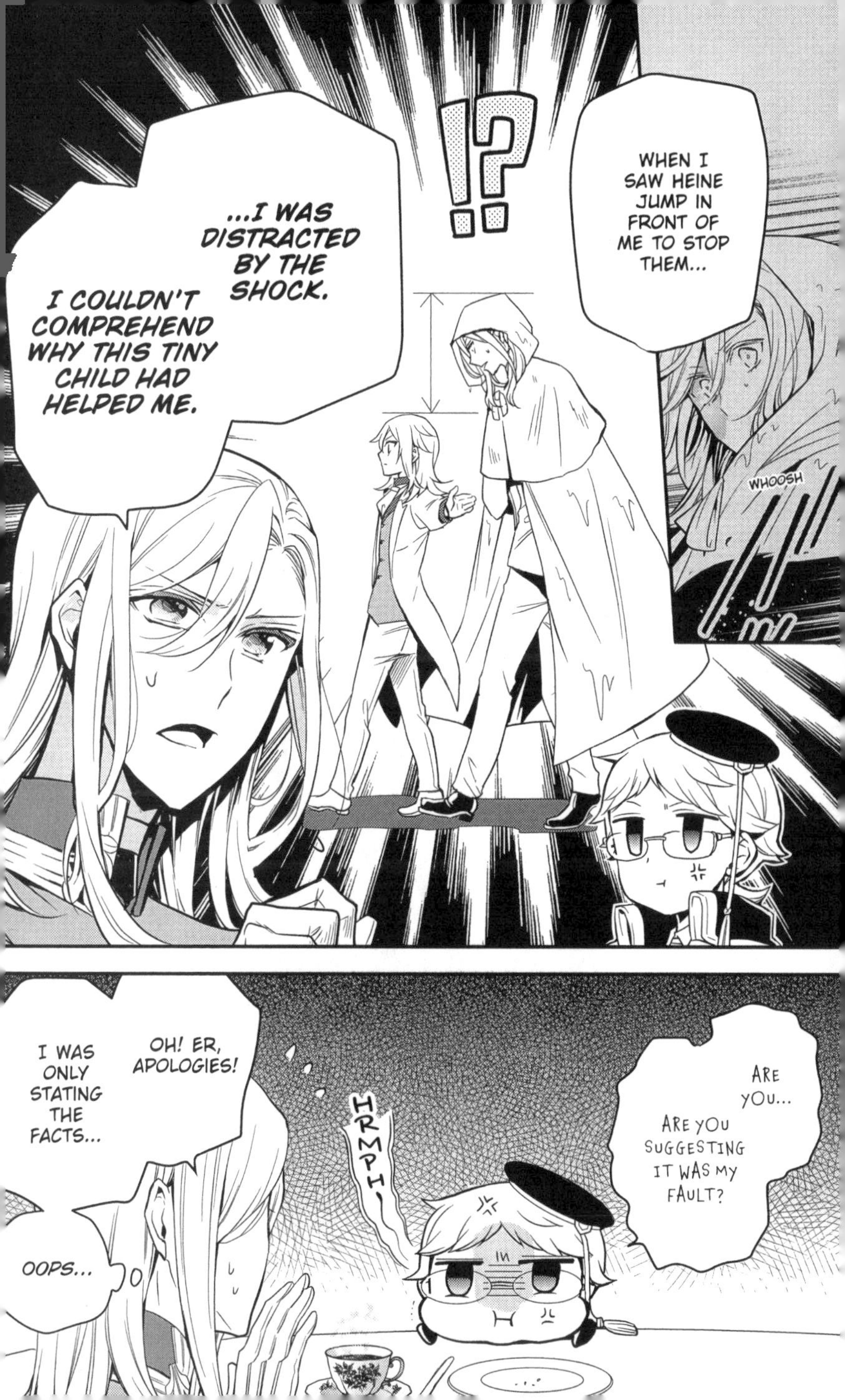
WHEN I SAW HEINE JUMP IN FRONT OF ME TO STOP THEM...
WHOOSH
!?
...I WAS DISTRACTED BY THE SHOCK.
I COULDN'T COMPREHEND WHY THIS TINY CHILD HAD HELPED ME.
ARE YOU...
ARE YOU SUGGESTING IT WAS MY FAULT?
HRMPH!
OH! ER, APOLOGIES!
I WAS ONLY STATING THE FACTS...
OOPS...

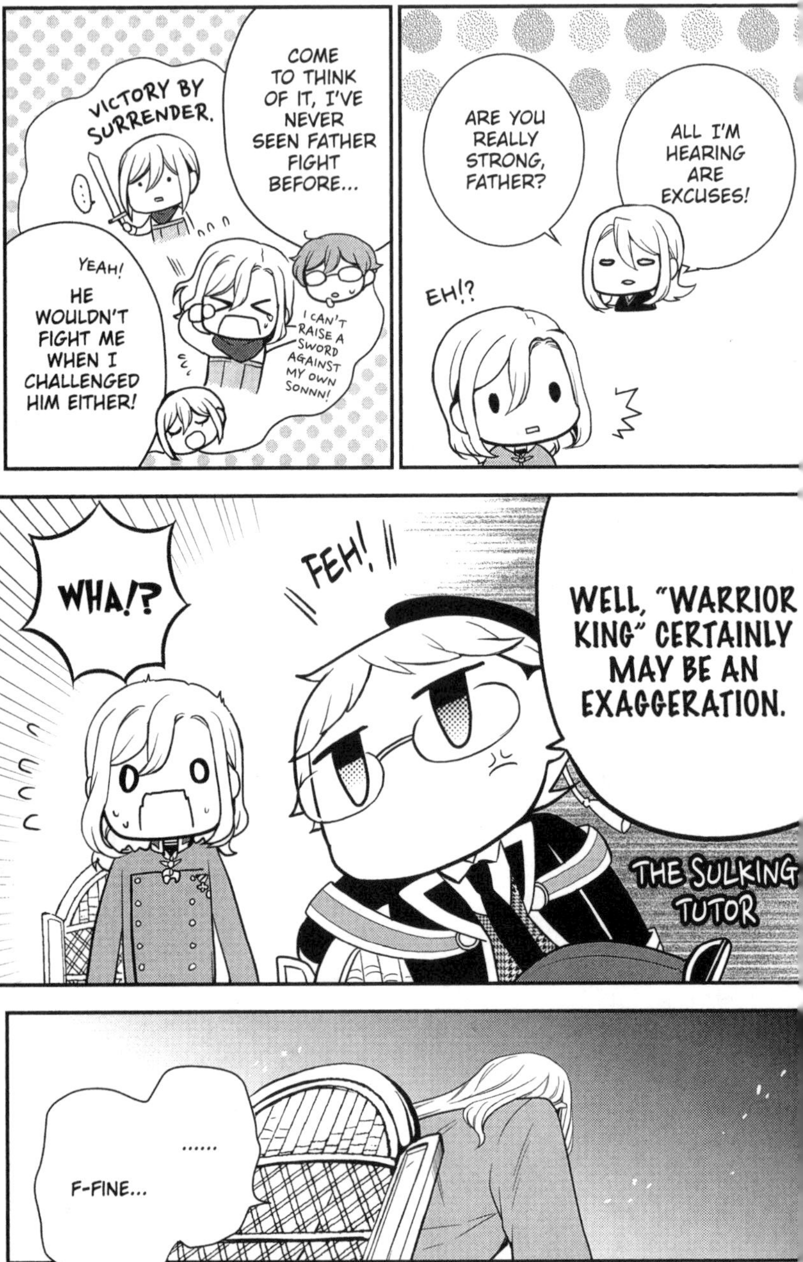
ALL I'M HEARING ARE EXCUSES!
ARE YOU REALLY STRONG, FATHER?
EH!?
COME TO THINK OF IT, I'VE NEVER SEEN FATHER FIGHT BEFORE...
VICTORY BY SURRENDER.
YEAH!
HE WOULDN'T FIGHT ME WHEN I CHALLENGED HIM EITHER!
I CAN'T RAISE A SWORD AGAINST MY OWN SONNN!
WELL, "WARRIOR KING" CERTAINLY MAY BE AN EXAGGERATION.
FEH!
WHA!?
THE SULKING TUTOR
......
F-FINE...

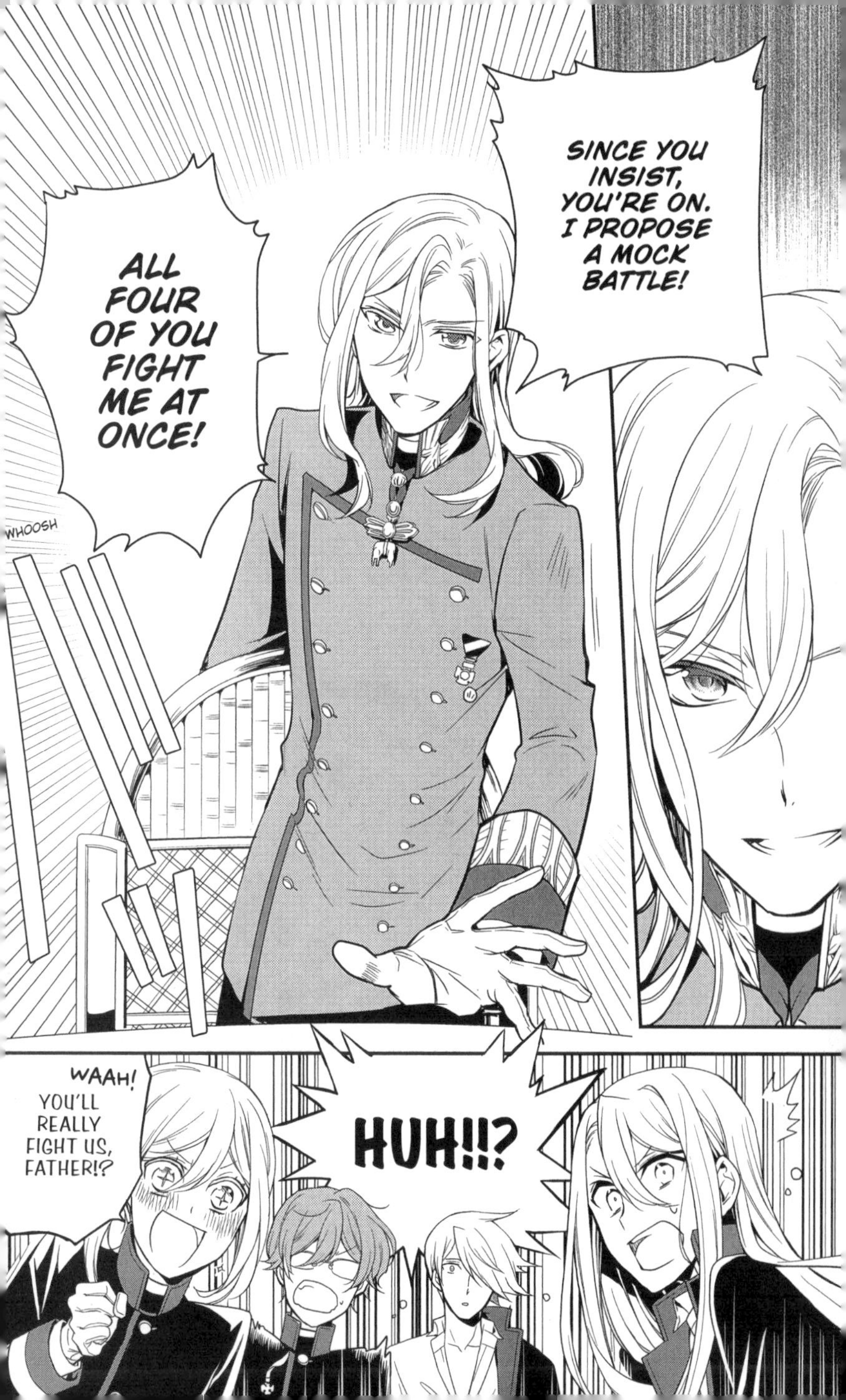
SINCE YOU INSIST, YOU'RE ON. I PROPOSE A MOCK BATTLE!
ALL FOUR OF YOU FIGHT ME AT ONCE!
WHOOSH
HUH!!?
WAAH!
YOU'LL REALLY FIGHT US, FATHER!?

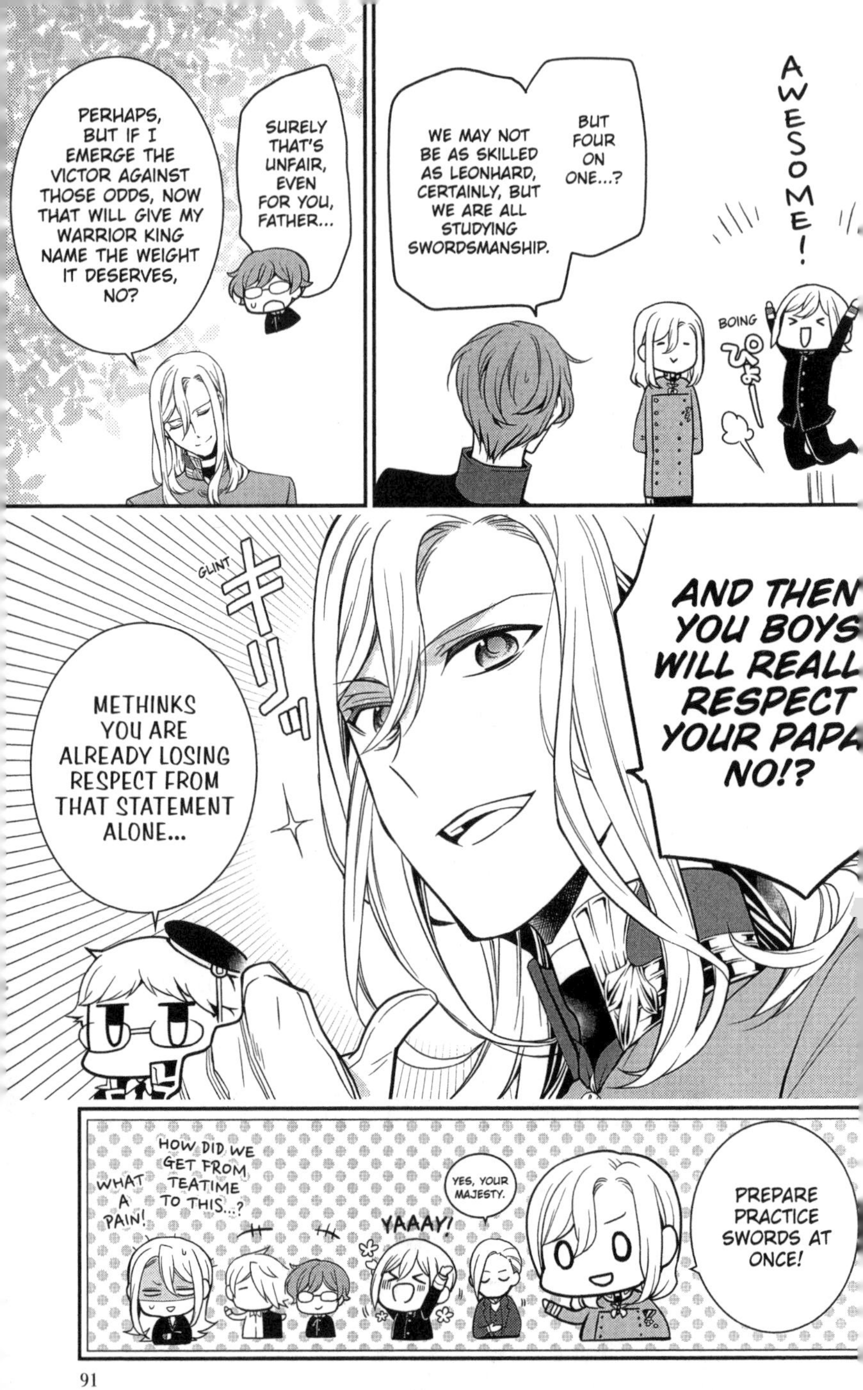

AWESOME!
BOING
BUT FOUR ON ONE...?
WE MAY NOT BE AS SKILLED AS LEONHARD, CERTAINLY, BUT WE ARE ALL STUDYING SWORDSMANSHIP.
SURELY THAT'S UNFAIR, EVEN FOR YOU, FATHER...
PERHAPS, BUT IF I EMERGE THE VICTOR AGAINST THOSE ODDS, NOW THAT WILL GIVE MY WARRIOR KING NAME THE WEIGHT IT DESERVES, NO?
AND THEN YOU BOYS WILL REALL RESPECT YOUR PAPA NO!?
GLINT
METHINKS YOU ARE ALREADY LOSING RESPECT FROM THAT STATEMENT ALONE...
PREPARE PRACTICE SWORDS AT ONCE!
YES, YOUR MAJESTY.
YAAAY!
HOW DID WE GET FROM TEATIME TO THIS...?
WHAT A PAIN!

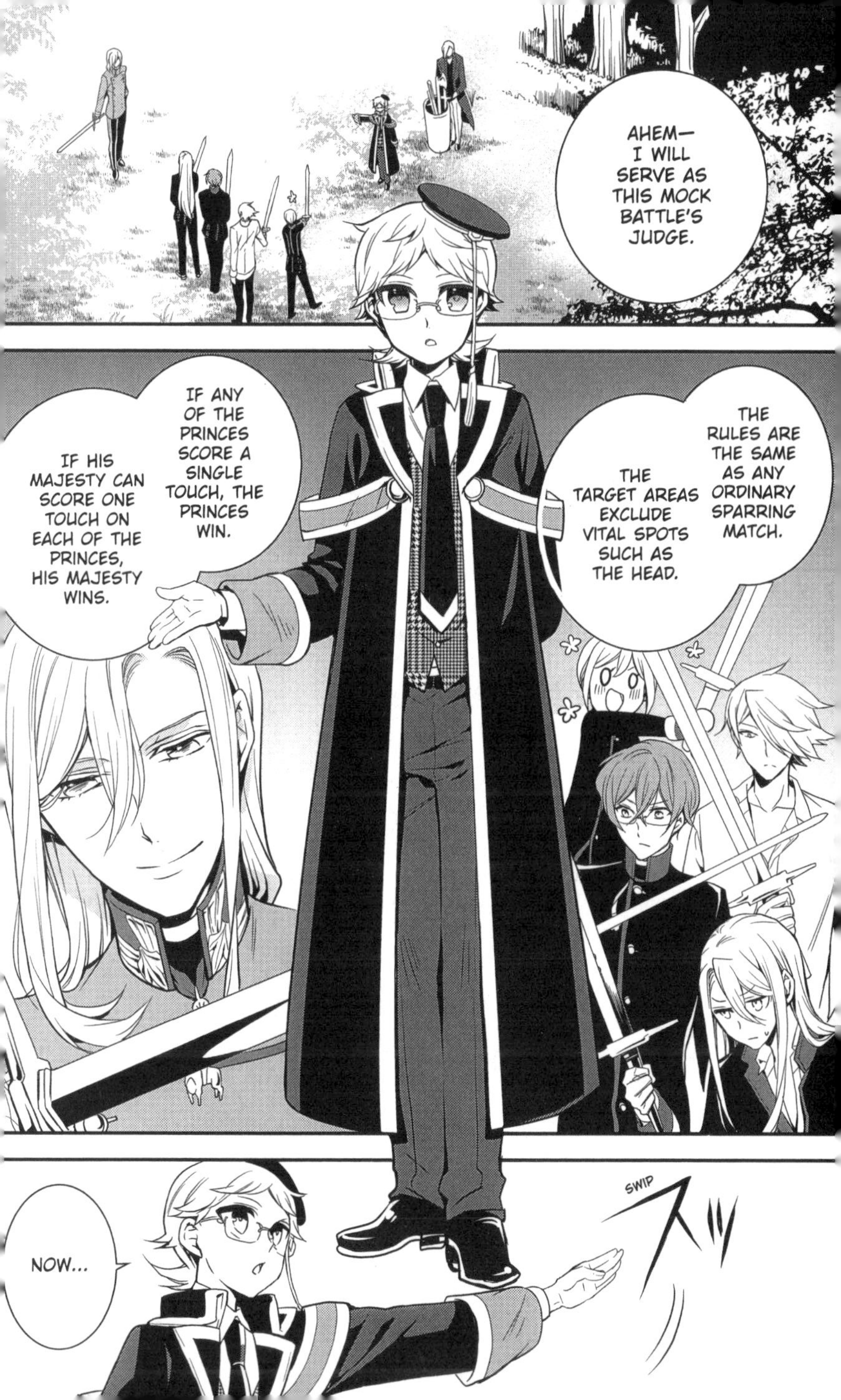
AHEM— I WILL SERVE AS THIS MOCK BATTLE'S JUDGE.
THE RULES ARE THE SAME AS ANY ORDINARY SPARRING MATCH.
THE TARGET AREAS EXCLUDE VITAL SPOTS SUCH AS THE HEAD.
IF ANY OF THE PRINCES SCORE A SINGLE TOUCH, THE PRINCES WIN.
IF HIS MAJESTY CAN SCORE ONE TOUCH ON EACH OF THE PRINCES, HIS MAJESTY WINS.
SWIP
NOW...

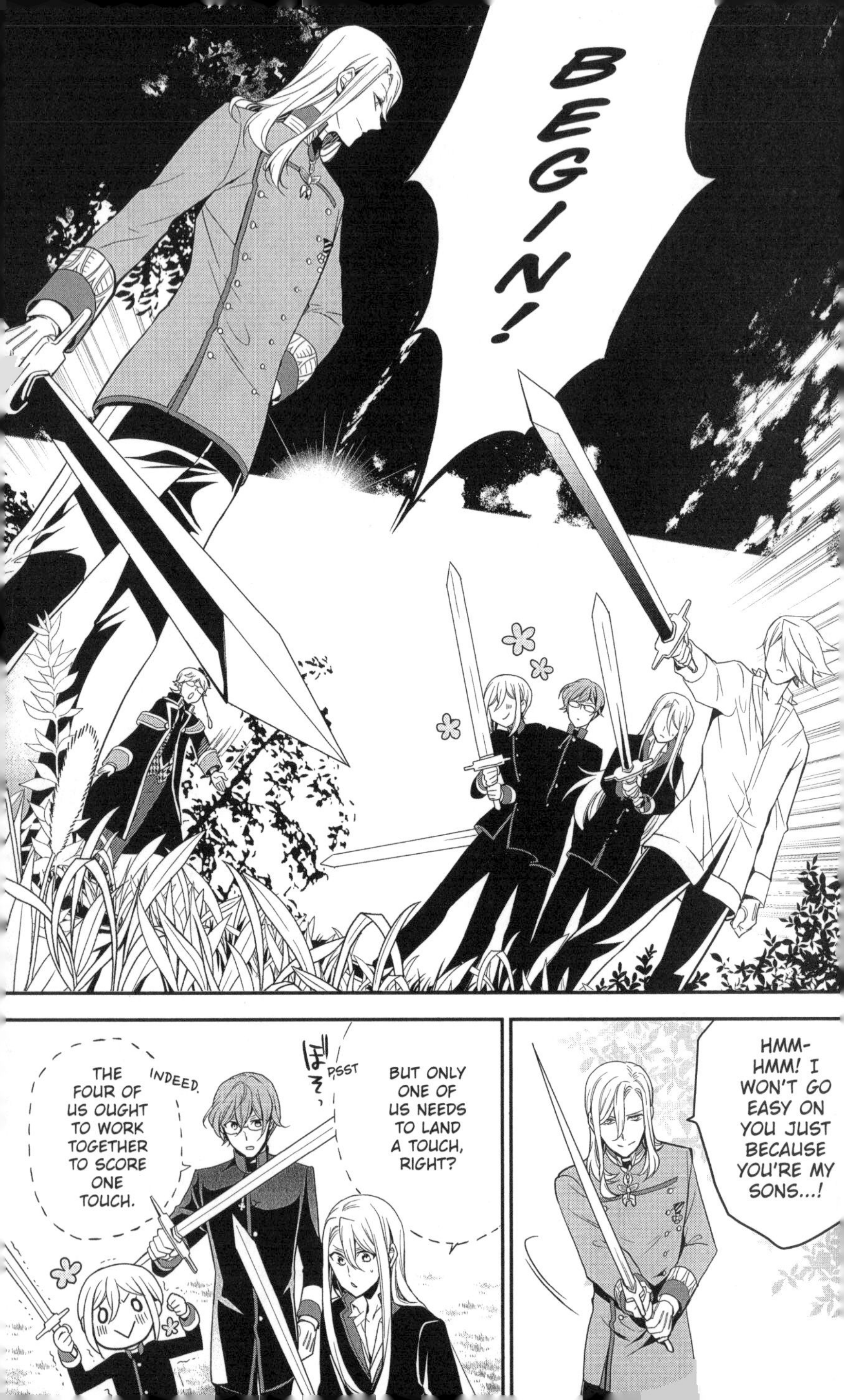
BEGIN!
HMM-HMM! I WON'T GO EASY ON YOU JUST BECAUSE YOU'RE MY SONS...!
ぼそ
PSST
BUT ONLY ONE OF US NEEDS TO LAND A TOUCH, RIGHT?
INDEED.
THE FOUR OF US OUGHT TO WORK TOGETHER TO SCORE ONE TOUCH.

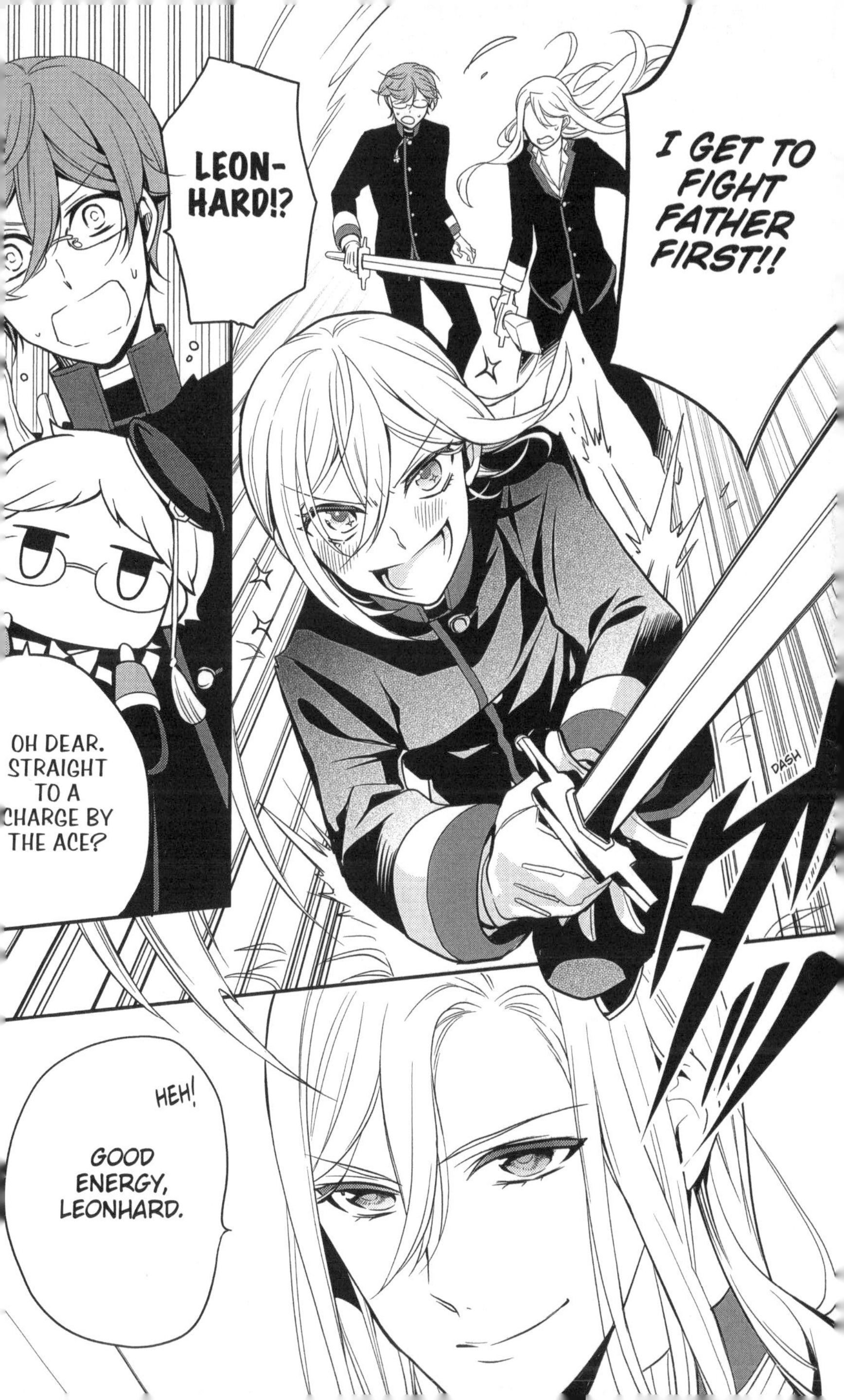
I GET TO FIGHT FATHER FIRST!!
DASH
LEON-HARD!?
OH DEAR. STRAIGHT TO A CHARGE BY THE ACE?
HEH!
GOOD ENERGY, LEONHARD.

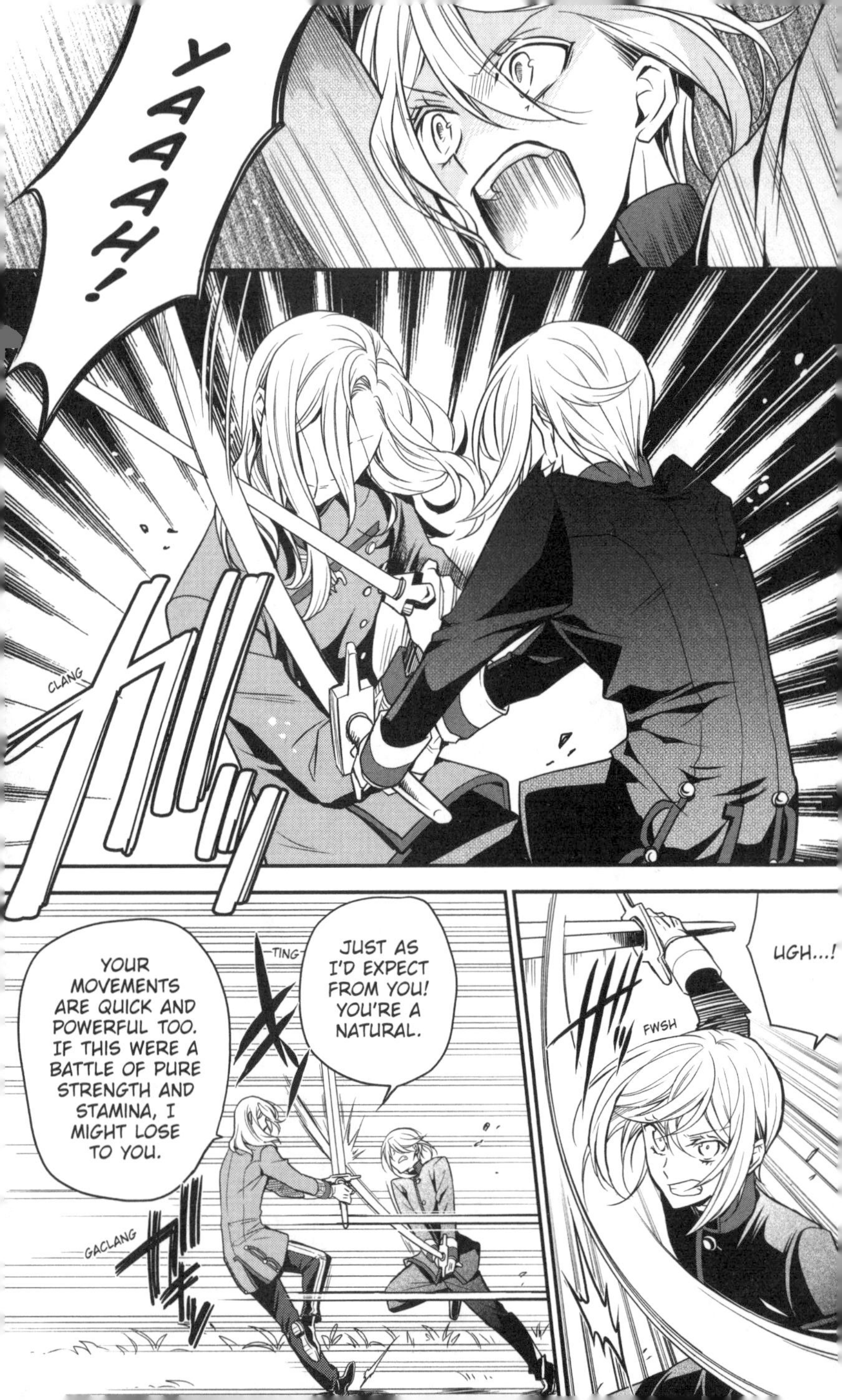
YAAAAH!
CLANG
UGH...!
FWSH
TING
JUST AS I'D EXPECT FROM YOU! YOU'RE A NATURAL.
YOUR MOVEMENTS ARE QUICK AND POWERFUL TOO. IF THIS WERE A BATTLE OF PURE STRENGTH AND STAMINA, I MIGHT LOSE TO YOU.
GACLANG

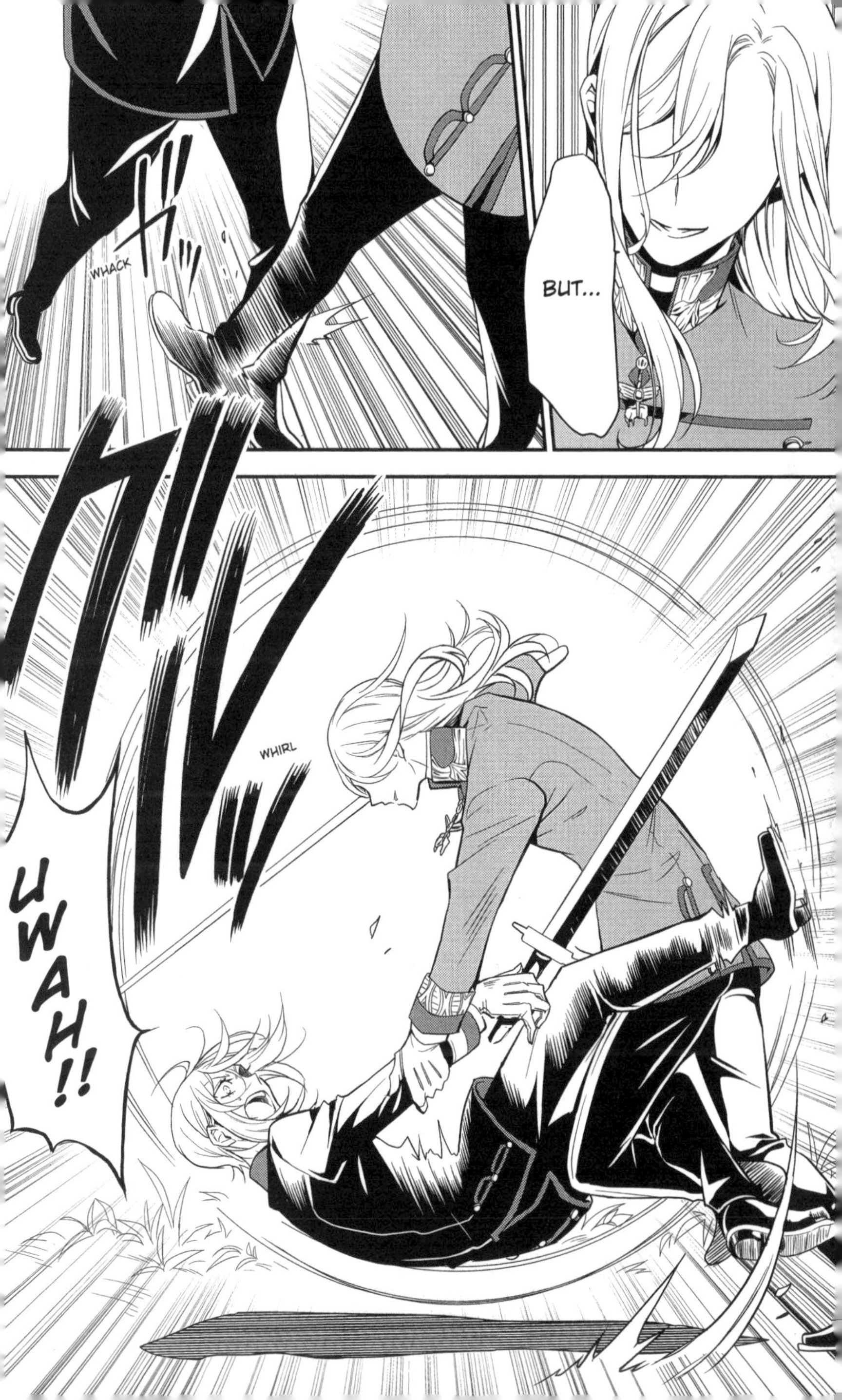
BUT...
WHACK
WHIRL
UWAH!!

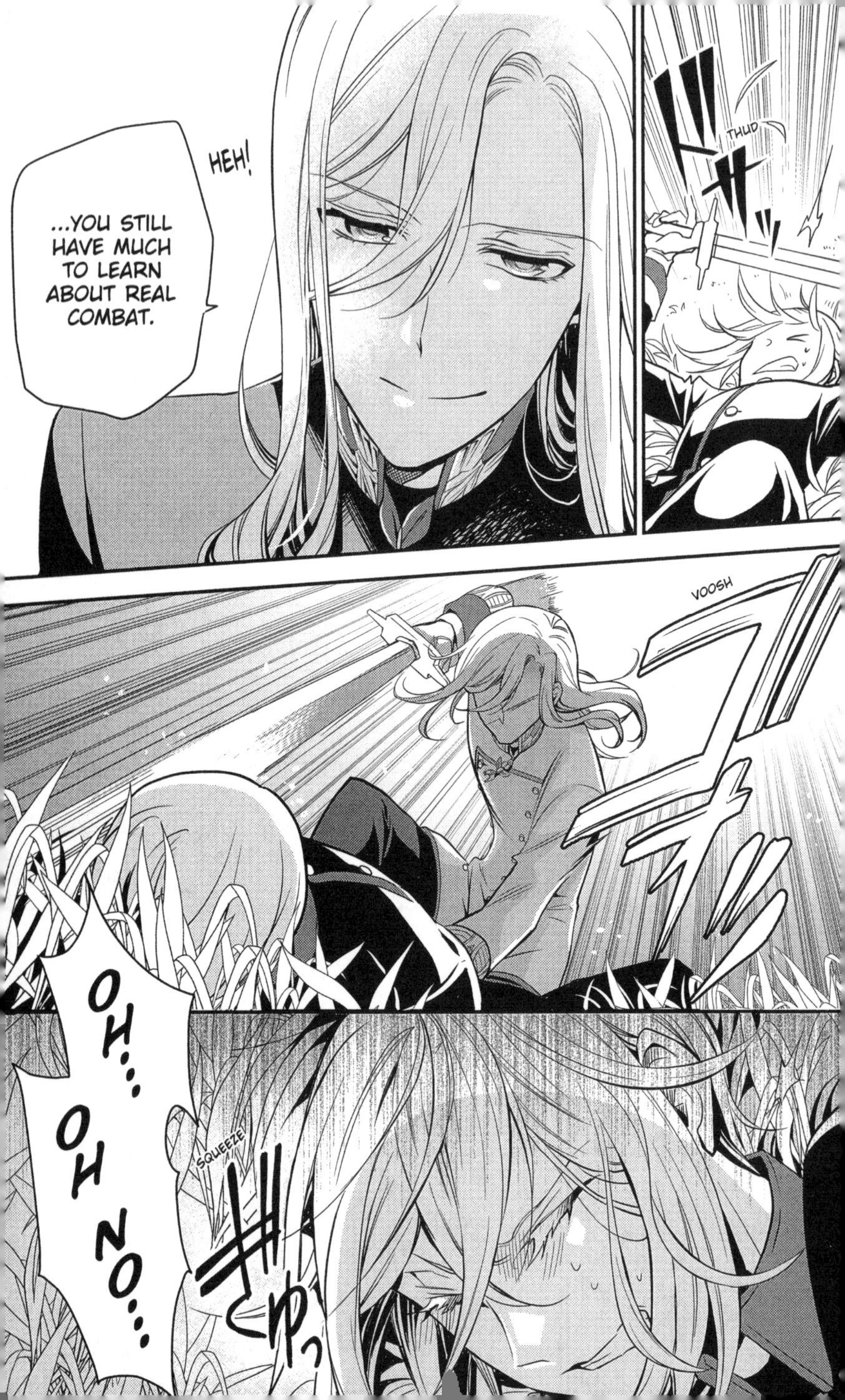
THUD
HEH!
...YOU STILL HAVE MUCH TO LEARN ABOUT REAL COMBAT.
VOOSH
OH... OH NO...
SQUEEZE

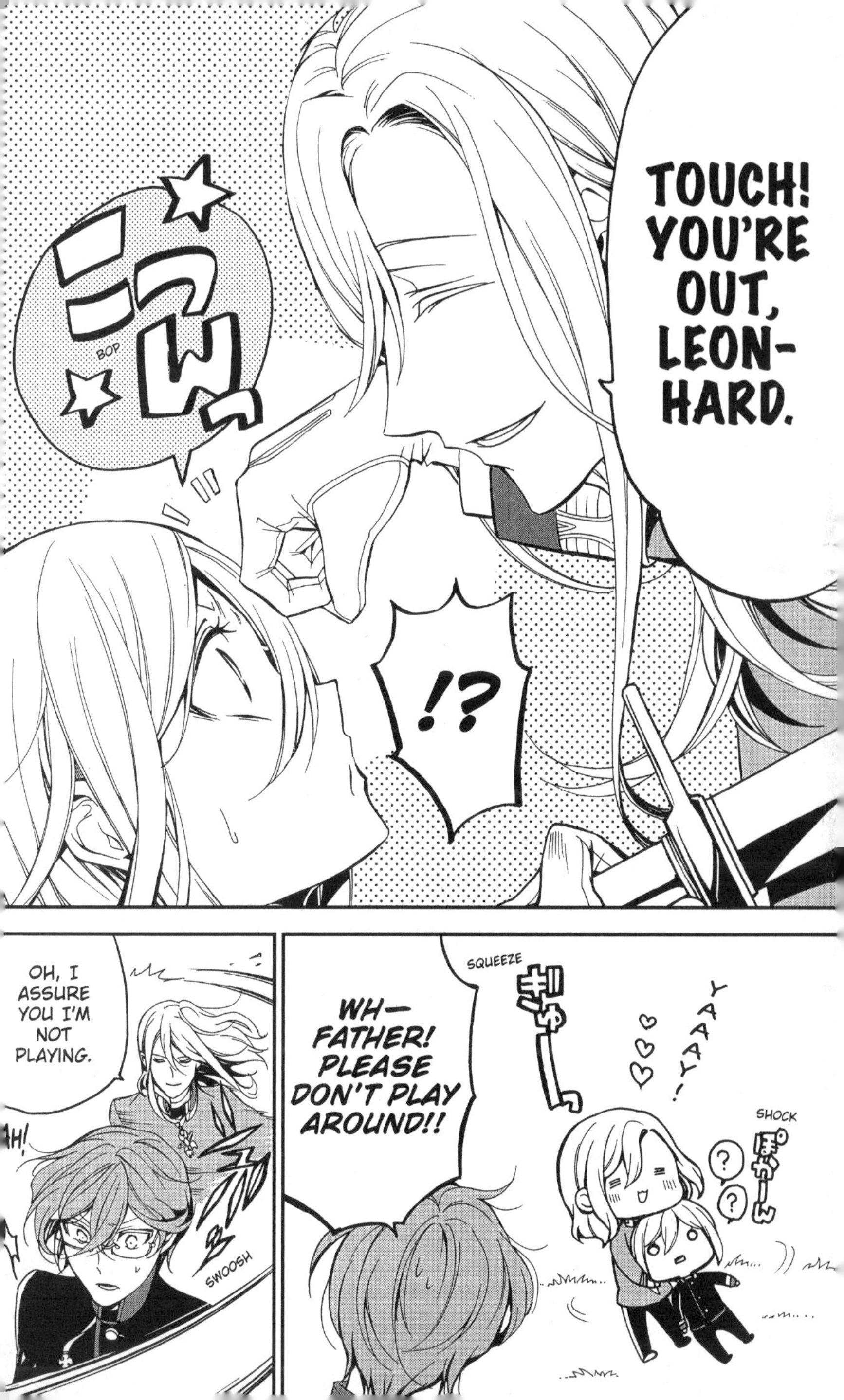
TOUCH! YOU'RE OUT, LEON-HARD.
こつん
BOP
!?
WH— FATHER! PLEASE DON'T PLAY AROUND!!
ぎゅっ
SQUEEZE
YAAAAY!
ぽかーん
SHOCK
OH, I ASSURE YOU I'M NOT PLAYING.
SWOOSH

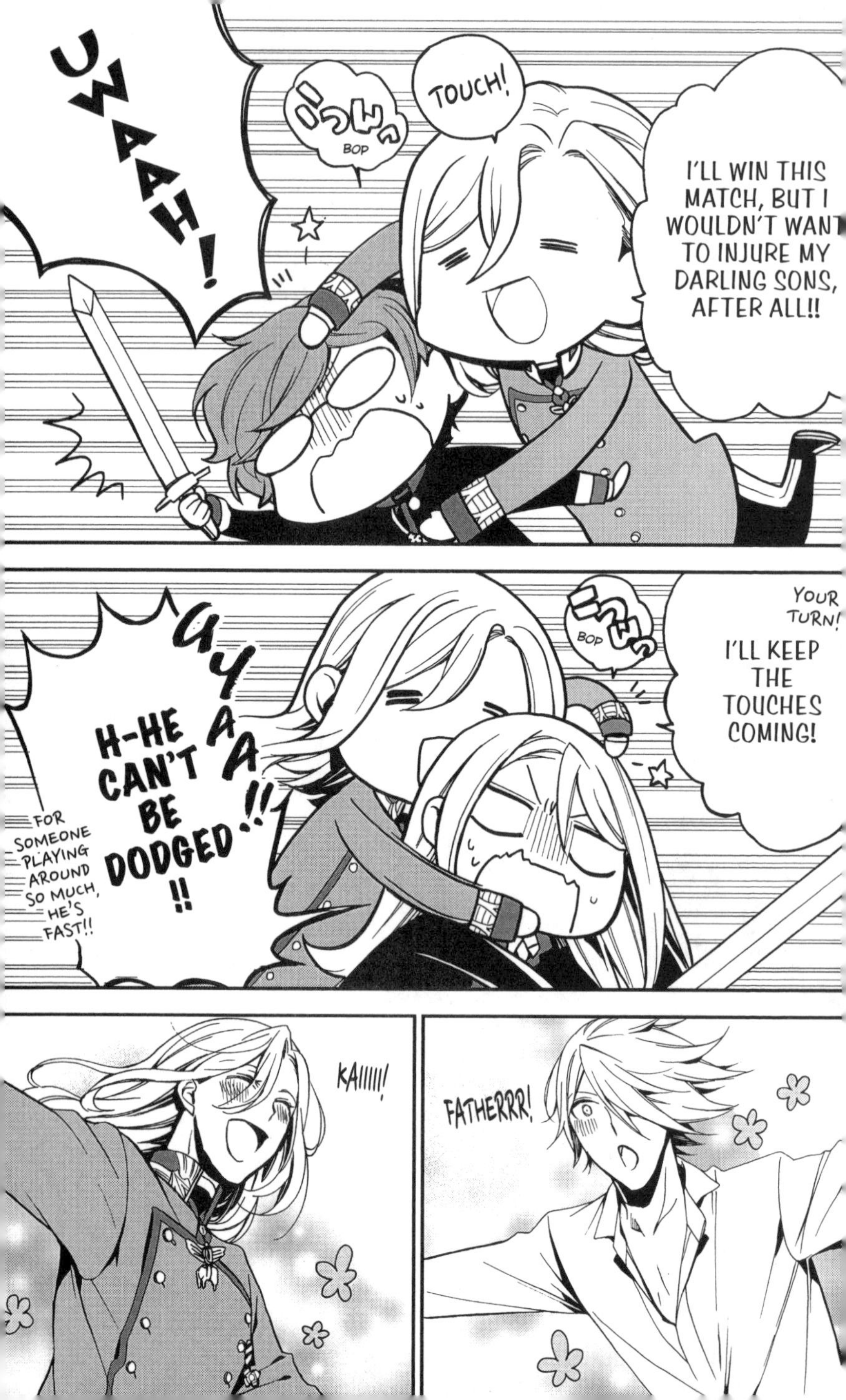

I'LL WIN THIS MATCH, BUT I WOULDN'T WANT TO INJURE MY DARLING SONS, AFTER ALL!!
TOUCH!
BOP
UWAAAH!
YOUR TURN!
I'LL KEEP THE TOUCHES COMING!
BOP
UYAAA!!
H-HE CAN'T BE DODGED!!
FOR SOMEONE PLAYING AROUND SO MUCH, HE'S FAST!!
FATHERRR!
KAIIIII!

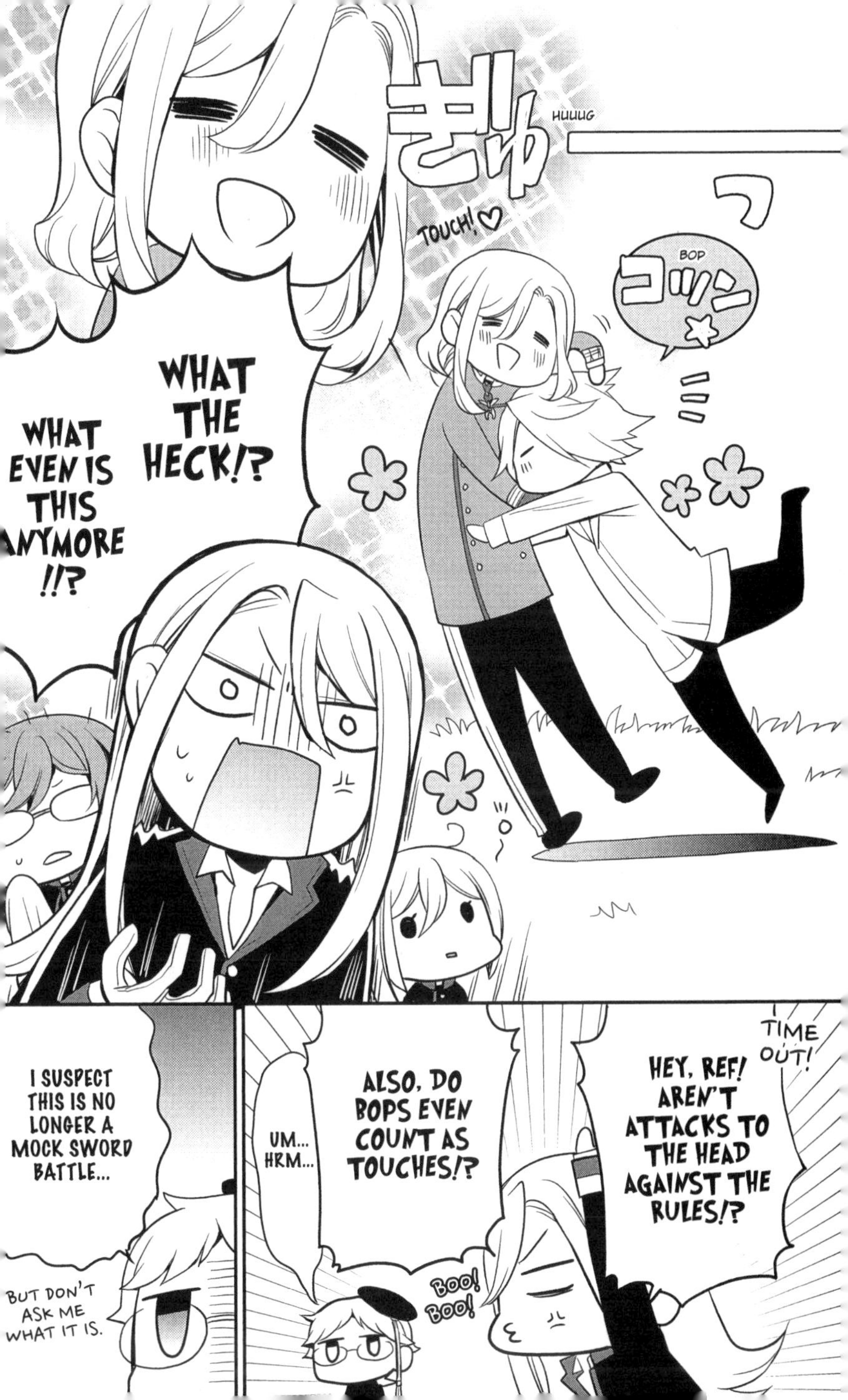
きゅーっ
HUUUG
TOUCH!♡
BOP
コツン
WHAT THE HECK!?
WHAT EVEN IS THIS ANYMORE!!?
TIME OUT!
HEY, REF! AREN'T ATTACKS TO THE HEAD AGAINST THE RULES!?
ALSO, DO BOPS EVEN COUNT AS TOUCHES!?
BOO! BOO!
UM... HRM...
I SUSPECT THIS IS NO LONGER A MOCK SWORD BATTLE...
BUT DON'T ASK ME WHAT IT IS.

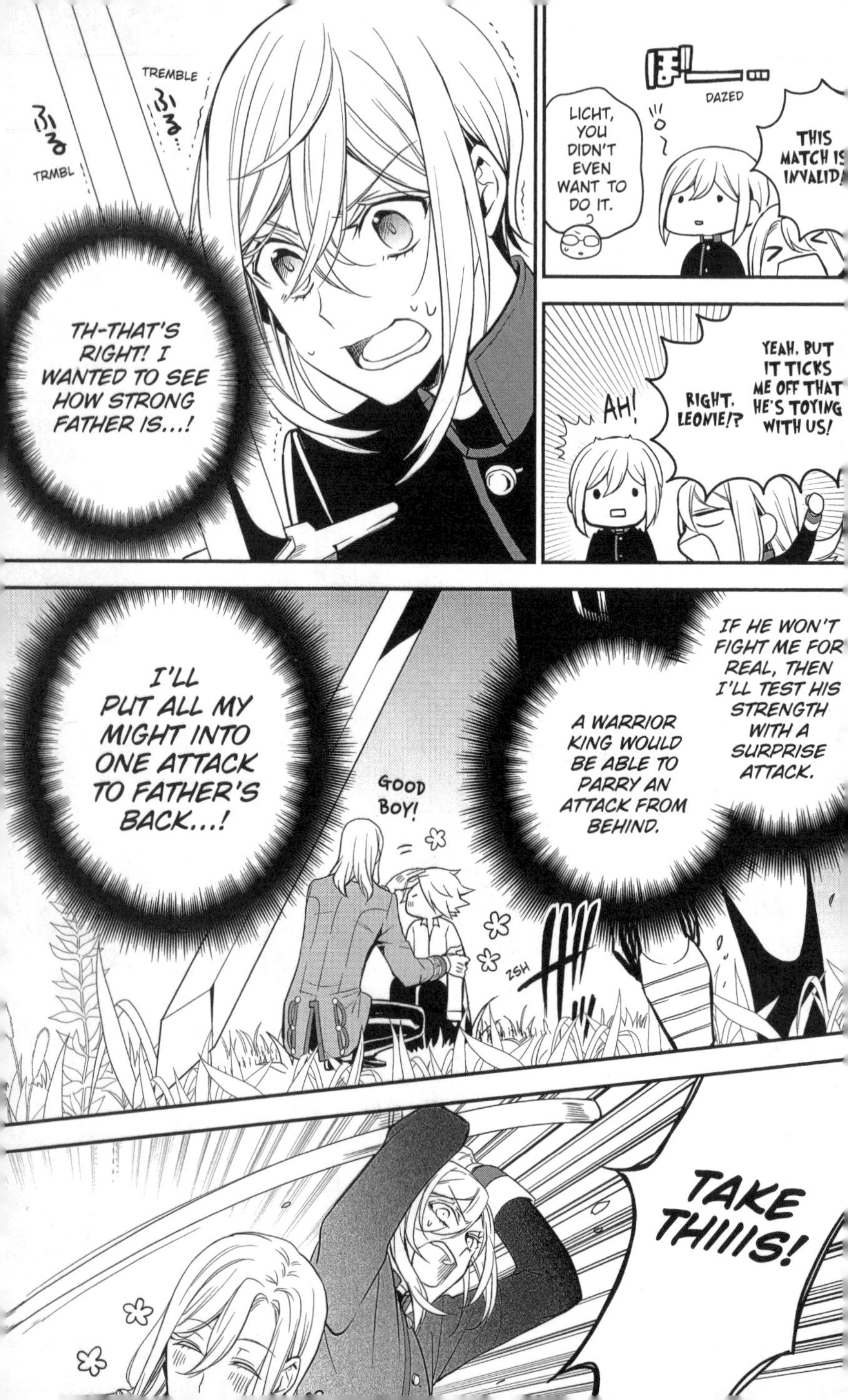
THIS MATCH IS INVALID!
DAZED
LICHT, YOU DIDN'T EVEN WANT TO DO IT.
YEAH, BUT IT TICKS ME OFF THAT HE'S TOYING WITH US!
RIGHT, LEONIE!?
AH!
ふる…
TREMBLE
ふる
TRMBL
TH-THAT'S RIGHT! I WANTED TO SEE HOW STRONG FATHER IS...!
IF HE WON'T FIGHT ME FOR REAL, THEN I'LL TEST HIS STRENGTH WITH A SURPRISE ATTACK.
A WARRIOR KING WOULD BE ABLE TO PARRY AN ATTACK FROM BEHIND.
ZSH
GOOD BOY!
I'LL PUT ALL MY MIGHT INTO ONE ATTACK TO FATHER'S BACK...!
TAKE THIIIS!

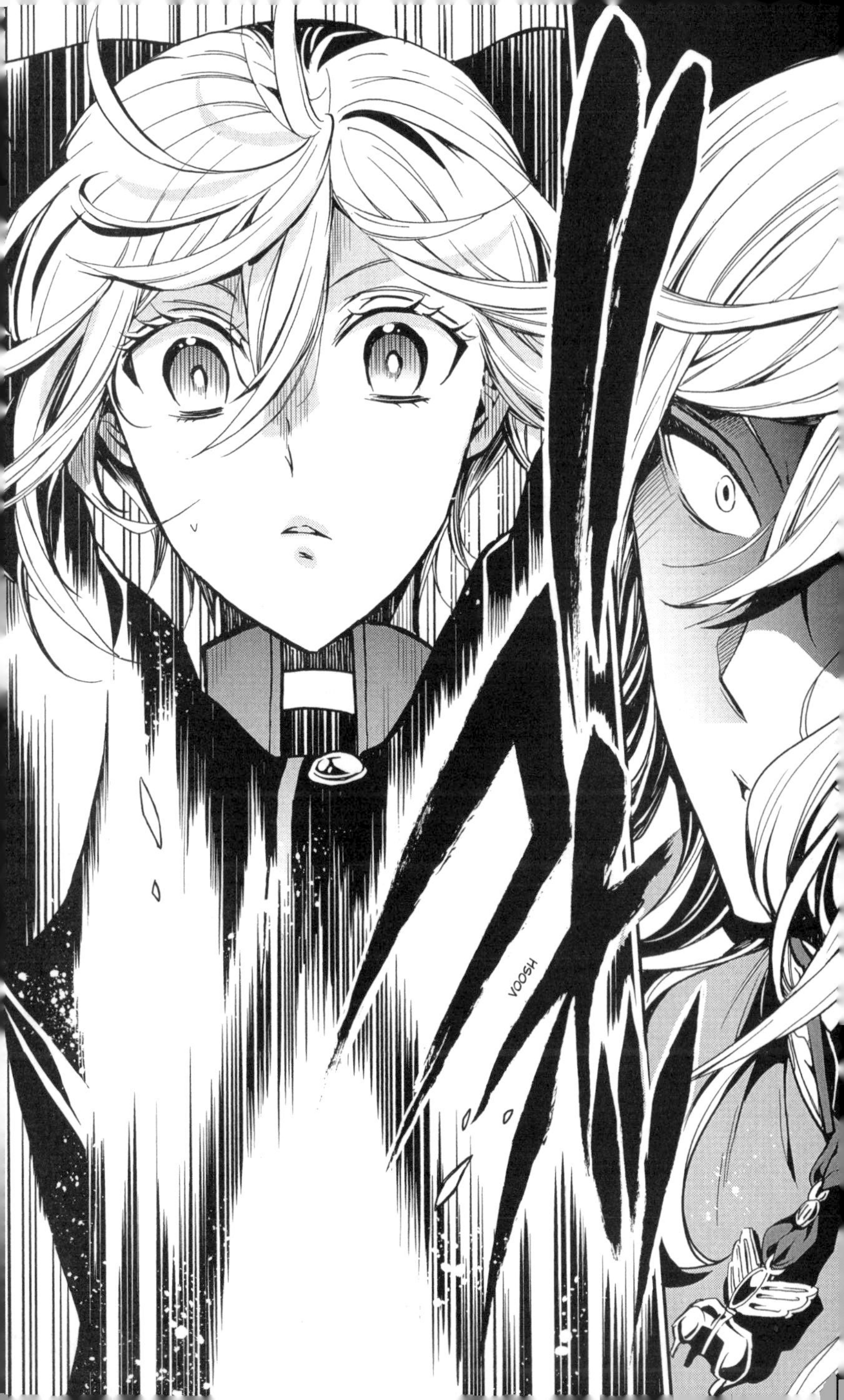
VOOSH

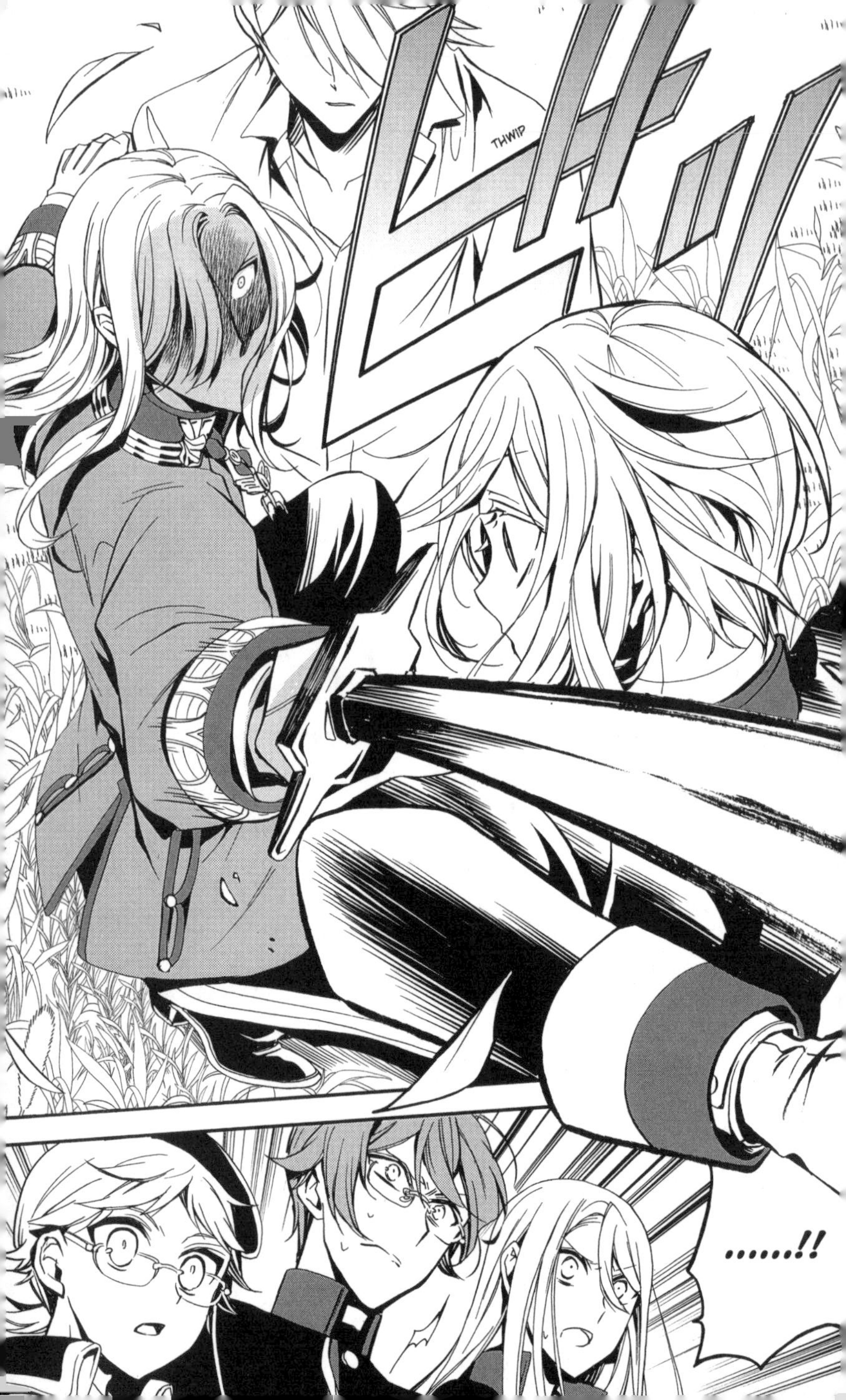
THWIP
......!!

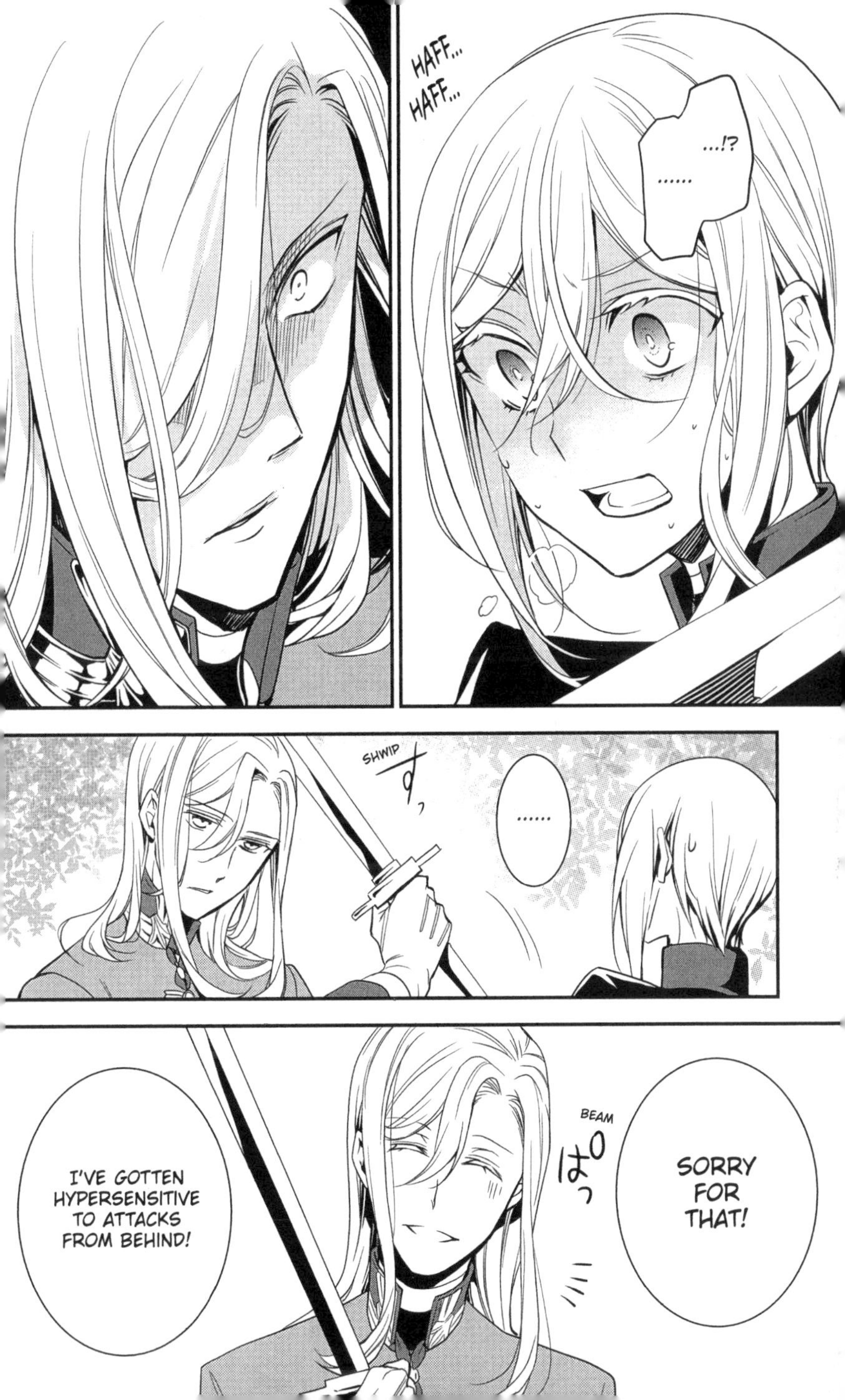
HAFF... HAFF...
...!?
......
......
SHWIP
SORRY FOR THAT!
BEAM
I'VE GOTTEN HYPERSENSITIVE TO ATTACKS FROM BEHIND!

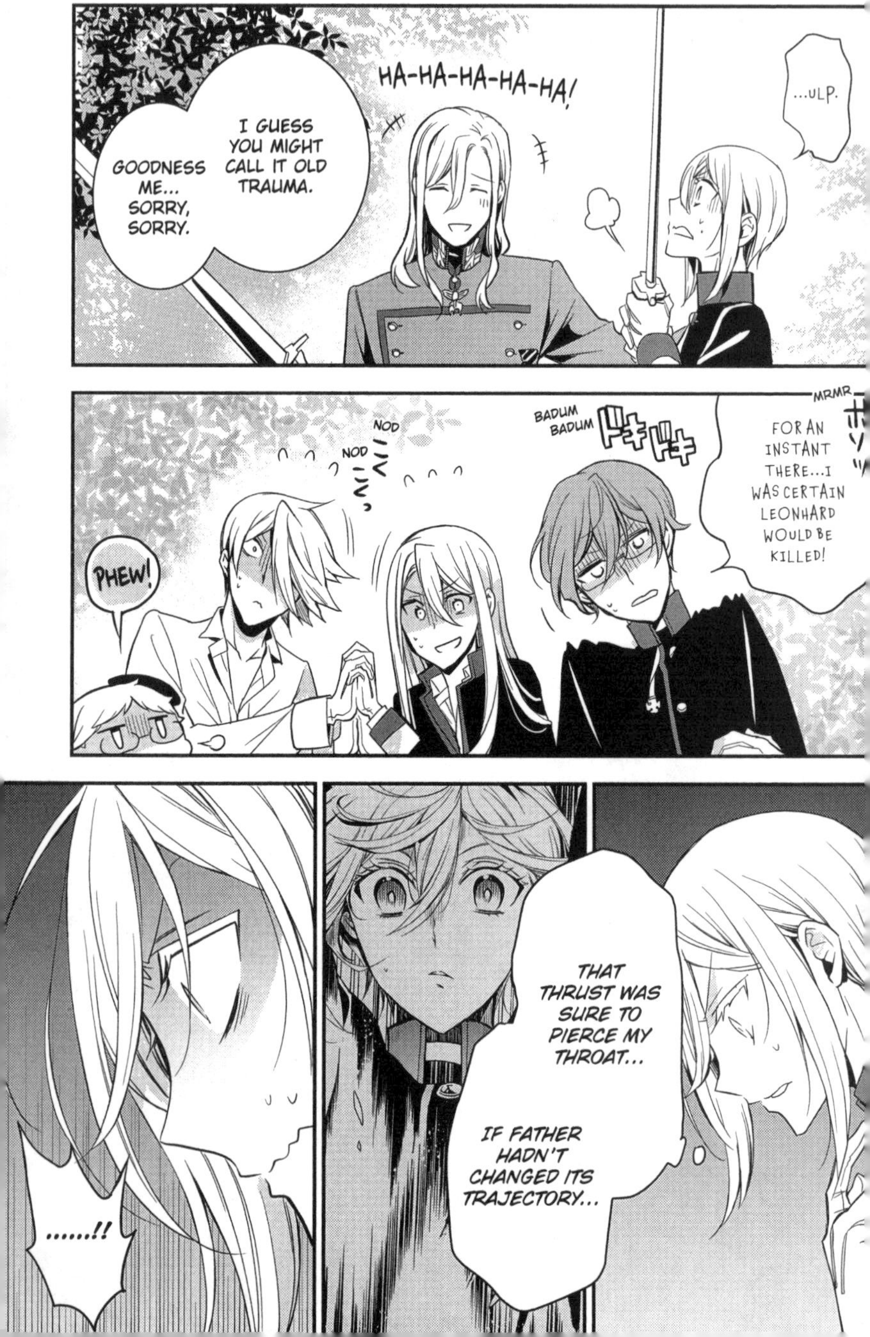
...ULP.
HA-HA-HA-HA-HA!
I GUESS YOU MIGHT CALL IT OLD TRAUMA.
GOODNESS ME... SORRY, SORRY.
MRMR
FOR AN INSTANT THERE...I WAS CERTAIN LEONHARD WOULD BE KILLED!
BADUM BADUM
ドキドキ
NOD NOD
PHEW!
THAT THRUST WAS SURE TO PIERCE MY THROAT...
IF FATHER HADN'T CHANGED ITS TRAJECTORY...
......!!

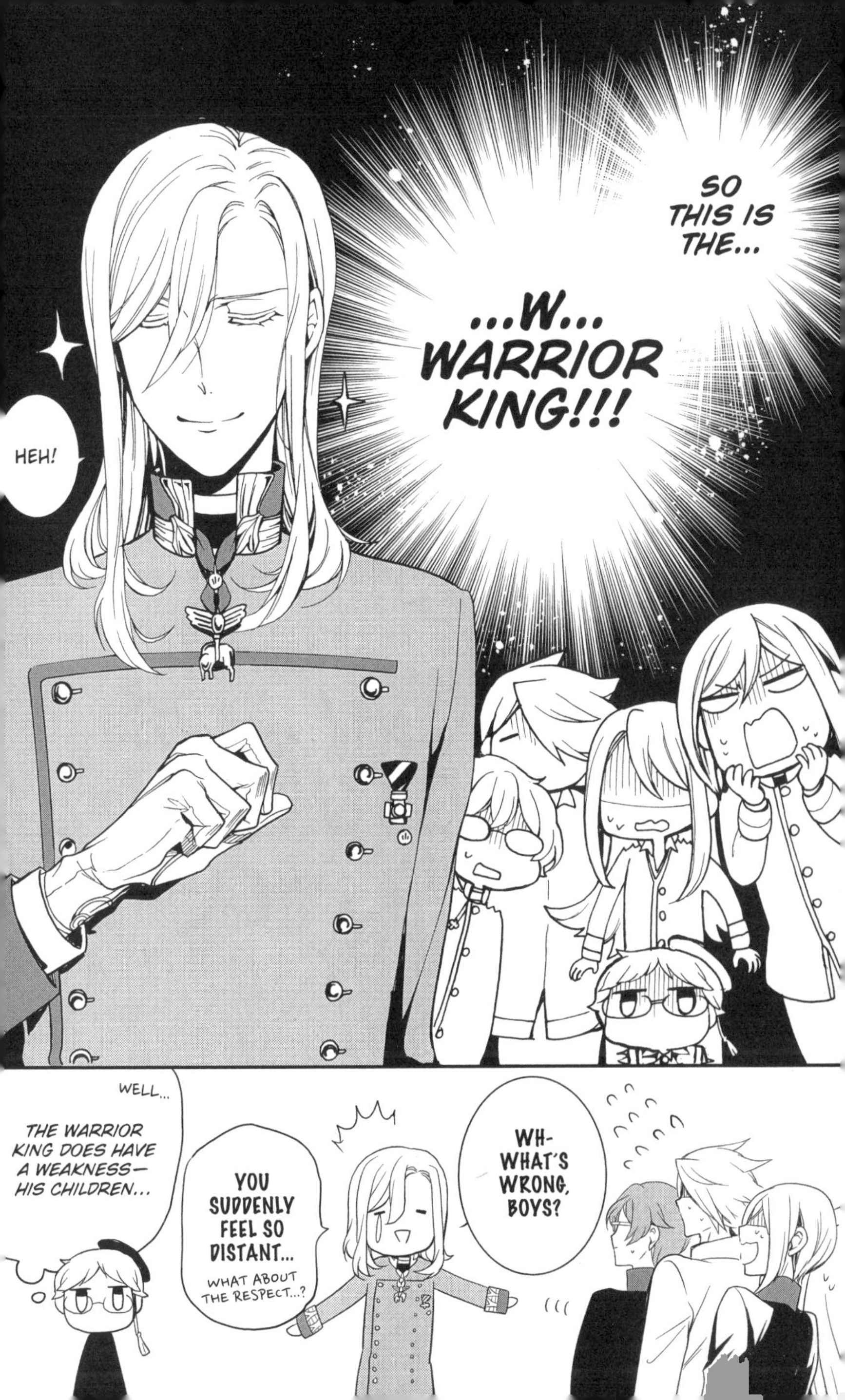
SO THIS IS THE...
...W... WARRIOR KING!!!
HEH!
WH- WHAT'S WRONG, BOYS?
YOU SUDDENLY FEEL SO DISTANT...
WHAT ABOUT THE RESPECT...?
WELL...
THE WARRIOR KING DOES HAVE A WEAKNESS— HIS CHILDREN...

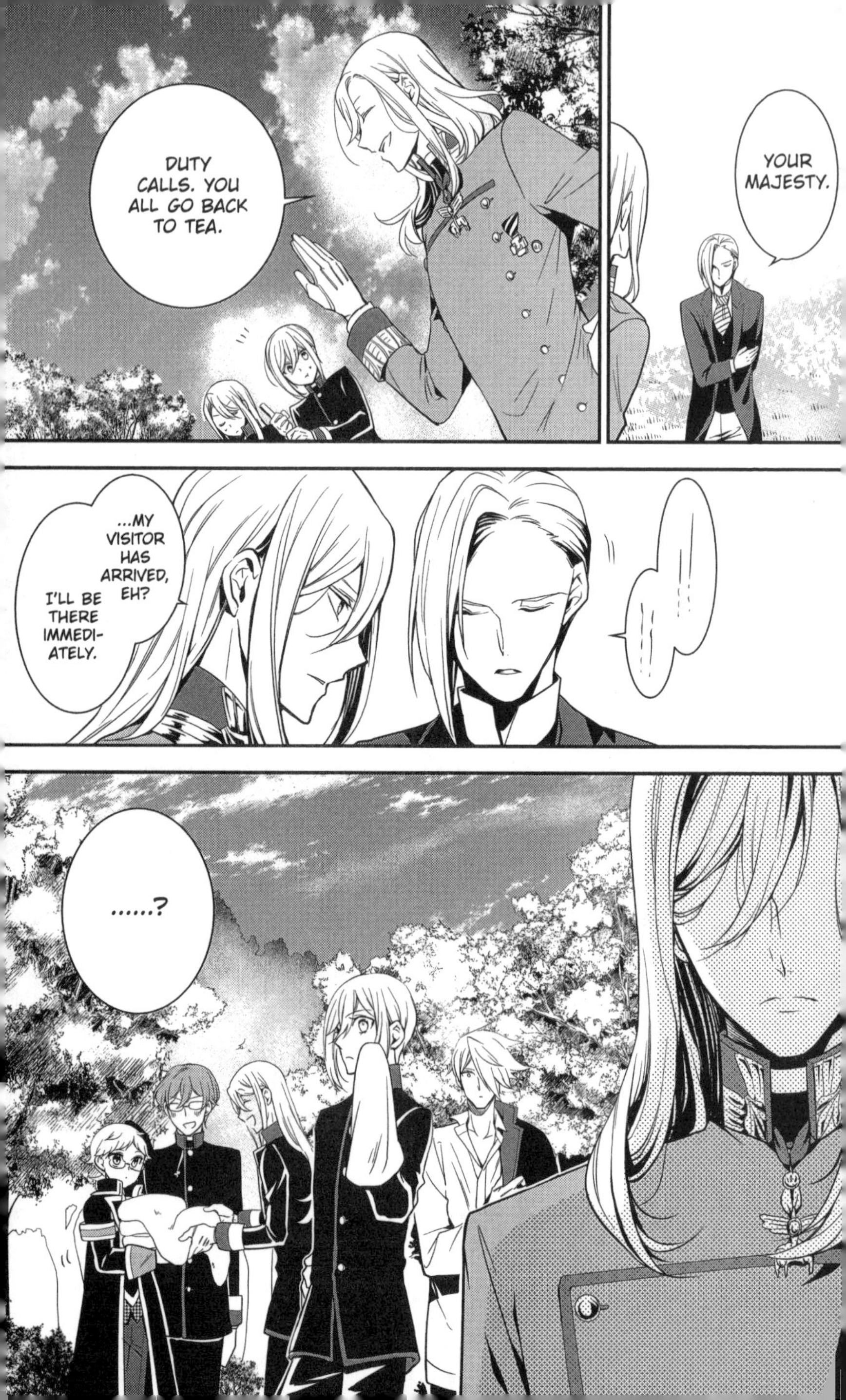
YOUR MAJESTY.
DUTY CALLS. YOU ALL GO BACK TO TEA.
...MY VISITOR HAS ARRIVED, EH?
I'LL BE THERE IMMEDIATELY.
......?

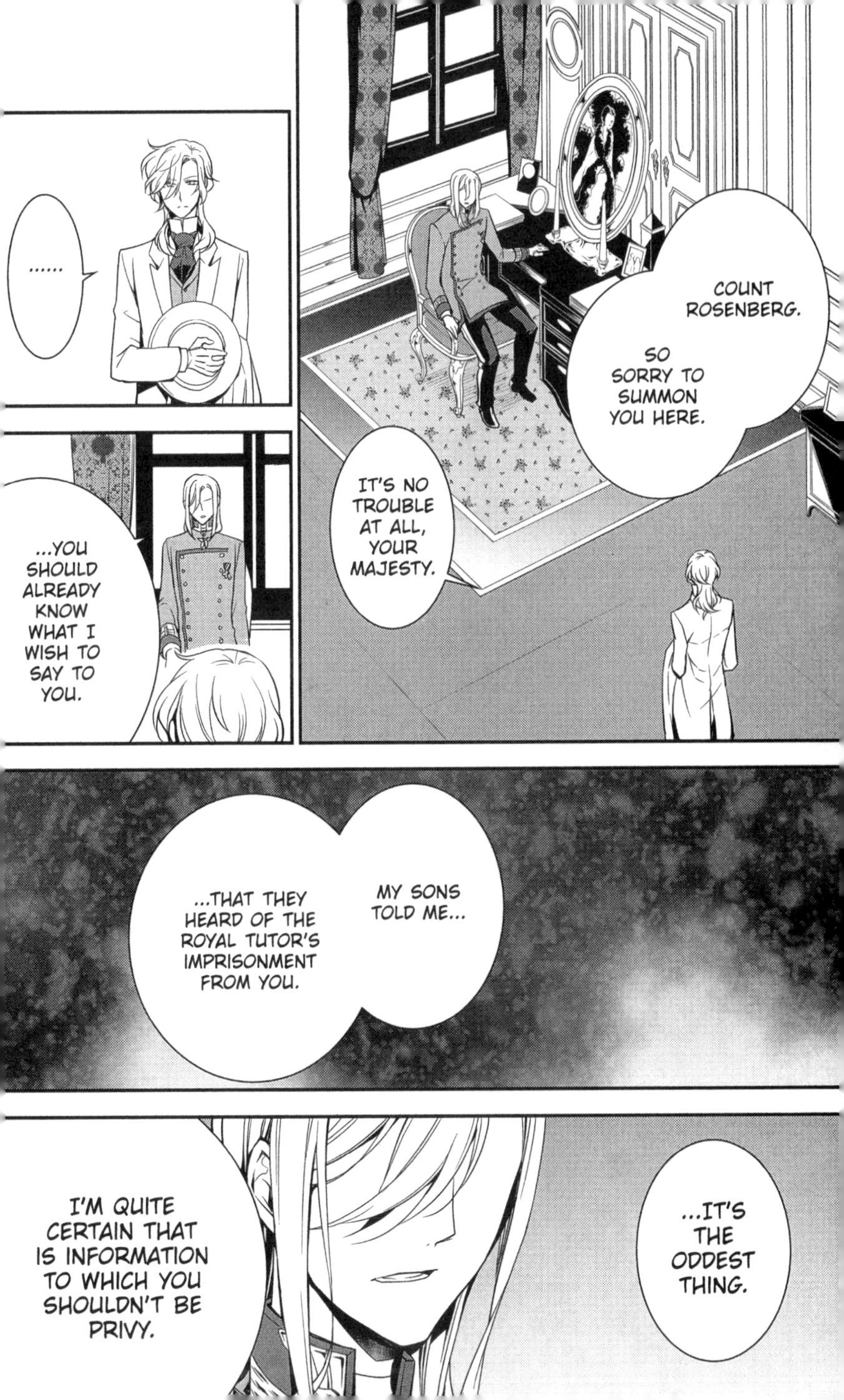
COUNT ROSENBERG.
SO SORRY TO SUMMON YOU HERE.
IT'S NO TROUBLE AT ALL, YOUR MAJESTY.
......
...YOU SHOULD ALREADY KNOW WHAT I WISH TO SAY TO YOU.
MY SONS TOLD ME...
...THAT THEY HEARD OF THE ROYAL TUTOR'S IMPRISONMENT FROM YOU.
...IT'S THE ODDEST THING.
I'M QUITE CERTAIN THAT IS INFORMATION TO WHICH YOU SHOULDN'T BE PRIVY.

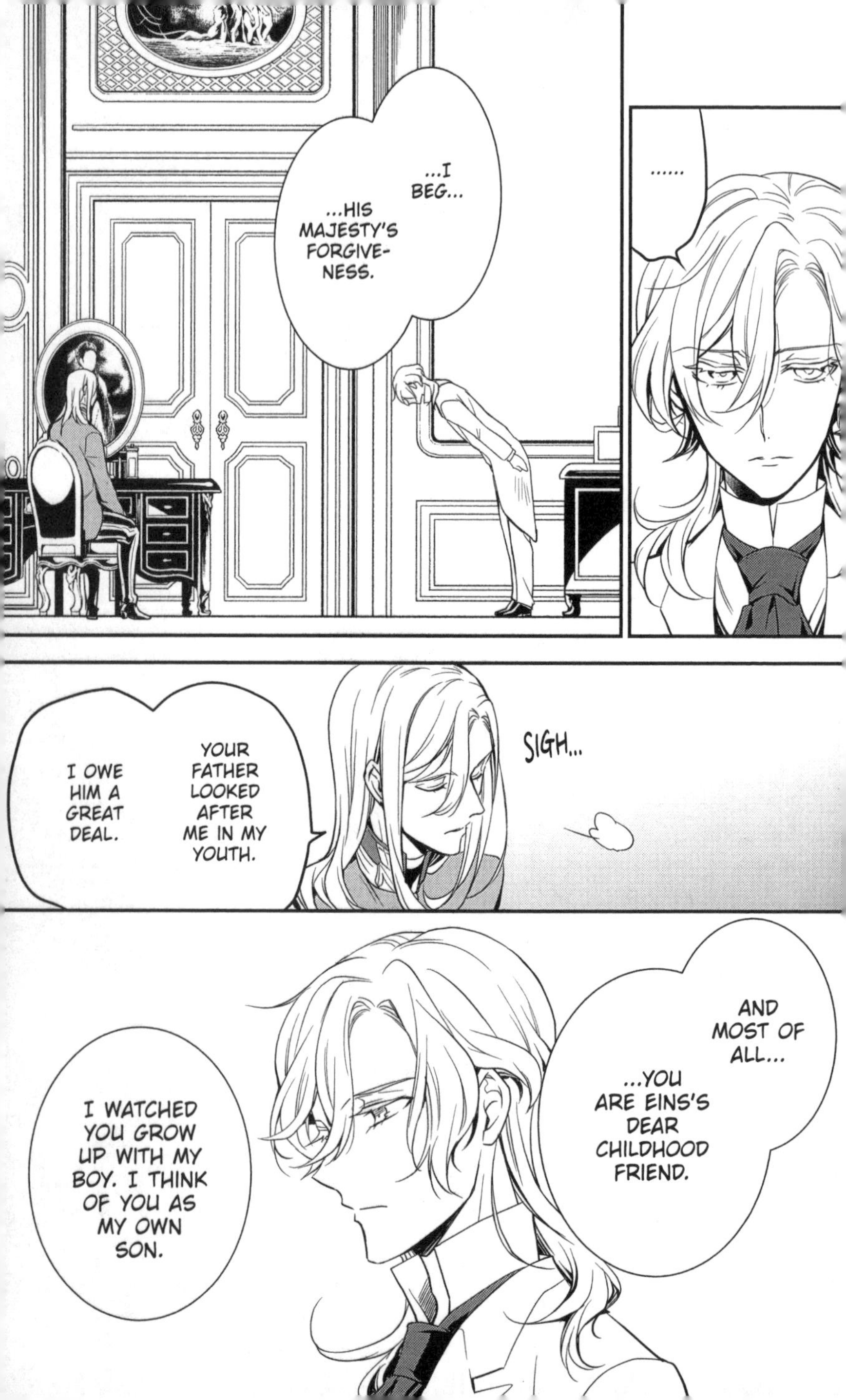
......
...I BEG...
...HIS MAJESTY'S FORGIVE-NESS.
SIGH...
YOUR FATHER LOOKED AFTER ME IN MY YOUTH.
I OWE HIM A GREAT DEAL.
AND MOST OF ALL...
...YOU ARE EINS'S DEAR CHILDHOOD FRIEND.
I WATCHED YOU GROW UP WITH MY BOY. I THINK OF YOU AS MY OWN SON.

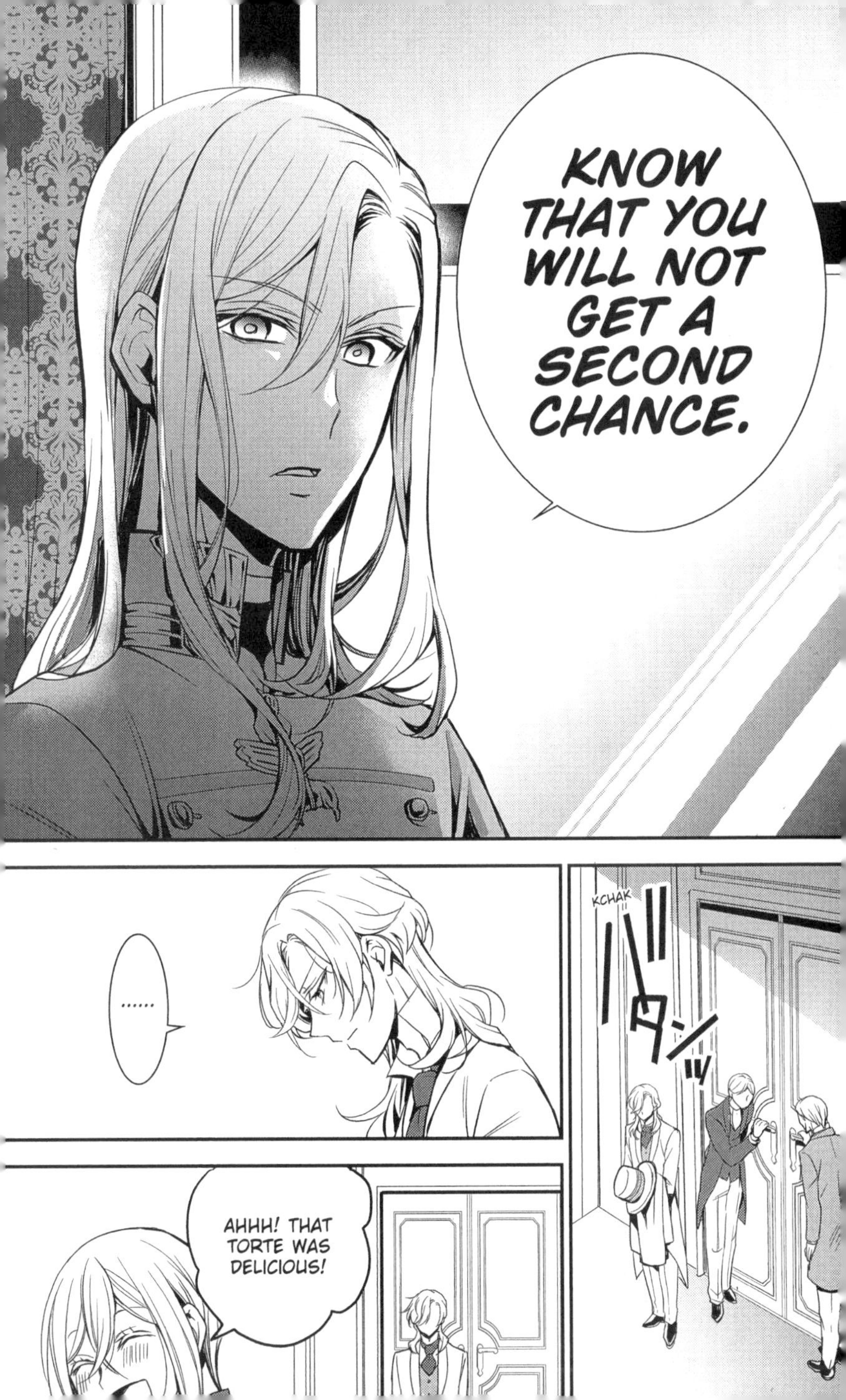
KNOW THAT YOU WILL NOT GET A SECOND CHANCE.
KCHAK
......
AHHH! THAT TORTE WAS DELICIOUS!

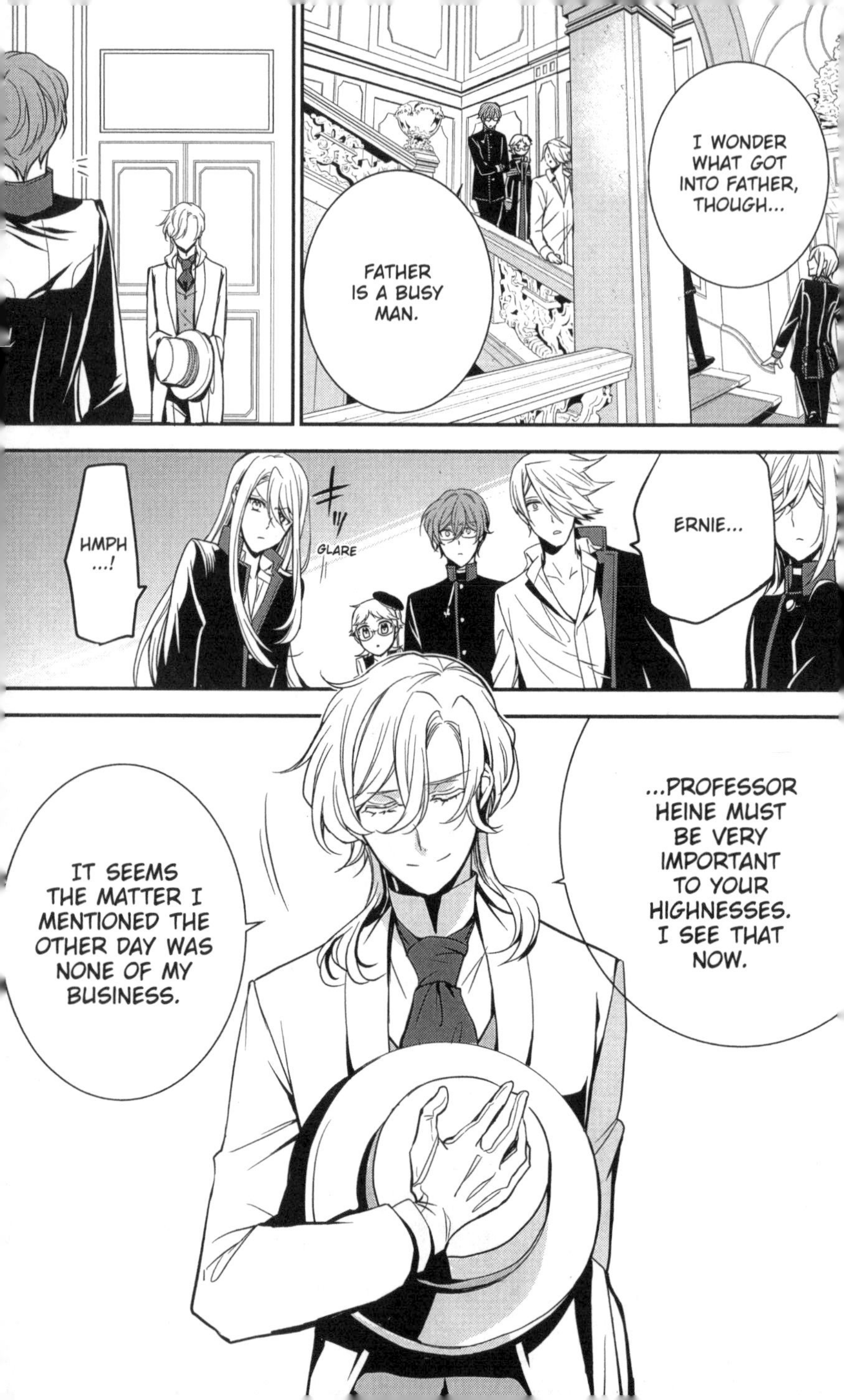
I WONDER WHAT GOT INTO FATHER, THOUGH...
FATHER IS A BUSY MAN.
ERNIE...
GLARE
HMPH ...!
...PROFESSOR HEINE MUST BE VERY IMPORTANT TO YOUR HIGHNESSES. I SEE THAT NOW.
IT SEEMS THE MATTER I MENTIONED THE OTHER DAY WAS NONE OF MY BUSINESS.

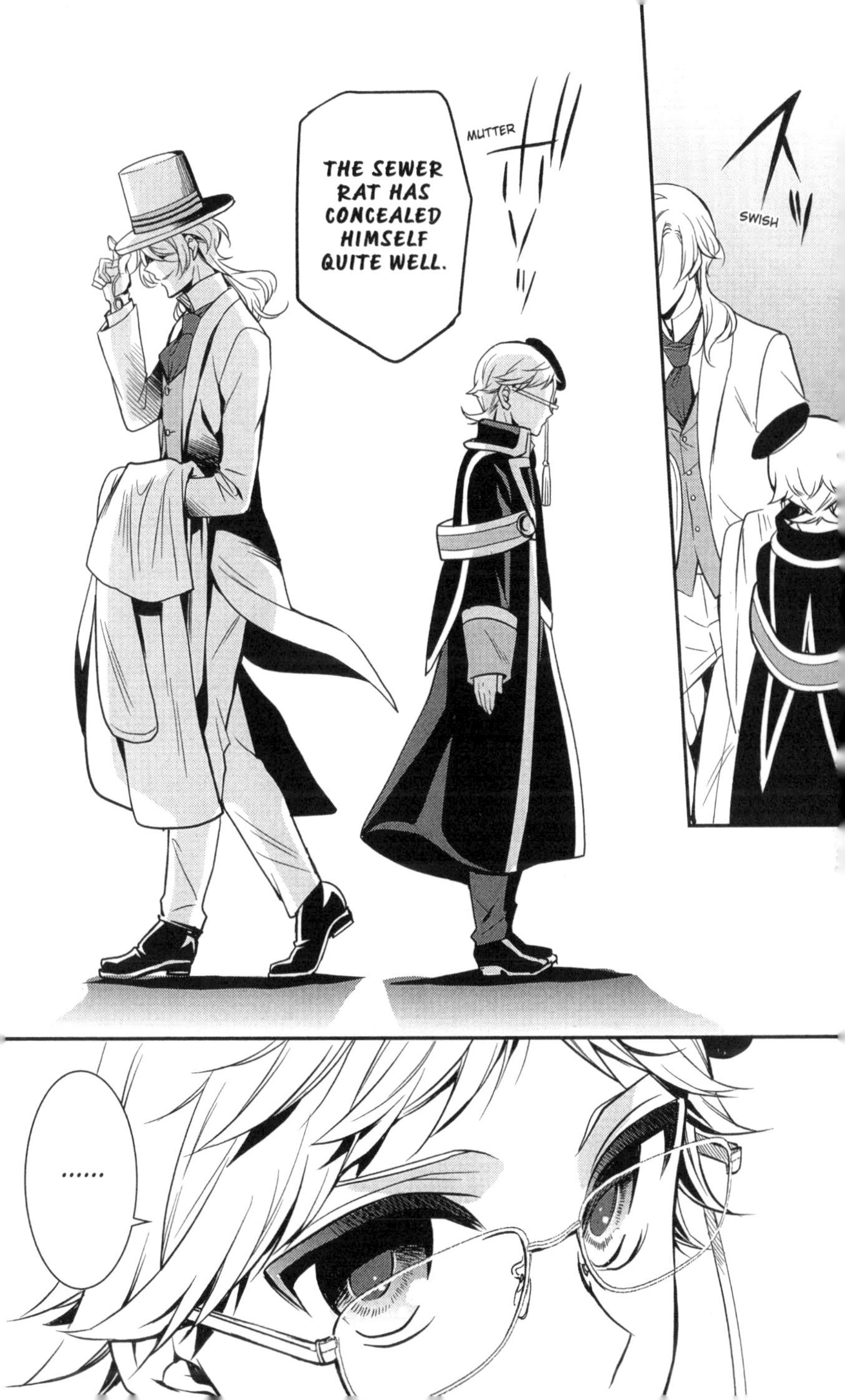
SWISH
MUTTER
THE SEWER RAT HAS CONCEALED HIMSELF QUITE WELL.
......

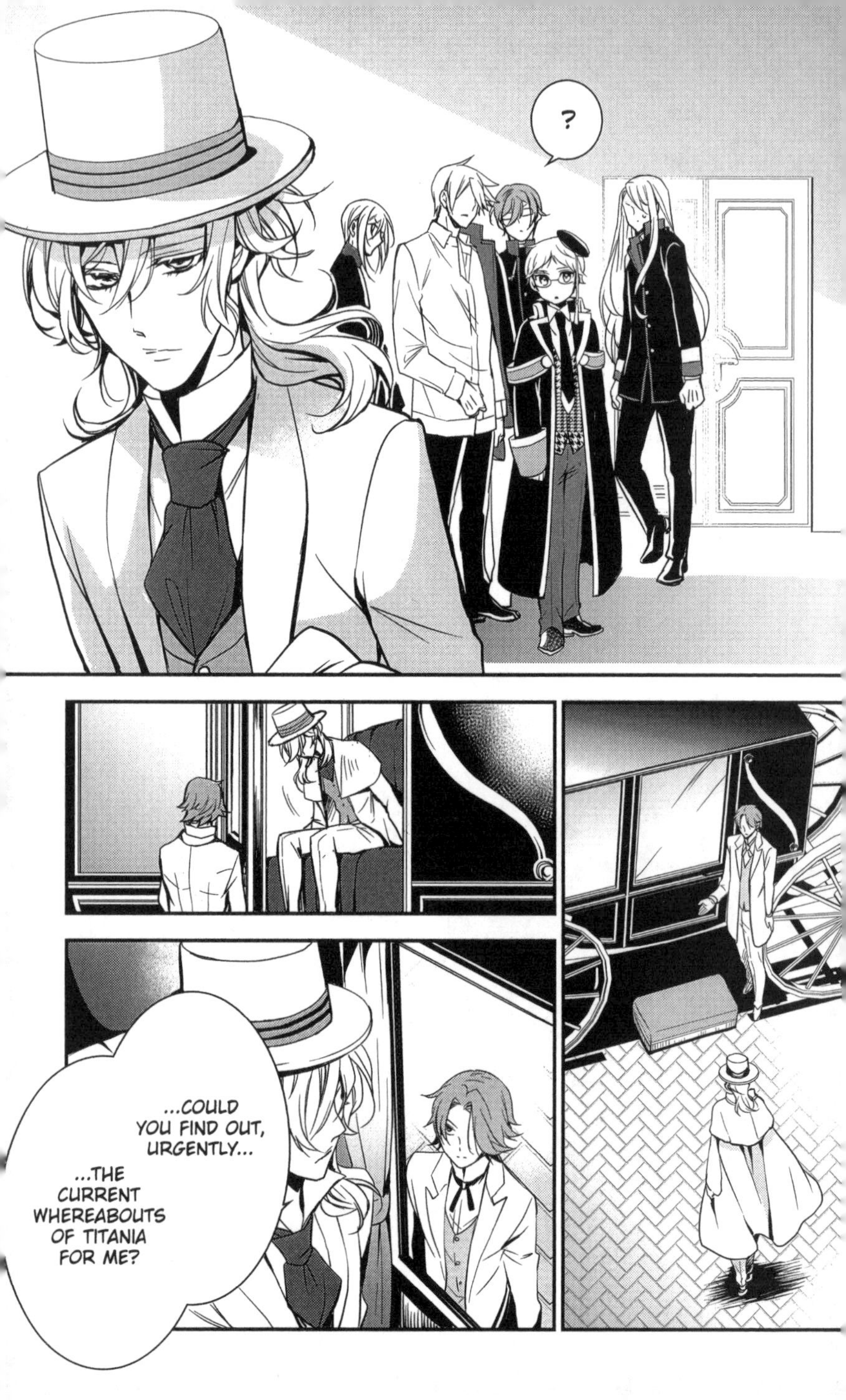
?
...COULD YOU FIND OUT, URGENTLY...
...THE CURRENT WHEREABOUTS OF TITANIA FOR ME?

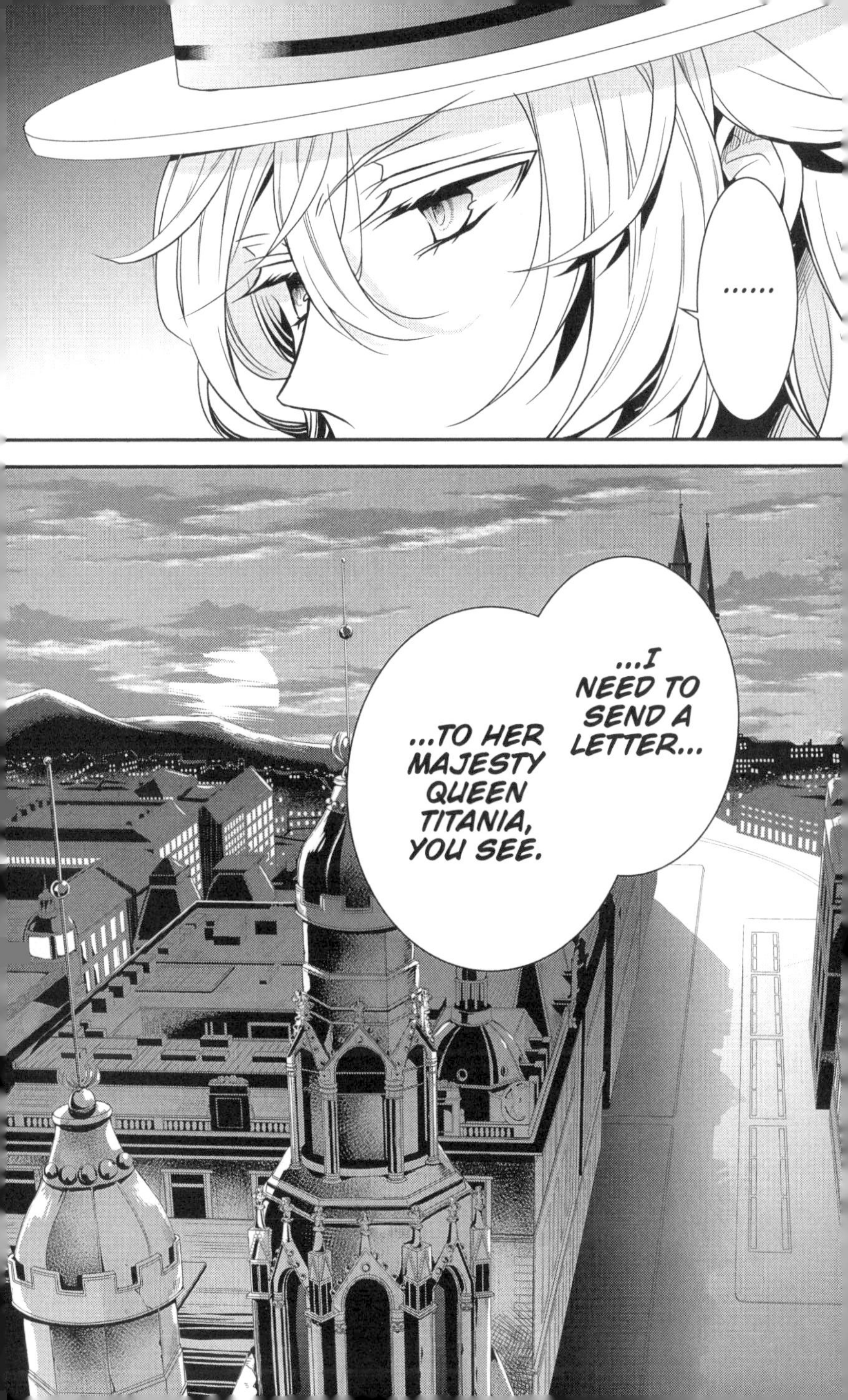
......
...I NEED TO SEND A LETTER...
...TO HER MAJESTY QUEEN TITANIA, YOU SEE.

Chapter 89
Qualification of a Mother

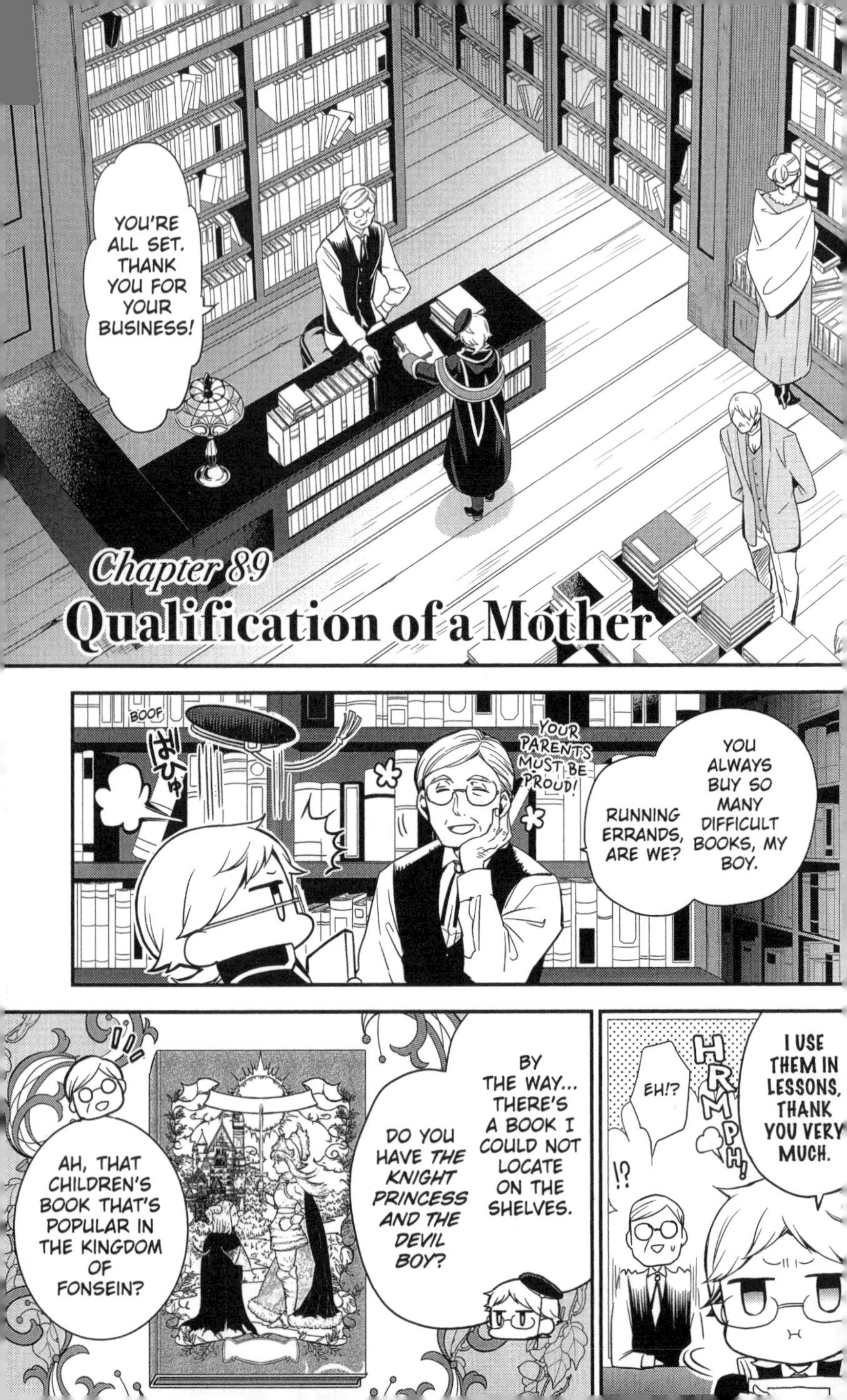
YOU'RE ALL SET. THANK YOU FOR YOUR BUSINESS!
YOU ALWAYS BUY SO MANY DIFFICULT BOOKS, MY BOY.
RUNNING ERRANDS, ARE WE?
YOUR PARENTS MUST BE PROUD!
BOOF
おひゅ
I USE THEM IN LESSONS, THANK YOU VERY MUCH.
HRMPH!
EH!?
!?
BY THE WAY... THERE'S A BOOK I COULD NOT LOCATE ON THE SHELVES.
DO YOU HAVE *THE KNIGHT PRINCESS AND THE DEVIL BOY?*
AH, THAT CHILDREN'S BOOK THAT'S POPULAR IN THE KINGDOM OF FONSEIN?

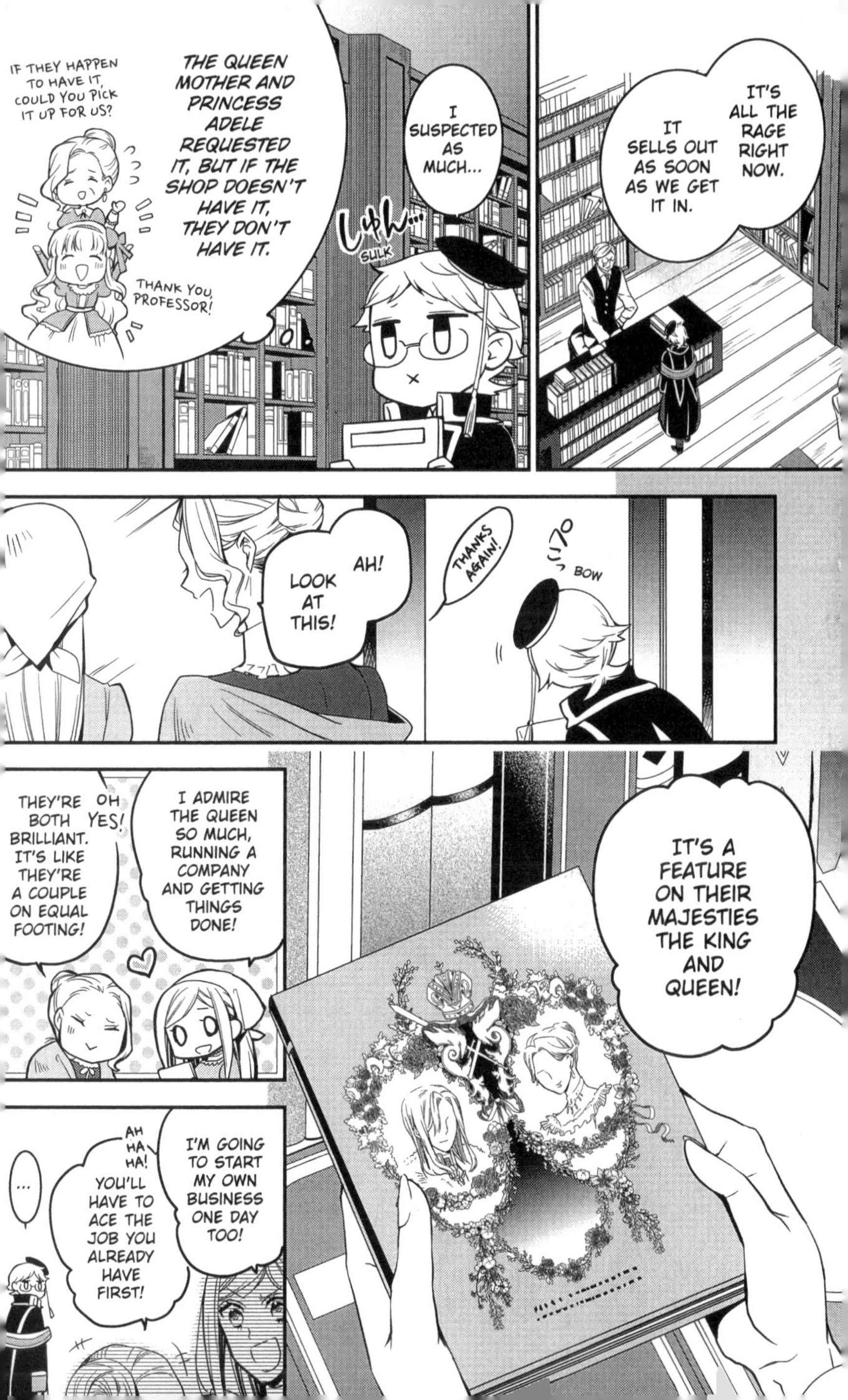
IT'S ALL THE RAGE RIGHT NOW.
IT SELLS OUT AS SOON AS WE GET IT IN.
I SUSPECTED AS MUCH...
しゅん… SULK
THE QUEEN MOTHER AND PRINCESS ADELE REQUESTED IT, BUT IF THE SHOP DOESN'T HAVE IT, THEY DON'T HAVE IT.
IF THEY HAPPEN TO HAVE IT, COULD YOU PICK IT UP FOR US?
THANK YOU, PROFESSOR!
ぺこ BOW
THANKS AGAIN!
AH!
LOOK AT THIS!
IT'S A FEATURE ON THEIR MAJESTIES THE KING AND QUEEN!
I ADMIRE THE QUEEN SO MUCH, RUNNING A COMPANY AND GETTING THINGS DONE!
OH YES!
THEY'RE BOTH BRILLIANT. IT'S LIKE THEY'RE A COUPLE ON EQUAL FOOTING!
I'M GOING TO START MY OWN BUSINESS ONE DAY TOO!
AH HA HA!
YOU'LL HAVE TO ACE THE JOB YOU ALREADY HAVE FIRST!
...

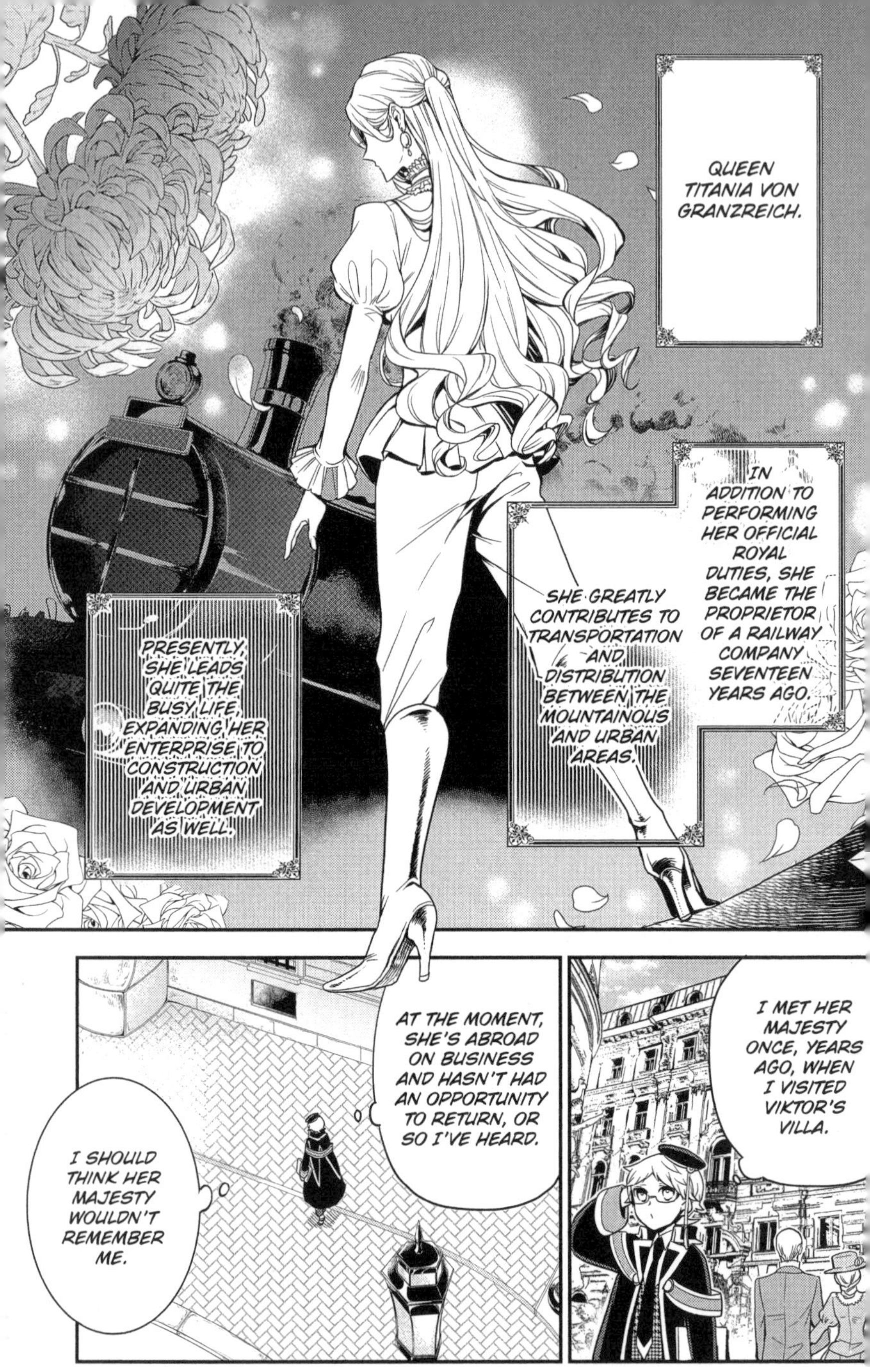
QUEEN TITANIA VON GRANZREICH.
IN ADDITION TO PERFORMING HER OFFICIAL ROYAL DUTIES, SHE BECAME THE PROPRIETOR OF A RAILWAY COMPANY SEVENTEEN YEARS AGO.
SHE GREATLY CONTRIBUTES TO TRANSPORTATION AND DISTRIBUTION BETWEEN THE MOUNTAINOUS AND URBAN AREAS.
PRESENTLY, SHE LEADS QUITE THE BUSY LIFE, EXPANDING HER ENTERPRISE TO CONSTRUCTION AND URBAN DEVELOPMENT AS WELL.
I MET HER MAJESTY ONCE, YEARS AGO, WHEN I VISITED VIKTOR'S VILLA.
AT THE MOMENT, SHE'S ABROAD ON BUSINESS AND HASN'T HAD AN OPPORTUNITY TO RETURN, OR SO I'VE HEARD.
I SHOULD THINK HER MAJESTY WOULDN'T REMEMBER ME.

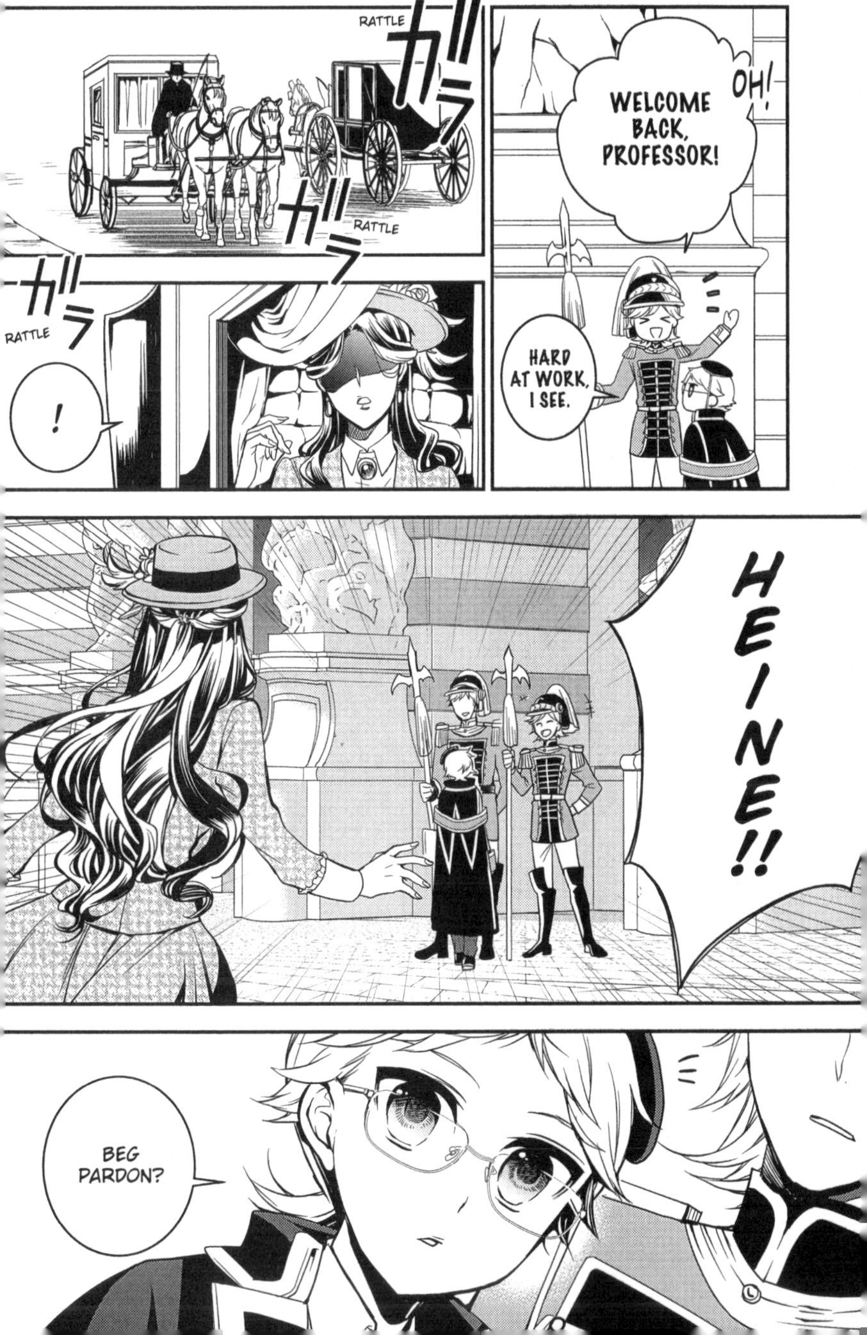
OH!
WELCOME BACK, PROFESSOR!
HARD AT WORK, I SEE.
ガラ
RATTLE
ガラ
RATTLE
ガラ
RATTLE
!
HEINE!!
BEG PARDON?

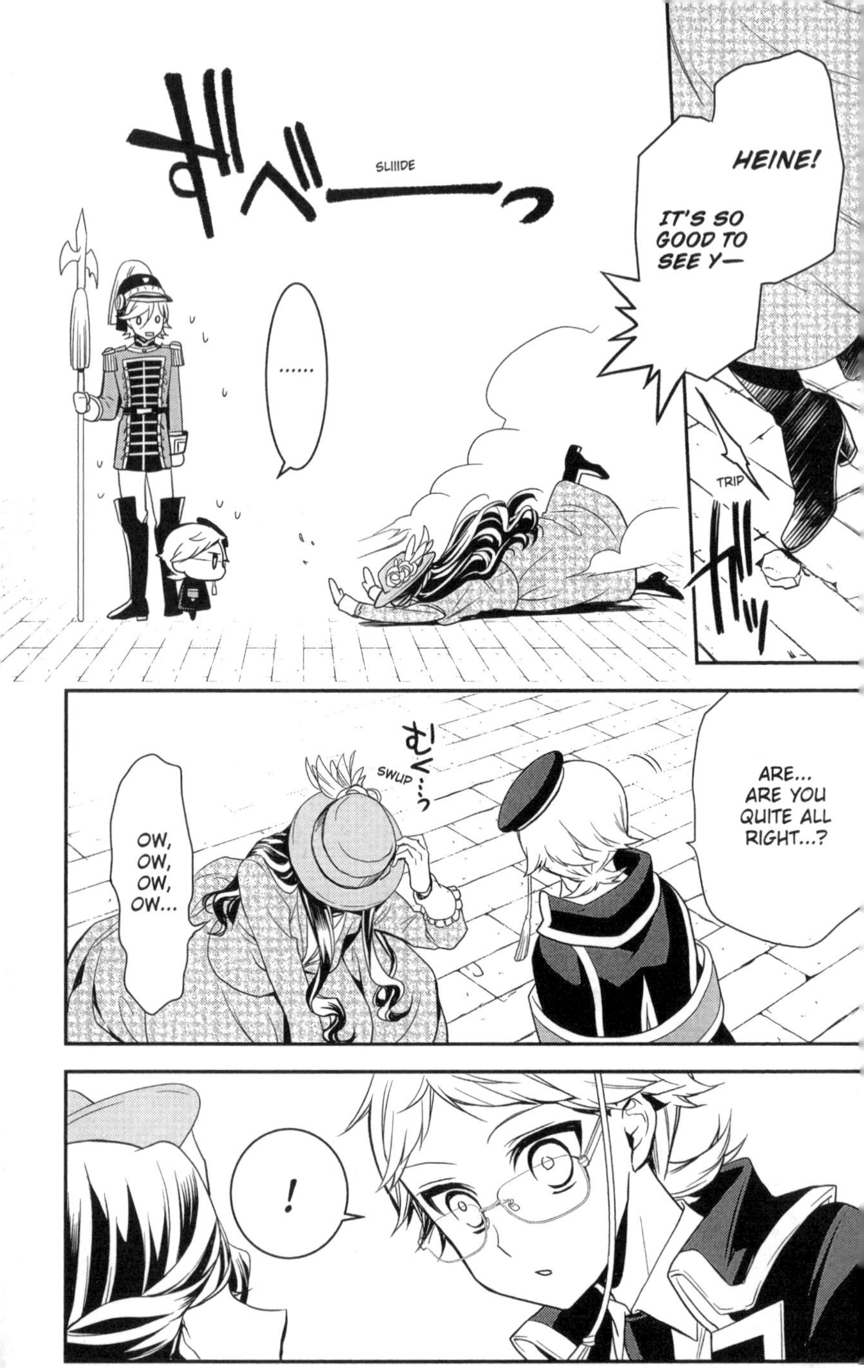
HEINE!
IT'S SO GOOD TO SEE Y—
TRIP
ずべーっ
SLIIIDE
......
ARE... ARE YOU QUITE ALL RIGHT...?
むく…っ
SWUP
OW, OW, OW, OW...
!

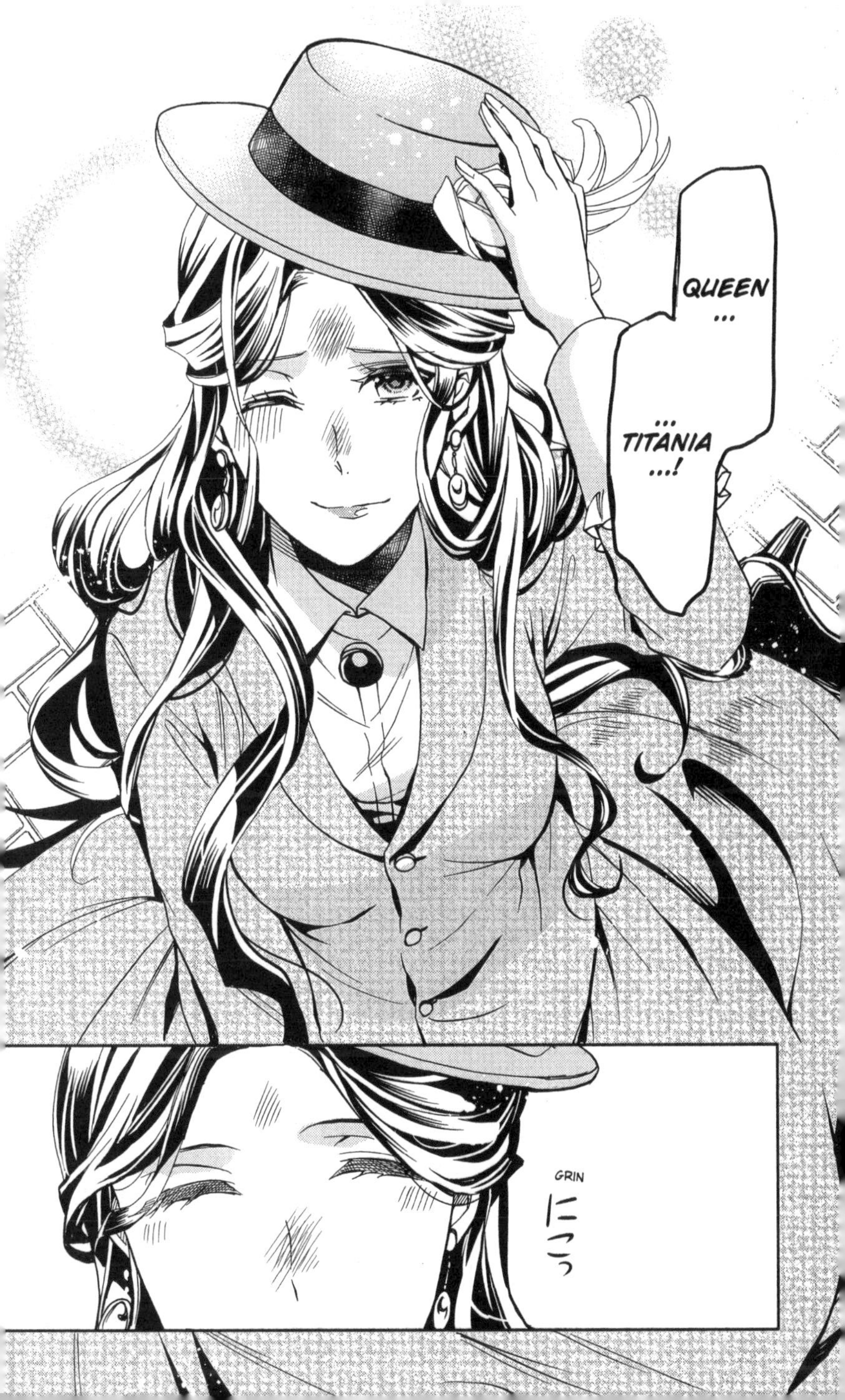
QUEEN ...
...TITANIA ...!
GRIN

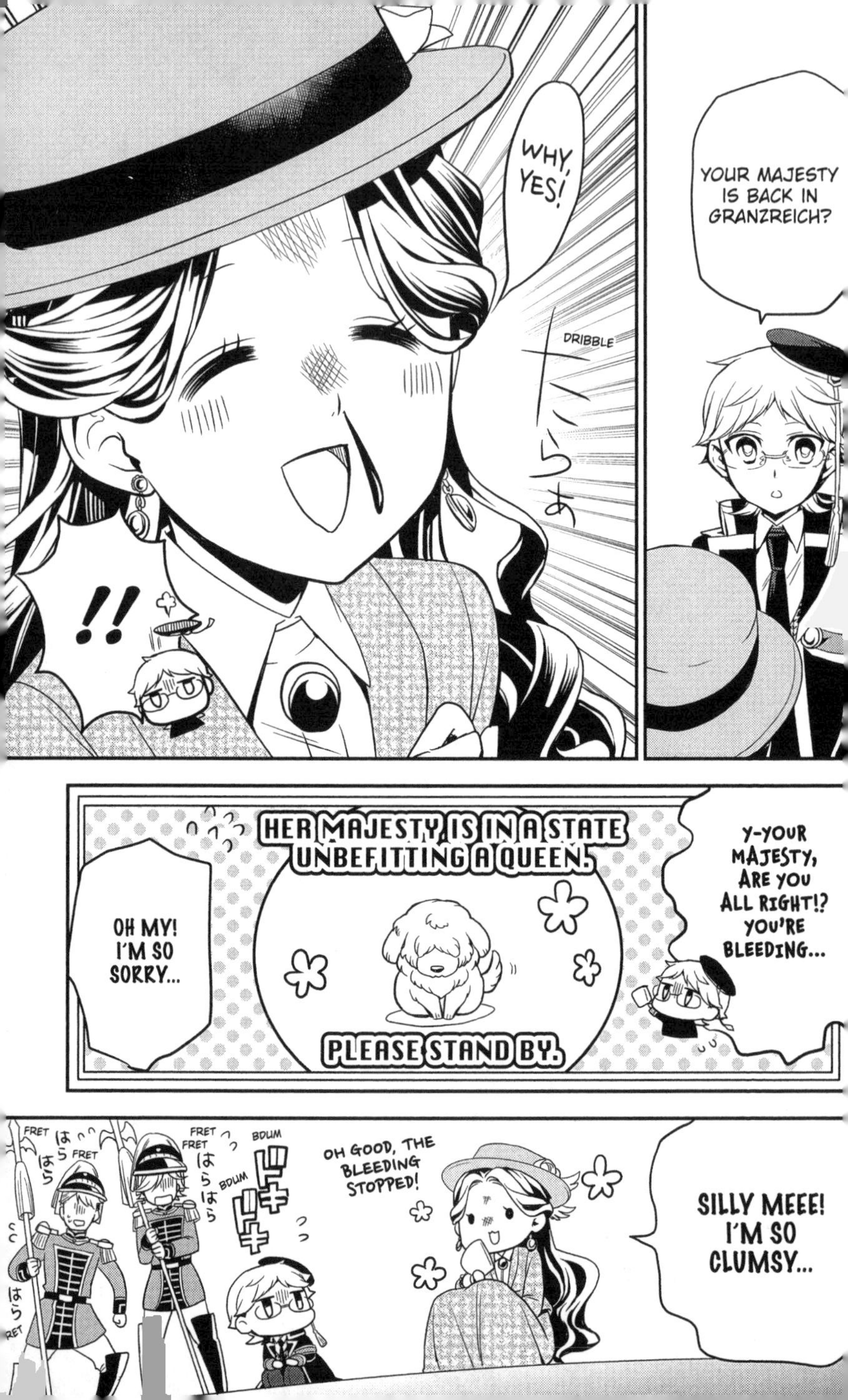
YOUR MAJESTY IS BACK IN GRANZREICH?
WHY, YES!
DRIBBLE
!!
Y-YOUR MAJESTY, ARE YOU ALL RIGHT!? YOU'RE BLEEDING...
HER MAJESTY IS IN A STATE UNBEFITTING A QUEEN.
PLEASE STAND BY.
OH MY! I'M SO SORRY...
SILLY MEEE! I'M SO CLUMSY...
OH GOOD, THE BLEEDING STOPPED!
BDUM
BDUM
FRET FRET
FRET
FRET

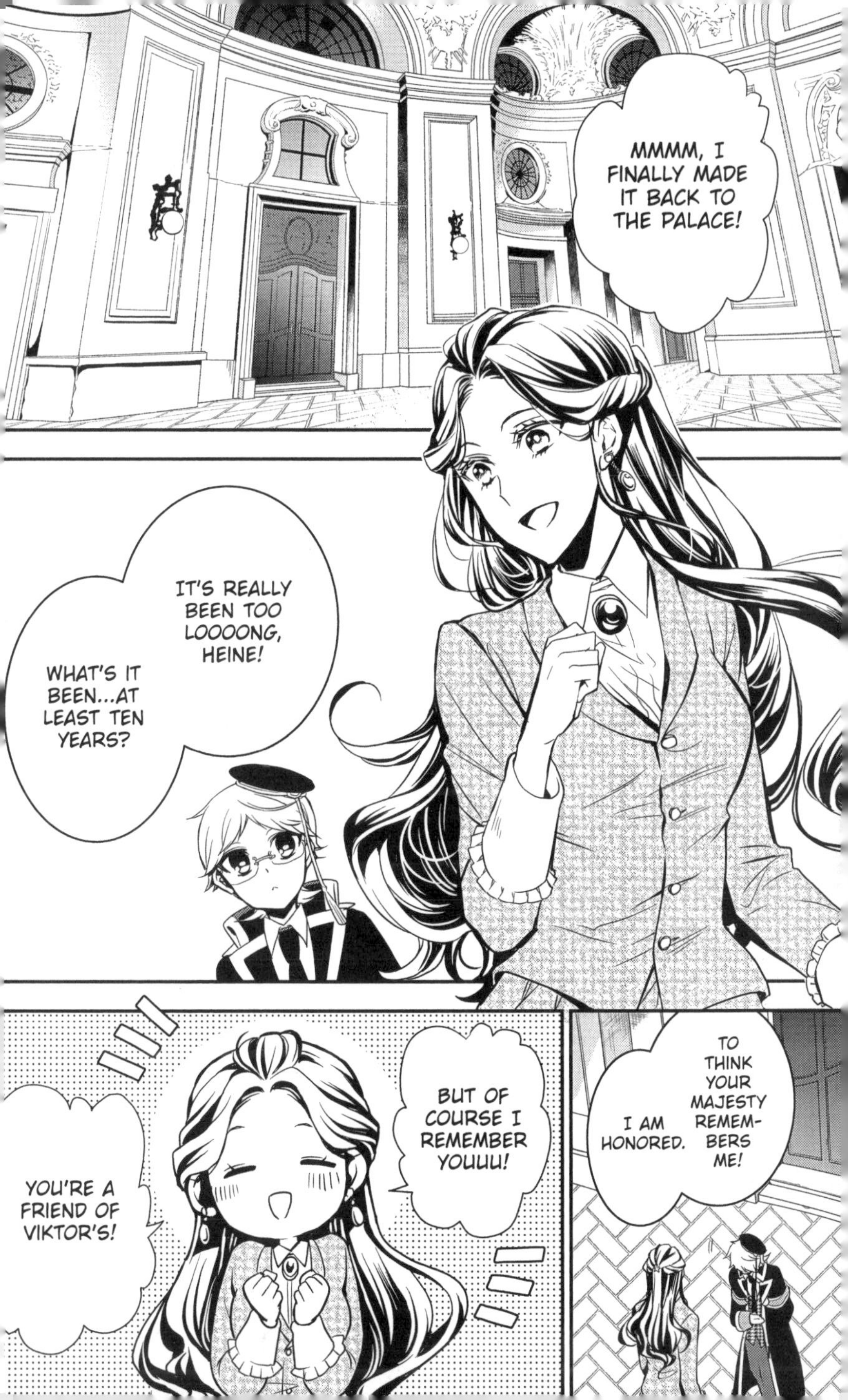
MMMM, I FINALLY MADE IT BACK TO THE PALACE!
IT'S REALLY BEEN TOO LOOOONG, HEINE!
WHAT'S IT BEEN...AT LEAST TEN YEARS?
TO THINK YOUR MAJESTY REMEM-BERS ME!
I AM HONORED.
BUT OF COURSE I REMEMBER YOUUU!
YOU'RE A FRIEND OF VIKTOR'S!

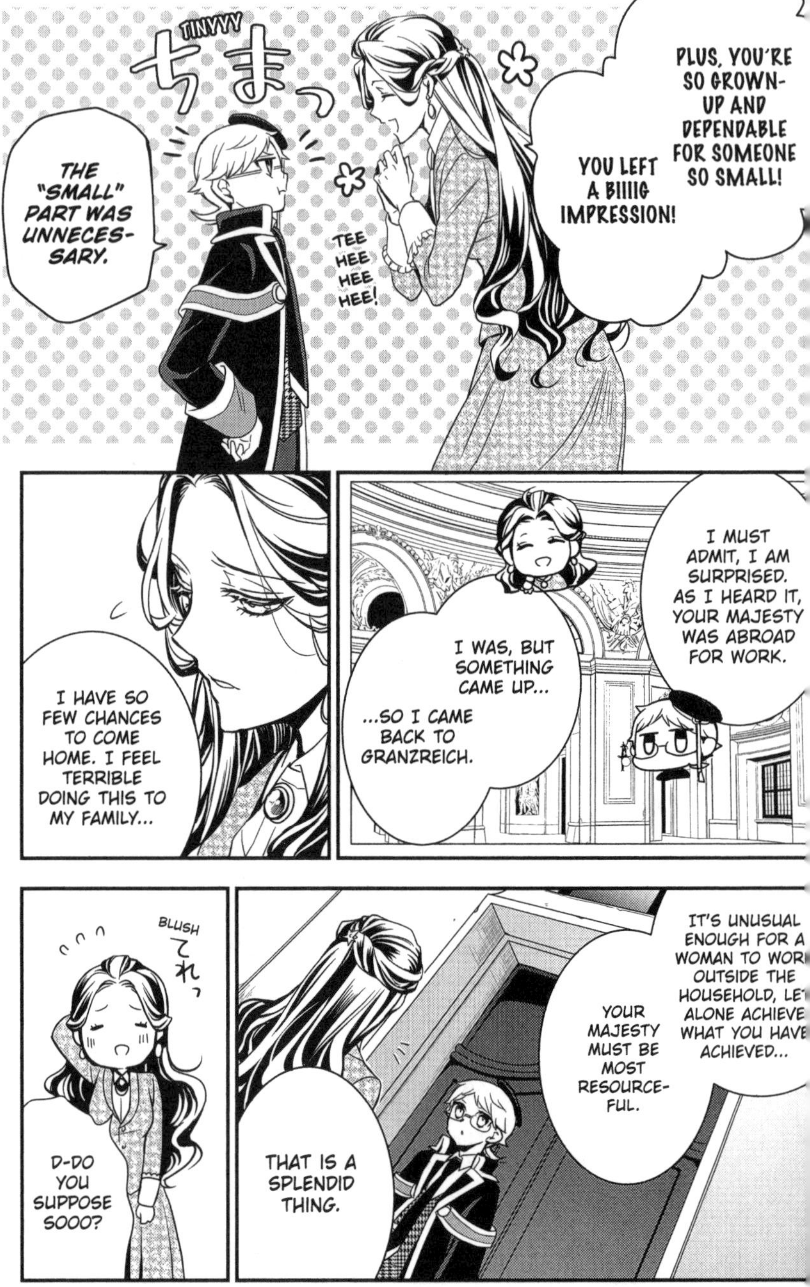
PLUS, YOU'RE SO GROWN-UP AND DEPENDABLE FOR SOMEONE SO SMALL!
YOU LEFT A BIIIIG IMPRESSION!
TINYYY
ちまっ
TEE HEE HEE HEE!
THE "SMALL" PART WAS UNNECESSARY.
I MUST ADMIT, I AM SURPRISED. AS I HEARD IT, YOUR MAJESTY WAS ABROAD FOR WORK.
I WAS, BUT SOMETHING CAME UP...
...SO I CAME BACK TO GRANZREICH.
I HAVE SO FEW CHANCES TO COME HOME. I FEEL TERRIBLE DOING THIS TO MY FAMILY...
IT'S UNUSUAL ENOUGH FOR A WOMAN TO WOR OUTSIDE THE HOUSEHOLD, LE ALONE ACHIEVE WHAT YOU HAVE ACHIEVED...
YOUR MAJESTY MUST BE MOST RESOURCEFUL.
THAT IS A SPLENDID THING.
BLUSH
てれっ
D-DO YOU SUPPOSE SOOO?

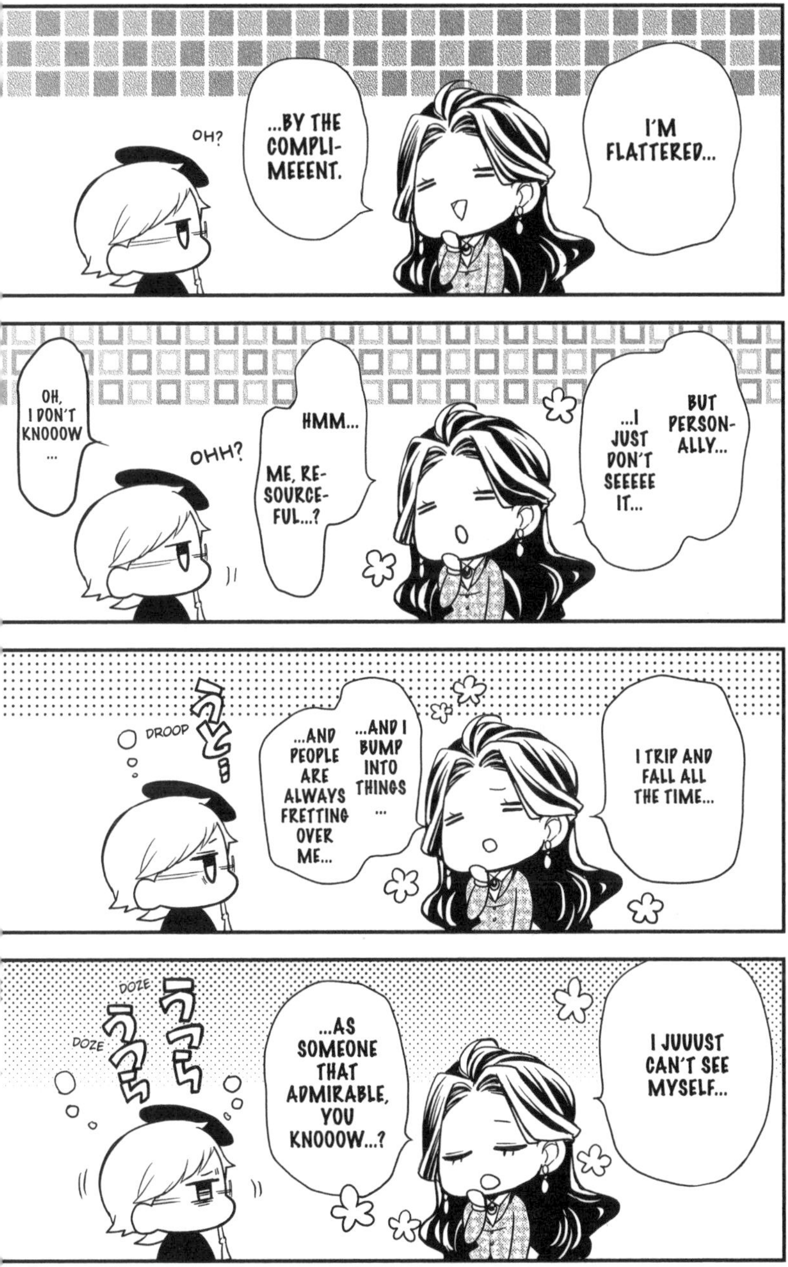
I'M FLATTERED...
...BY THE COMPLIMEEENT.
OH?
BUT PERSONALLY...
...I JUST DON'T SEEEEE IT...
HMM...
ME, RESOURCEFUL...?
OHH?
OH, I DON'T KNOOOW ...
I TRIP AND FALL ALL THE TIME...
...AND I BUMP INTO THINGS ...
...AND PEOPLE ARE ALWAYS FRETTING OVER ME...
うと
DROOP
I JUUUST CAN'T SEE MYSELF...
...AS SOMEONE THAT ADMIRABLE, YOU KNOOOW...?
うつら
DOZE
うつら
DOZE

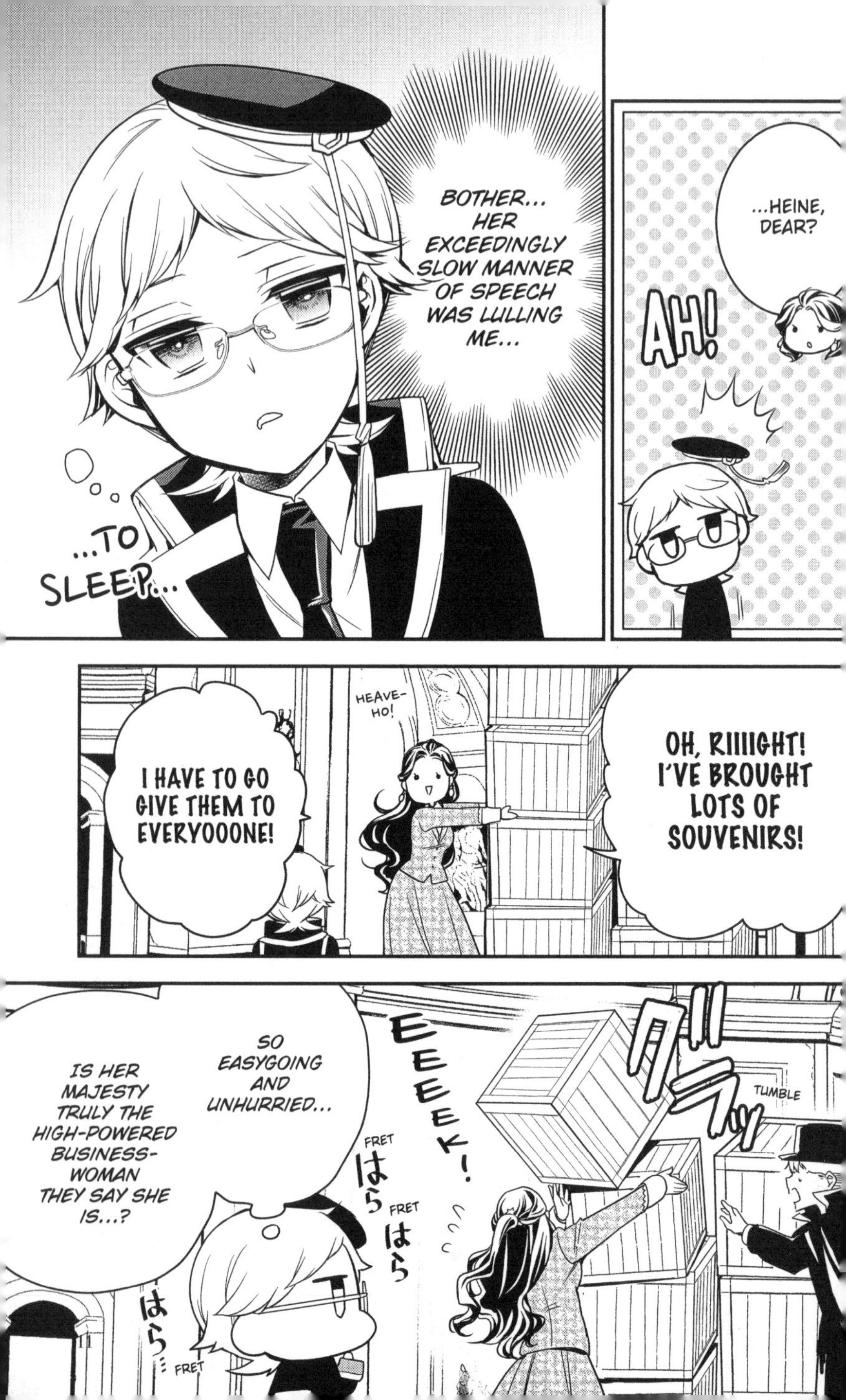

...HEINE, DEAR?
AH!
BOTHER... HER EXCEEDINGLY SLOW MANNER OF SPEECH WAS LULLING ME...
...TO SLEEP...
OH, RIIIIGHT! I'VE BROUGHT LOTS OF SOUVENIRS!
HEAVE-HO!
I HAVE TO GO GIVE THEM TO EVERYOOONE!
グラッ
TUMBLE
EEEEEK!
はら FRET
はら FRET
SO EASYGOING AND UNHURRIED...
IS HER MAJESTY TRULY THE HIGH-POWERED BUSINESS-WOMAN THEY SAY SHE IS...?
はら FRET

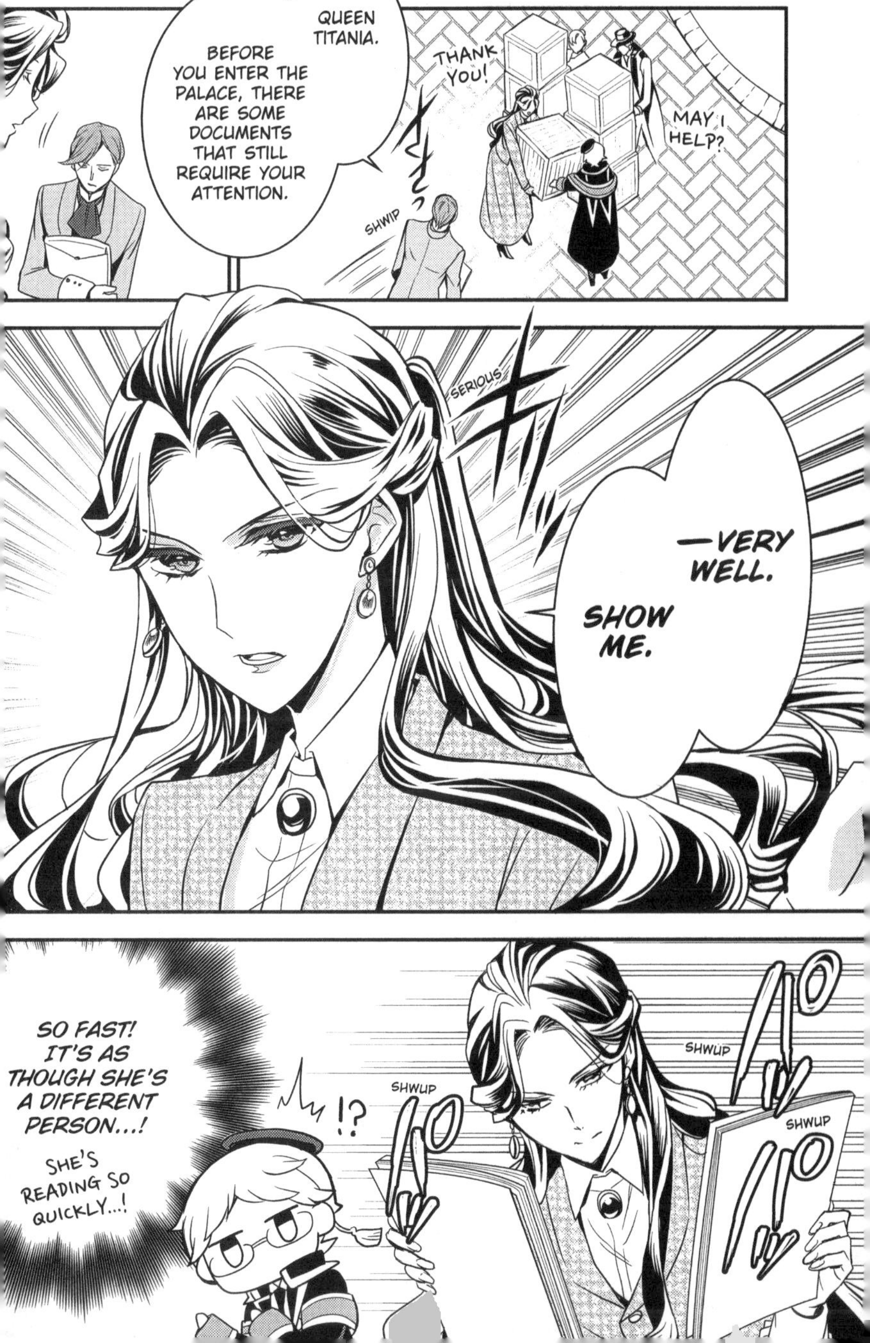

MAY I HELP?
THANK YOU!
QUEEN TITANIA.
BEFORE YOU ENTER THE PALACE, THERE ARE SOME DOCUMENTS THAT STILL REQUIRE YOUR ATTENTION.
SHWIP
—VERY WELL.
SHOW ME.
SERIOUS
SHWUP
SHWUP
SHWUP
!?
SO FAST! IT'S AS THOUGH SHE'S A DIFFERENT PERSON...!
SHE'S READING SO QUICKLY...!

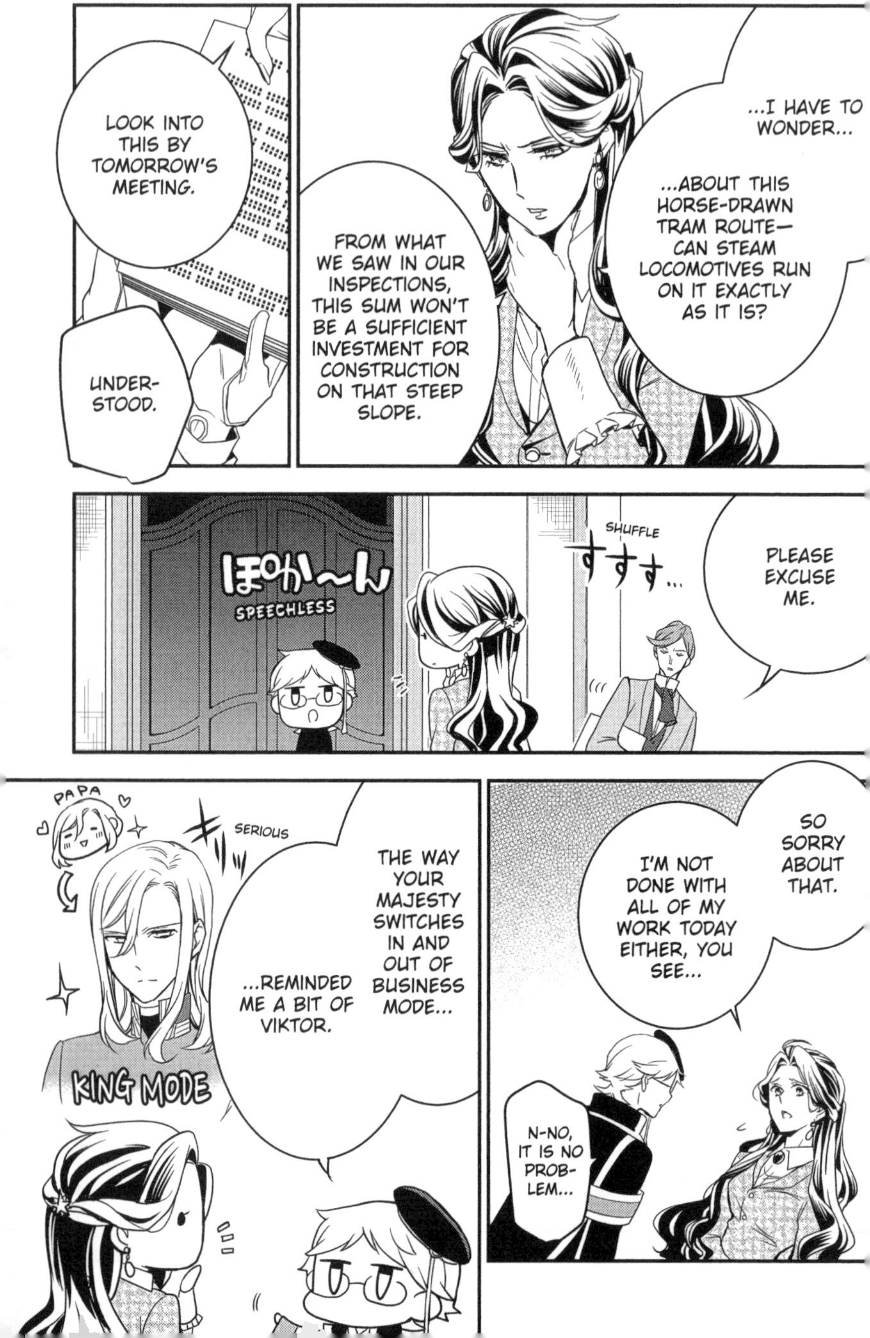
...I HAVE TO WONDER...
...ABOUT THIS HORSE-DRAWN TRAM ROUTE—CAN STEAM LOCOMOTIVES RUN ON IT EXACTLY AS IT IS?
FROM WHAT WE SAW IN OUR INSPECTIONS, THIS SUM WON'T BE A SUFFICIENT INVESTMENT FOR CONSTRUCTION ON THAT STEEP SLOPE.
LOOK INTO THIS BY TOMORROW'S MEETING.
UNDER-STOOD.
PLEASE EXCUSE ME.
すすす...
SHUFFLE
ぽか～ん
SPEECHLESS
SO SORRY ABOUT THAT.
I'M NOT DONE WITH ALL OF MY WORK TODAY EITHER, YOU SEE...
N-NO, IT IS NO PROB-LEM...
THE WAY YOUR MAJESTY SWITCHES IN AND OUT OF BUSINESS MODE...
...REMINDED ME A BIT OF VIKTOR.
PAPA
SERIOUS
KING MODE

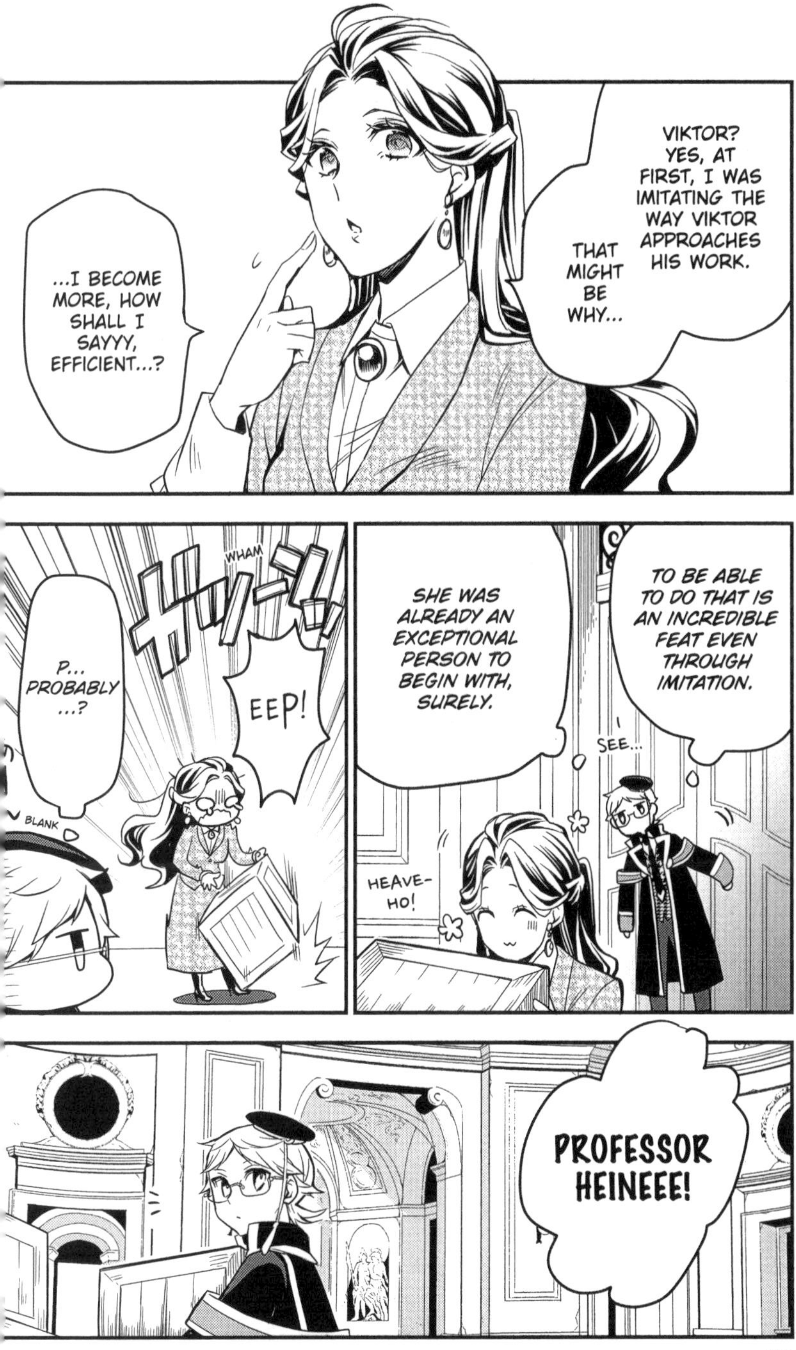

VIKTOR? YES, AT FIRST, I WAS IMITATING THE WAY VIKTOR APPROACHES HIS WORK.
THAT MIGHT BE WHY...
...I BECOME MORE, HOW SHALL I SAYYY, EFFICIENT...?
TO BE ABLE TO DO THAT IS AN INCREDIBLE FEAT EVEN THROUGH IMITATION.
SHE WAS ALREADY AN EXCEPTIONAL PERSON TO BEGIN WITH, SURELY.
I SEE...
HEAVE-HO!
WHAM
EEP!
P... PROBABLY ...?
BLANK
PROFESSOR HEINEEE!

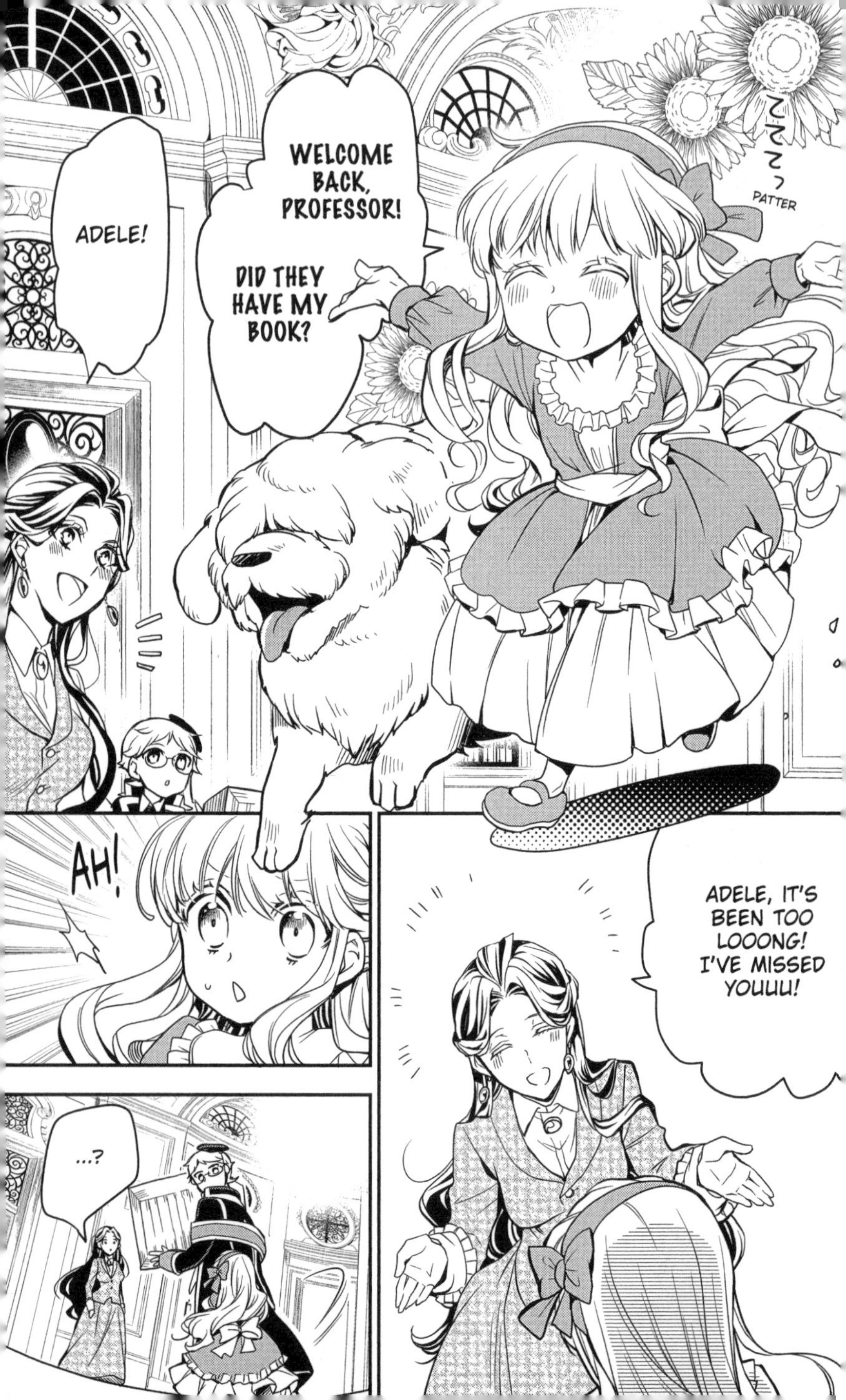
PATTER
WELCOME BACK, PROFESSOR!
DID THEY HAVE MY BOOK?
ADELE!
ADELE, IT'S BEEN TOO LOOONG! I'VE MISSED YOUUU!
AH!
...?

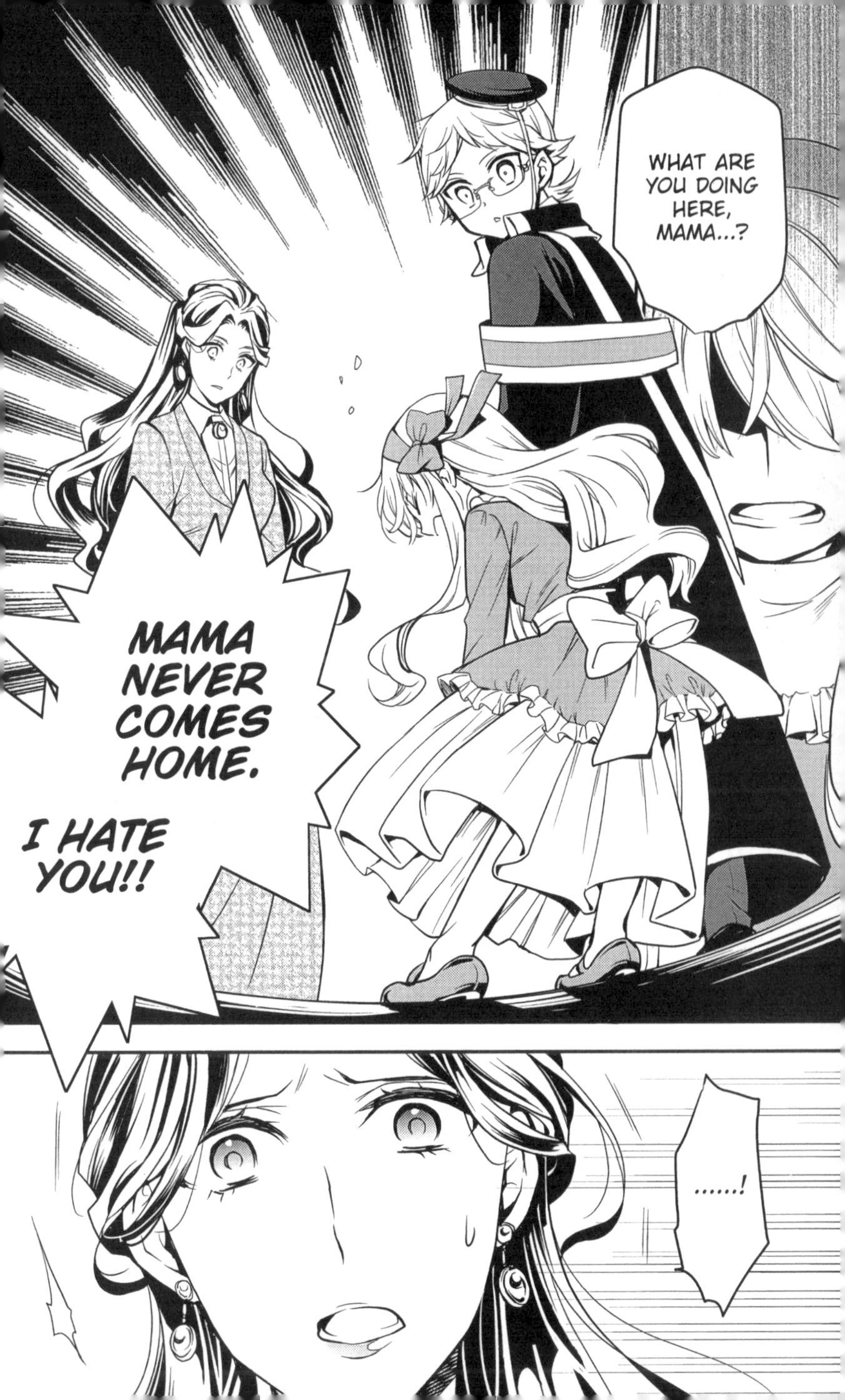
WHAT ARE YOU DOING HERE, MAMA...?
MAMA NEVER COMES HOME.
I HATE YOU!!
......!

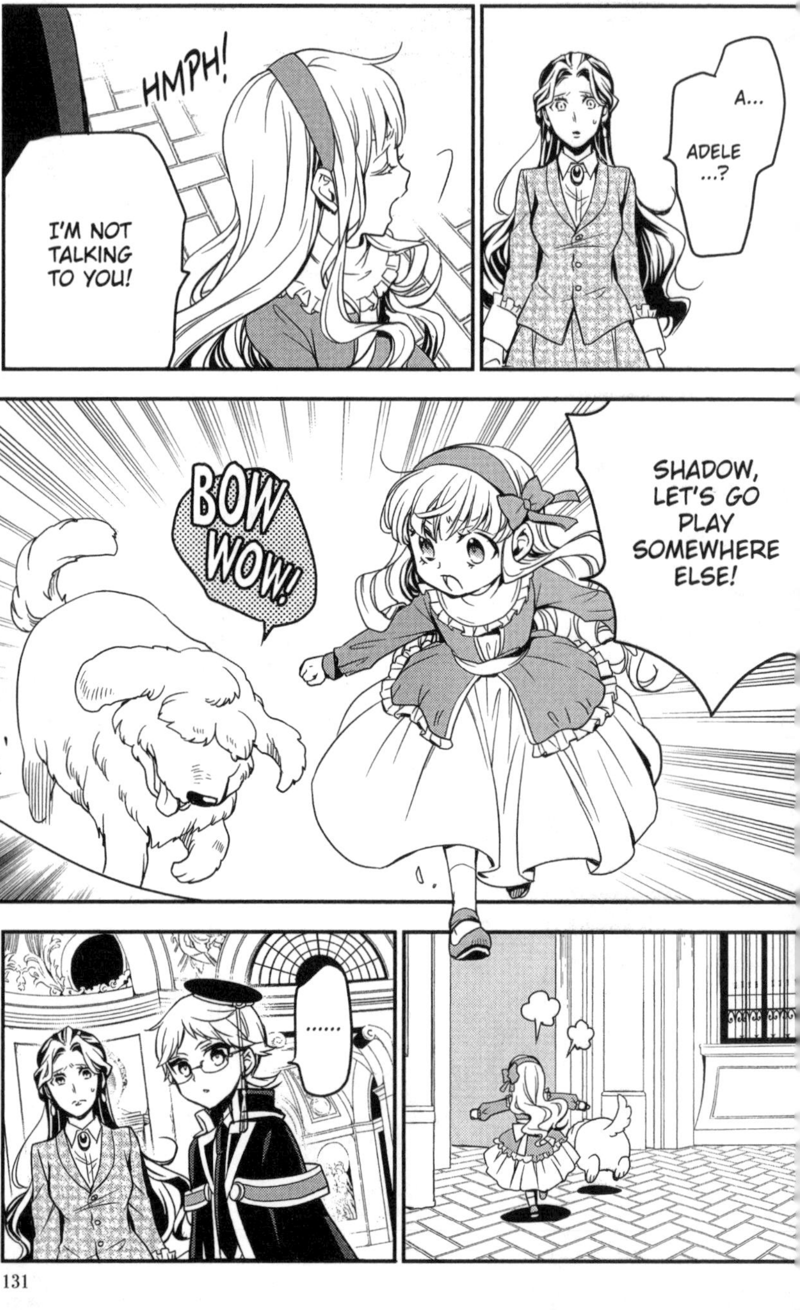
A...
ADELE ...?
HMPH!
I'M NOT TALKING TO YOU!
SHADOW, LET'S GO PLAY SOMEWHERE ELSE!
BOW WOW!
......

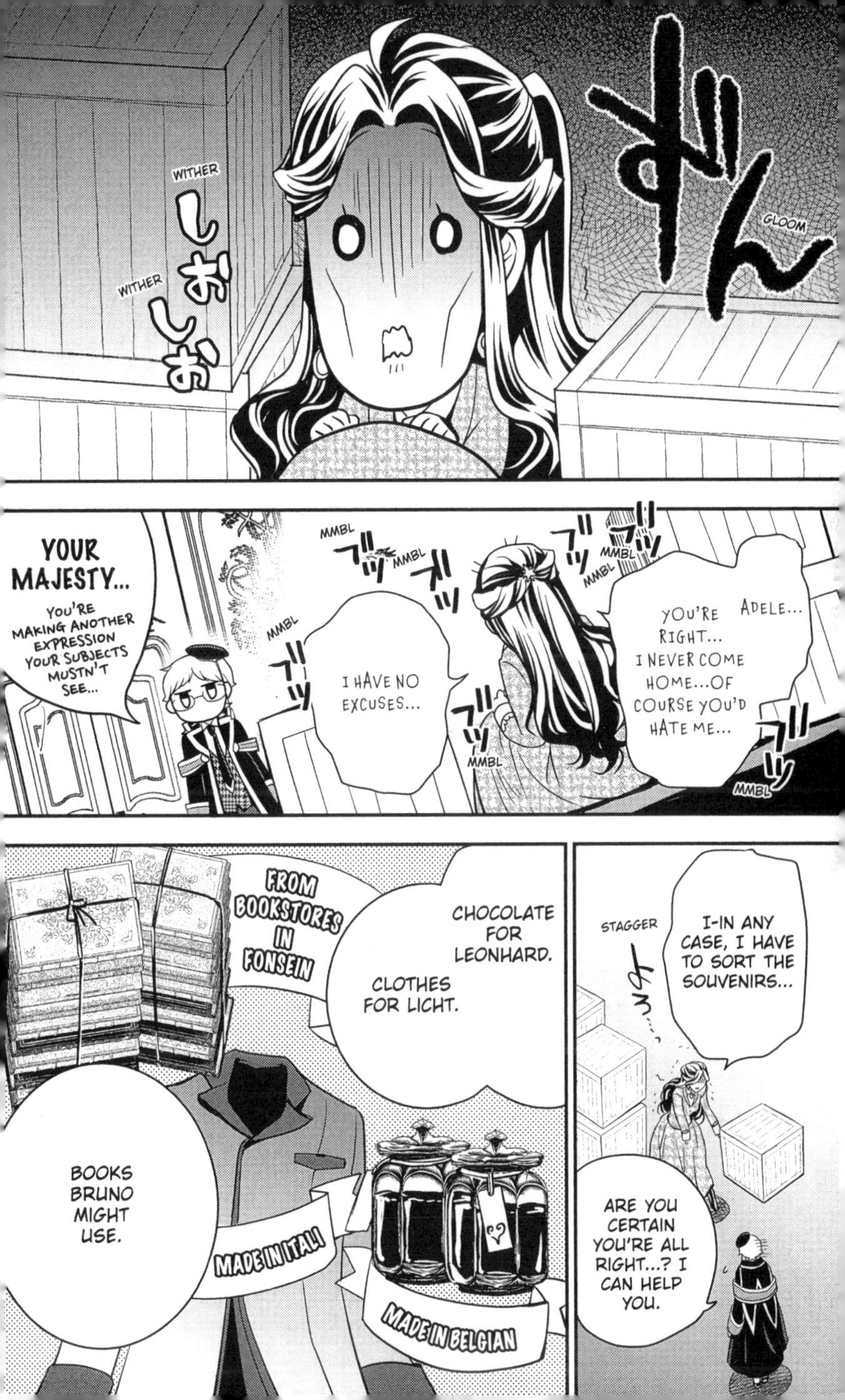
ずん
GLOOM
しおしお
WITHER
WITHER
ブツ
MMBL
ADELE... YOU'RE RIGHT... I NEVER COME HOME...OF COURSE YOU'D HATE ME...
I HAVE NO EXCUSES...
YOUR MAJESTY... YOU'RE MAKING ANOTHER EXPRESSION YOUR SUBJECTS MUSTN'T SEE...
I-IN ANY CASE, I HAVE TO SORT THE SOUVENIRS...
STAGGER
ARE YOU CERTAIN YOU'RE ALL RIGHT...? I CAN HELP YOU.
CHOCOLATE FOR LEONHARD.
CLOTHES FOR LICHT.
FROM BOOKSTORES IN FONSEIN
BOOKS BRUNO MIGHT USE.
MADE IN ITALI
MADE IN BELGIAN

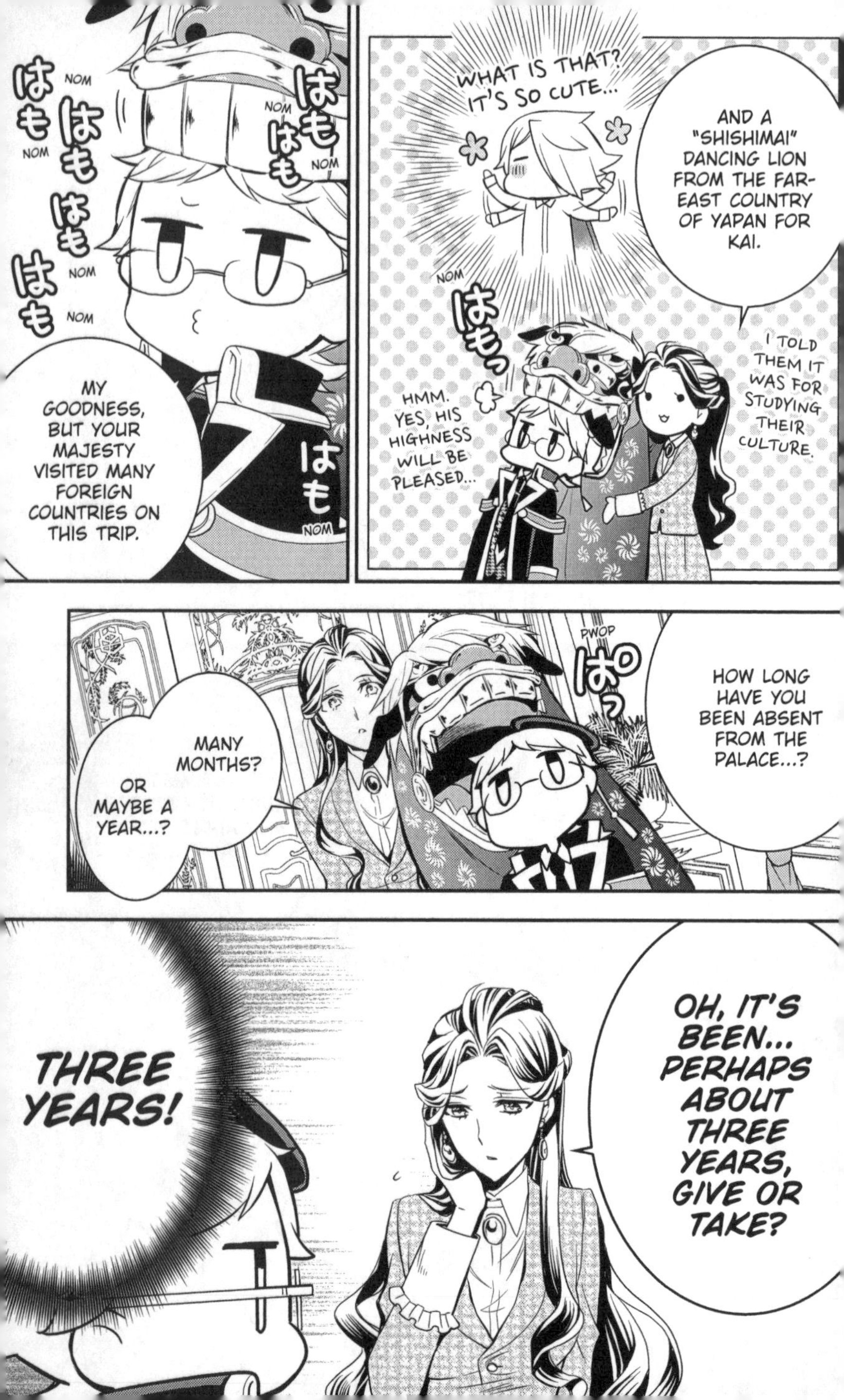
AND A "SHISHIMAI" DANCING LION FROM THE FAR-EAST COUNTRY OF YAPAN FOR KAI.
WHAT IS THAT? IT'S SO CUTE...
I TOLD THEM IT WAS FOR STUDYING THEIR CULTURE.
NOM
はもっ
HMM. YES, HIS HIGHNESS WILL BE PLEASED...
はもはも NOM NOM
はもはもはもはも NOM NOM NOM NOM
はもはもはも NOM NOM
はも NOM
MY GOODNESS, BUT YOUR MAJESTY VISITED MANY FOREIGN COUNTRIES ON THIS TRIP.
HOW LONG HAVE YOU BEEN ABSENT FROM THE PALACE...?
PWOP
ぱっ
MANY MONTHS?
OR MAYBE A YEAR...?
OH, IT'S BEEN... PERHAPS ABOUT THREE YEARS, GIVE OR TAKE?
THREE YEARS!

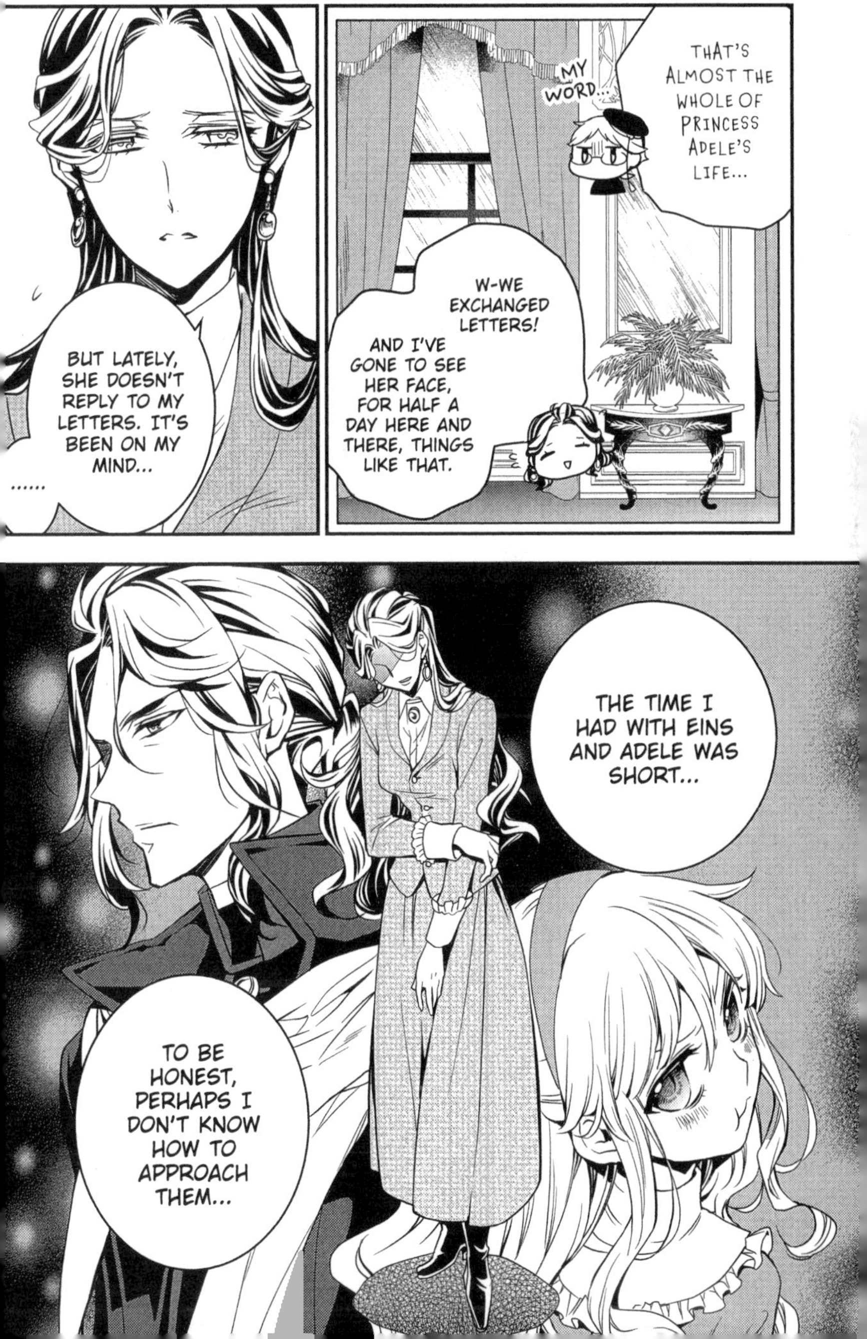
THAT'S ALMOST THE WHOLE OF PRINCESS ADELE'S LIFE...
MY WORD...
W-WE EXCHANGED LETTERS!
AND I'VE GONE TO SEE HER FACE, FOR HALF A DAY HERE AND THERE, THINGS LIKE THAT.
BUT LATELY, SHE DOESN'T REPLY TO MY LETTERS. IT'S BEEN ON MY MIND...
......
THE TIME I HAD WITH EINS AND ADELE WAS SHORT...
TO BE HONEST, PERHAPS I DON'T KNOW HOW TO APPROACH THEM...

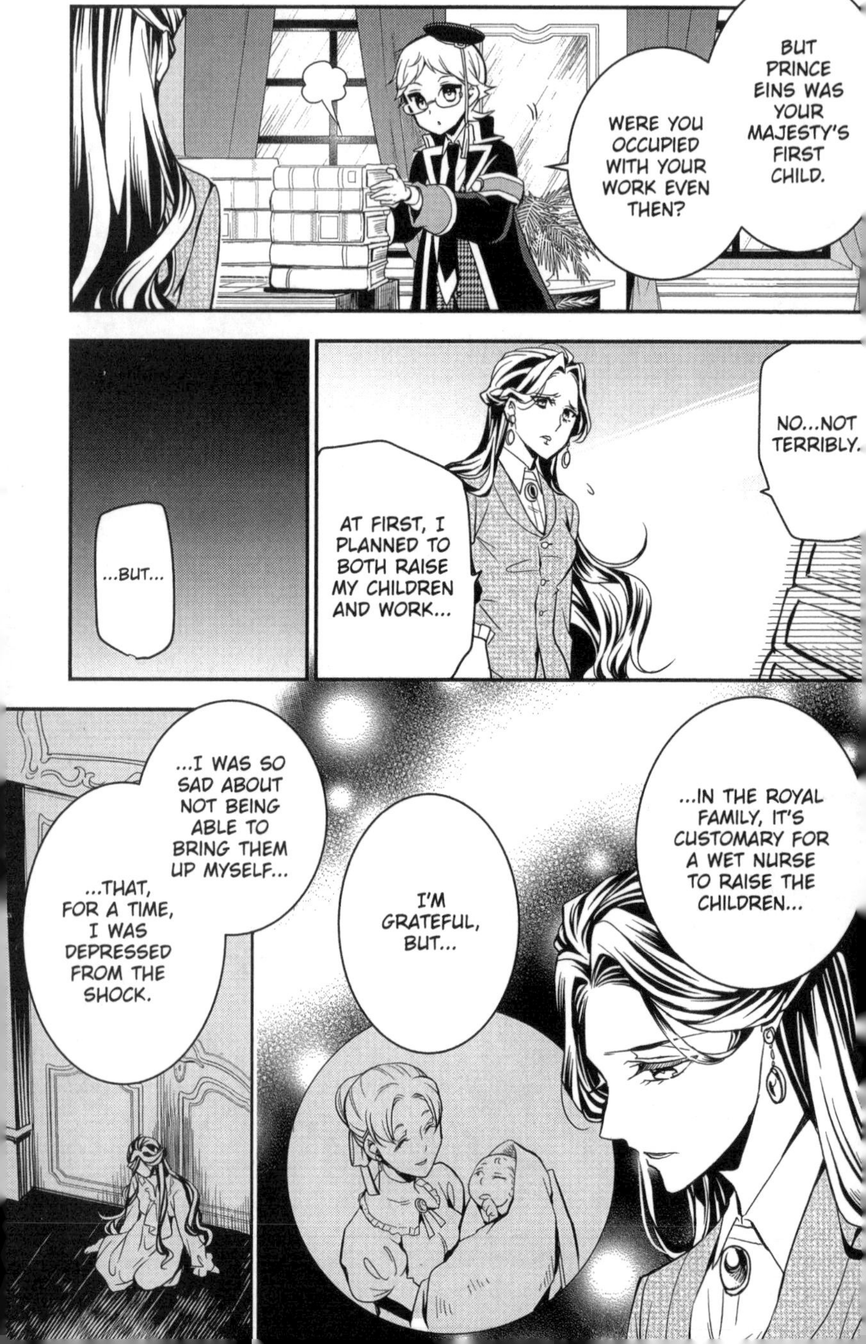
BUT PRINCE EINS WAS YOUR MAJESTY'S FIRST CHILD.
WERE YOU OCCUPIED WITH YOUR WORK EVEN THEN?
NO...NOT TERRIBLY.
AT FIRST, I PLANNED TO BOTH RAISE MY CHILDREN AND WORK...
...BUT...
...IN THE ROYAL FAMILY, IT'S CUSTOMARY FOR A WET NURSE TO RAISE THE CHILDREN...
I'M GRATEFUL, BUT...
...I WAS SO SAD ABOUT NOT BEING ABLE TO BRING THEM UP MYSELF...
...THAT, FOR A TIME, I WAS DEPRESSED FROM THE SHOCK.

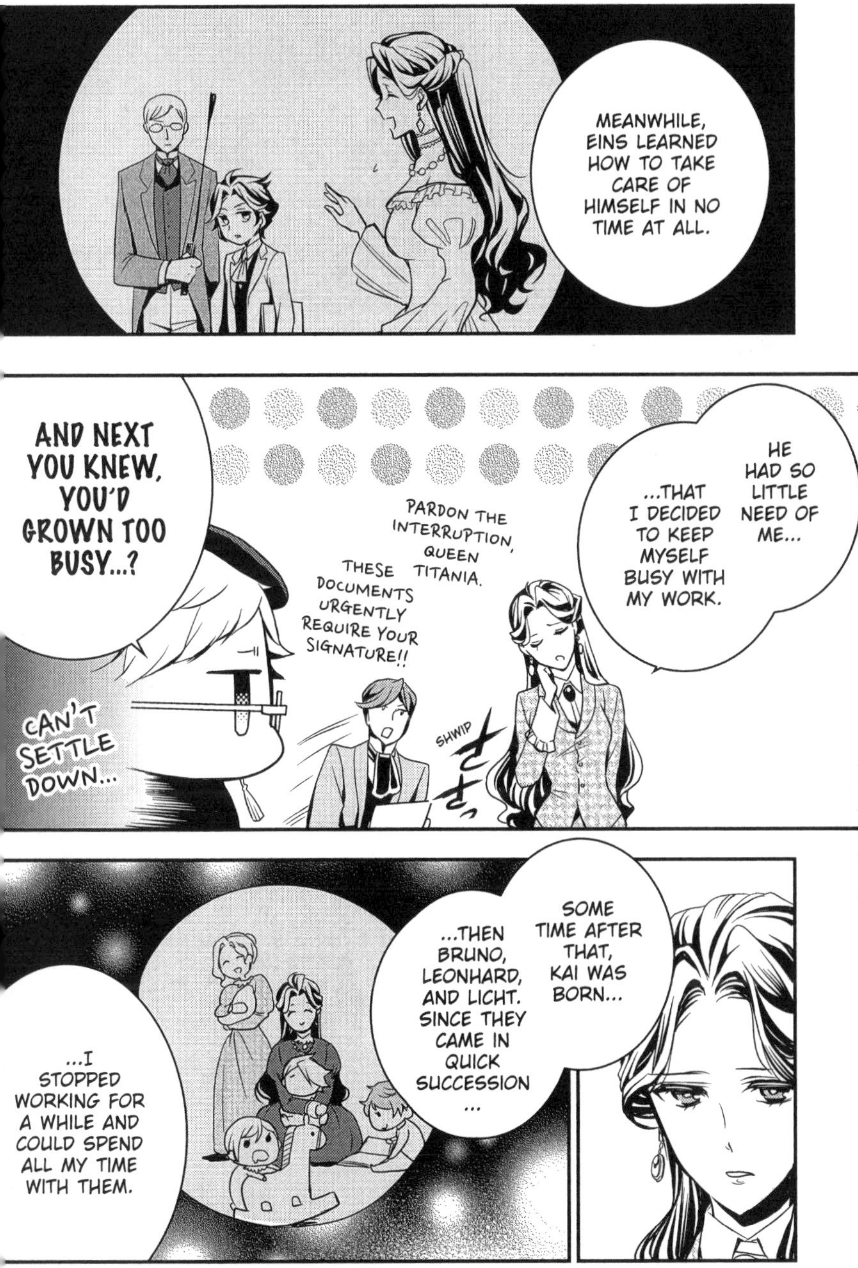
MEANWHILE, EINS LEARNED HOW TO TAKE CARE OF HIMSELF IN NO TIME AT ALL.
HE HAD SO LITTLE NEED OF ME...
...THAT I DECIDED TO KEEP MYSELF BUSY WITH MY WORK.
PARDON THE INTERRUPTION, QUEEN TITANIA.
THESE DOCUMENTS URGENTLY REQUIRE YOUR SIGNATURE!!
SHWIP
AND NEXT YOU KNEW, YOU'D GROWN TOO BUSY...?
CAN'T SETTLE DOWN...
SOME TIME AFTER THAT, KAI WAS BORN...
...THEN BRUNO, LEONHARD, AND LICHT. SINCE THEY CAME IN QUICK SUCCESSION...
...I STOPPED WORKING FOR A WHILE AND COULD SPEND ALL MY TIME WITH THEM.

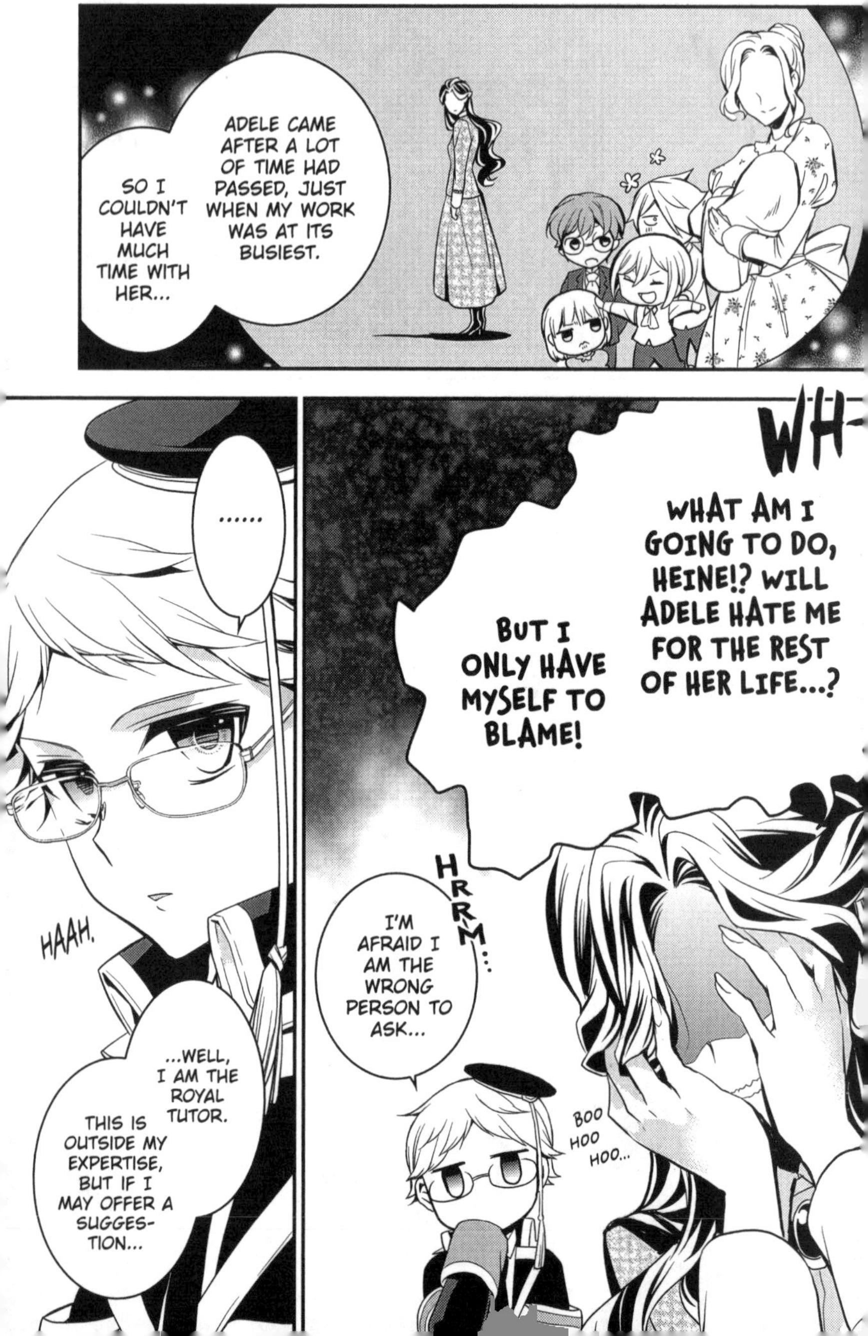
ADELE CAME AFTER A LOT OF TIME HAD PASSED, JUST WHEN MY WORK WAS AT ITS BUSIEST.
SO I COULDN'T HAVE MUCH TIME WITH HER...
WH-
WHAT AM I GOING TO DO, HEINE!? WILL ADELE HATE ME FOR THE REST OF HER LIFE...?
BUT I ONLY HAVE MYSELF TO BLAME!
HRRM...
I'M AFRAID I AM THE WRONG PERSON TO ASK...
BOO HOO HOO...
......
HAAH.
...WELL, I AM THE ROYAL TUTOR.
THIS IS OUTSIDE MY EXPERTISE, BUT IF I MAY OFFER A SUGGES-TION...

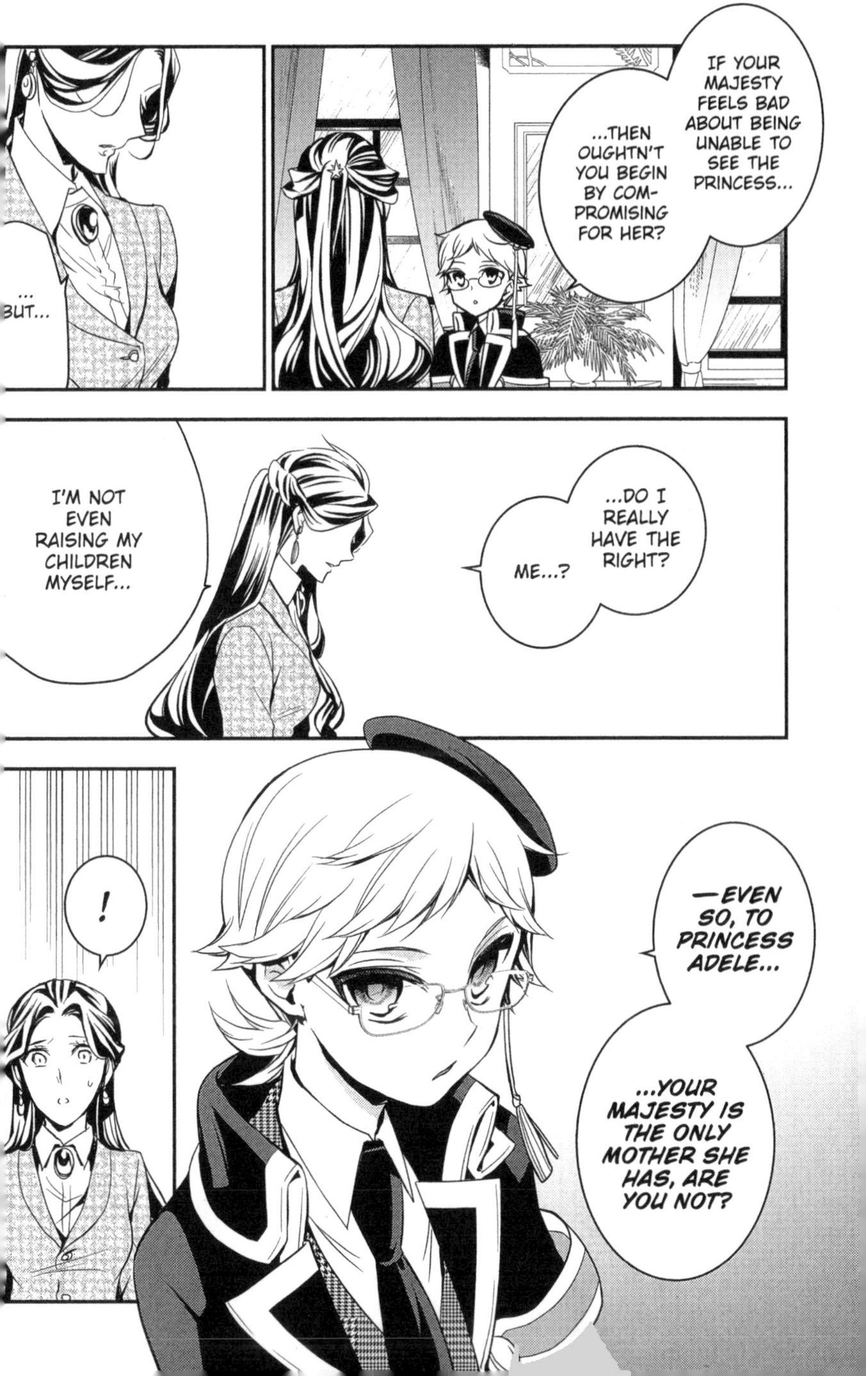
IF YOUR MAJESTY FEELS BAD ABOUT BEING UNABLE TO SEE THE PRINCESS...
...THEN OUGHTN'T YOU BEGIN BY COM-PROMISING FOR HER?
... BUT...
...DO I REALLY HAVE THE RIGHT?
ME...?
I'M NOT EVEN RAISING MY CHILDREN MYSELF...
—EVEN SO, TO PRINCESS ADELE...
...YOUR MAJESTY IS THE ONLY MOTHER SHE HAS, ARE YOU NOT?
!

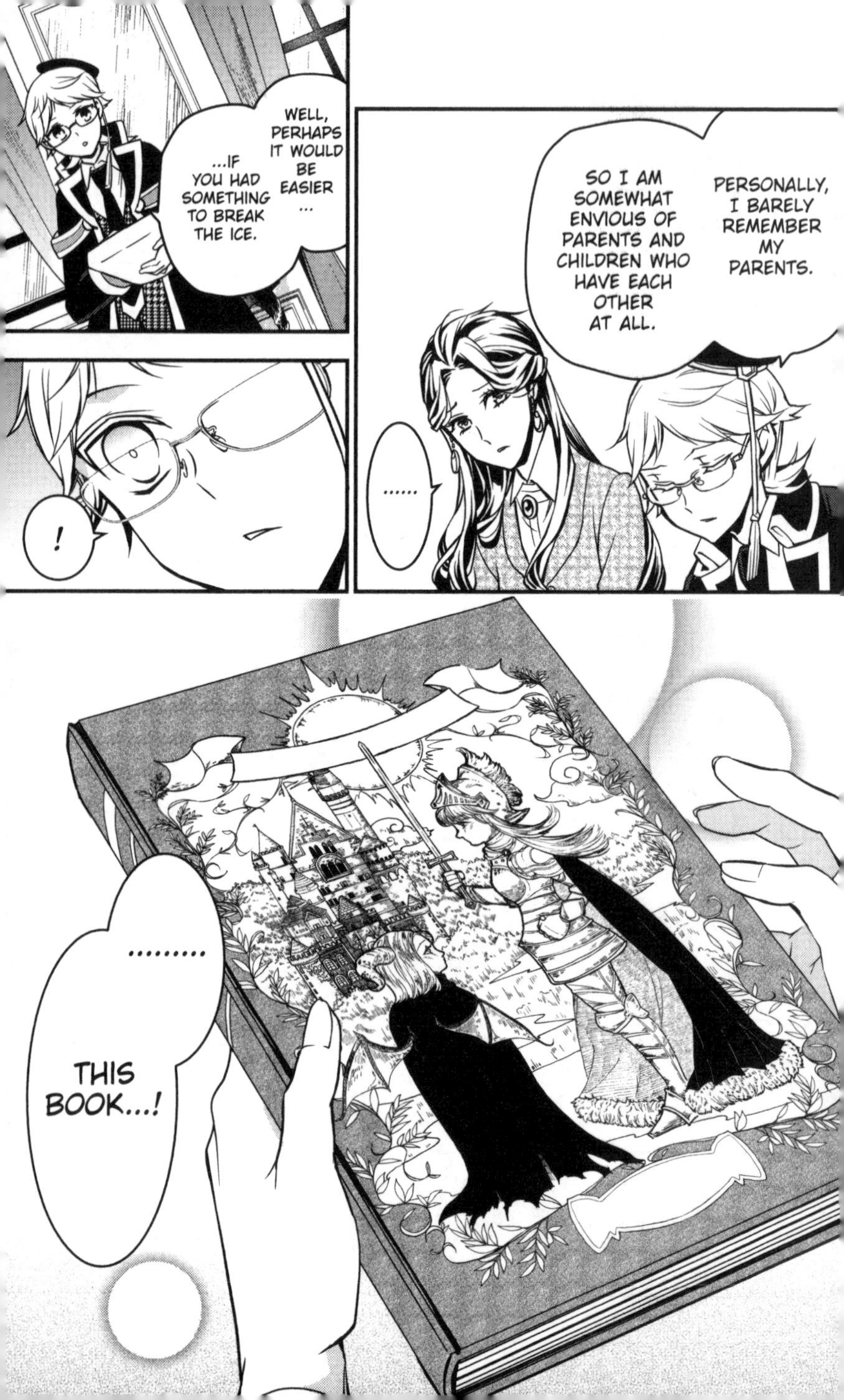
PERSONALLY, I BARELY REMEMBER MY PARENTS.
SO I AM SOMEWHAT ENVIOUS OF PARENTS AND CHILDREN WHO HAVE EACH OTHER AT ALL.
......
WELL, PERHAPS IT WOULD BE EASIER...
...IF YOU HAD SOMETHING TO BREAK THE ICE.
!
....
THIS BOOK...!

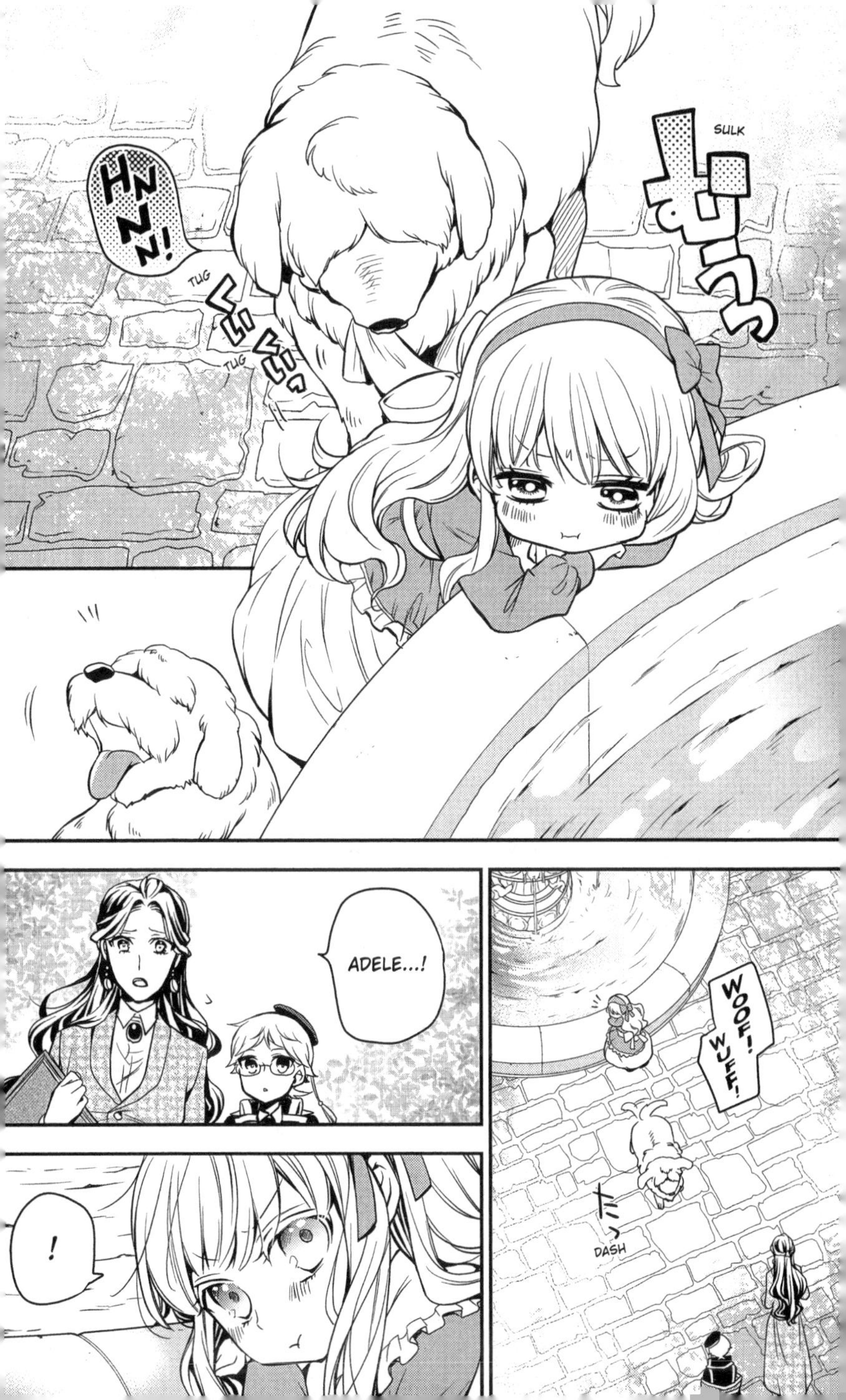
SULK
HNNN!
TUG
TUG
WOOF!
WUFF!
DASH
ADELE...!
!

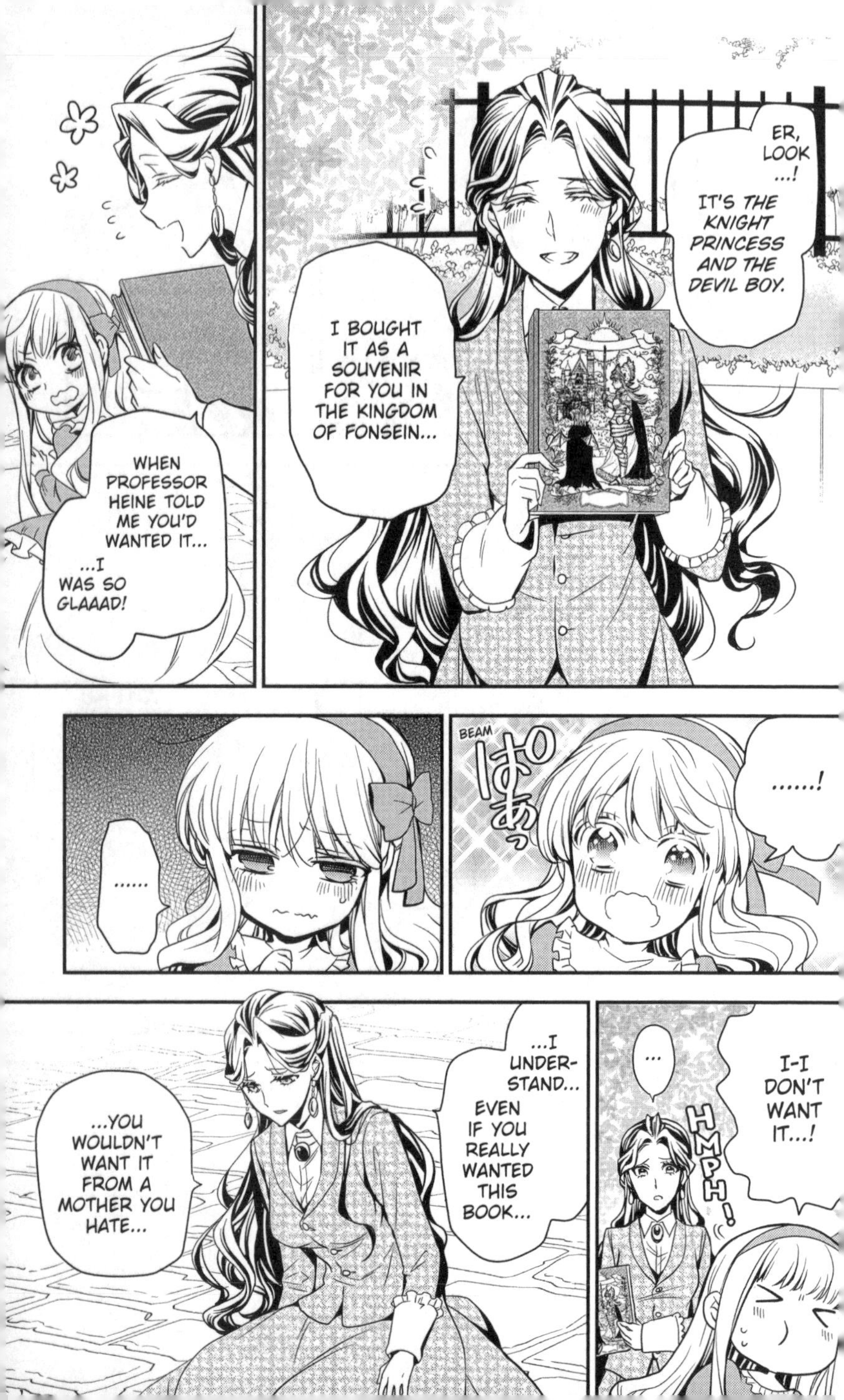
ER, LOOK...!
IT'S THE KNIGHT PRINCESS AND THE DEVIL BOY.
I BOUGHT IT AS A SOUVENIR FOR YOU IN THE KINGDOM OF FONSEIN...
WHEN PROFESSOR HEINE TOLD ME YOU'D WANTED IT...
...I WAS SO GLAAAD!
......!
BEAM
ぱあっ
......
I-I DON'T WANT IT...!
...
HMPH!
...I UNDERSTAND...
EVEN IF YOU REALLY WANTED THIS BOOK...
...YOU WOULDN'T WANT IT FROM A MOTHER YOU HATE...

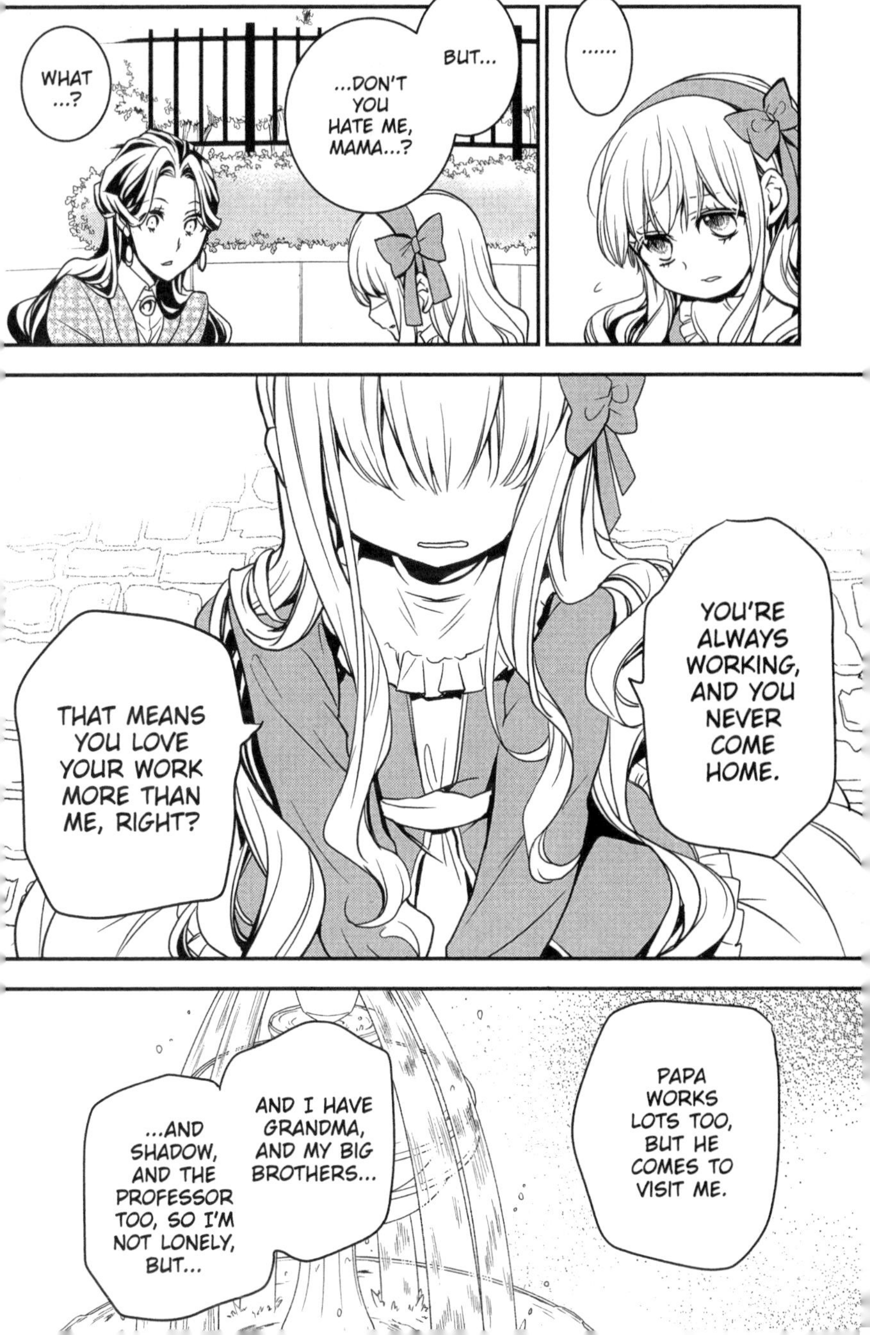
......
BUT...
...DON'T YOU HATE ME, MAMA...?
WHAT ...?
YOU'RE ALWAYS WORKING, AND YOU NEVER COME HOME.
THAT MEANS YOU LOVE YOUR WORK MORE THAN ME, RIGHT?
PAPA WORKS LOTS TOO, BUT HE COMES TO VISIT ME.
AND I HAVE GRANDMA, AND MY BIG BROTHERS...
...AND SHADOW, AND THE PROFESSOR TOO, SO I'M NOT LONELY, BUT...

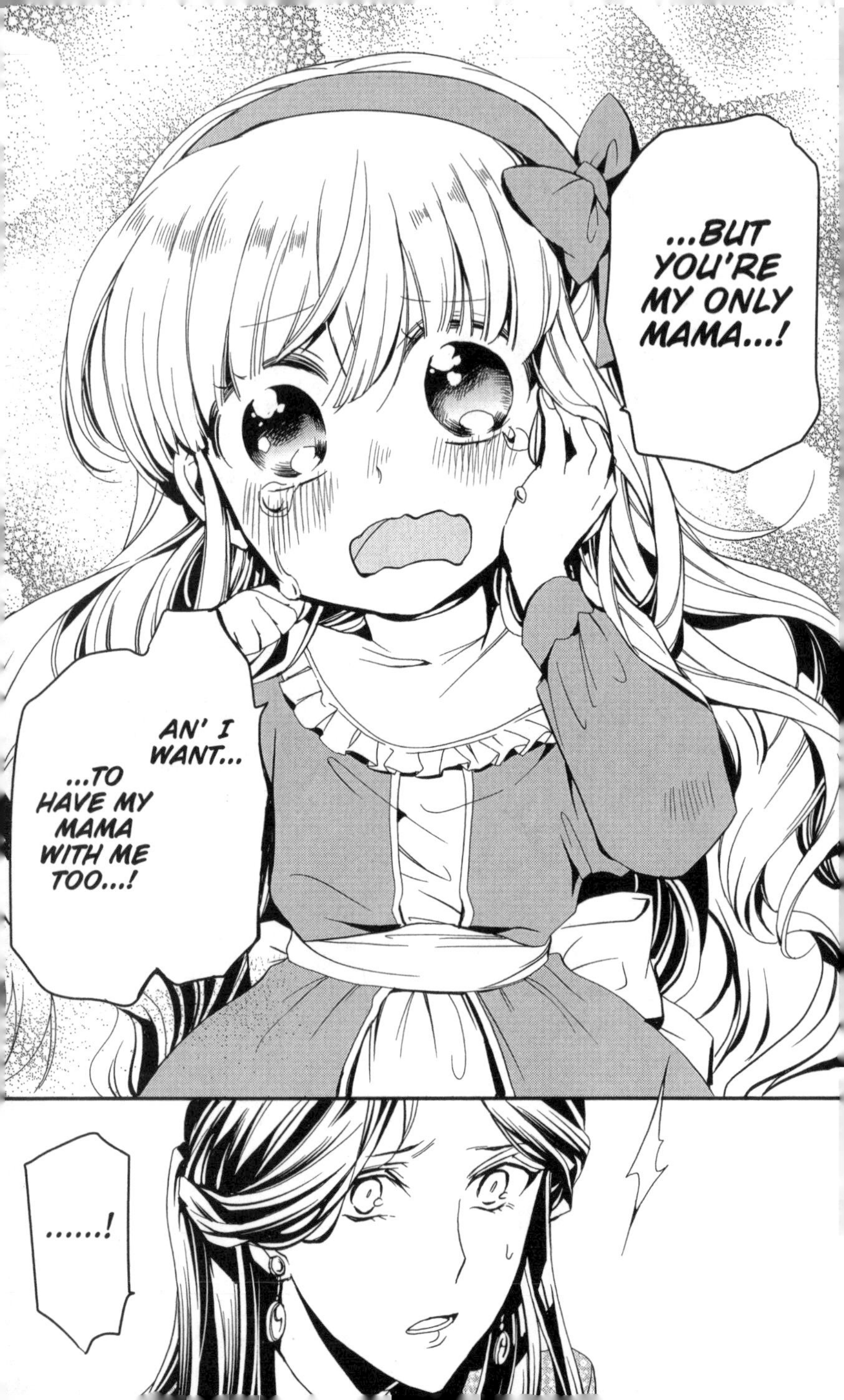
...BUT YOU'RE MY ONLY MAMA...!
AN' I WANT... ...TO HAVE MY MAMA WITH ME TOO...!
......!

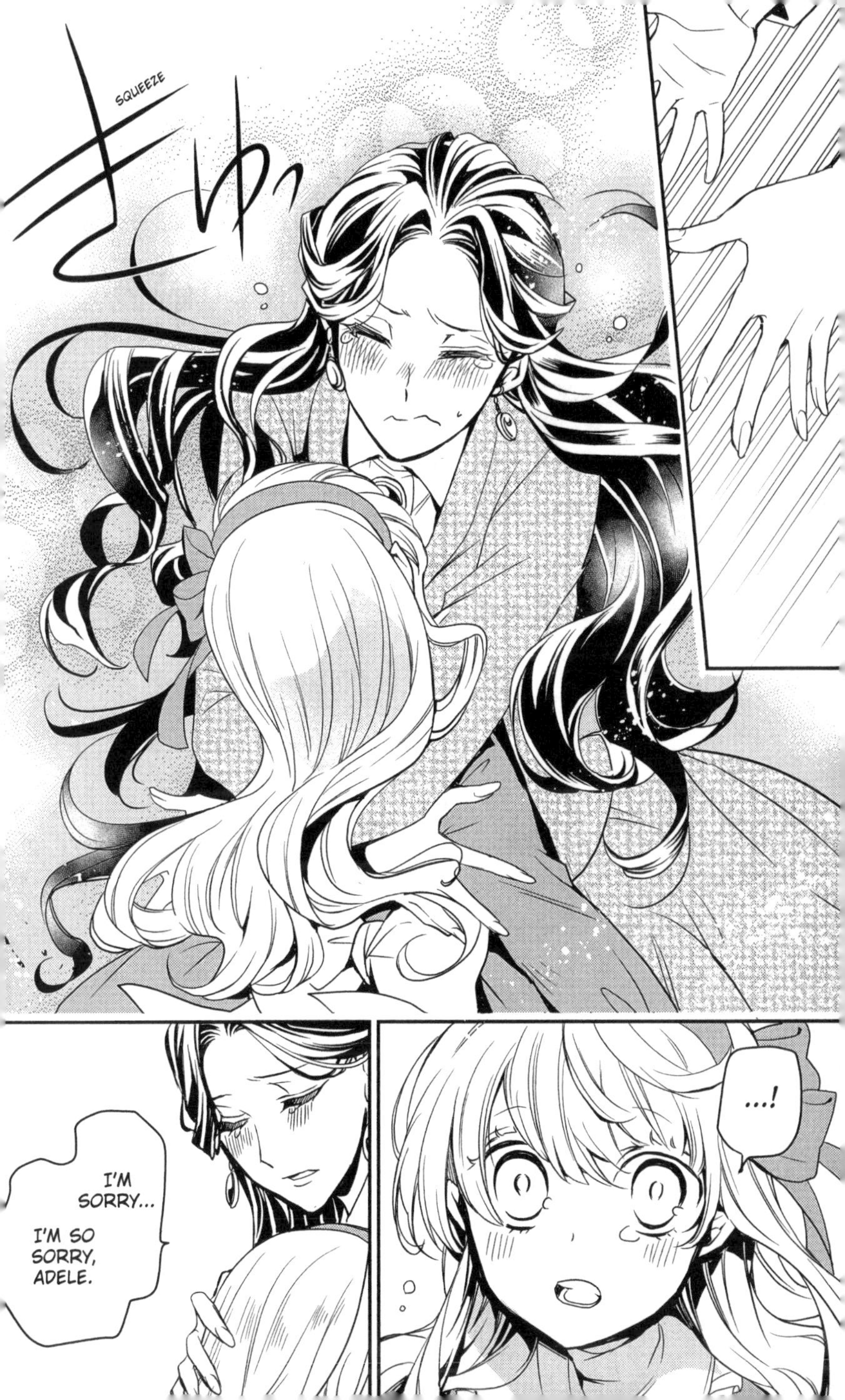
SQUEEZE
...!
I'M SORRY...
I'M SO SORRY, ADELE.

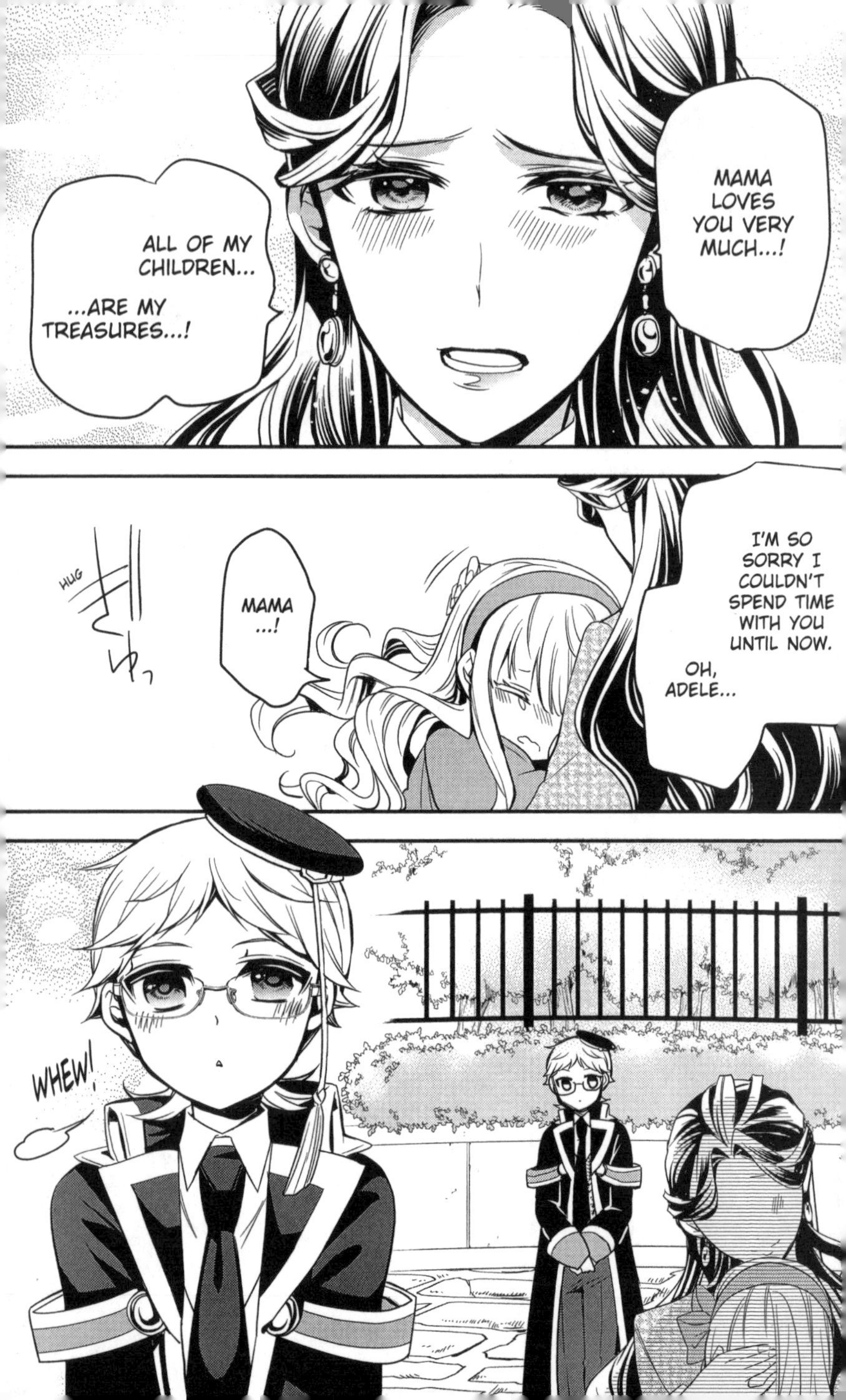
MAMA LOVES YOU VERY MUCH...!
ALL OF MY CHILDREN...
...ARE MY TREASURES...!
I'M SO SORRY I COULDN'T SPEND TIME WITH YOU UNTIL NOW.
OH, ADELE...
MAMA ...!
ぎゅっ
HUG
WHEW!

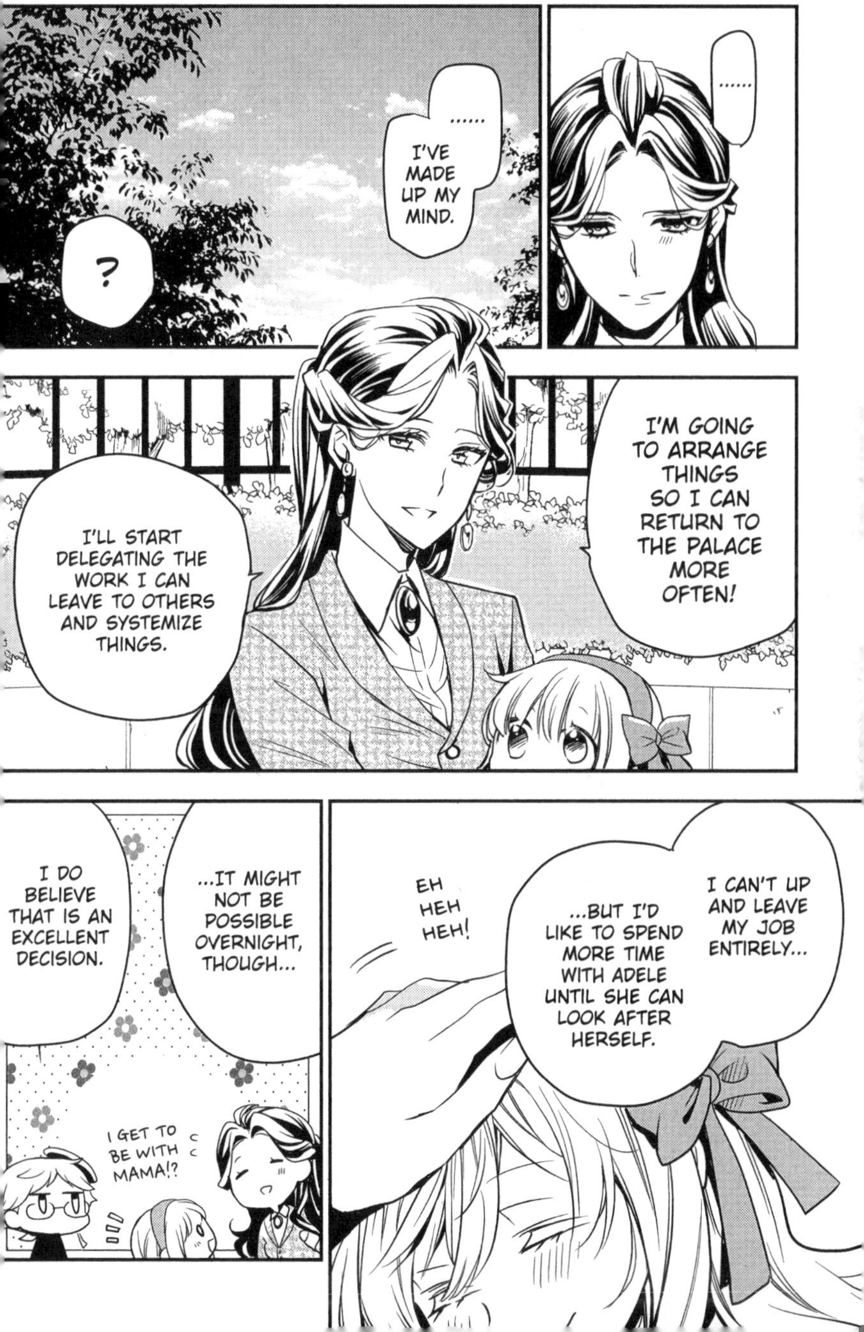
......
......
I'VE MADE UP MY MIND.
?
I'M GOING TO ARRANGE THINGS SO I CAN RETURN TO THE PALACE MORE OFTEN!
I'LL START DELEGATING THE WORK I CAN LEAVE TO OTHERS AND SYSTEMIZE THINGS.
I CAN'T UP AND LEAVE MY JOB ENTIRELY...
...BUT I'D LIKE TO SPEND MORE TIME WITH ADELE UNTIL SHE CAN LOOK AFTER HERSELF.
EH HEH HEH!
...IT MIGHT NOT BE POSSIBLE OVERNIGHT, THOUGH...
I DO BELIEVE THAT IS AN EXCELLENT DECISION.
I GET TO BE WITH MAMA!?

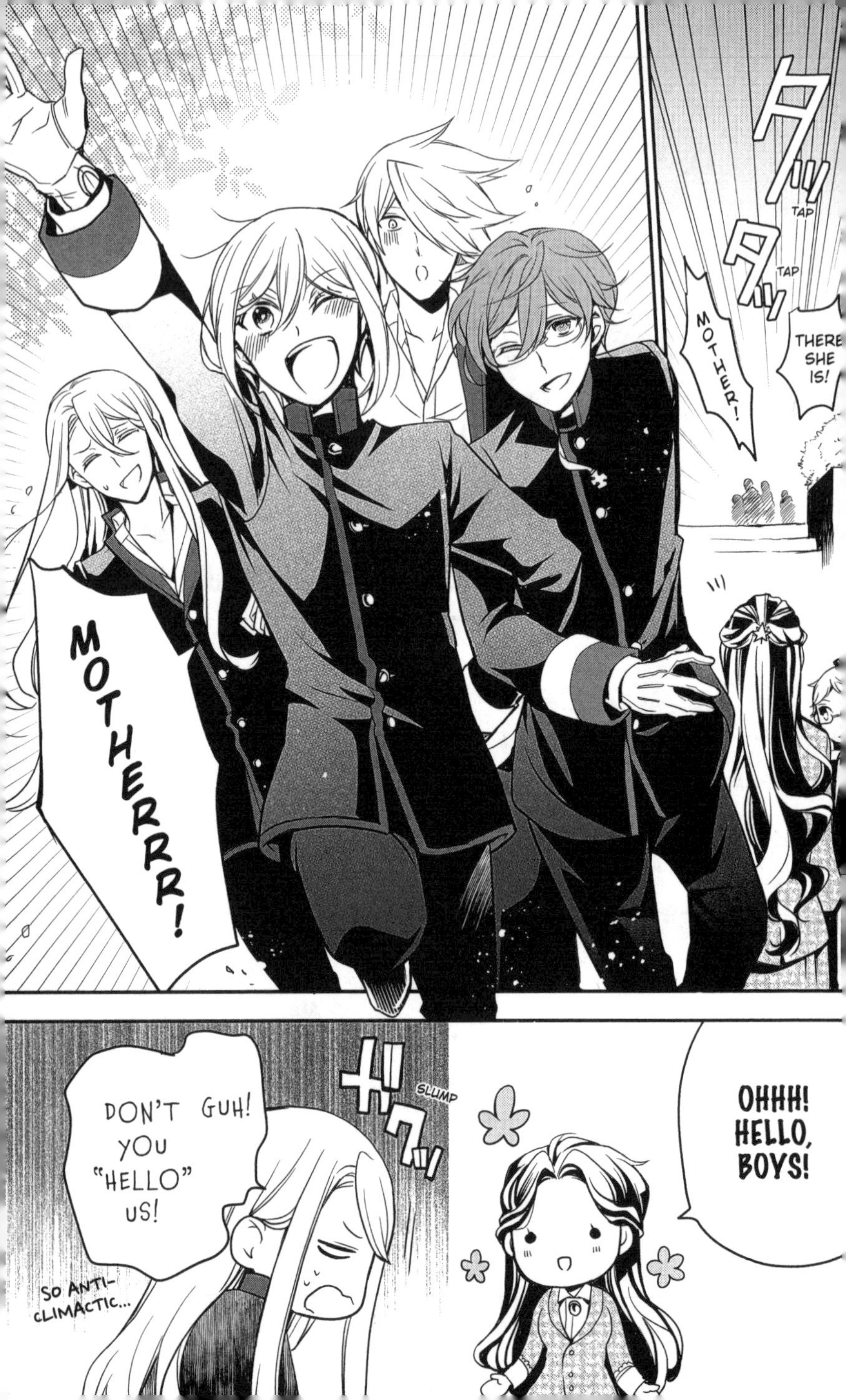
TAP
TAP
THERE SHE IS!
MOTHER!
MOTHERRR!
OHHH! HELLO, BOYS!
SLUMP
DON'T GUH! YOU "HELLO" US!
SO ANTI-CLIMACTIC...

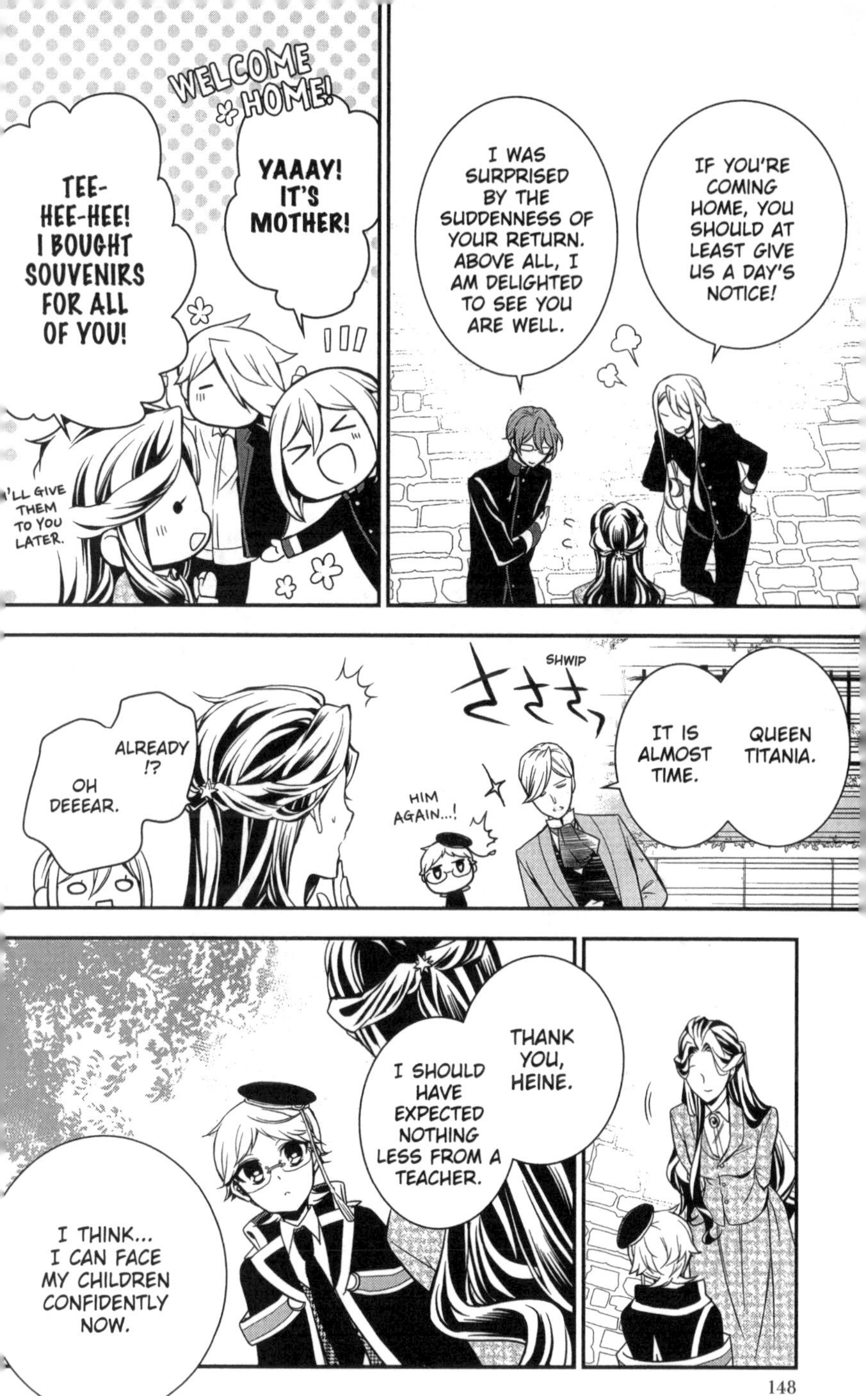
IF YOU'RE COMING HOME, YOU SHOULD AT LEAST GIVE US A DAY'S NOTICE!
I WAS SURPRISED BY THE SUDDENNESS OF YOUR RETURN. ABOVE ALL, I AM DELIGHTED TO SEE YOU ARE WELL.
WELCOME HOME!
YAAAY! IT'S MOTHER!
TEE-HEE-HEE! I BOUGHT SOUVENIRS FOR ALL OF YOU!
I'LL GIVE THEM TO YOU LATER.
QUEEN TITANIA.
IT IS ALMOST TIME.
SHWIP
HIM AGAIN...!
ALREADY!?
OH DEEEAR.
THANK YOU, HEINE.
I SHOULD HAVE EXPECTED NOTHING LESS FROM A TEACHER.
I THINK... I CAN FACE MY CHILDREN CONFIDENTLY NOW.

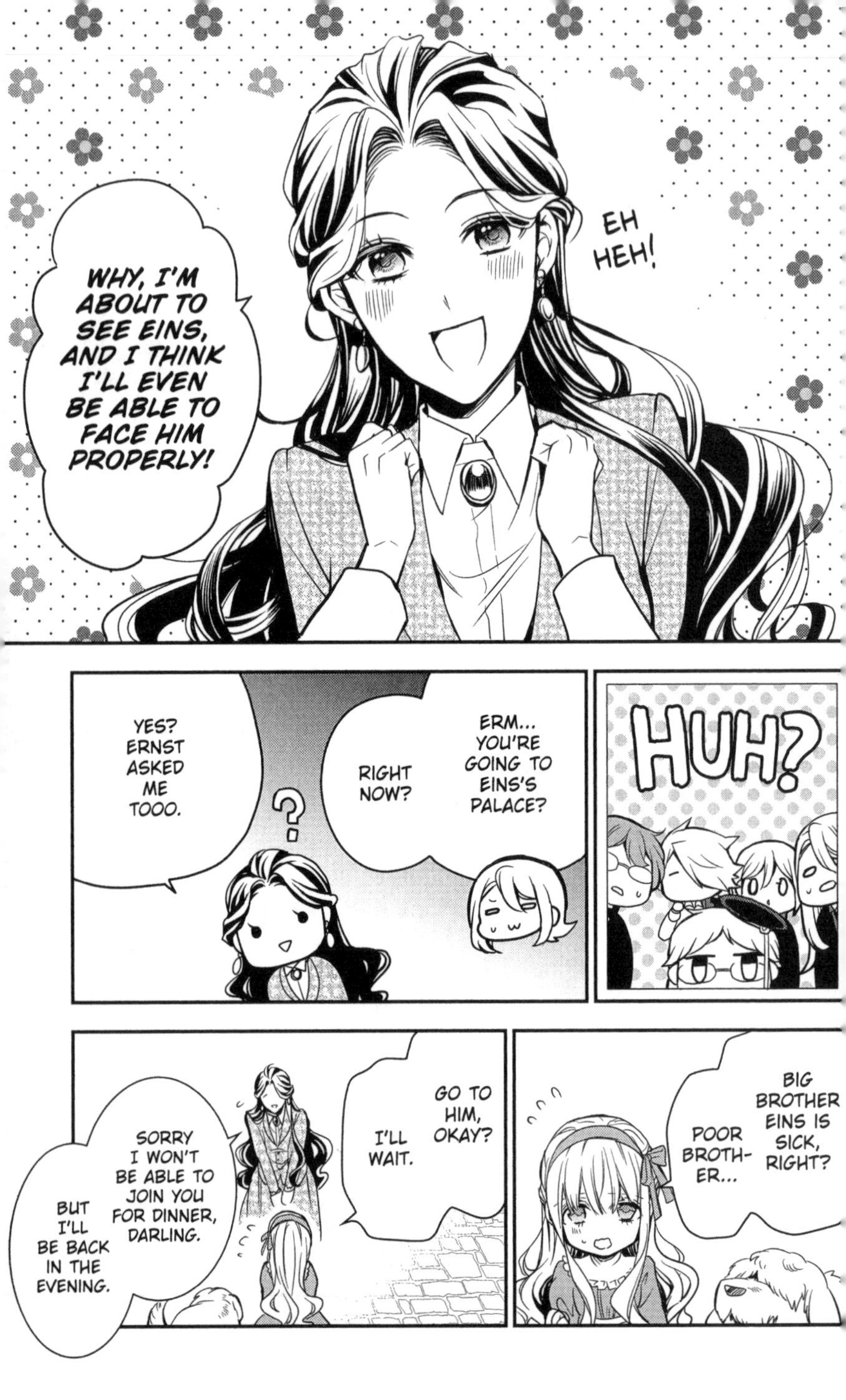
EH HEH!
WHY, I'M ABOUT TO SEE EINS, AND I THINK I'LL EVEN BE ABLE TO FACE HIM PROPERLY!
HUH?
ERM... YOU'RE GOING TO EINS'S PALACE?
RIGHT NOW?
YES? ERNST ASKED ME TOOO.
BIG BROTHER EINS IS SICK, RIGHT?
POOR BROTH-ER...
GO TO HIM, OKAY?
I'LL WAIT.
SORRY I WON'T BE ABLE TO JOIN YOU FOR DINNER, DARLING.
BUT I'LL BE BACK IN THE EVENING.

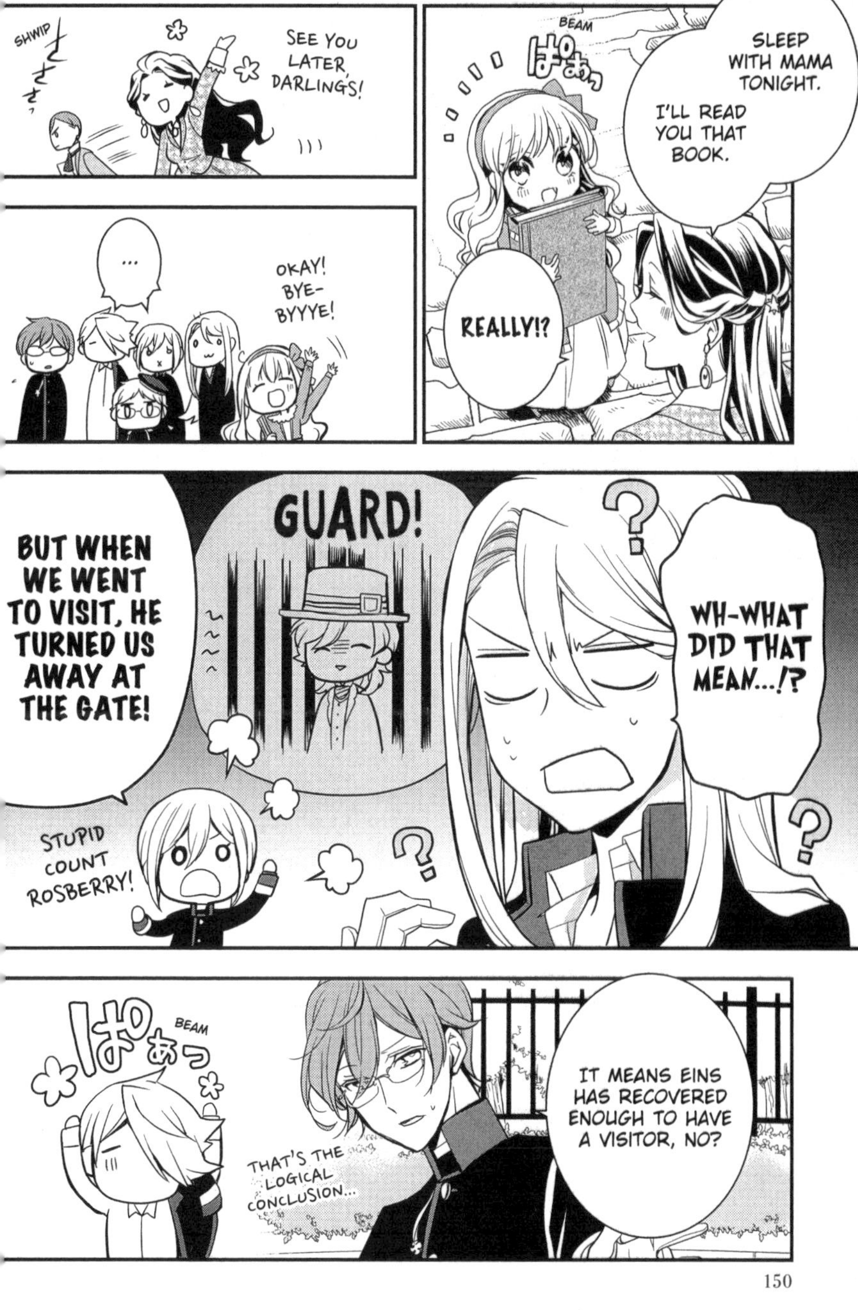
BEAM
SLEEP WITH MAMA TONIGHT.
I'LL READ YOU THAT BOOK.
REALLY!?
SHWIP
SEE YOU LATER, DARLINGS!
...
OKAY! BYE-BYYYE!
WH-WHAT DID THAT MEAN...!?
GUARD!
BUT WHEN WE WENT TO VISIT, HE TURNED US AWAY AT THE GATE!
STUPID COUNT ROSBERRY!
IT MEANS EINS HAS RECOVERED ENOUGH TO HAVE A VISITOR, NO?
THAT'S THE LOGICAL CONCLUSION...
BEAM

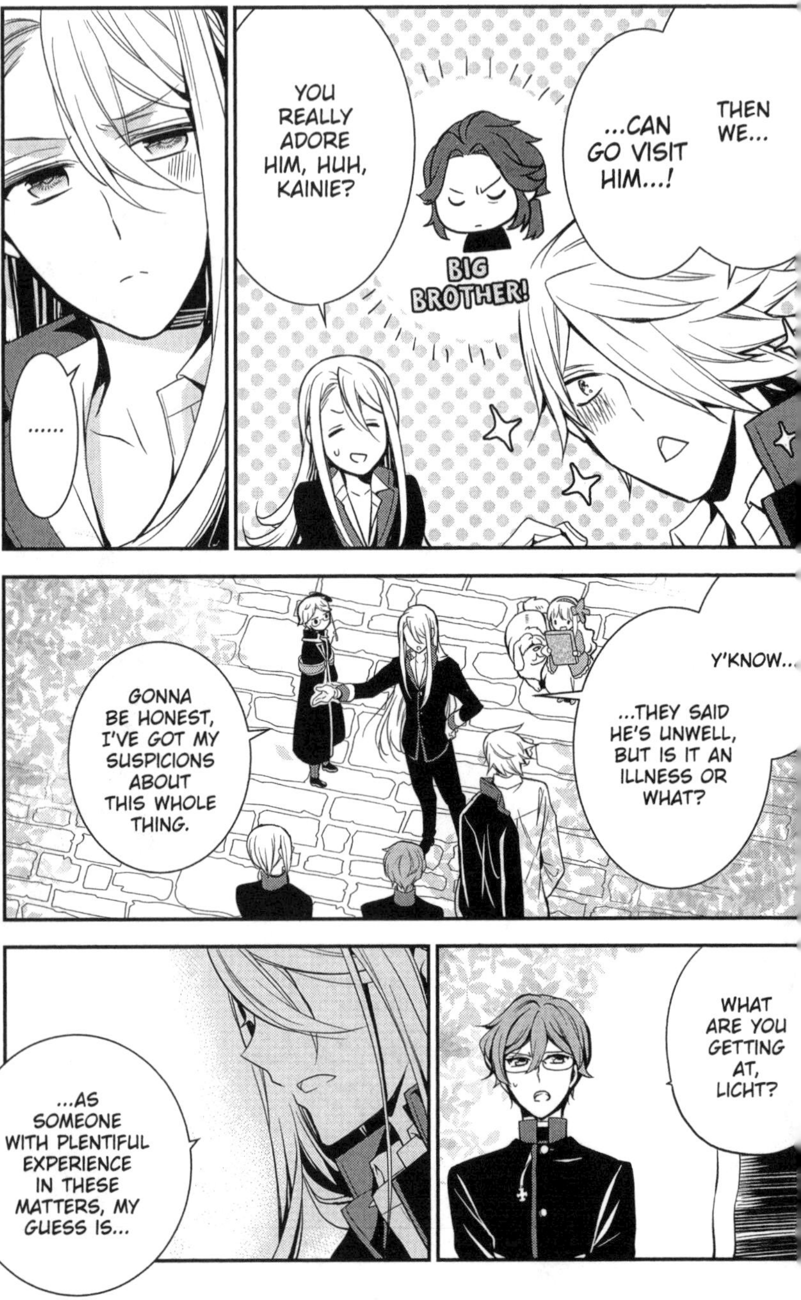
THEN WE...
...CAN GO VISIT HIM...!
BIG BROTHER!
YOU REALLY ADORE HIM, HUH, KAINIE?
......
Y'KNOW...
...THEY SAID HE'S UNWELL, BUT IS IT AN ILLNESS OR WHAT?
GONNA BE HONEST, I'VE GOT MY SUSPICIONS ABOUT THIS WHOLE THING.
WHAT ARE YOU GETTING AT, LICHT?
...AS SOMEONE WITH PLENTIFUL EXPERIENCE IN THESE MATTERS, MY GUESS IS...

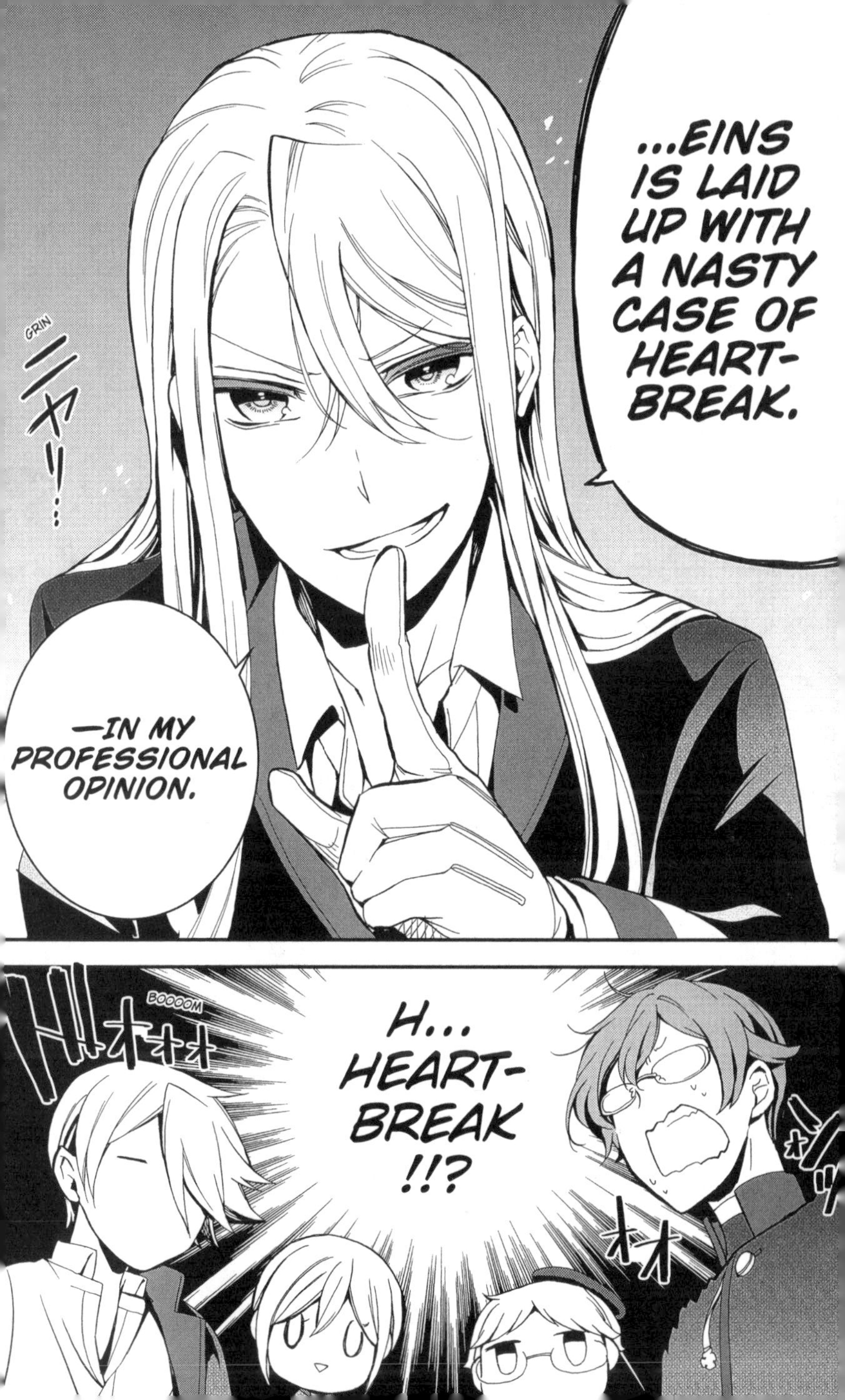
...EINS IS LAID UP WITH A NASTY CASE OF HEART-BREAK.
GRIN
—IN MY PROFESSIONAL OPINION.
H... HEART-BREAK!!?
BOOOOM

Chapter 90
A Rose in Full Bloom

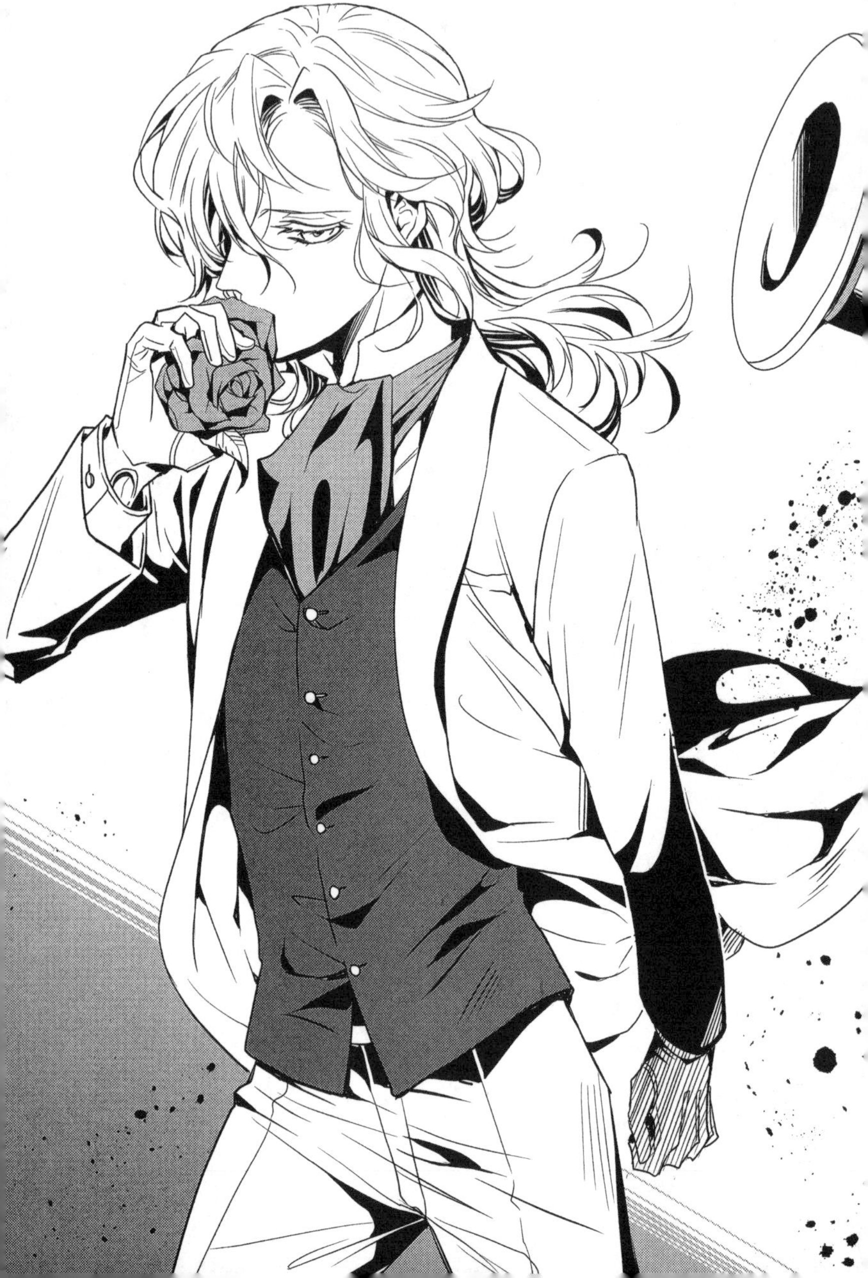

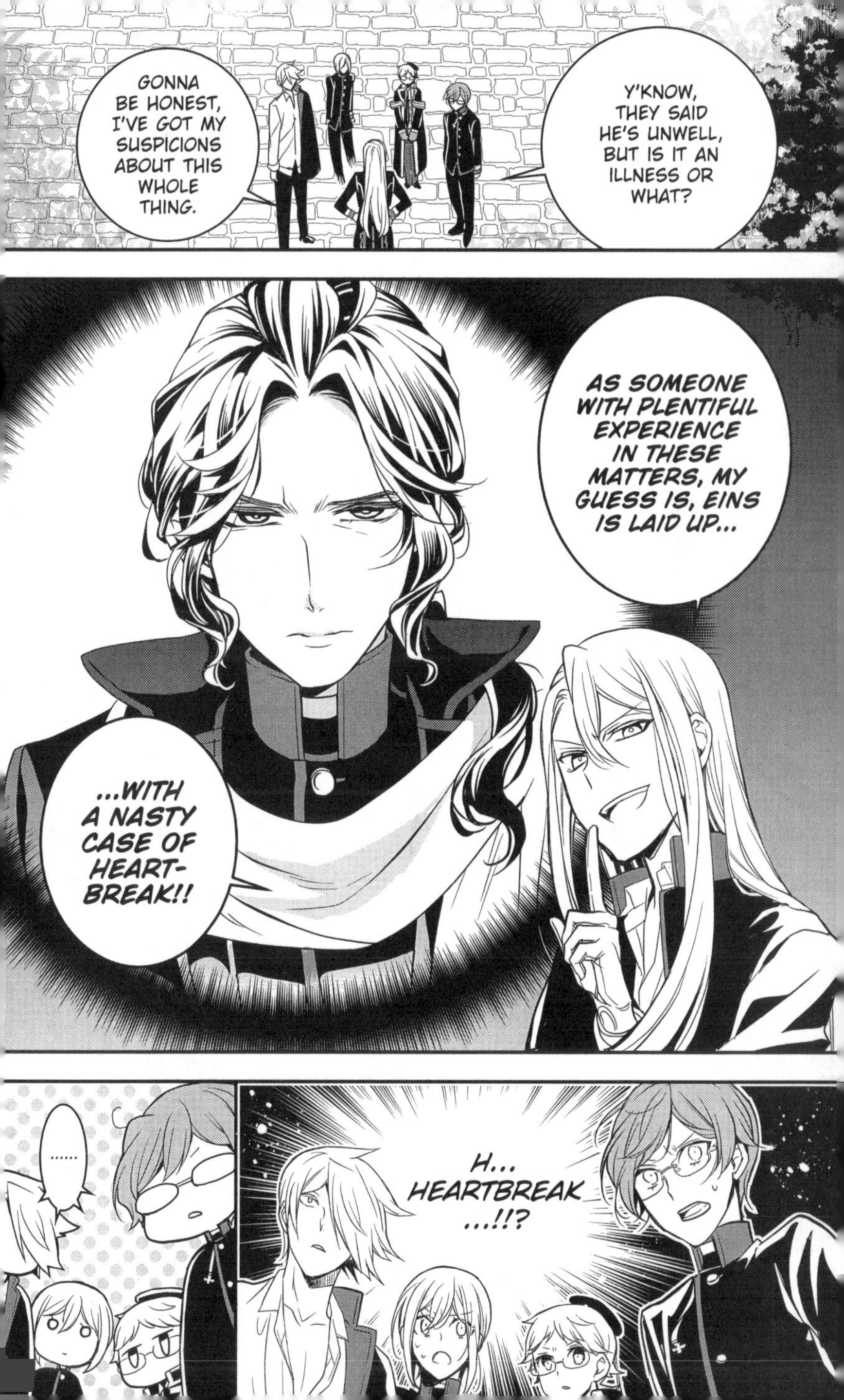
Y'KNOW, THEY SAID HE'S UNWELL, BUT IS IT AN ILLNESS OR WHAT?
GONNA BE HONEST, I'VE GOT MY SUSPICIONS ABOUT THIS WHOLE THING.
AS SOMEONE WITH PLENTIFUL EXPERIENCE IN THESE MATTERS, MY GUESS IS, EINS IS LAID UP...
...WITH A NASTY CASE OF HEART-BREAK!!
H... HEARTBREAK ...!!?
......

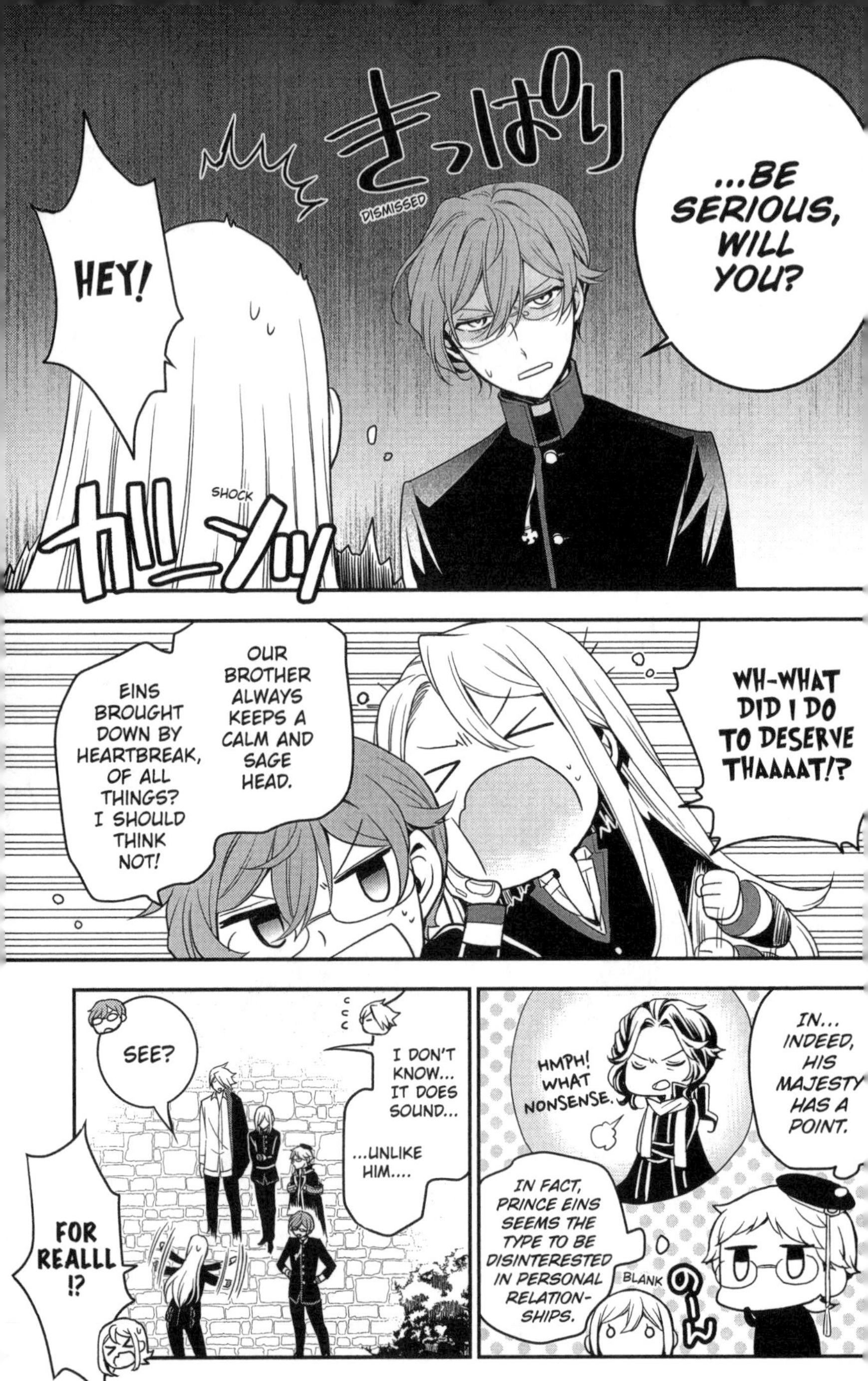
...BE SERIOUS, WILL YOU?
きっぱり
DISMISSED
HEY!
SHOCK
WH-WHAT DID I DO TO DESERVE THAAAAT!?
OUR BROTHER ALWAYS KEEPS A CALM AND SAGE HEAD.
EINS BROUGHT DOWN BY HEARTBREAK, OF ALL THINGS? I SHOULD THINK NOT!
IN... INDEED, HIS MAJESTY HAS A POINT.
HMPH! WHAT NONSENSE.
IN FACT, PRINCE EINS SEEMS THE TYPE TO BE DISINTERESTED IN PERSONAL RELATION-SHIPS.
BLANK
I DON'T KNOW... IT DOES SOUND...
...UNLIKE HIM....
SEE?
FOR REALLL !?

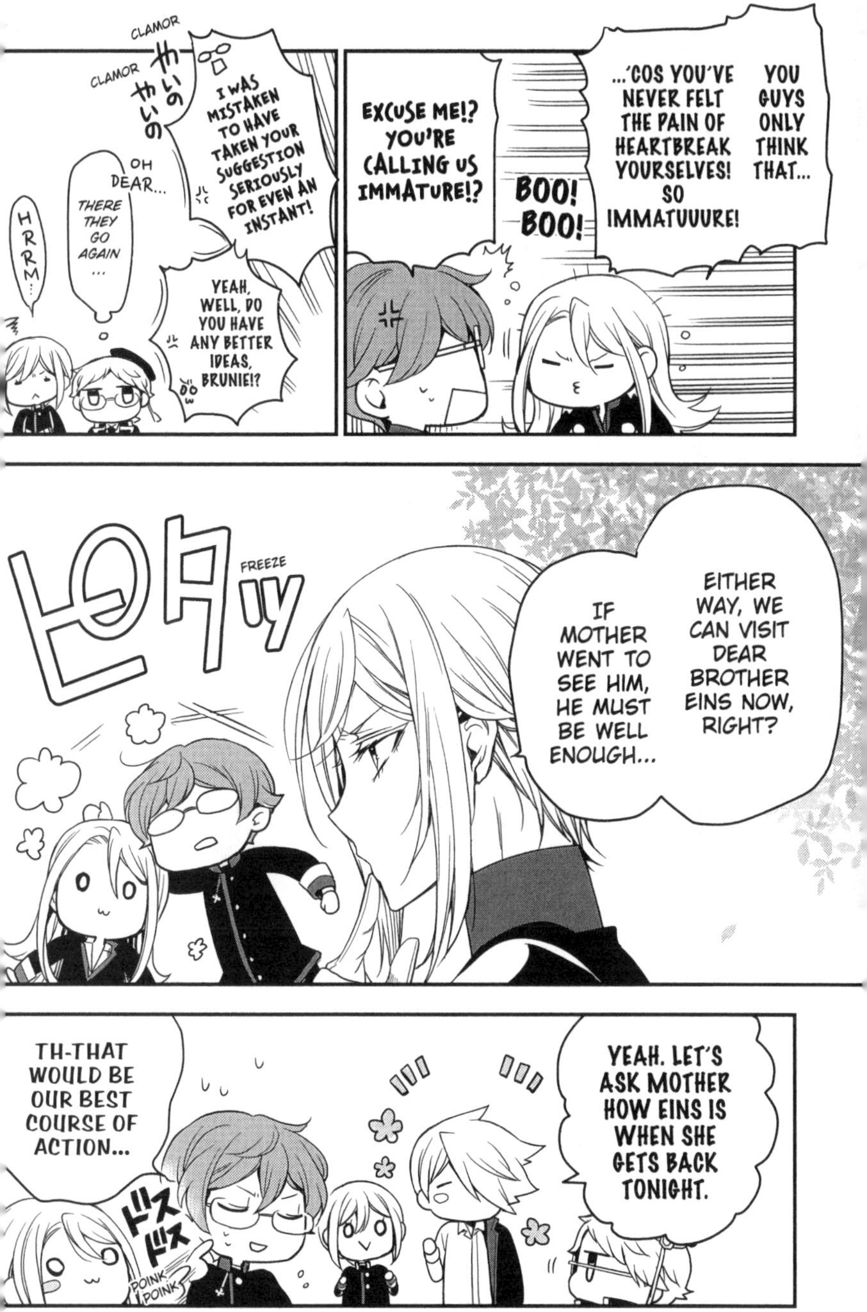
YOU GUYS ONLY THINK THAT...
...'COS YOU'VE NEVER FELT THE PAIN OF HEARTBREAK YOURSELVES! SO IMMATUUURE!
BOO! BOO!
EXCUSE ME!? YOU'RE CALLING US IMMATURE!?
I WAS MISTAKEN TO HAVE TAKEN YOUR SUGGESTION SERIOUSLY FOR EVEN AN INSTANT!
やいのやいの
CLAMOR
CLAMOR
YEAH, WELL, DO YOU HAVE ANY BETTER IDEAS, BRUNIE!?
OH DEAR...
THERE THEY GO AGAIN...
HRRM...
EITHER WAY, WE CAN VISIT DEAR BROTHER EINS NOW, RIGHT?
IF MOTHER WENT TO SEE HIM, HE MUST BE WELL ENOUGH...
ピタッ
FREEZE
YEAH. LET'S ASK MOTHER HOW EINS IS WHEN SHE GETS BACK TONIGHT.
TH-THAT WOULD BE OUR BEST COURSE OF ACTION...
ドスドス
POINK POINK

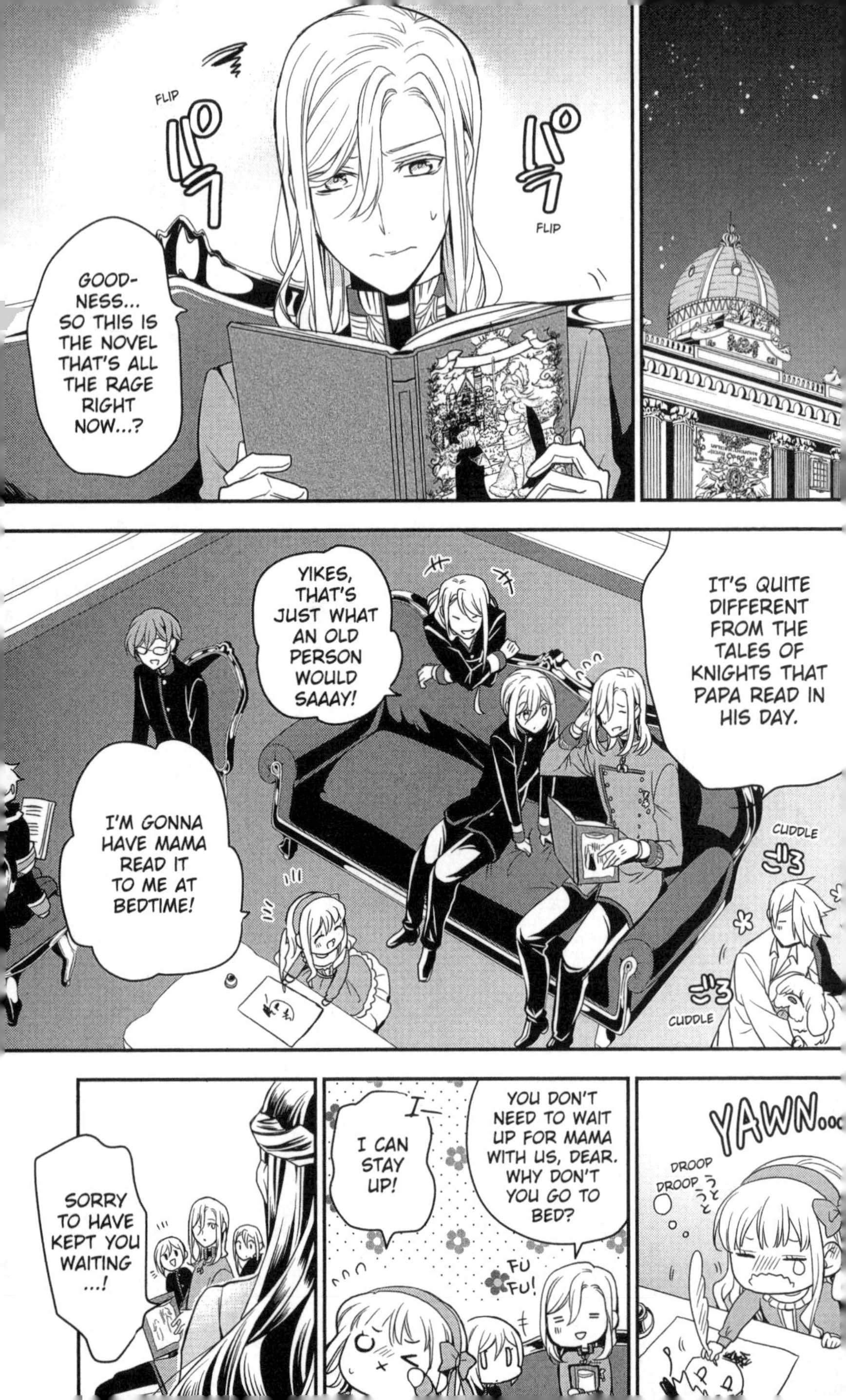
FLIP
FLIP
GOOD-NESS... SO THIS IS THE NOVEL THAT'S ALL THE RAGE RIGHT NOW...?
IT'S QUITE DIFFERENT FROM THE TALES OF KNIGHTS THAT PAPA READ IN HIS DAY.
YIKES, THAT'S JUST WHAT AN OLD PERSON WOULD SAAAY!
CUDDLE
CUDDLE
I'M GONNA HAVE MAMA READ IT TO ME AT BEDTIME!
YAWN...
DROOP DROOP
YOU DON'T NEED TO WAIT UP FOR MAMA WITH US, DEAR. WHY DON'T YOU GO TO BED?
I CAN STAY UP!
FU FU!
SORRY TO HAVE KEPT YOU WAITING ...!

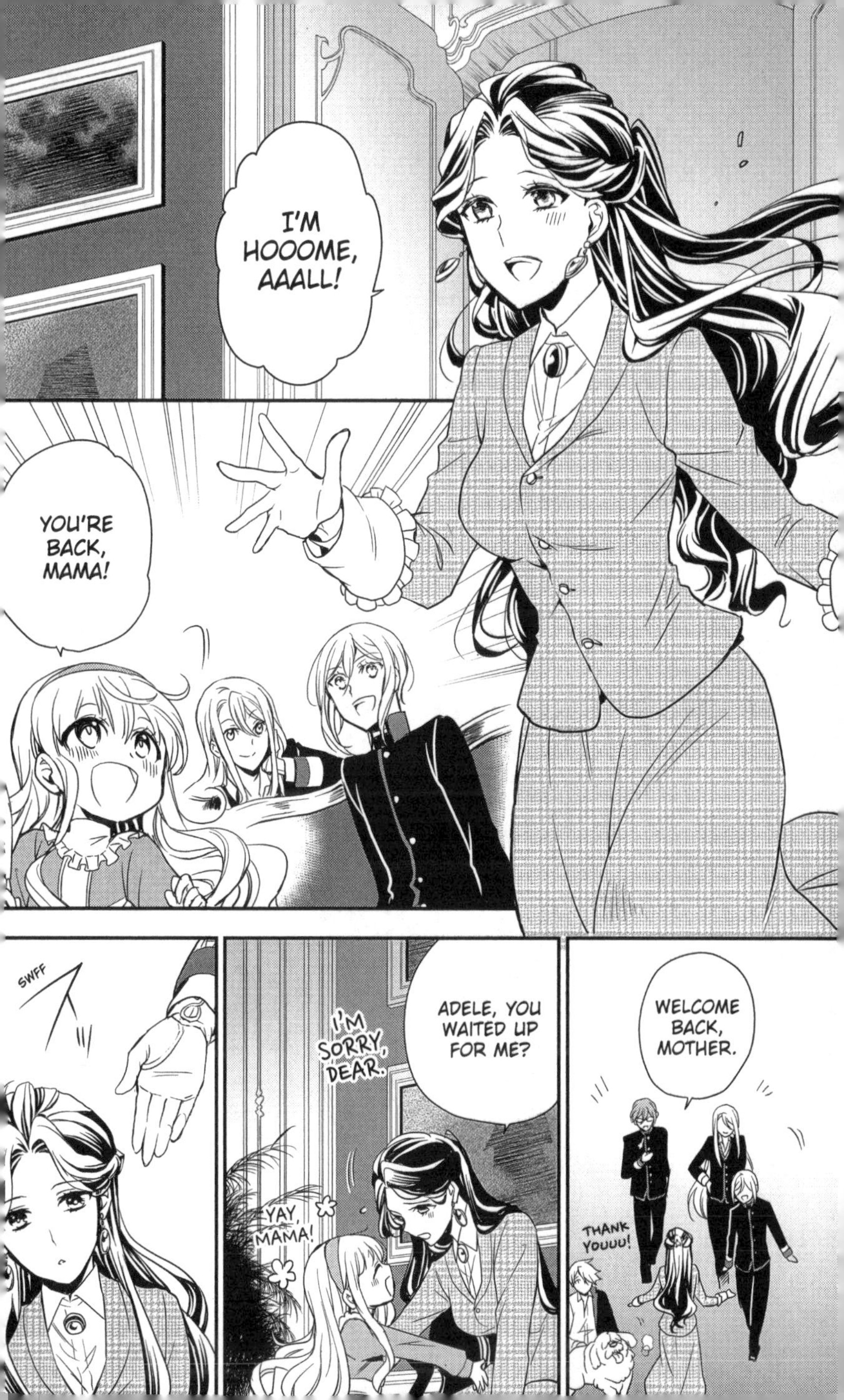
I'M HOOOME, AAALL!
YOU'RE BACK, MAMA!
WELCOME BACK, MOTHER.
THANK YOUUU!
ADELE, YOU WAITED UP FOR ME?
I'M SORRY, DEAR.
YAY, MAMA!
SWFF

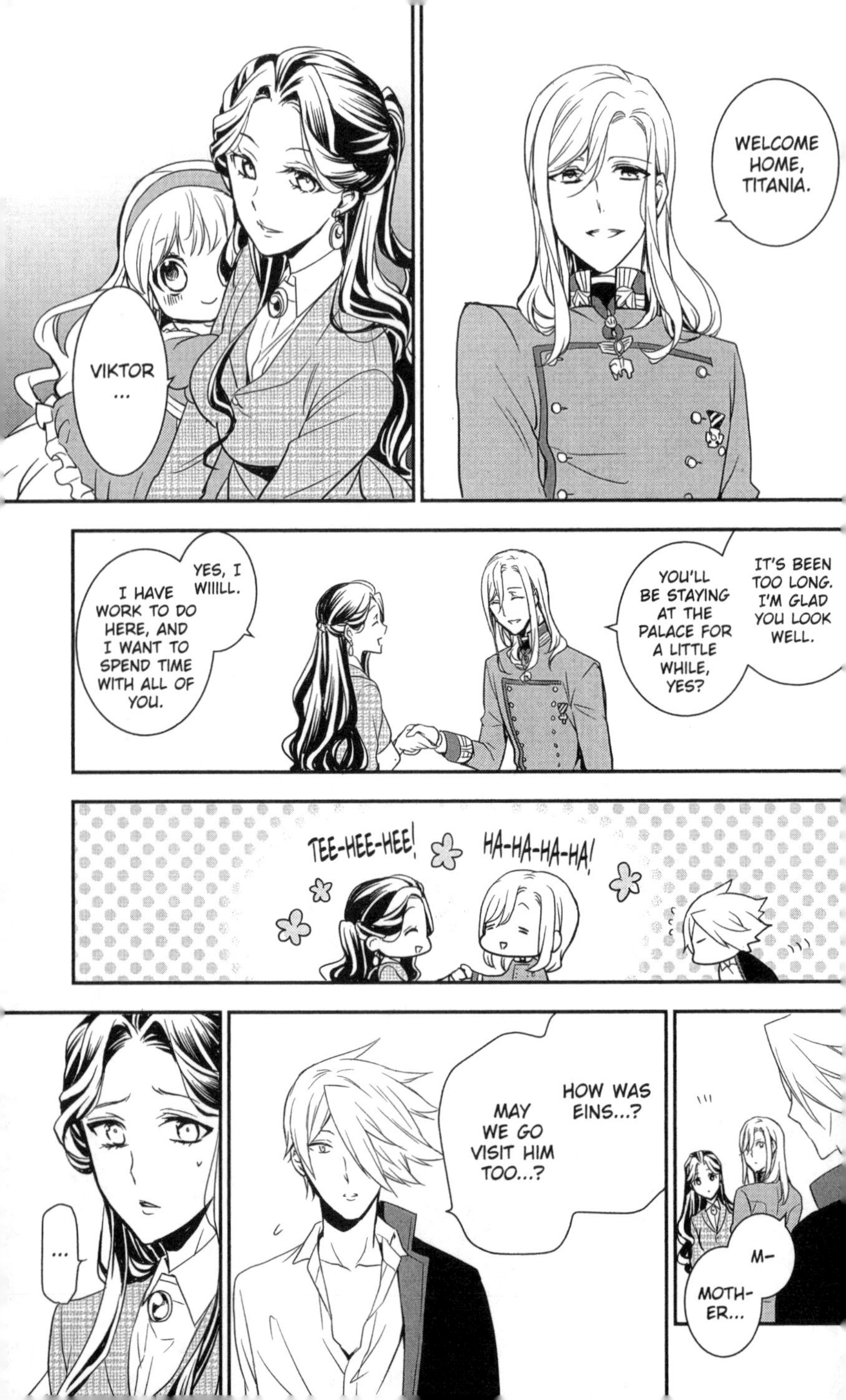
WELCOME HOME, TITANIA.
VIKTOR...
IT'S BEEN TOO LONG. I'M GLAD YOU LOOK WELL.
YOU'LL BE STAYING AT THE PALACE FOR A LITTLE WHILE, YES?
YES, I WIIILL.
I HAVE WORK TO DO HERE, AND I WANT TO SPEND TIME WITH ALL OF YOU.
HA-HA-HA-HA!
TEE-HEE-HEE!
M-MOTHER...
HOW WAS EINS...?
MAY WE GO VISIT HIM TOO...?
...

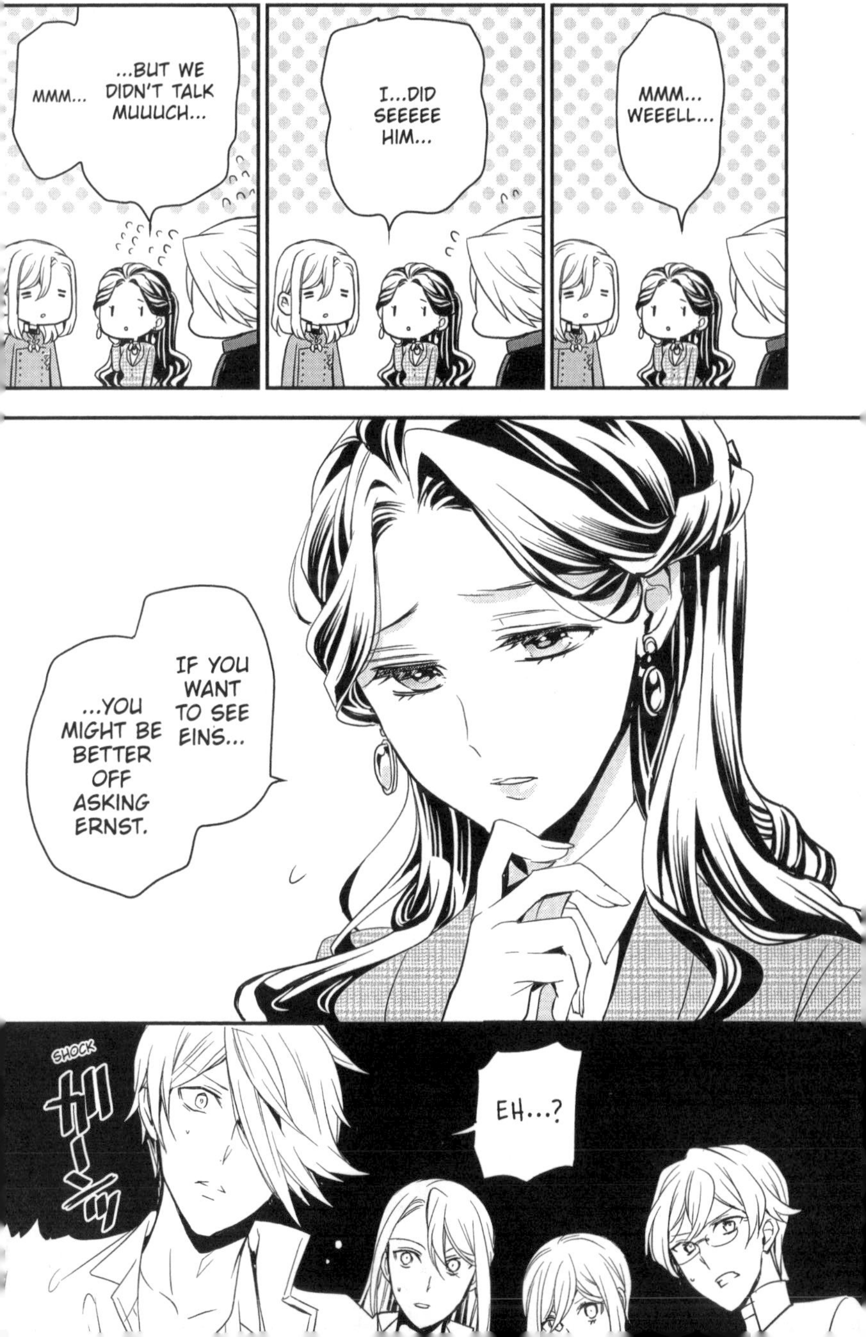
MMM... WEEELL...
I...DID SEEEEE HIM...
MMM... ...BUT WE DIDN'T TALK MUUUCH...
IF YOU WANT TO SEE EINS... ...YOU MIGHT BE BETTER OFF ASKING ERNST.
EH...?
SHOCK

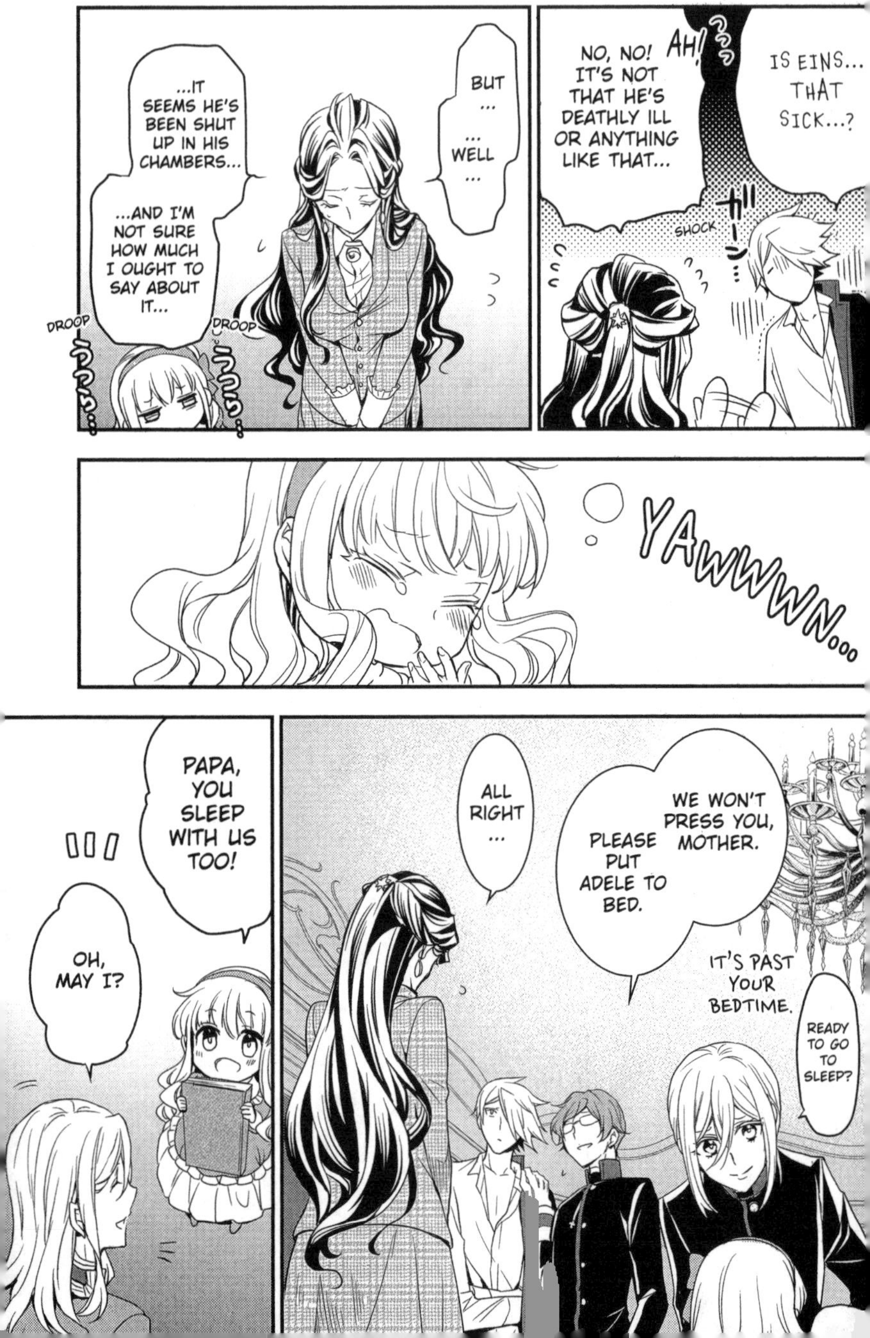
IS EINS... THAT SICK...?
AH!
NO, NO! IT'S NOT THAT HE'S DEATHLY ILL OR ANYTHING LIKE THAT...
SHOCK
BUT ... ... WELL ...
...IT SEEMS HE'S BEEN SHUT UP IN HIS CHAMBERS...
...AND I'M NOT SURE HOW MUCH I OUGHT TO SAY ABOUT IT...
DROOP
DROOP
YAWWWN...
READY TO GO TO SLEEP?
IT'S PAST YOUR BEDTIME.
WE WON'T PRESS YOU, MOTHER.
PLEASE PUT ADELE TO BED.
ALL RIGHT ...
PAPA, YOU SLEEP WITH US TOO!
OH, MAY I?

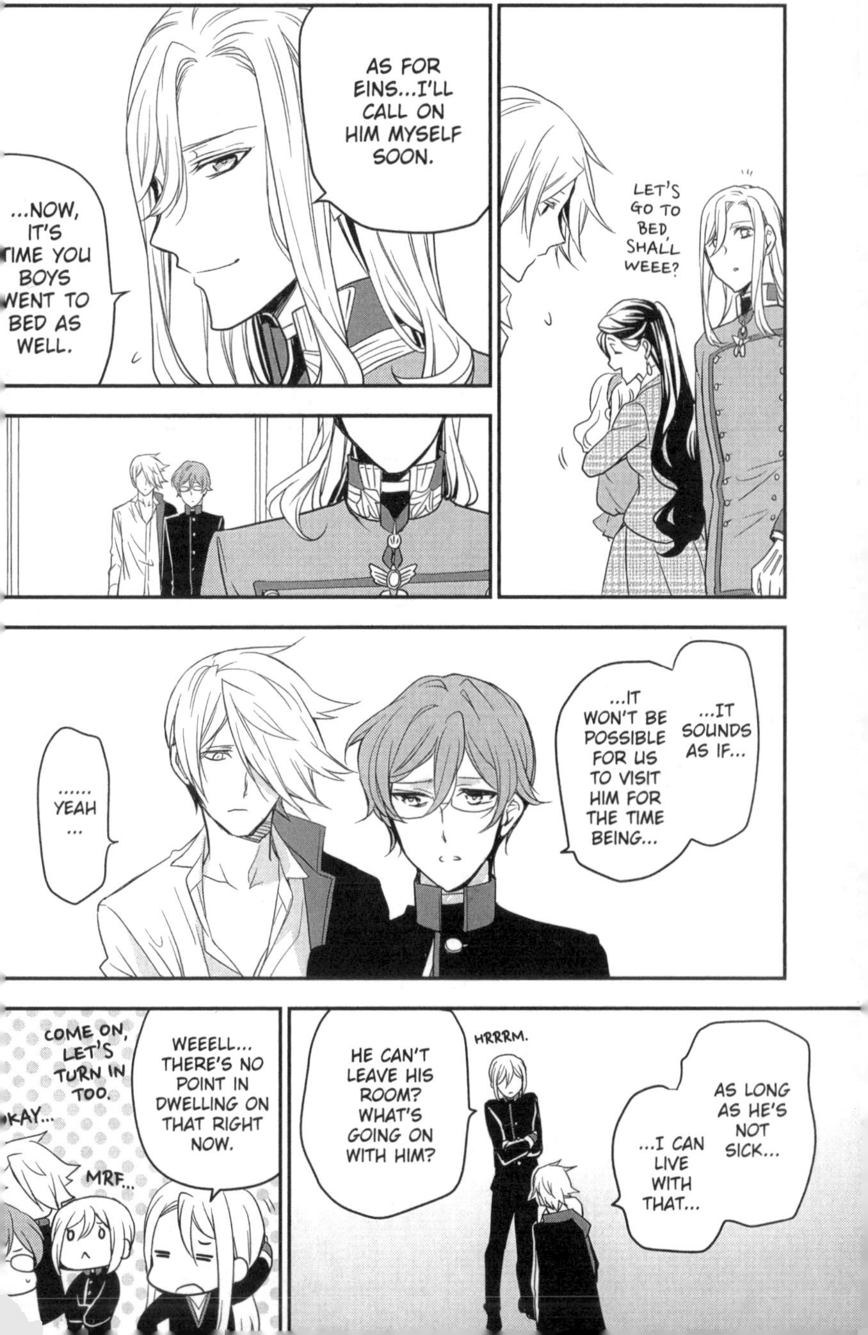
LET'S GO TO BED SHALL WEEE?
AS FOR EINS...I'LL CALL ON HIM MYSELF SOON.
...NOW, IT'S TIME YOU BOYS WENT TO BED AS WELL.
...IT SOUNDS AS IF...
...IT WON'T BE POSSIBLE FOR US TO VISIT HIM FOR THE TIME BEING...
......YEAH...
AS LONG AS HE'S NOT SICK...
...I CAN LIVE WITH THAT...
HRRRM.
HE CAN'T LEAVE HIS ROOM? WHAT'S GOING ON WITH HIM?
WEEELL... THERE'S NO POINT IN DWELLING ON THAT RIGHT NOW.
COME ON, LET'S TURN IN TOO.
KAY...
MRF...

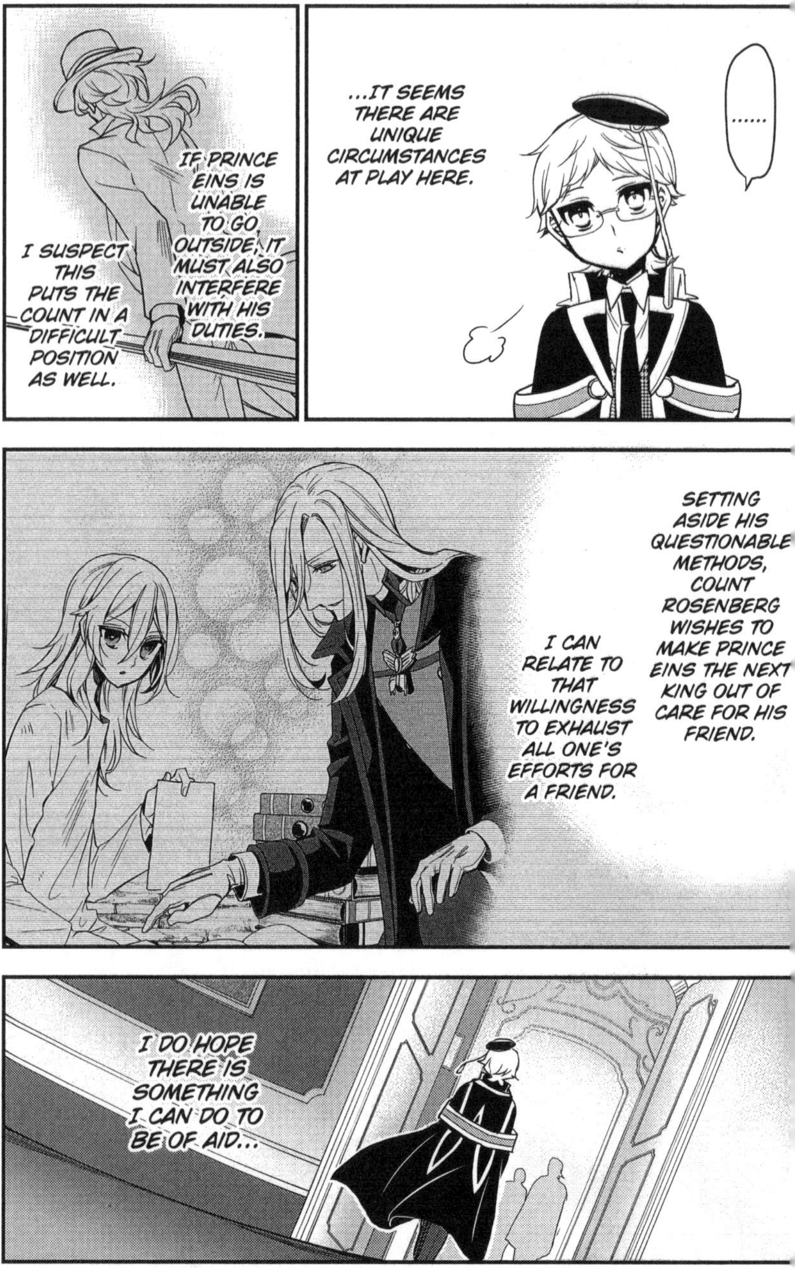
......
...IT SEEMS THERE ARE UNIQUE CIRCUMSTANCES AT PLAY HERE.
IF PRINCE EINS IS UNABLE TO GO OUTSIDE, IT MUST ALSO INTERFERE WITH HIS DUTIES.
I SUSPECT THIS PUTS THE COUNT IN A DIFFICULT POSITION AS WELL.
SETTING ASIDE HIS QUESTIONABLE METHODS, COUNT ROSENBERG WISHES TO MAKE PRINCE EINS THE NEXT KING OUT OF CARE FOR HIS FRIEND.
I CAN RELATE TO THAT WILLINGNESS TO EXHAUST ALL ONE'S EFFORTS FOR A FRIEND.
I DO HOPE THERE IS SOMETHING I CAN DO TO BE OF AID...

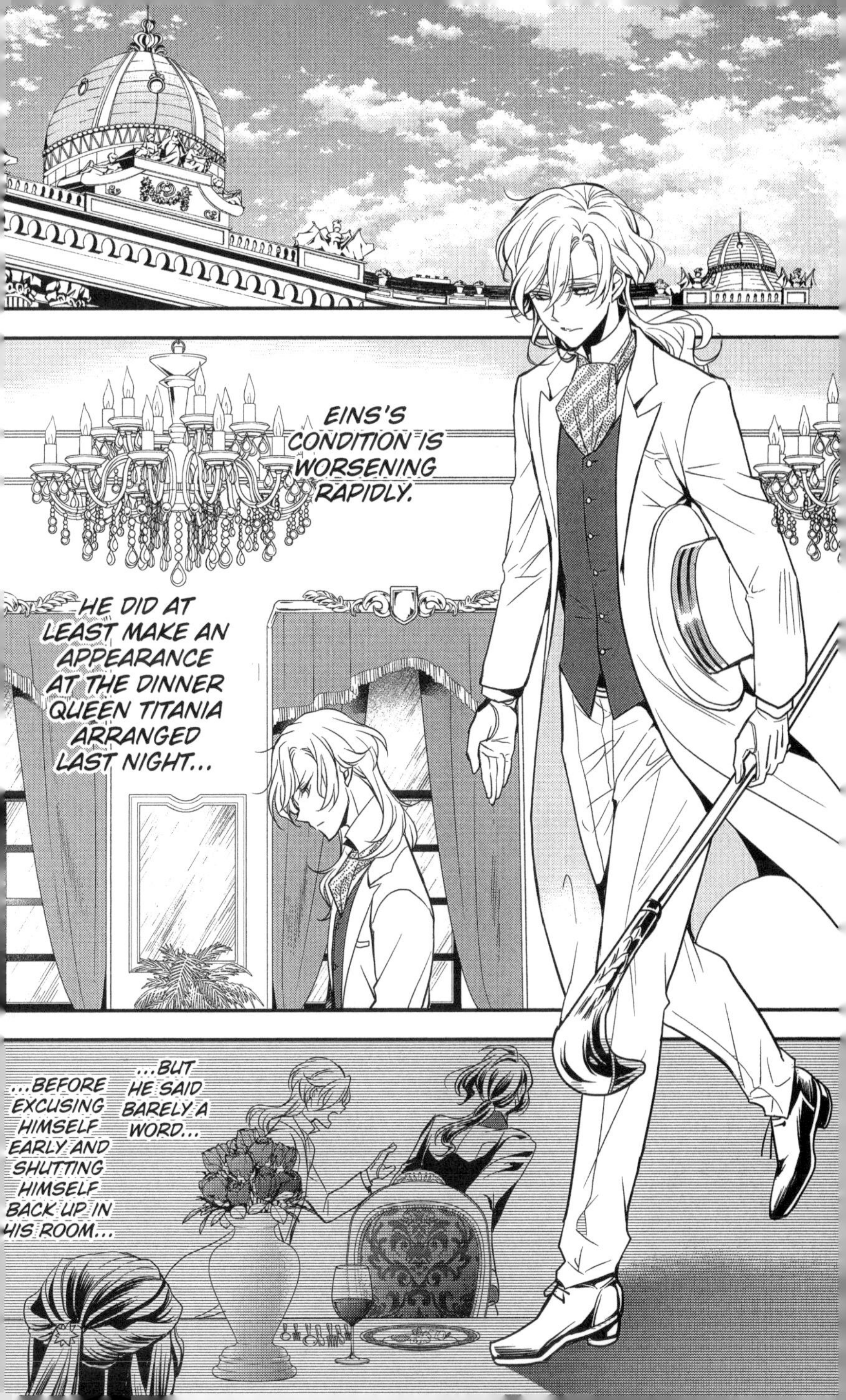
EINS'S CONDITION IS WORSENING RAPIDLY.
HE DID AT LEAST MAKE AN APPEARANCE AT THE DINNER QUEEN TITANIA ARRANGED LAST NIGHT...
...BUT HE SAID BARELY A WORD...
...BEFORE EXCUSING HIMSELF EARLY AND SHUTTING HIMSELF BACK UP IN HIS ROOM...

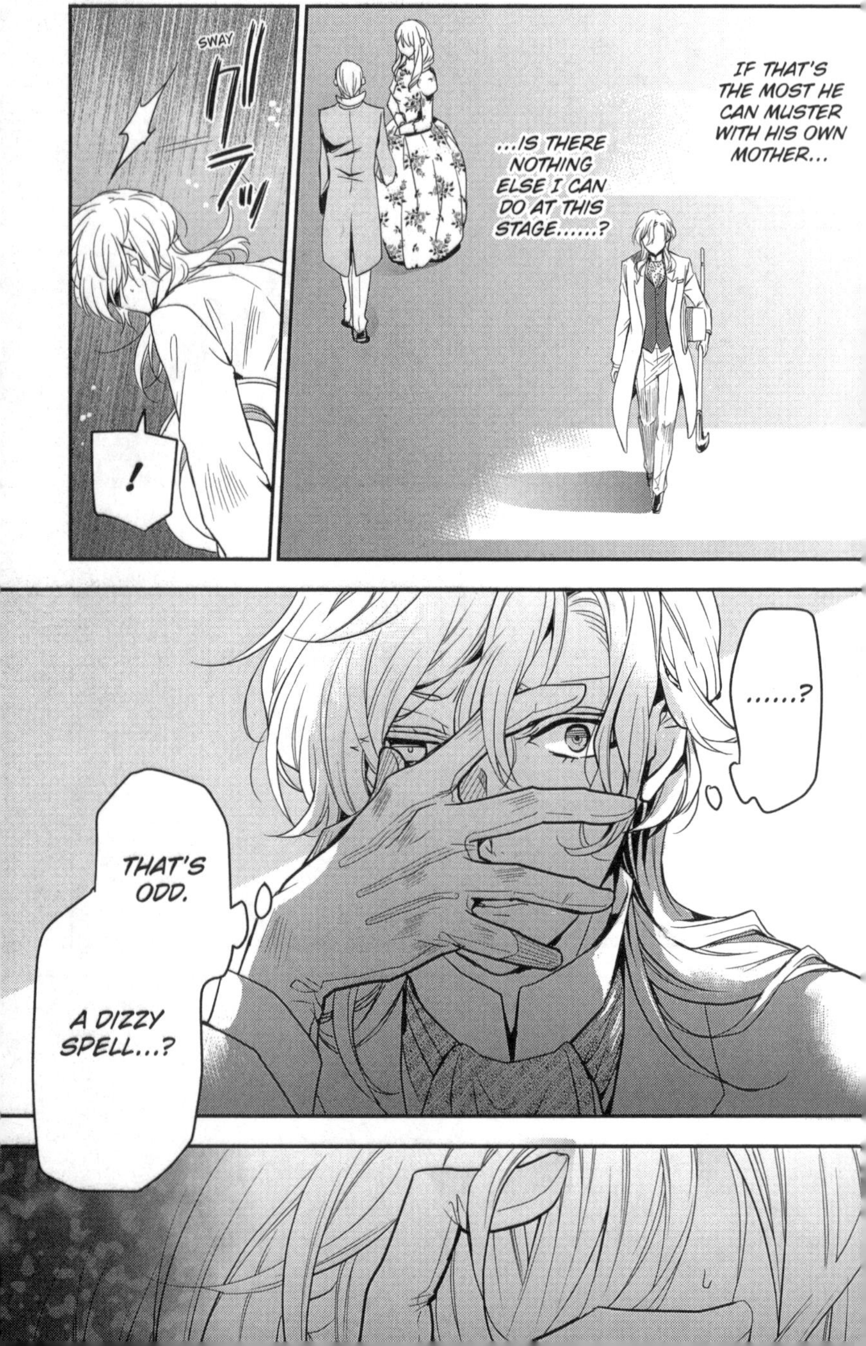
IF THAT'S THE MOST HE CAN MUSTER WITH HIS OWN MOTHER...
...IS THERE NOTHING ELSE I CAN DO AT THIS STAGE......?
SWAY
グラッ
!
......?
THAT'S ODD.
A DIZZY SPELL...?

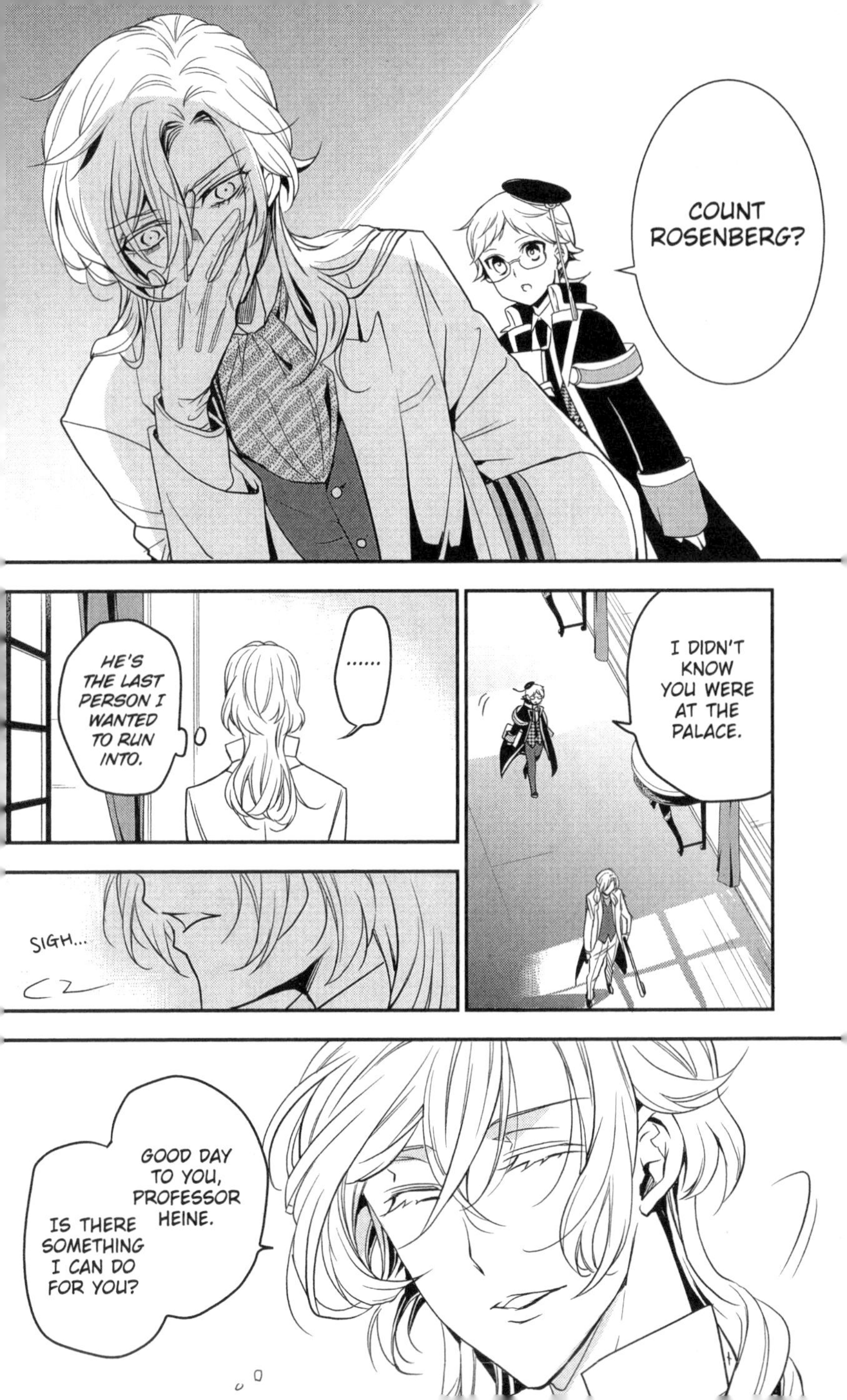
COUNT ROSENBERG?
I DIDN'T KNOW YOU WERE AT THE PALACE.
......
HE'S THE LAST PERSON I WANTED TO RUN INTO.
SIGH...
GOOD DAY TO YOU, PROFESSOR HEINE.
IS THERE SOMETHING I CAN DO FOR YOU?

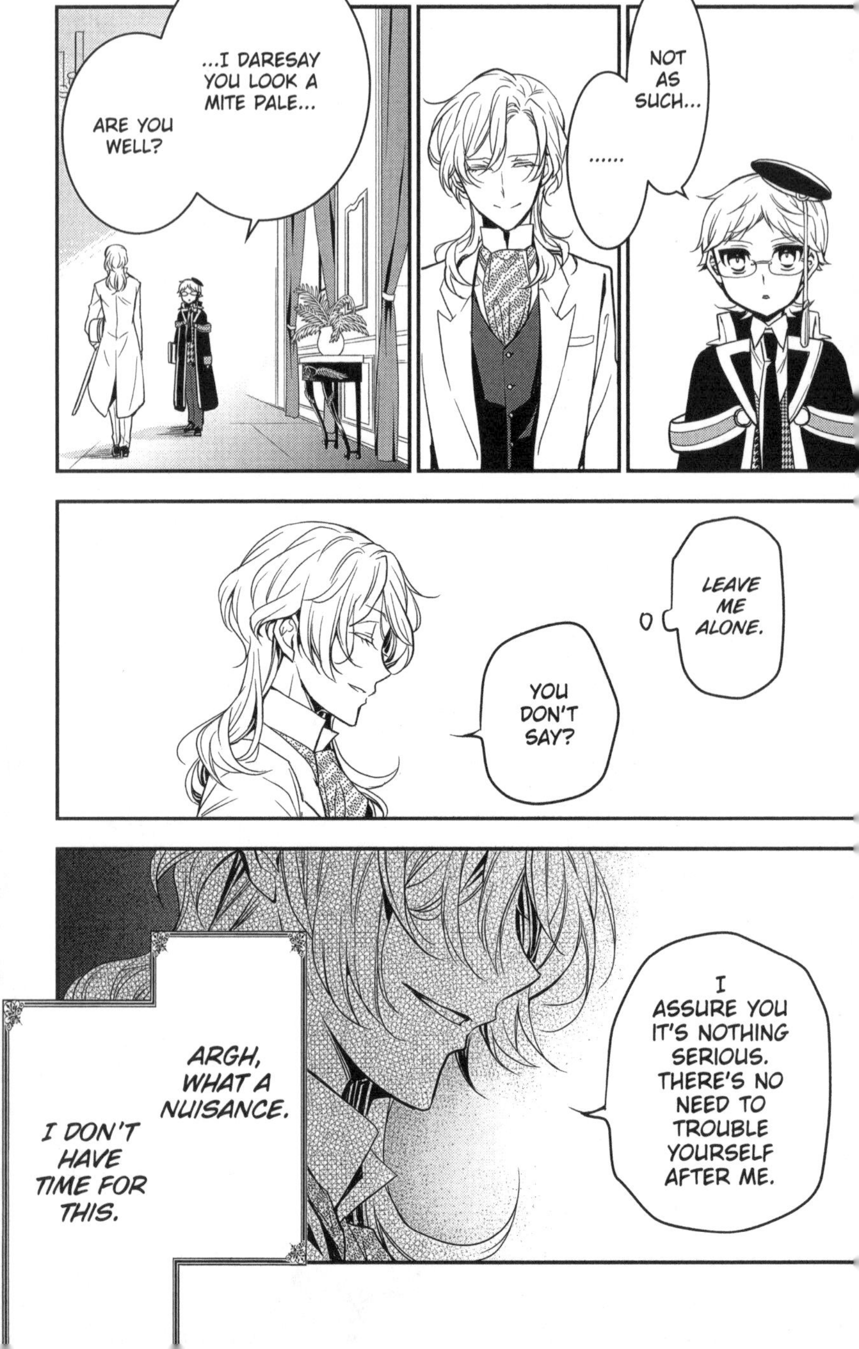
NOT AS SUCH...
......
...I DARESAY YOU LOOK A MITE PALE...
ARE YOU WELL?
LEAVE ME ALONE.
YOU DON'T SAY?
I ASSURE YOU IT'S NOTHING SERIOUS. THERE'S NO NEED TO TROUBLE YOURSELF AFTER ME.
ARGH, WHAT A NUISANCE.
I DON'T HAVE TIME FOR THIS.

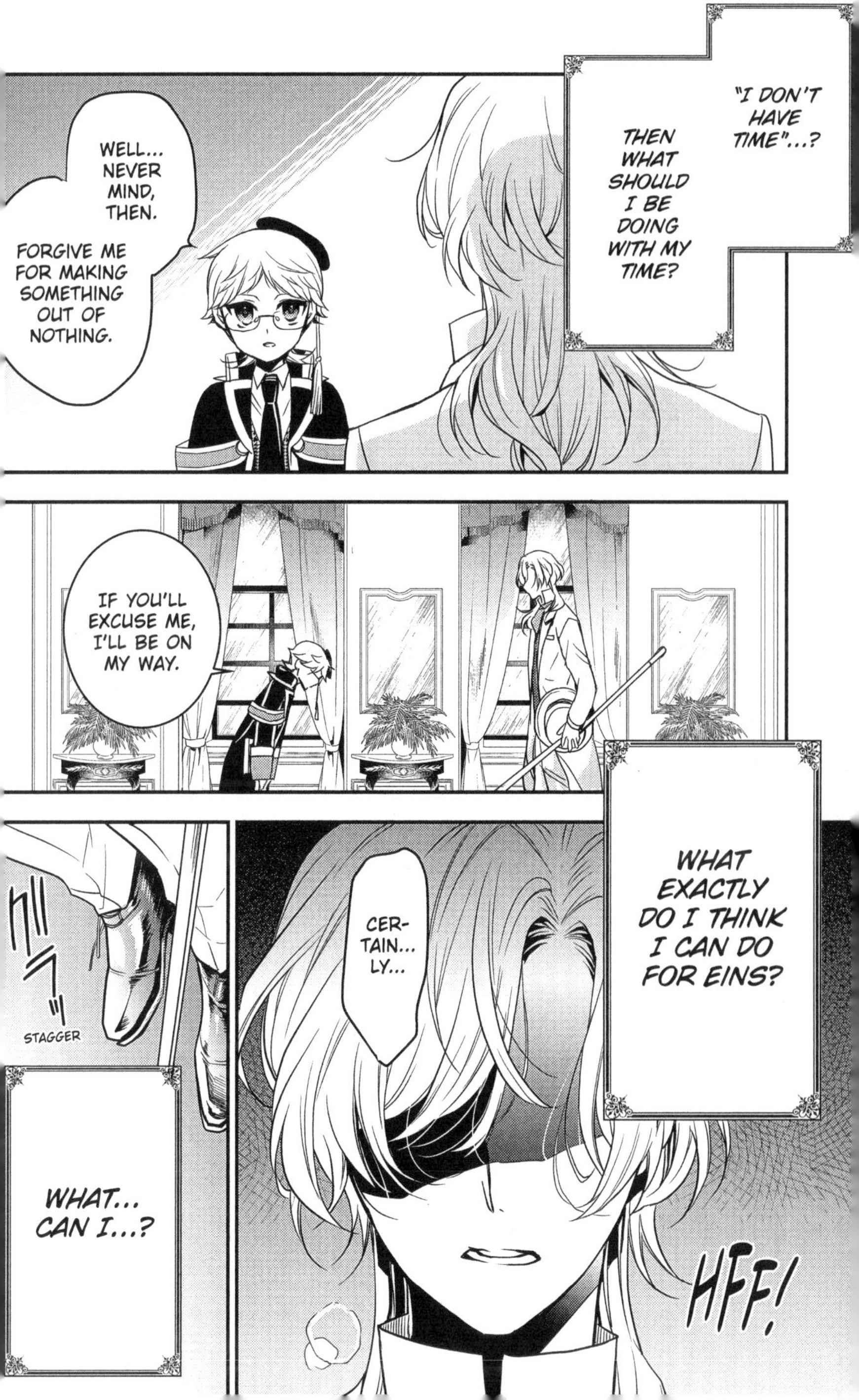
"I DON'T HAVE TIME"...?
THEN WHAT SHOULD I BE DOING WITH MY TIME?
WELL... NEVER MIND, THEN.
FORGIVE ME FOR MAKING SOMETHING OUT OF NOTHING.
IF YOU'LL EXCUSE ME, I'LL BE ON MY WAY.
WHAT EXACTLY DO I THINK I CAN DO FOR EINS?
CER-TAIN... LY...
HFF!
STAGGER
WHAT... CAN I...?

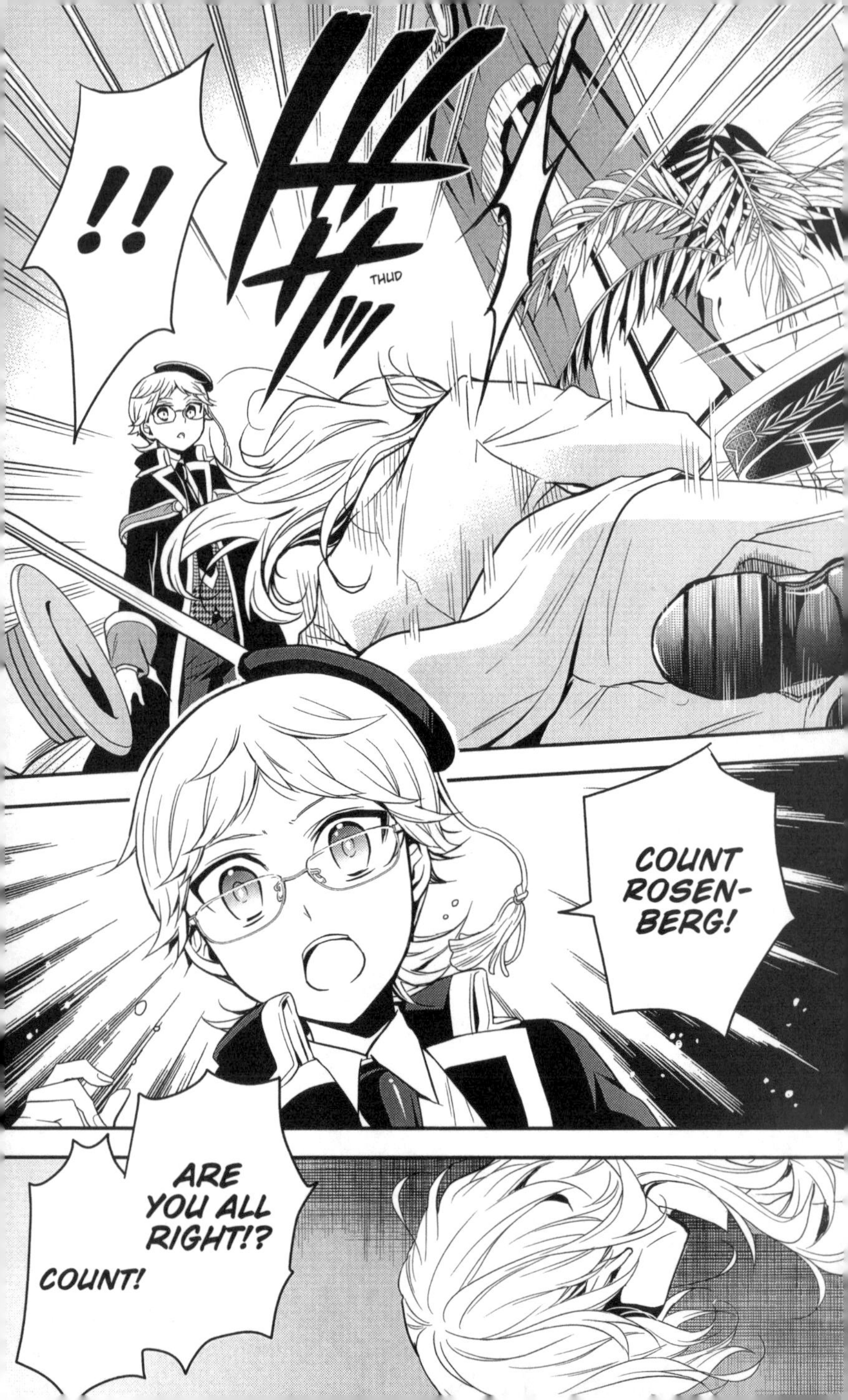
THUD
!!
COUNT ROSEN-BERG!
ARE YOU ALL RIGHT!?
COUNT!

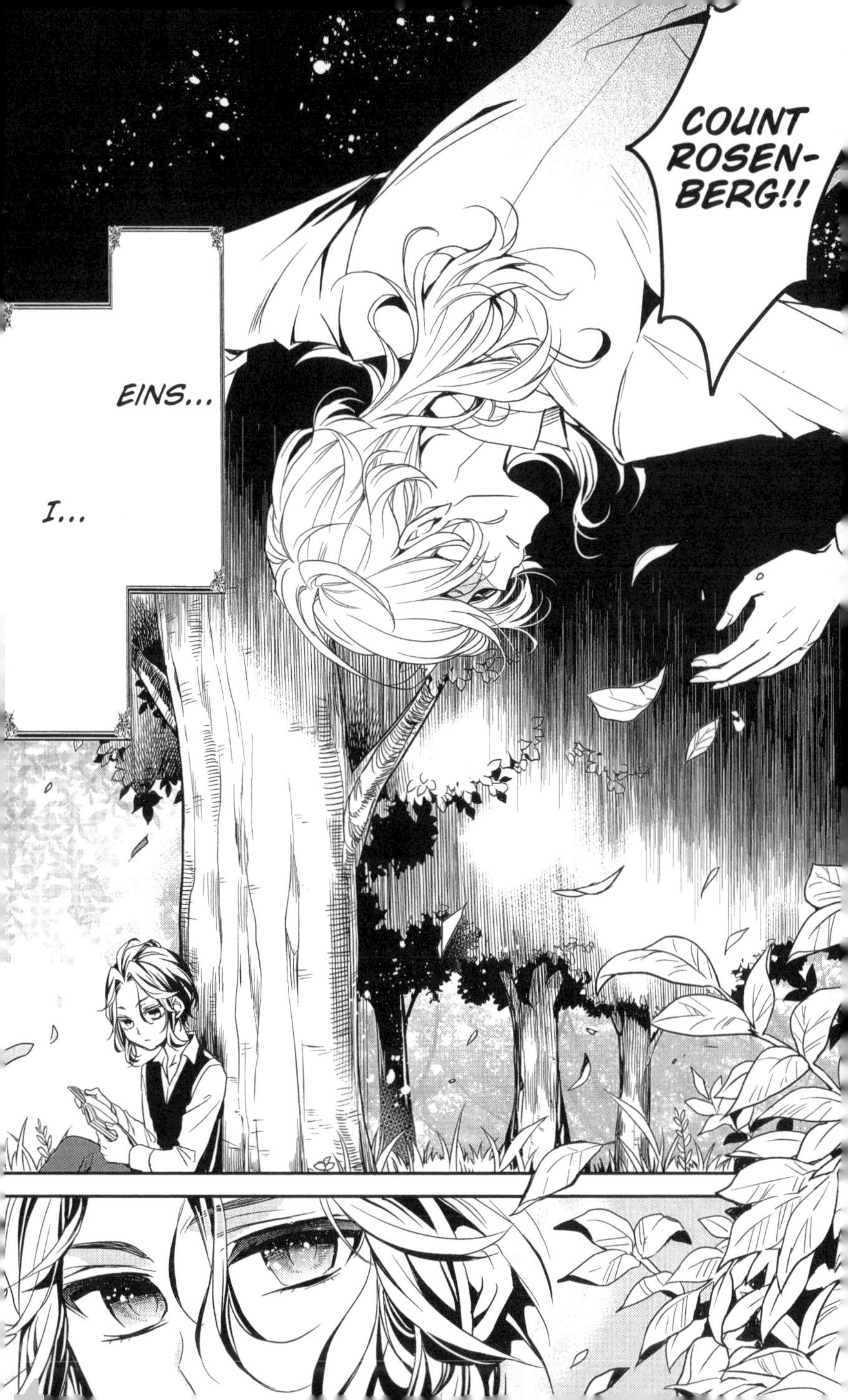
COUNT ROSEN-BERG!!
EINS...
I...

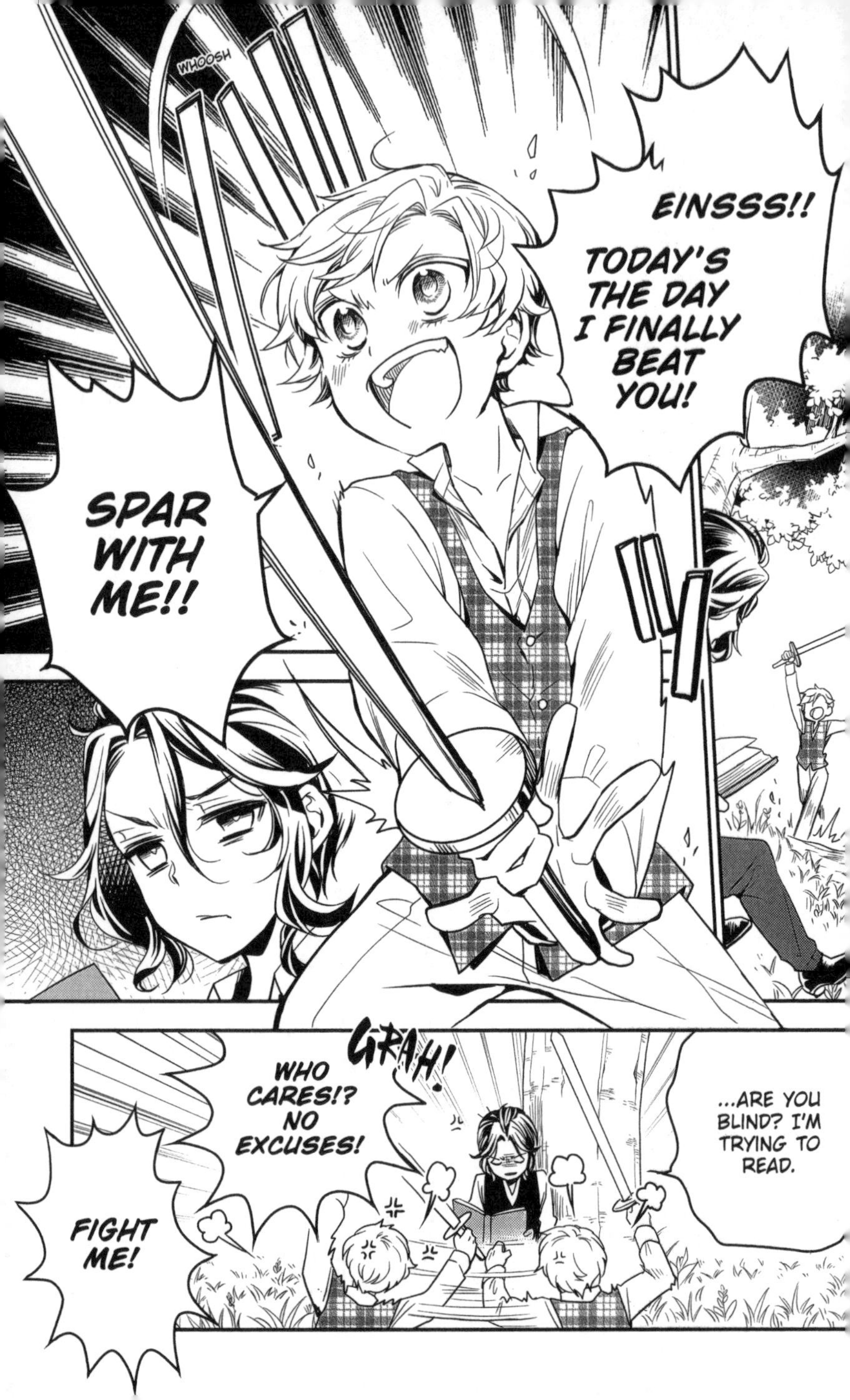
EINSSS!!
TODAY'S THE DAY I FINALLY BEAT YOU!
WHOOSH
SPAR WITH ME!!
...ARE YOU BLIND? I'M TRYING TO READ.
GRAH!
WHO CARES!? NO EXCUSES!
FIGHT ME!

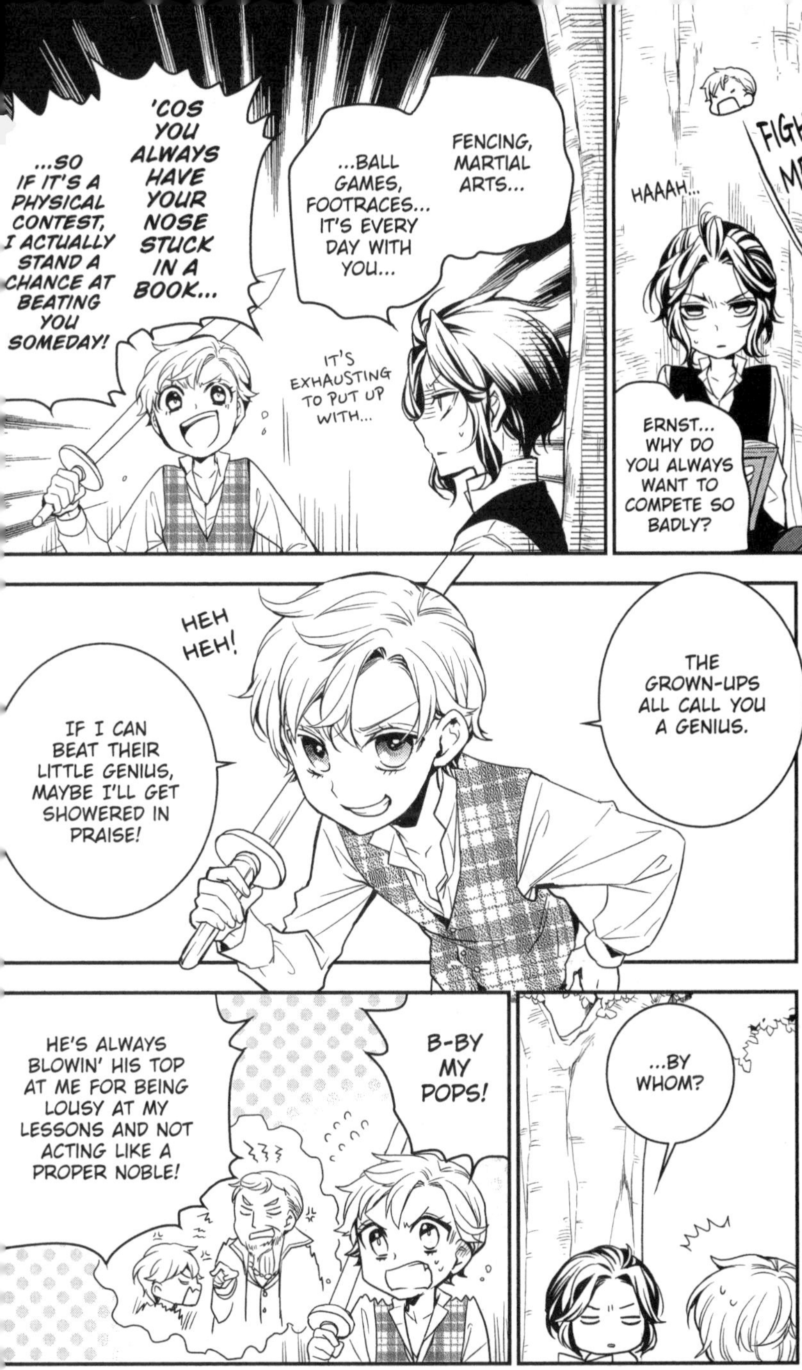

FIGHT ME!!
HAAAH...
ERNST... WHY DO YOU ALWAYS WANT TO COMPETE SO BADLY?
FENCING, MARTIAL ARTS...
...BALL GAMES, FOOTRACES... IT'S EVERY DAY WITH YOU...
'COS YOU ALWAYS HAVE YOUR NOSE STUCK IN A BOOK...
...SO IF IT'S A PHYSICAL CONTEST, I ACTUALLY STAND A CHANCE AT BEATING YOU SOMEDAY!
IT'S EXHAUSTING TO PUT UP WITH...
THE GROWN-UPS ALL CALL YOU A GENIUS.
HEH HEH!
IF I CAN BEAT THEIR LITTLE GENIUS, MAYBE I'LL GET SHOWERED IN PRAISE!
...BY WHOM?
B-BY MY POPS!
HE'S ALWAYS BLOWIN' HIS TOP AT ME FOR BEING LOUSY AT MY LESSONS AND NOT ACTING LIKE A PROPER NOBLE!

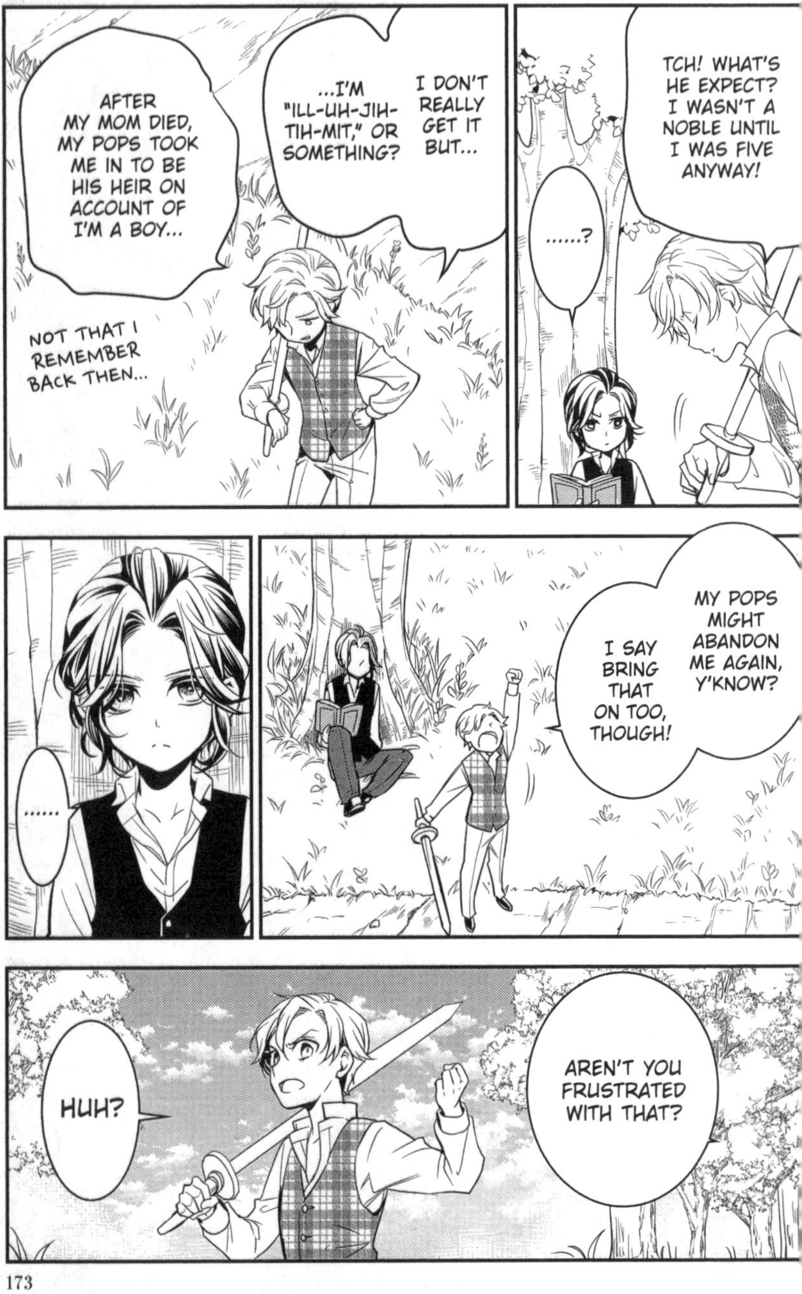
TCH! WHAT'S HE EXPECT? I WASN'T A NOBLE UNTIL I WAS FIVE ANYWAY!
......?
I DON'T REALLY GET IT BUT...
...I'M "ILL-UH-JIH-TIH-MIT," OR SOMETHING?
AFTER MY MOM DIED, MY POPS TOOK ME IN TO BE HIS HEIR ON ACCOUNT OF I'M A BOY...
NOT THAT I REMEMBER BACK THEN...
MY POPS MIGHT ABANDON ME AGAIN, Y'KNOW?
I SAY BRING THAT ON TOO, THOUGH!
......
AREN'T YOU FRUSTRATED WITH THAT?
HUH?

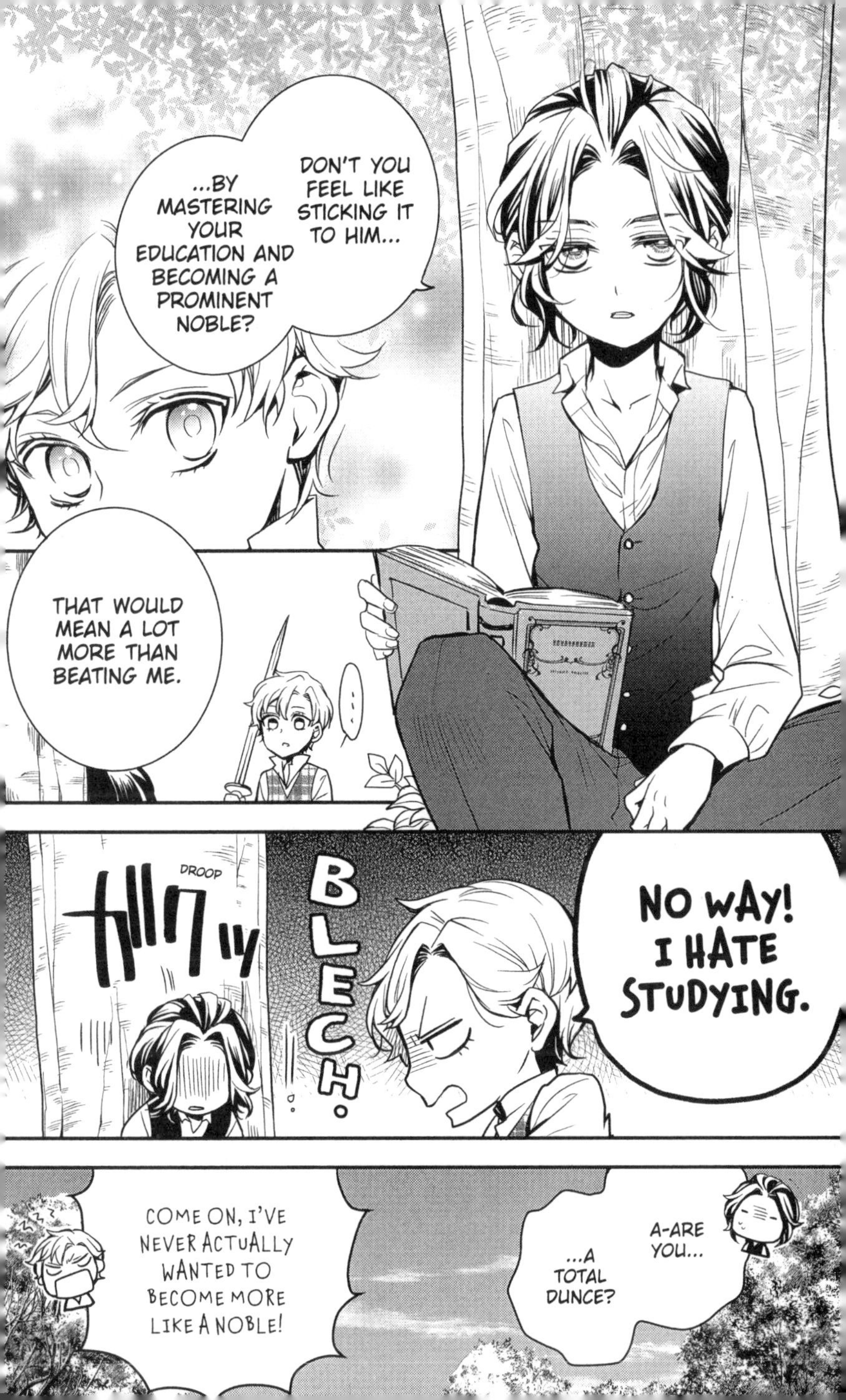

DON'T YOU FEEL LIKE STICKING IT TO HIM...
...BY MASTERING YOUR EDUCATION AND BECOMING A PROMINENT NOBLE?
THAT WOULD MEAN A LOT MORE THAN BEATING ME.
...
NO WAY! I HATE STUDYING.
BLECH.
DROOP
A-ARE YOU...
...A TOTAL DUNCE?
COME ON, I'VE NEVER ACTUALLY WANTED TO BECOME MORE LIKE A NOBLE!

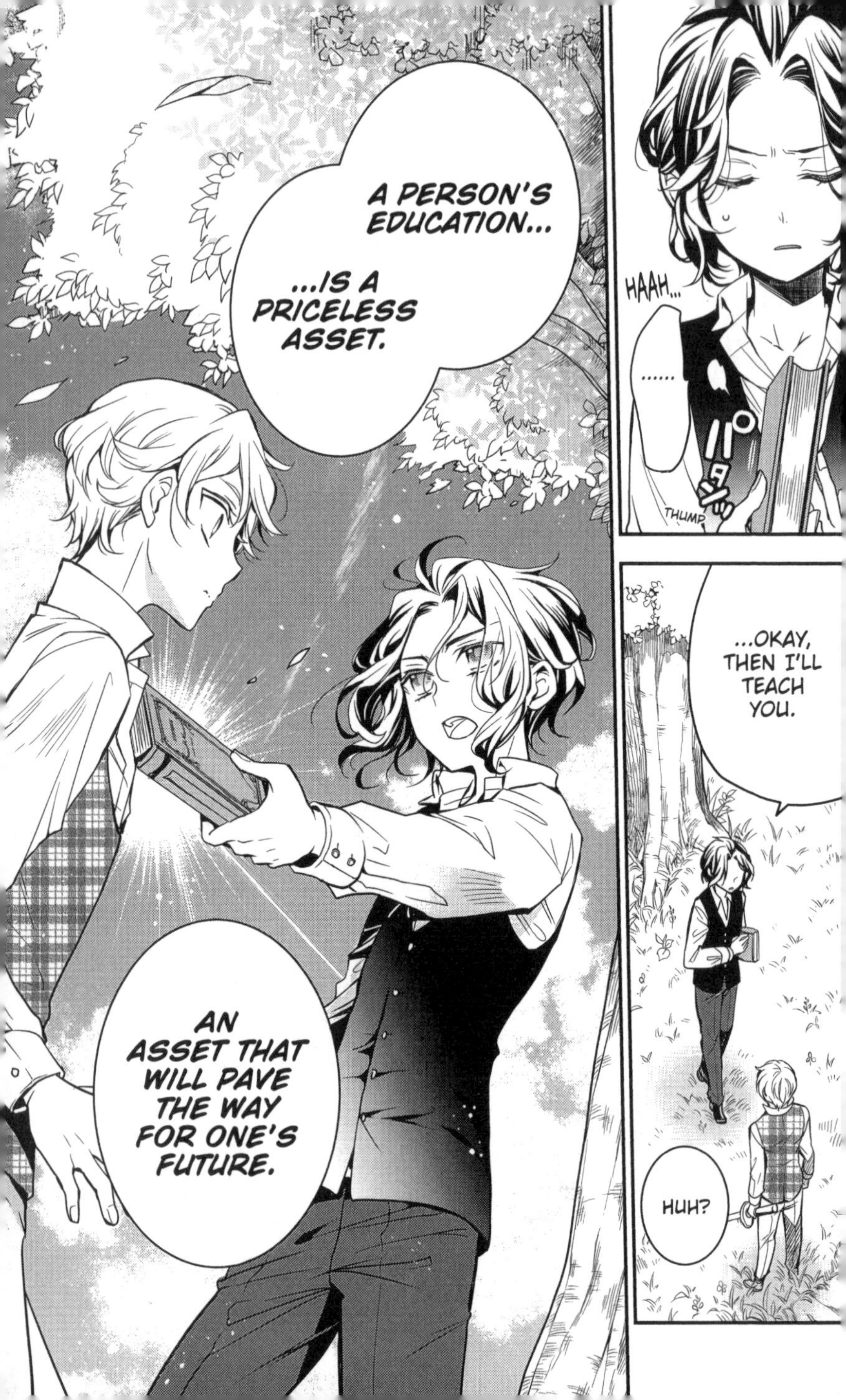
HAAH...
......
パタン
THUMP
...OKAY, THEN I'LL TEACH YOU.
HUH?
A PERSON'S EDUCATION...
...IS A PRICELESS ASSET.
AN ASSET THAT WILL PAVE THE WAY FOR ONE'S FUTURE.

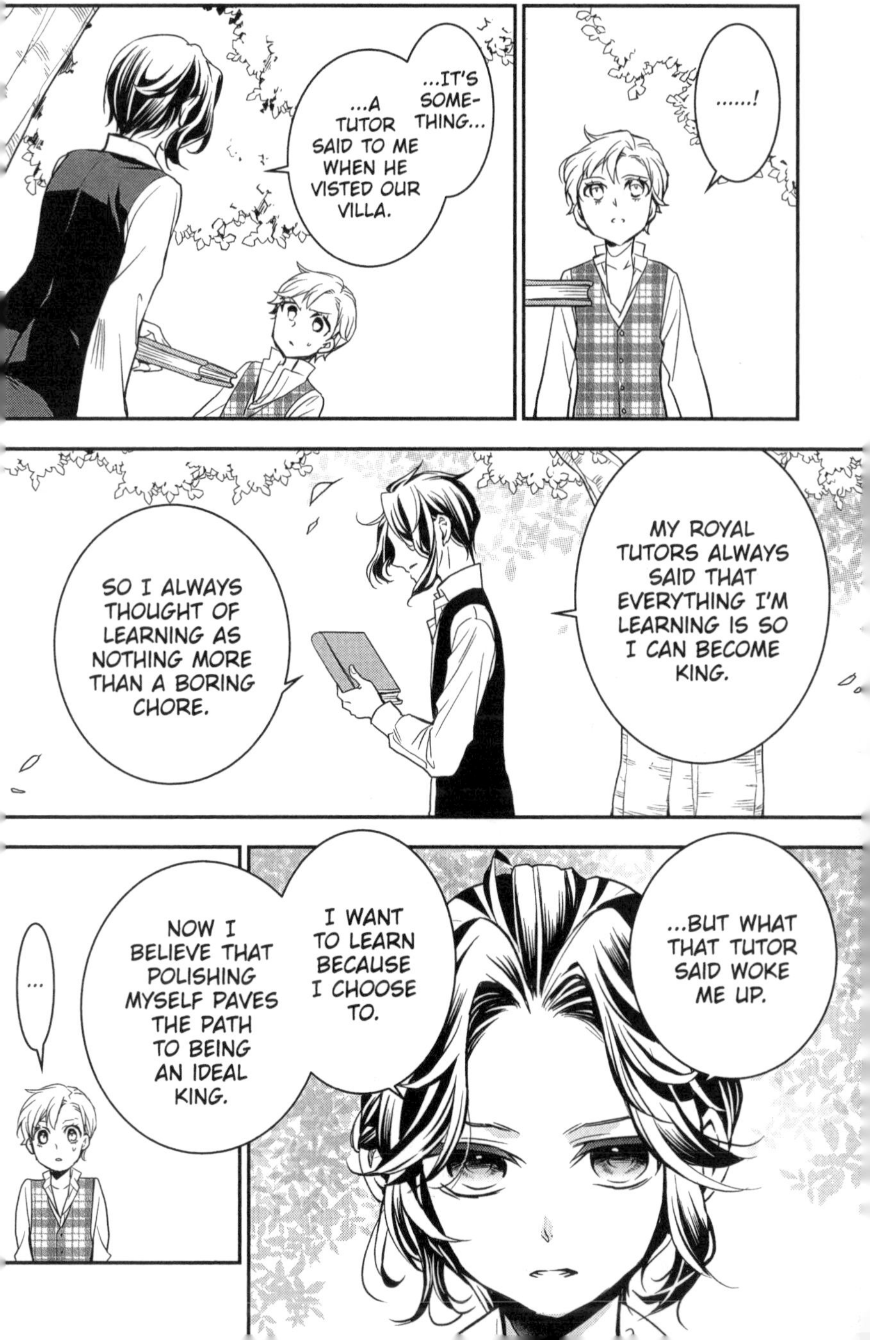
......!
...IT'S SOMETHING... ...A TUTOR SAID TO ME WHEN HE VISTED OUR VILLA.
MY ROYAL TUTORS ALWAYS SAID THAT EVERYTHING I'M LEARNING IS SO I CAN BECOME KING.
SO I ALWAYS THOUGHT OF LEARNING AS NOTHING MORE THAN A BORING CHORE.
...BUT WHAT THAT TUTOR SAID WOKE ME UP.
I WANT TO LEARN BECAUSE I CHOOSE TO.
NOW I BELIEVE THAT POLISHING MYSELF PAVES THE PATH TO BEING AN IDEAL KING.
...

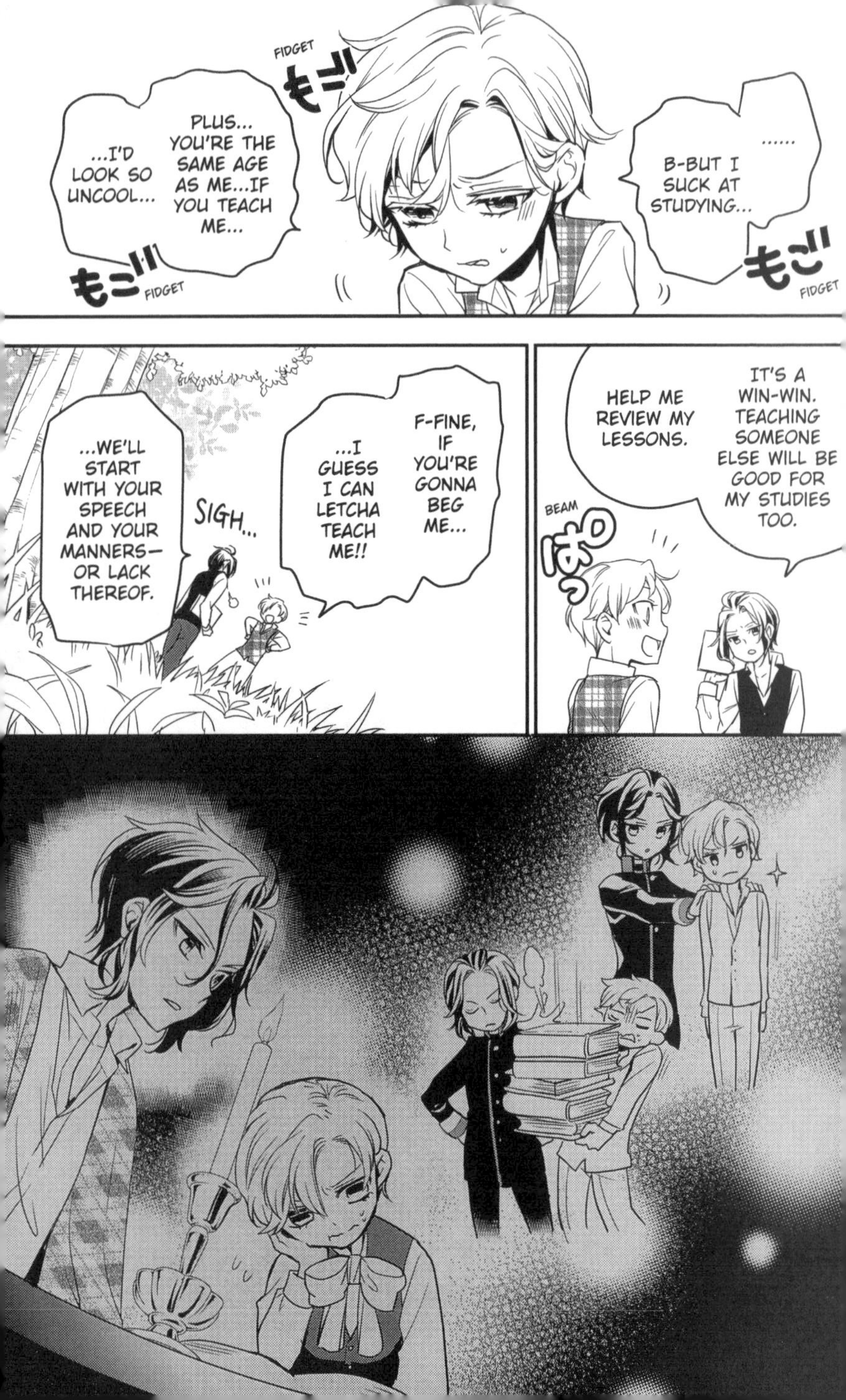
......
B-BUT I SUCK AT STUDYING...
もご
FIDGET
もご
FIDGET
PLUS... YOU'RE THE SAME AGE AS ME...IF YOU TEACH ME...
...I'D LOOK SO UNCOOL...
もご
FIDGET
IT'S A WIN-WIN. TEACHING SOMEONE ELSE WILL BE GOOD FOR MY STUDIES TOO.
HELP ME REVIEW MY LESSONS.
ぱっ
BEAM
F-FINE, IF YOU'RE GONNA BEG ME...
...I GUESS I CAN LETCHA TEACH ME!!
SIGH...
...WE'LL START WITH YOUR SPEECH AND YOUR MANNERS—OR LACK THEREOF.

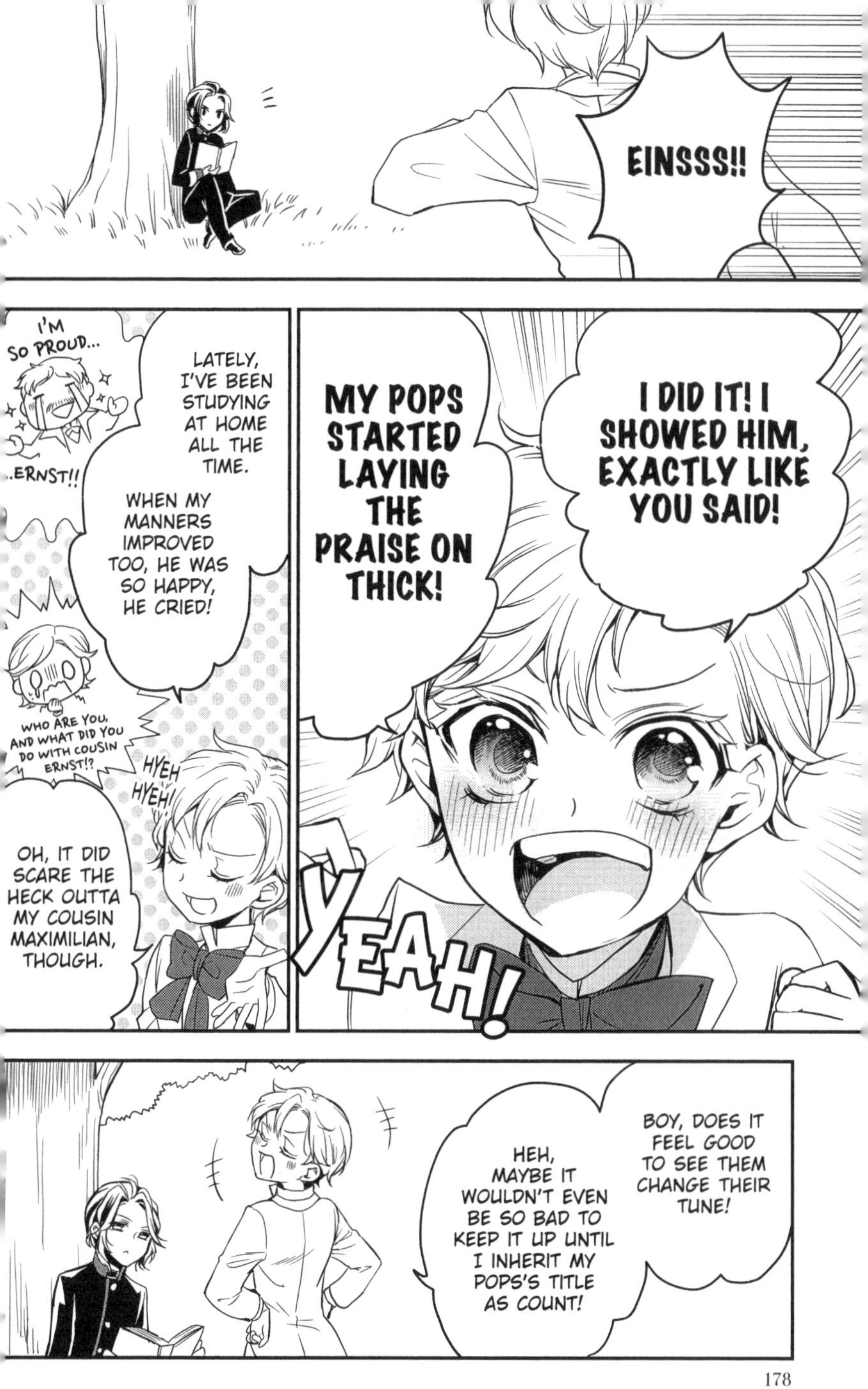
EINSSS!!
I DID IT! I SHOWED HIM, EXACTLY LIKE YOU SAID!
MY POPS STARTED LAYING THE PRAISE ON THICK!
YEAH!
LATELY, I'VE BEEN STUDYING AT HOME ALL THE TIME.
I'M SO PROUD... ...ERNST!!
WHEN MY MANNERS IMPROVED TOO, HE WAS SO HAPPY, HE CRIED!
WHO ARE YOU, AND WHAT DID YOU DO WITH COUSIN ERNST!?
HYEH HYEH!
OH, IT DID SCARE THE HECK OUTTA MY COUSIN MAXIMILIAN, THOUGH.
BOY, DOES IT FEEL GOOD TO SEE THEM CHANGE THEIR TUNE!
HEH, MAYBE IT WOULDN'T EVEN BE SO BAD TO KEEP IT UP UNTIL I INHERIT MY POPS'S TITLE AS COUNT!

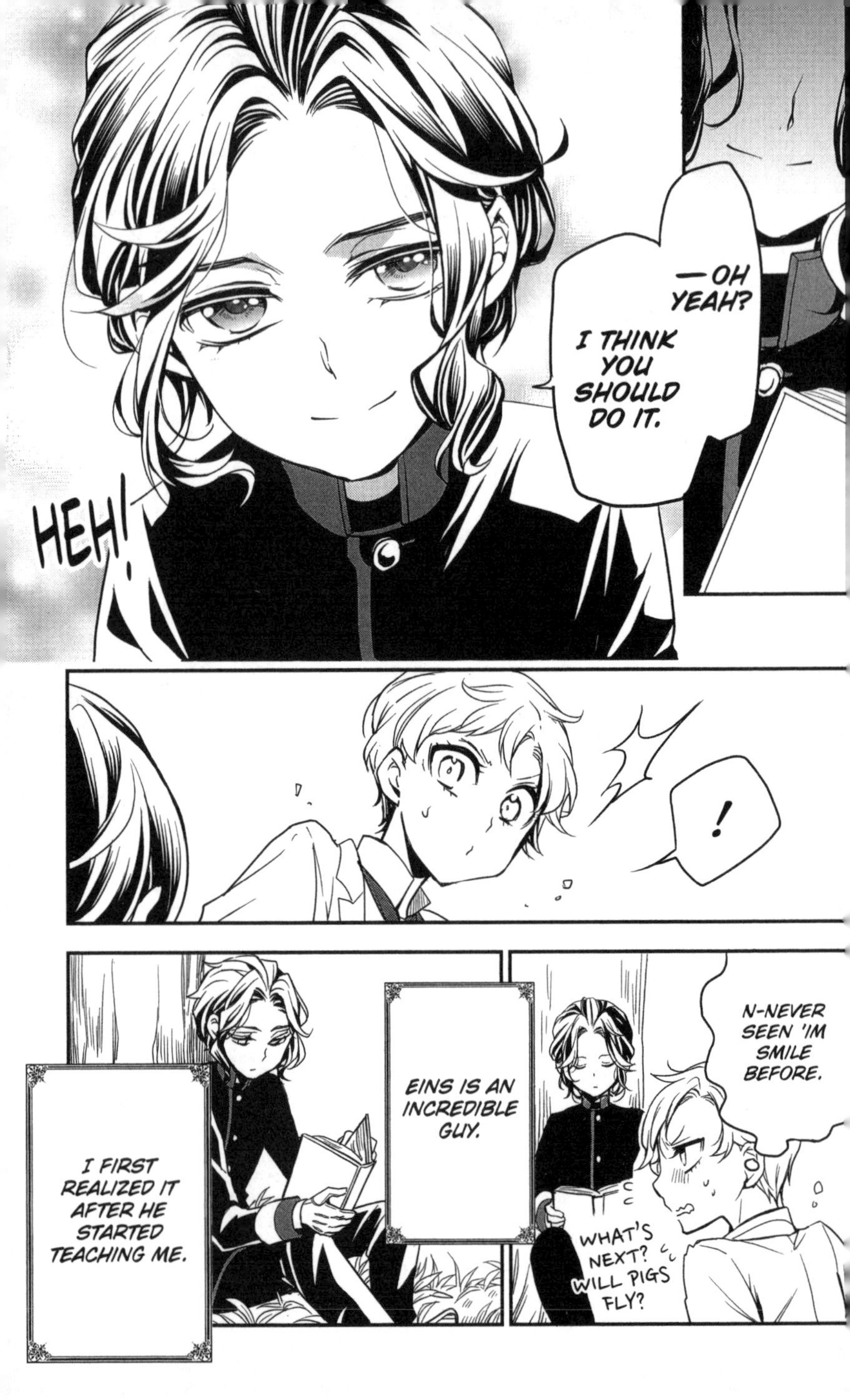
—OH YEAH?
I THINK YOU SHOULD DO IT.
HEH!
!
N-NEVER SEEN 'IM SMILE BEFORE.
WHAT'S NEXT? WILL PIGS FLY?
EINS IS AN INCREDIBLE GUY.
I FIRST REALIZED IT AFTER HE STARTED TEACHING ME.

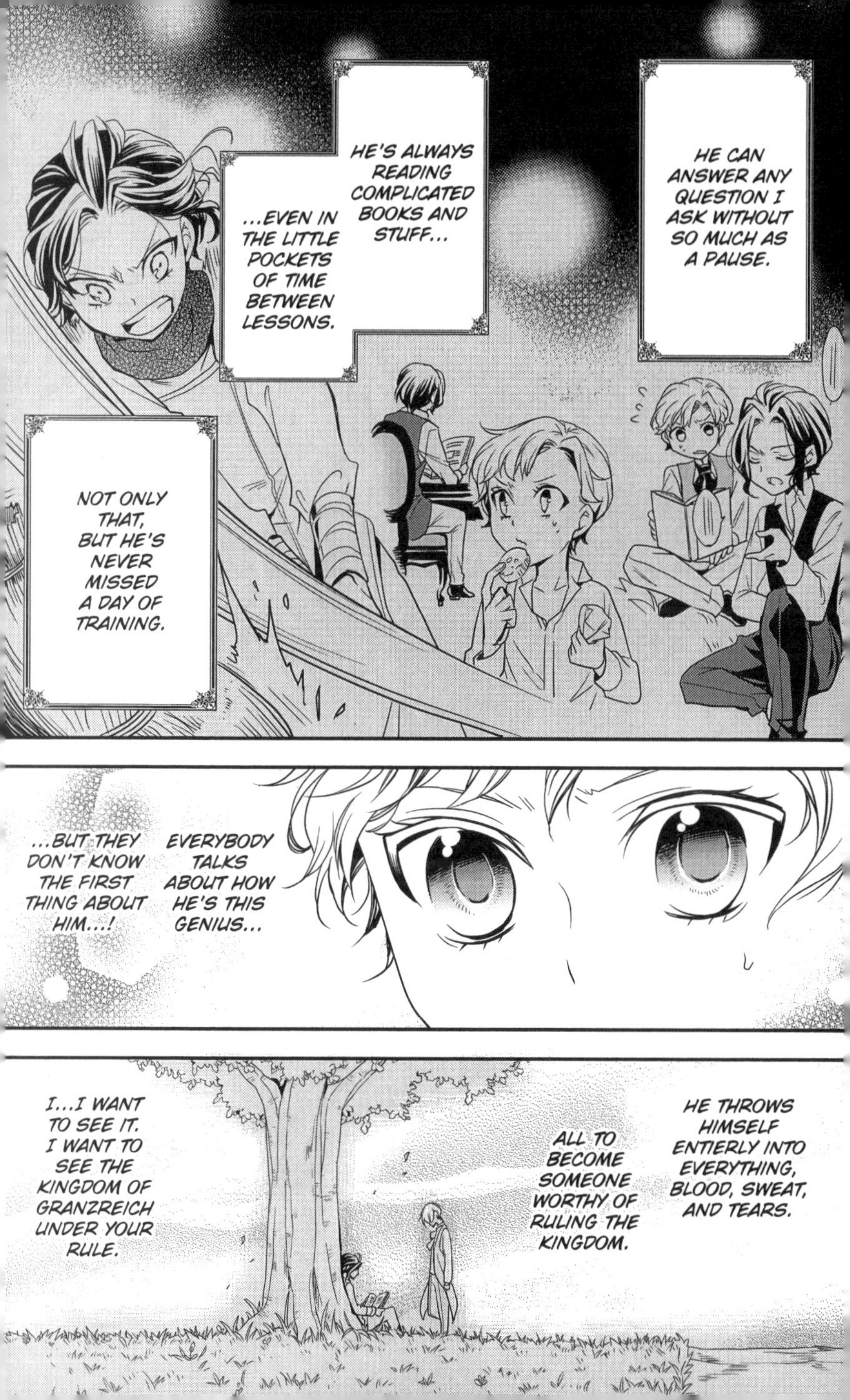
HE CAN ANSWER ANY QUESTION I ASK WITHOUT SO MUCH AS A PAUSE.
HE'S ALWAYS READING COMPLICATED BOOKS AND STUFF...
...EVEN IN THE LITTLE POCKETS OF TIME BETWEEN LESSONS.
NOT ONLY THAT, BUT HE'S NEVER MISSED A DAY OF TRAINING.
EVERYBODY TALKS ABOUT HOW HE'S THIS GENIUS...
...BUT THEY DON'T KNOW THE FIRST THING ABOUT HIM...!
HE THROWS HIMSELF ENTIERLY INTO EVERYTHING, BLOOD, SWEAT, AND TEARS.
ALL TO BECOME SOMEONE WORTHY OF RULING THE KINGDOM.
I...I WANT TO SEE IT. I WANT TO SEE THE KINGDOM OF GRANZREICH UNDER YOUR RULE.

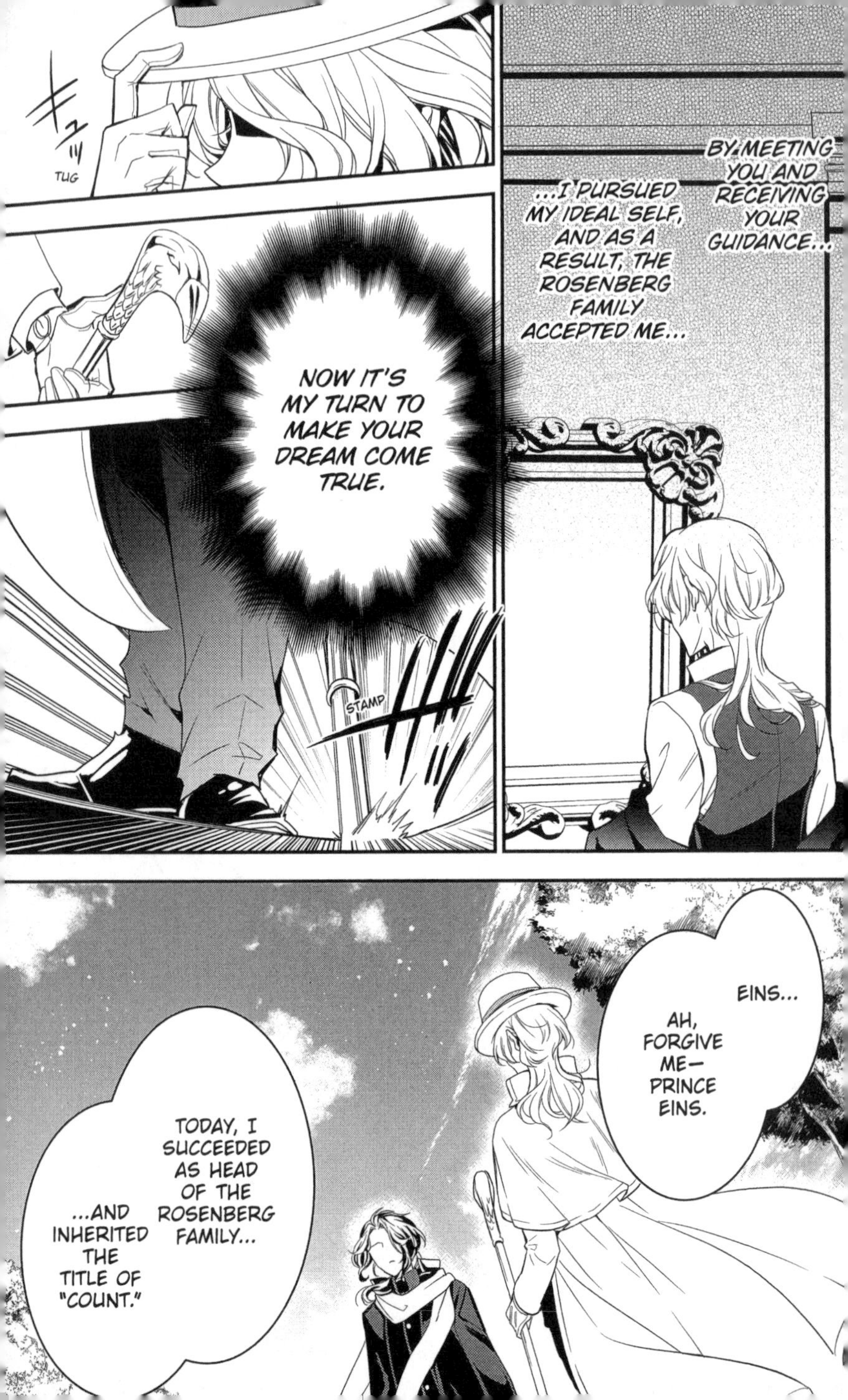
BY MEETING YOU AND RECEIVING YOUR GUIDANCE...
...I PURSUED MY IDEAL SELF, AND AS A RESULT, THE ROSENBERG FAMILY ACCEPTED ME...
TUG
NOW IT'S MY TURN TO MAKE YOUR DREAM COME TRUE.
STAMP
EINS...
AH, FORGIVE ME—PRINCE EINS.
TODAY, I SUCCEEDED AS HEAD OF THE ROSENBERG FAMILY...
...AND INHERITED THE TITLE OF "COUNT."

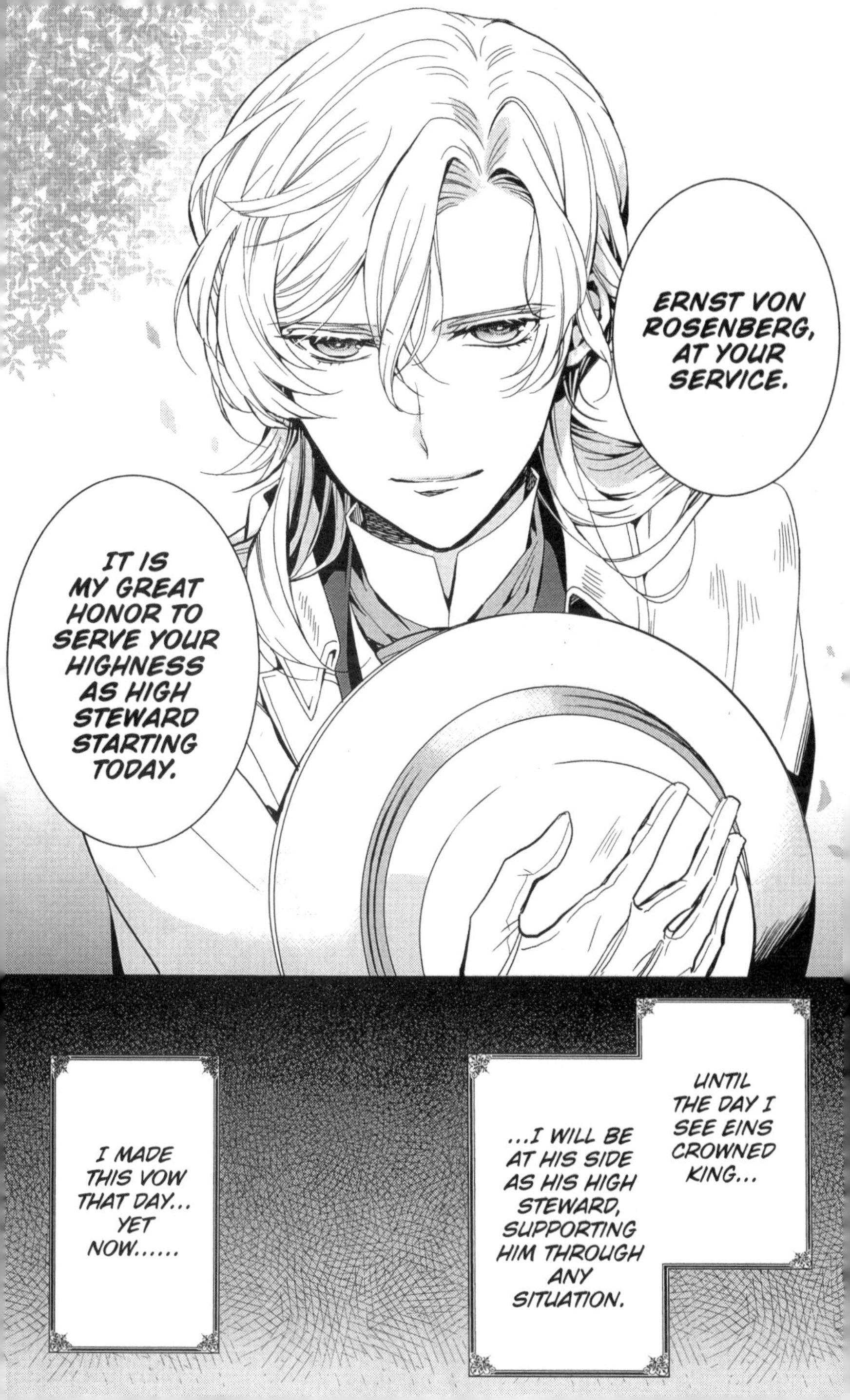
ERNST VON ROSENBERG, AT YOUR SERVICE.
IT IS MY GREAT HONOR TO SERVE YOUR HIGHNESS AS HIGH STEWARD STARTING TODAY.
UNTIL THE DAY I SEE EINS CROWNED KING...
...I WILL BE AT HIS SIDE AS HIS HIGH STEWARD, SUPPORTING HIM THROUGH ANY SITUATION.
I MADE THIS VOW THAT DAY... YET NOW......

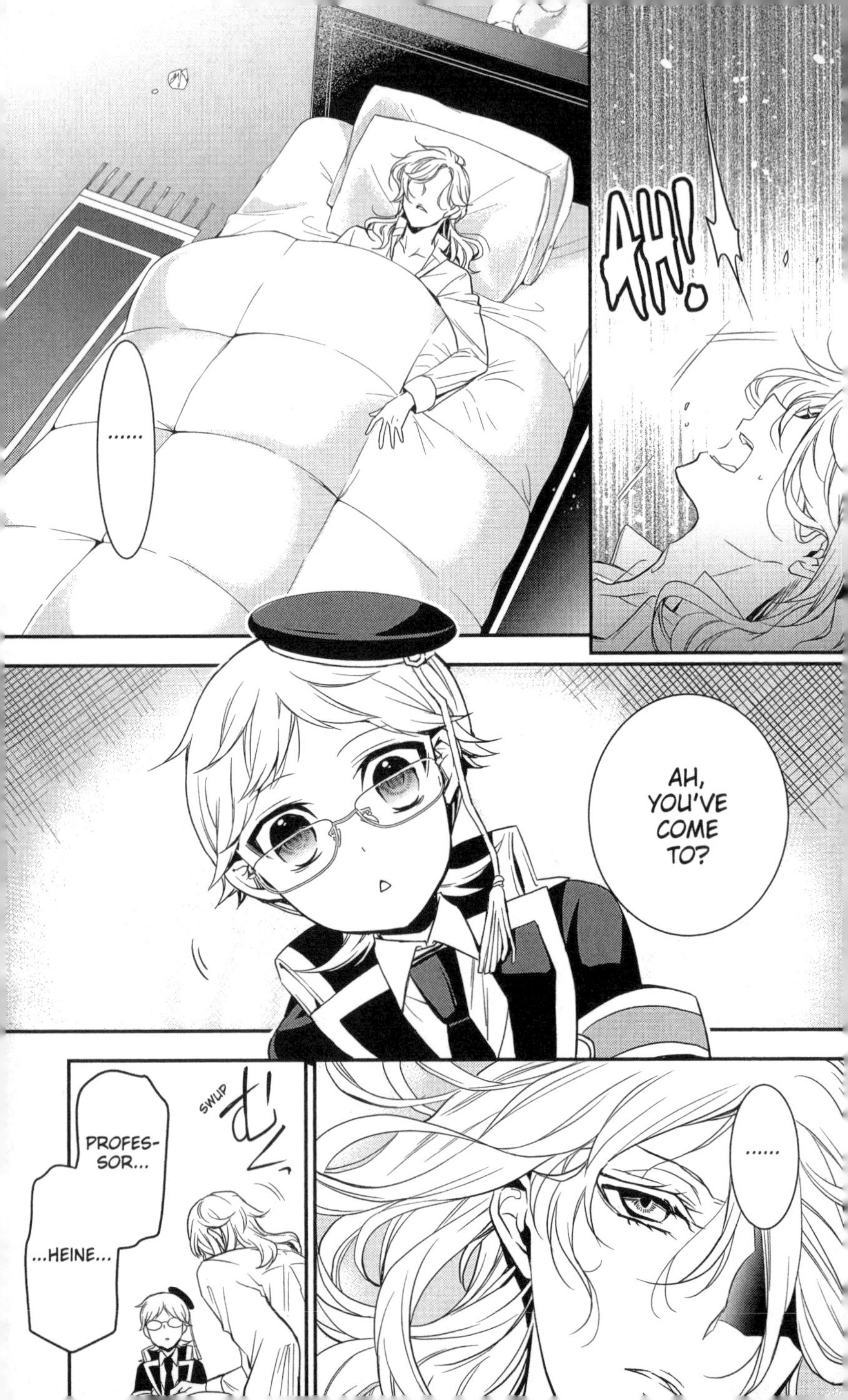
AH!
......
AH, YOU'VE COME TO?
......
SWUP
PROFES-SOR...
...HEINE...

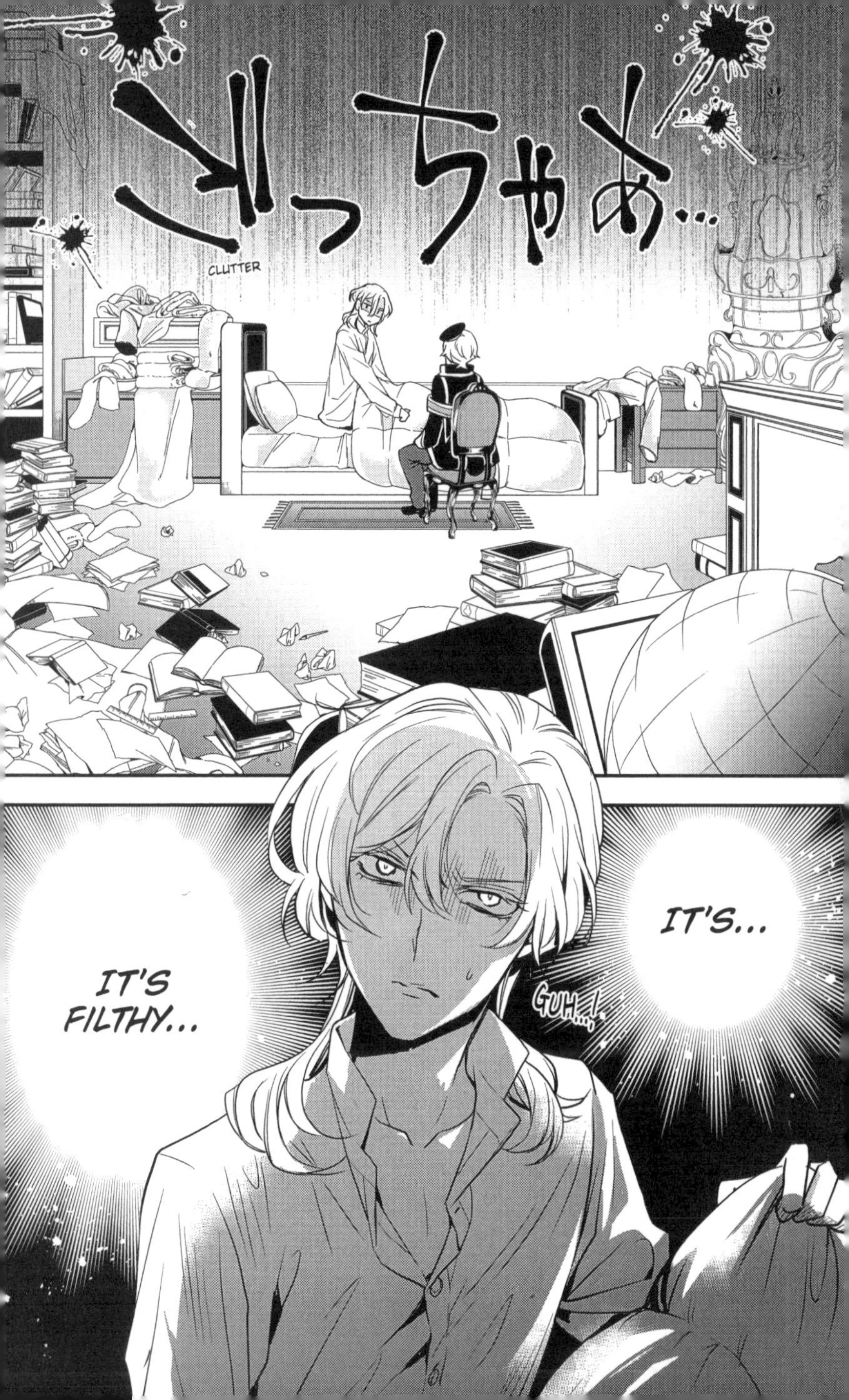
ごっちゃあ…
CLUTTER
IT'S...
GUH...!
IT'S FILTHY...

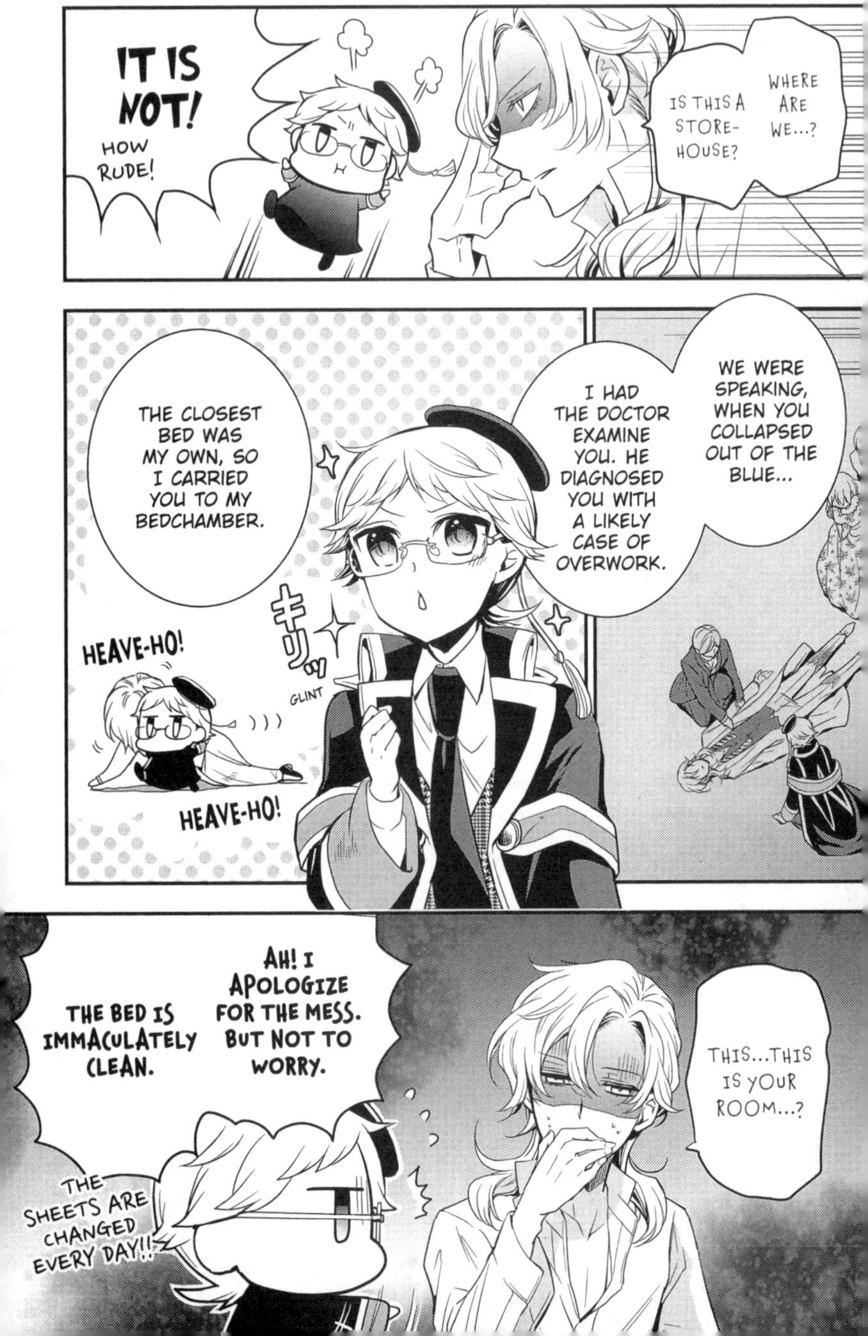
WHERE ARE WE...?
IS THIS A STOREHOUSE?
IT IS NOT!
HOW RUDE!
WE WERE SPEAKING, WHEN YOU COLLAPSED OUT OF THE BLUE...
I HAD THE DOCTOR EXAMINE YOU. HE DIAGNOSED YOU WITH A LIKELY CASE OF OVERWORK.
THE CLOSEST BED WAS MY OWN, SO I CARRIED YOU TO MY BEDCHAMBER.
GLINT
HEAVE-HO!
HEAVE-HO!
THIS...THIS IS YOUR ROOM...?
AH! I APOLOGIZE FOR THE MESS. BUT NOT TO WORRY.
THE BED IS IMMACULATELY CLEAN.
THE SHEETS ARE CHANGED EVERY DAY!!

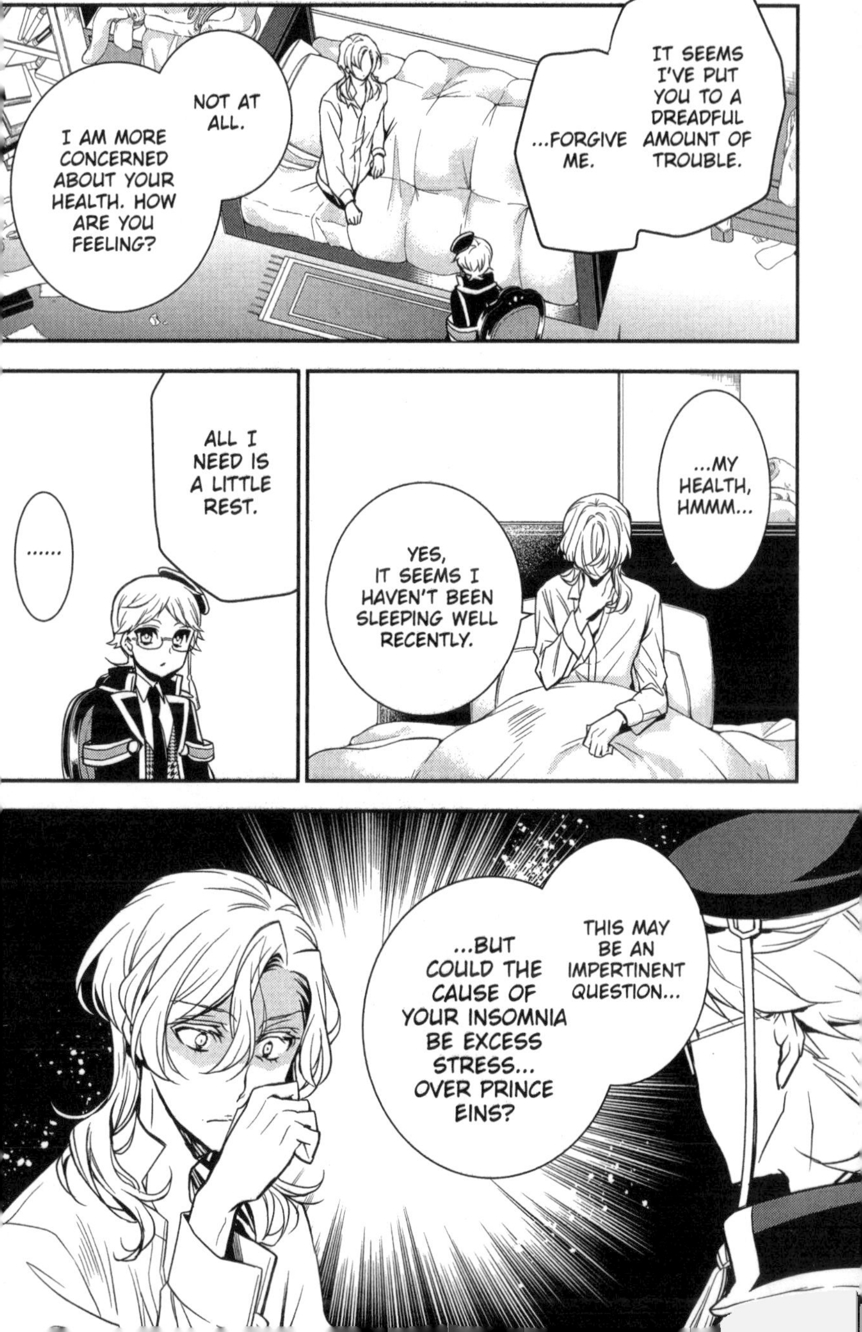
IT SEEMS I'VE PUT YOU TO A DREADFUL AMOUNT OF TROUBLE.
...FORGIVE ME.
NOT AT ALL.
I AM MORE CONCERNED ABOUT YOUR HEALTH. HOW ARE YOU FEELING?
...MY HEALTH, HMMM...
YES, IT SEEMS I HAVEN'T BEEN SLEEPING WELL RECENTLY.
ALL I NEED IS A LITTLE REST.
......
THIS MAY BE AN IMPERTINENT QUESTION...
...BUT COULD THE CAUSE OF YOUR INSOMNIA BE EXCESS STRESS... OVER PRINCE EINS?

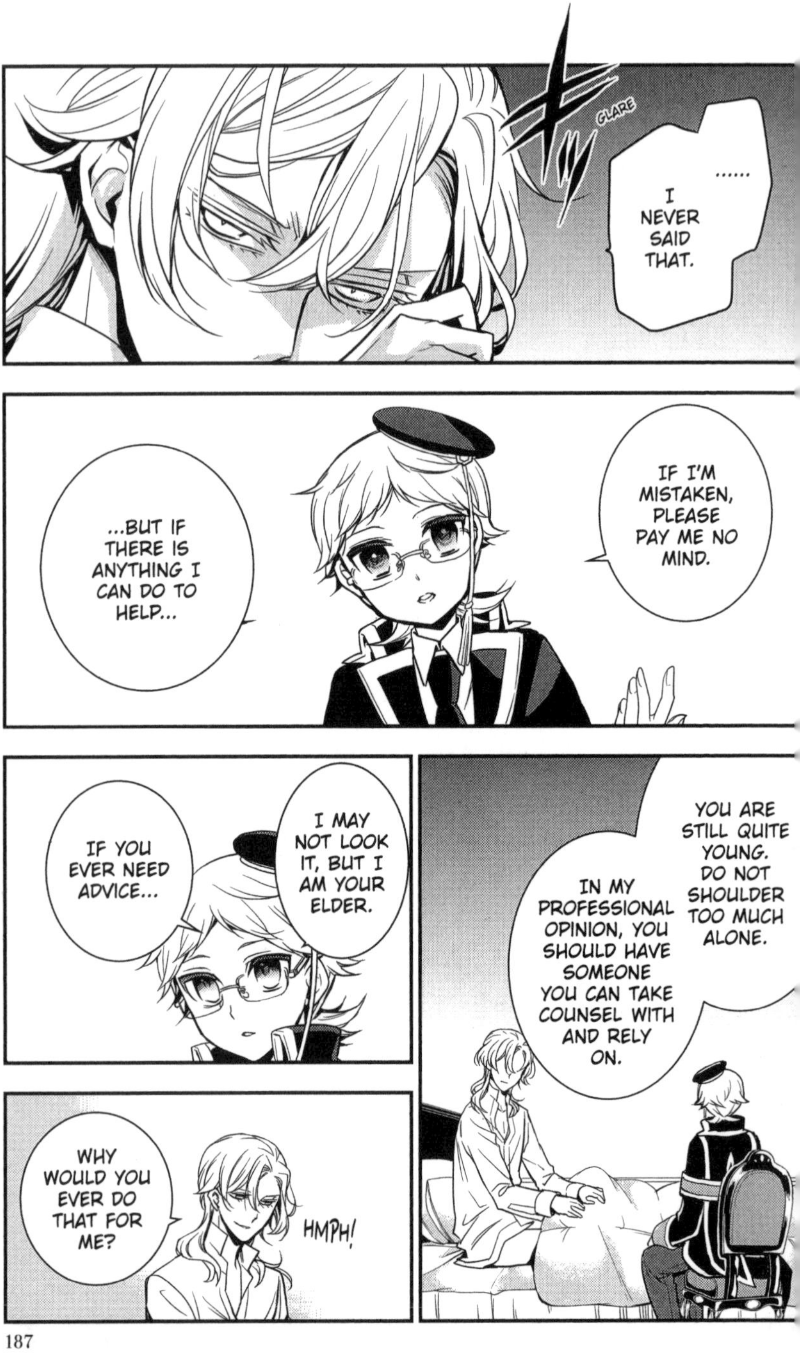
GLARE
......
I NEVER SAID THAT.
IF I'M MISTAKEN, PLEASE PAY ME NO MIND.
...BUT IF THERE IS ANYTHING I CAN DO TO HELP...
YOU ARE STILL QUITE YOUNG. DO NOT SHOULDER TOO MUCH ALONE.
IN MY PROFESSIONAL OPINION, YOU SHOULD HAVE SOMEONE YOU CAN TAKE COUNSEL WITH AND RELY ON.
I MAY NOT LOOK IT, BUT I AM YOUR ELDER.
IF YOU EVER NEED ADVICE...
HMPH!
WHY WOULD YOU EVER DO THAT FOR ME?

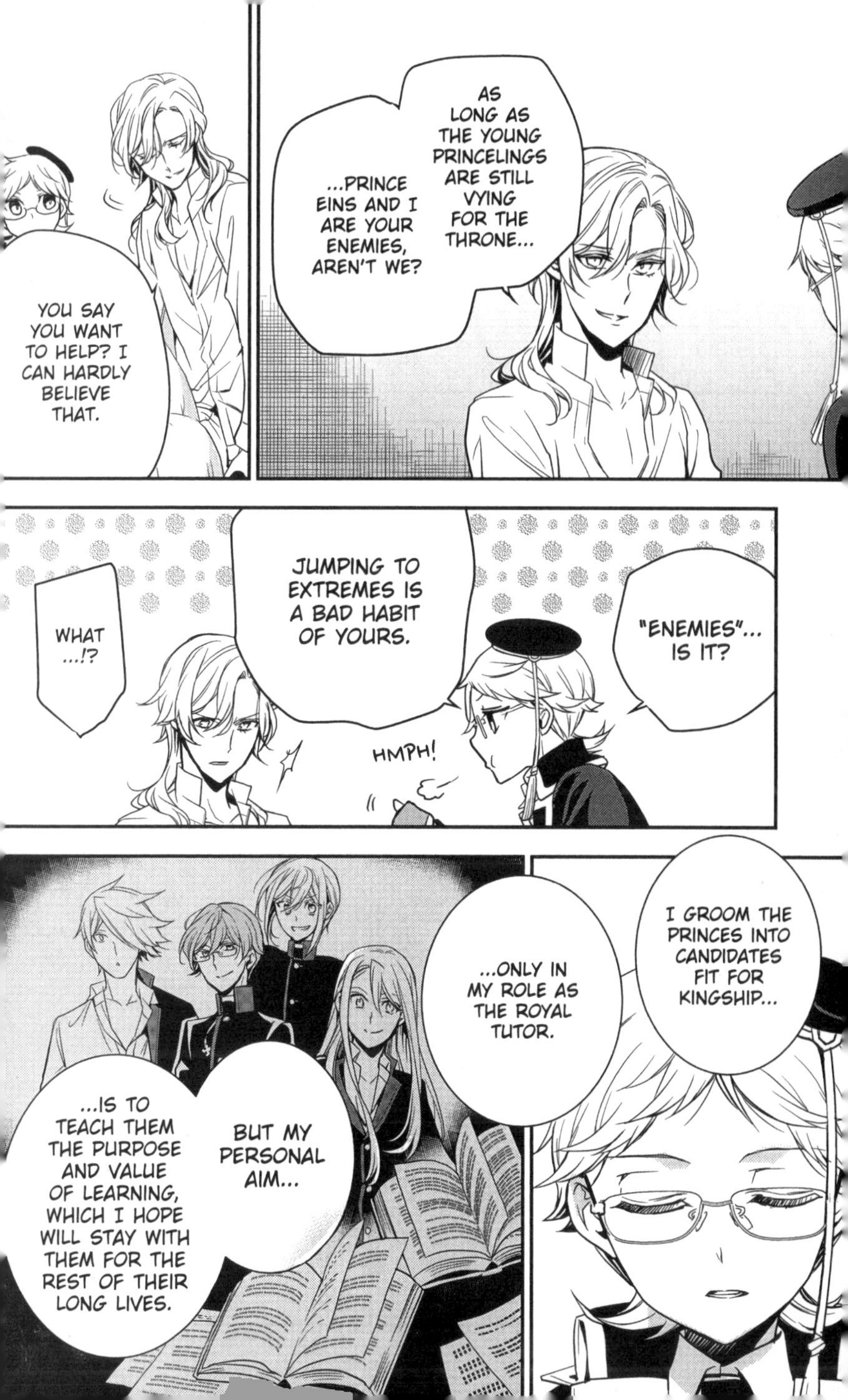
AS LONG AS THE YOUNG PRINCELINGS ARE STILL VYING FOR THE THRONE...
...PRINCE EINS AND I ARE YOUR ENEMIES, AREN'T WE?
YOU SAY YOU WANT TO HELP? I CAN HARDLY BELIEVE THAT.
"ENEMIES"... IS IT?
HMPH!
JUMPING TO EXTREMES IS A BAD HABIT OF YOURS.
WHAT ...!?
I GROOM THE PRINCES INTO CANDIDATES FIT FOR KINGSHIP...
...ONLY IN MY ROLE AS THE ROYAL TUTOR.
BUT MY PERSONAL AIM...
...IS TO TEACH THEM THE PURPOSE AND VALUE OF LEARNING, WHICH I HOPE WILL STAY WITH THEM FOR THE REST OF THEIR LONG LIVES.

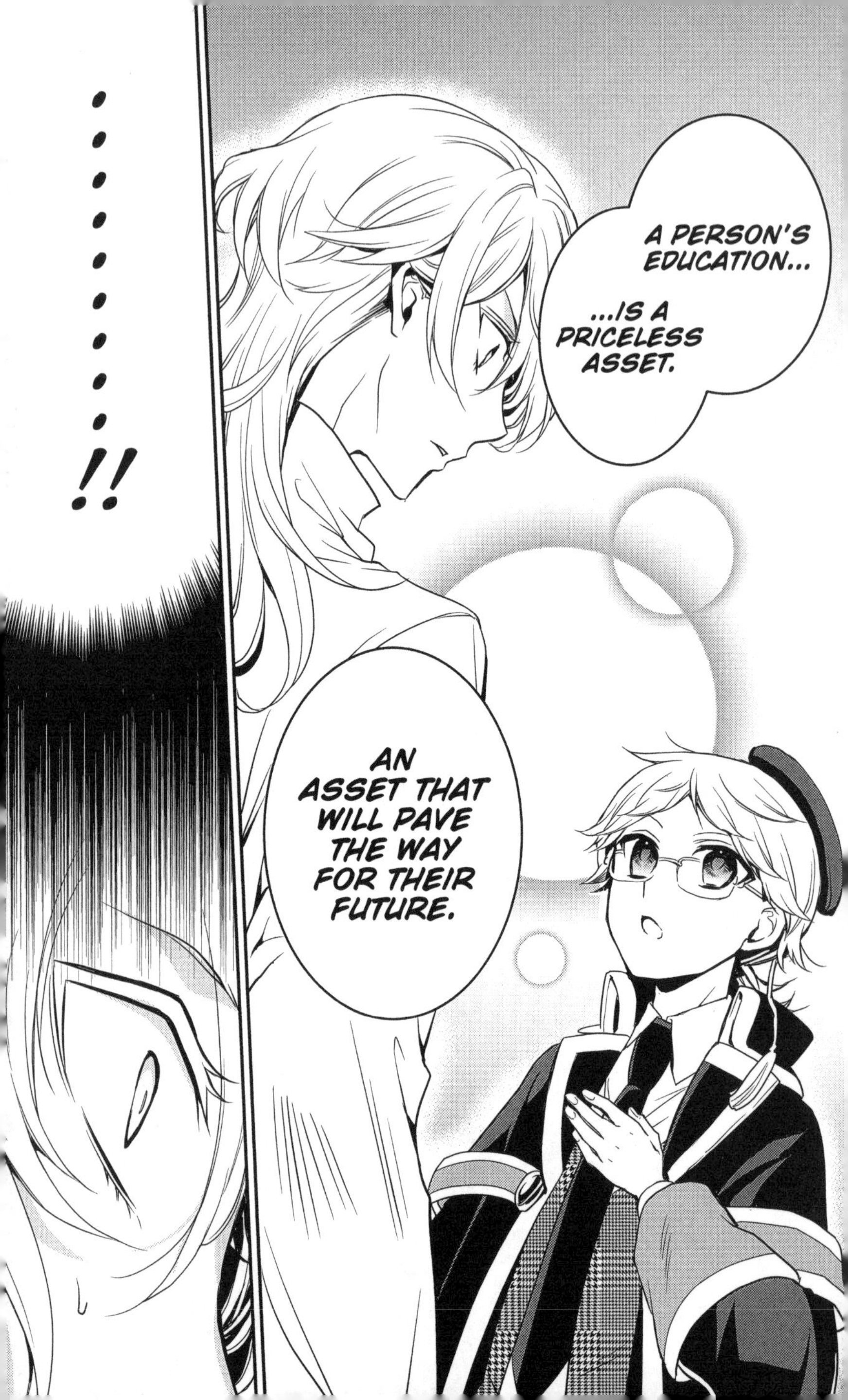
A PERSON'S EDUCATION...
...IS A PRICELESS ASSET.
AN ASSET THAT WILL PAVE THE WAY FOR THEIR FUTURE.
.........!!

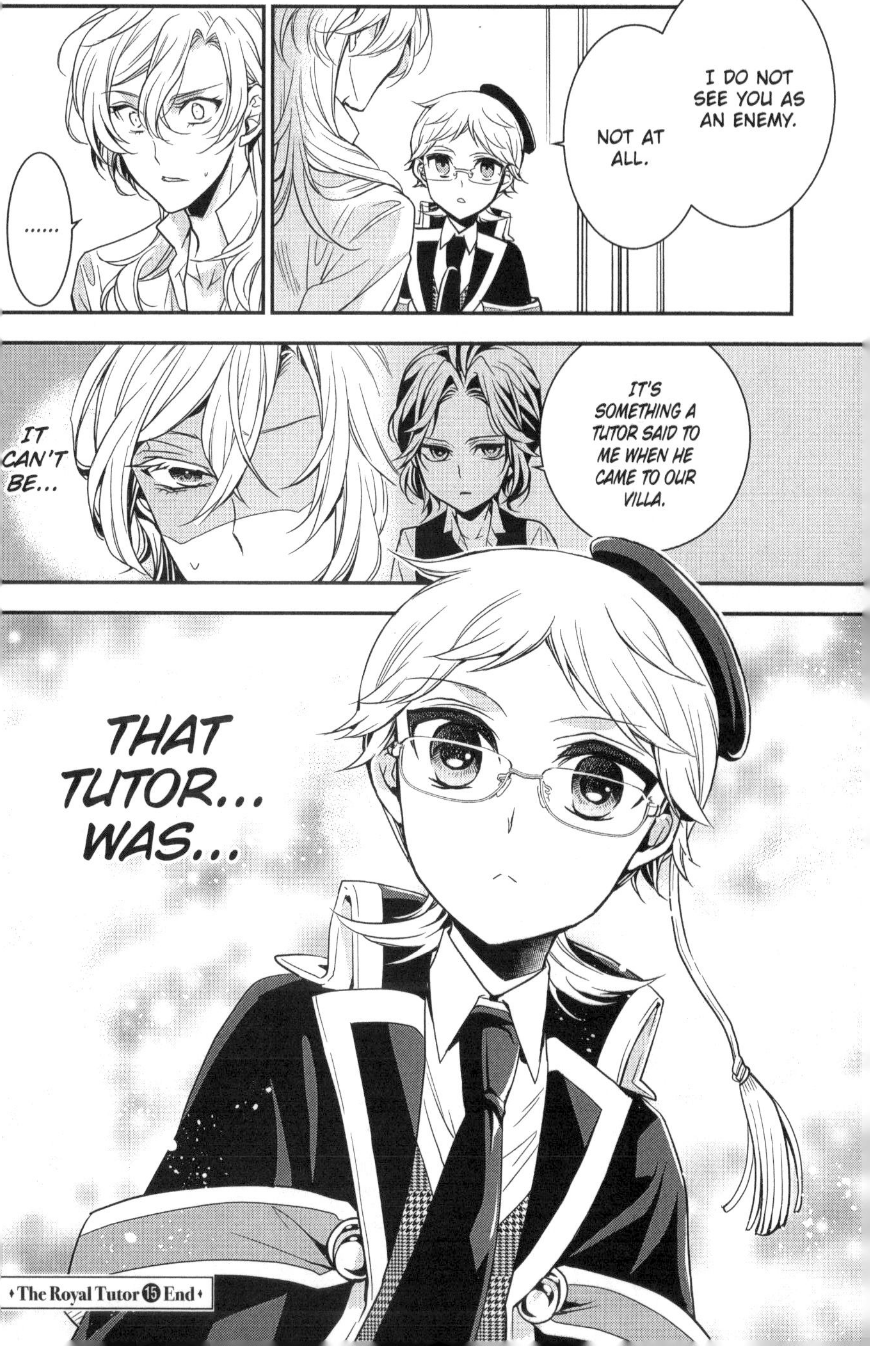
I DO NOT SEE YOU AS AN ENEMY.
NOT AT ALL.
......
IT'S SOMETHING A TUTOR SAID TO ME WHEN HE CAME TO OUR VILLA.
IT CAN'T BE...
THAT TUTOR... WAS...
• The Royal Tutor 15 End •

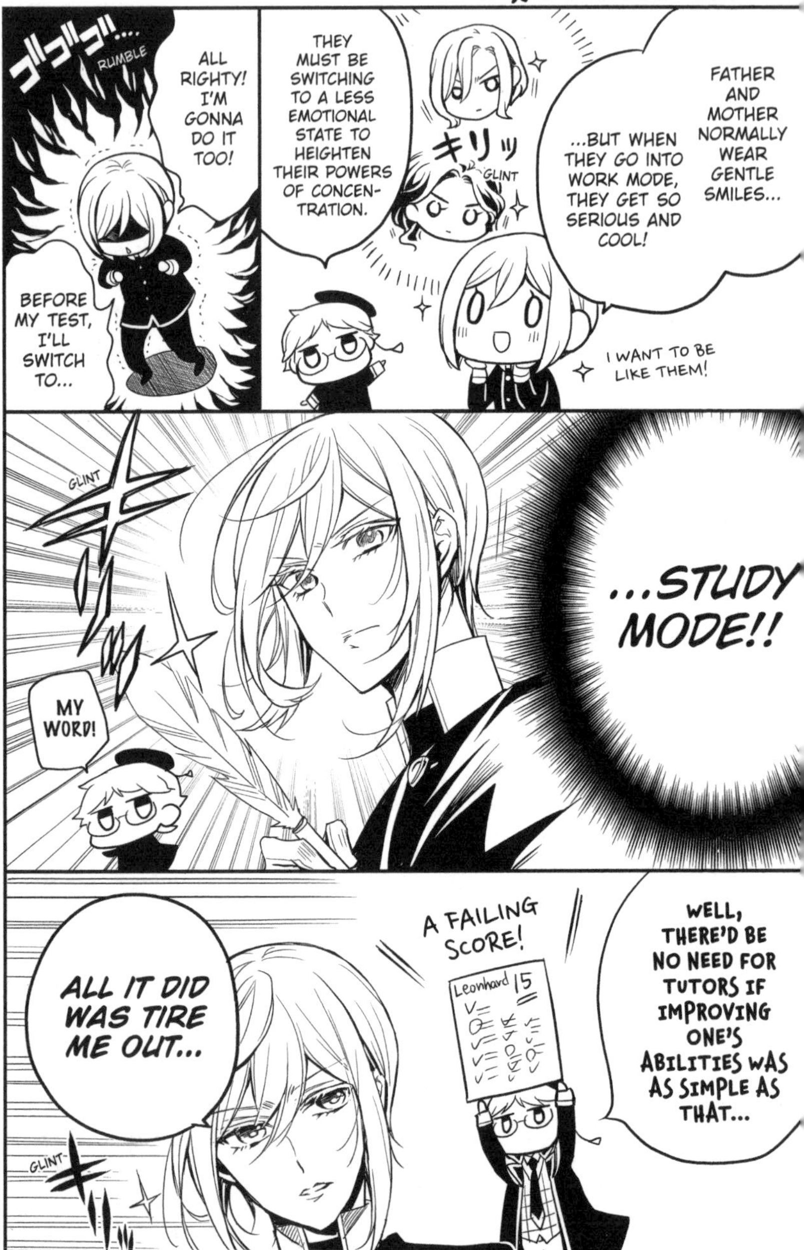
FATHER AND MOTHER NORMALLY WEAR GENTLE SMILES...
...BUT WHEN THEY GO INTO WORK MODE, THEY GET SO SERIOUS AND COOL!
キリッ
GLINT
I WANT TO BE LIKE THEM!
THEY MUST BE SWITCHING TO A LESS EMOTIONAL STATE TO HEIGHTEN THEIR POWERS OF CONCENTRATION.
ゴゴゴ....
RUMBLE
ALL RIGHTY! I'M GONNA DO IT TOO!
BEFORE MY TEST, I'LL SWITCH TO...
...STUDY MODE!!
GLINT
MY WORD!
WELL, THERE'D BE NO NEED FOR TUTORS IF IMPROVING ONE'S ABILITIES WAS AS SIMPLE AS THAT...
A FAILING SCORE!
Leonhard 15
ALL IT DID WAS TIRE ME OUT...
GLINT-

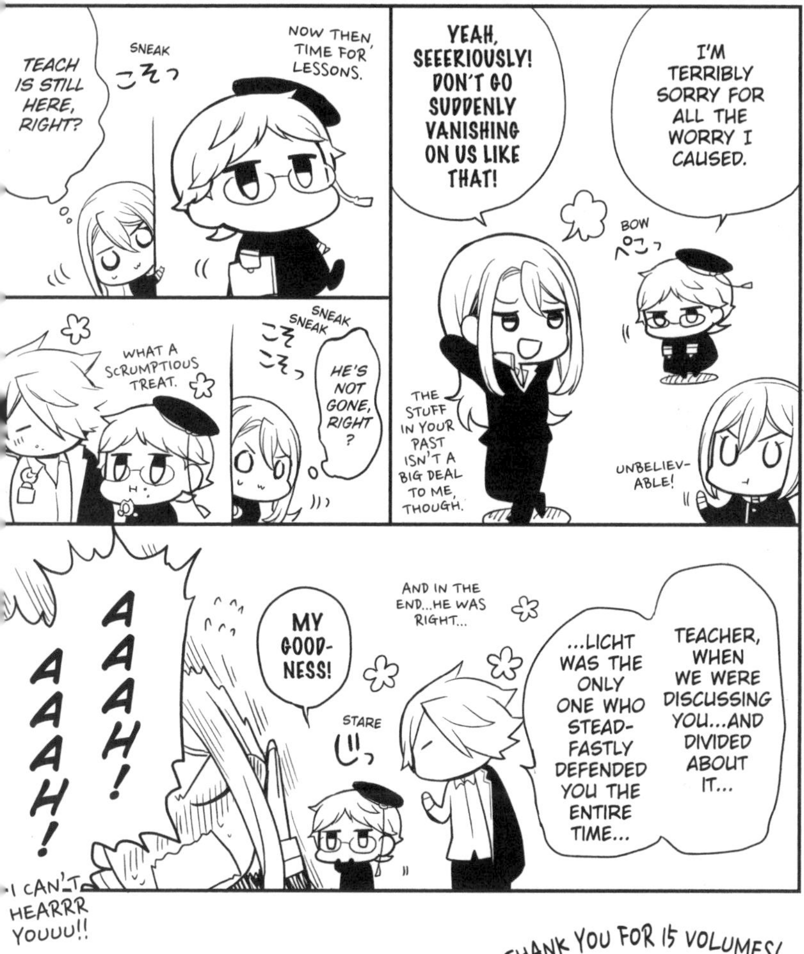
I'M TERRIBLY SORRY FOR ALL THE WORRY I CAUSED.
YEAH, SEEERIOUSLY! DON'T GO SUDDENLY VANISHING ON US LIKE THAT!
BOW
UNBELIEV-ABLE!
THE STUFF IN YOUR PAST ISN'T A BIG DEAL TO ME, THOUGH.
NOW THEN, TIME FOR LESSONS.
SNEAK
TEACH IS STILL HERE, RIGHT?
SNEAK SNEAK
HE'S NOT GONE, RIGHT?
WHAT A SCRUMPTIOUS TREAT.
TEACHER, WHEN WE WERE DISCUSSING YOU...AND DIVIDED ABOUT IT...
...LICHT WAS THE ONLY ONE WHO STEAD-FASTLY DEFENDED YOU THE ENTIRE TIME...
AND IN THE END...HE WAS RIGHT...
STARE
MY GOOD-NESS!
AAAAH!
AAAAH!
I CAN'T HEARRR YOUUU!!

♡ SPECIAL THANKS ♡

TSUCHIYA-SAN • K-SAN •
AO-SAN
MY EDITOR, AKIYAMA-SAN

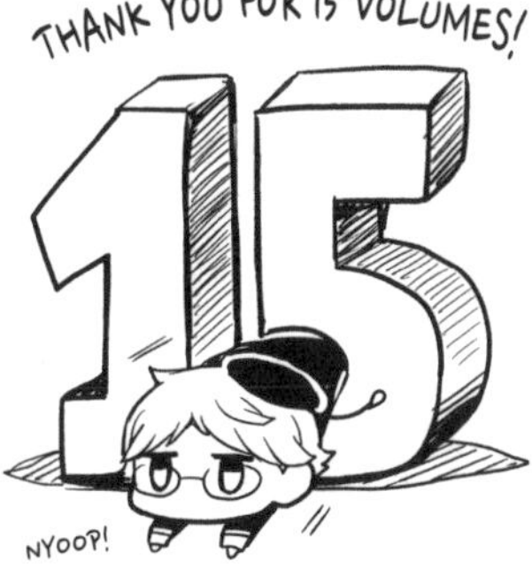
THANK YOU FOR 15 VOLUMES!
NYOOP!

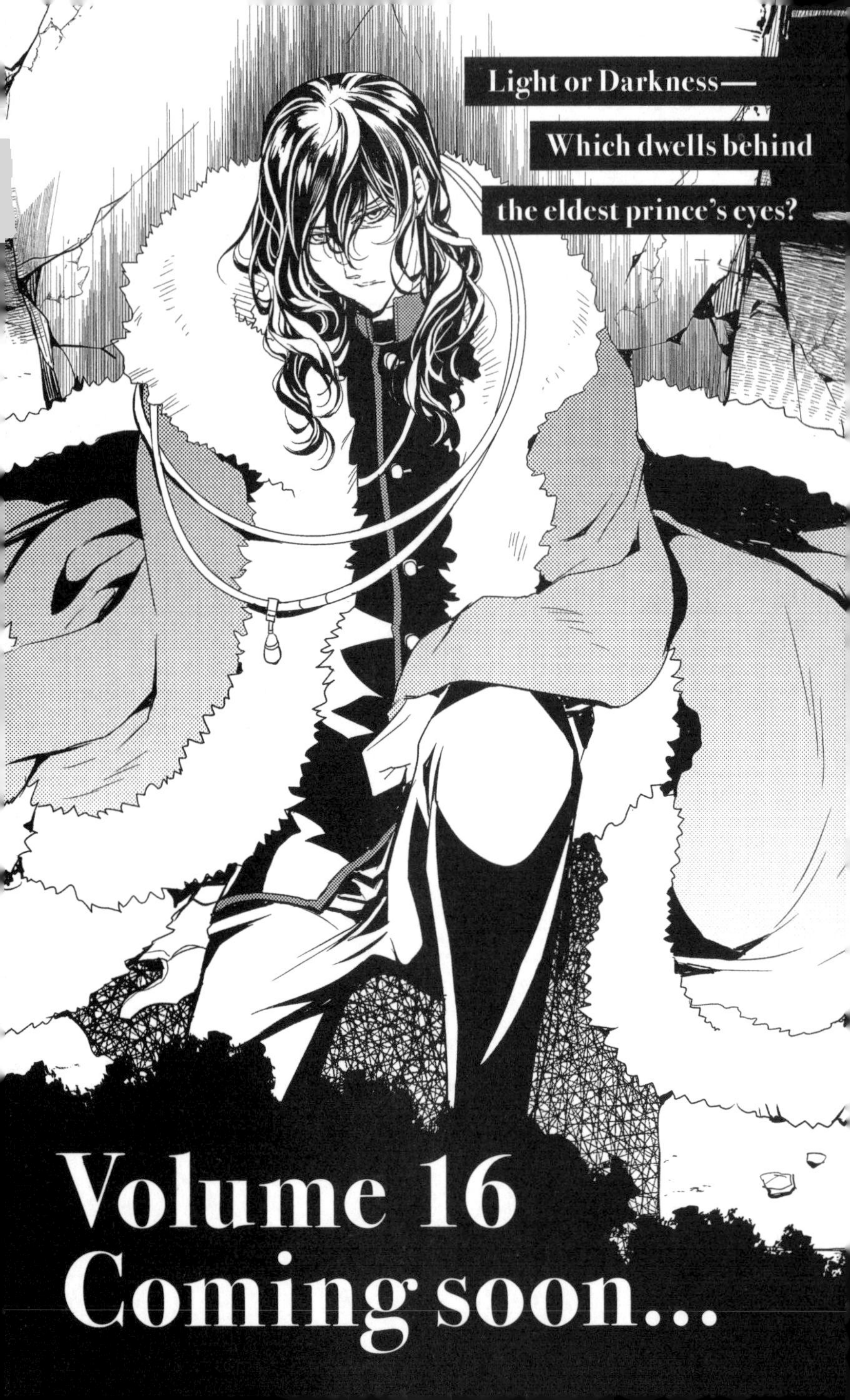
Light or Darkness—
Which dwells behind
the eldest prince's eyes?
Volume 16
Coming soon...

The Royal Tutor ⑮

Higasa Akai

Translation: Amanda Haley • Lettering: Abigail Blackman

THE ROYAL TUTOR Vol. 15 © 2020 Higasa Akai / SQUARE ENIX CO., LTD. First published in Japan in 2020 by SQUARE ENIX CO., LTD. English translation rights arranged with SQUARE ENIX CO., LTD. and Yen Press, LLC through Tuttle-Mori Agency, Inc., Tokyo.

English translation © 2021 by SQUARE ENIX CO., LTD.

Yen Press
150 West 30th Street, 19th Floor
New York, NY 10001

Visit us at yenpress.com
facebook.com/yenpress
twitter.com/yenpress
yenpress.tumblr.com
instagram.com/yenpress

First Yen Press Print Edition: May 2021
The chapters in this volume were originally published as ebooks by Yen Press.

Yen Press is an imprint of Yen Press, LLC.
The Yen Press name and logo are trademarks of Yen Press, LLC.

Library of Congress Control Number: 2017938422

ISBNs: 978-1-9753-2454-4 (paperback)
       978-1-9753-2455-1 (ebook)

10 9 8 7 6 5 4 3 2 1

BVG

Printed in the United States of America